Derivatives and Alternative Investments

CFA® PROGRAM CURRICULUM • VOLUME 6

LEVEL I
2010

Custom Publishing

New York   Boston   San Francisco
London   Toronto   Sydney   Tokyo   Singapore   Madrid
Mexico City   Munich   Paris   Cape Town   Hong Kong   Montreal

10 9 8 7 6 5

2008160754

AG/RH

Please visit our website at *www.pearsoncustom.com*

Pearson
Custom Publishing
is a division of

PEARSON

www.pearsonhighered.com

ISBN 10: 0-558-16022-0
ISBN 13: 978-0-558-16022-7

CONTENTS

READING 70

HOW TO USE THE CFA PROGRAM CURRICULUM

Congratulations on your decision to enter the Chartered Financial Analyst (CFA®) Program. This exciting and rewarding program of study reflects your desire to become a serious investment professional. You are embarking on a program noted for its high ethical standards and the breadth of knowledge, skills, and abilities it develops. Your commitment to the CFA Program should be educationally and professionally rewarding.

The credential you seek is respected around the world as a mark of accomplishment and dedication. Each level of the program represents a distinct achievement in professional development. Successful completion of the program is rewarded with membership in a prestigious global community of investment professionals. CFA charterholders are dedicated to life-long learning and maintaining currency with the ever-changing dynamics of a challenging profession. The CFA Program represents the first step towards a career-long commitment to professional education.

The CFA examination measures your degree of mastery of the assigned CFA Program curriculum. Effective study and preparation based on that curriculum are keys to your success on the examination.

Curriculum Development

The CFA Program curriculum is grounded in the practice of the investment profession. Utilizing a collaborative website, CFA Institute performs a continuous practice analysis with investment professionals around the world to determine the knowledge, skills, and abilities that are relevant to the profession. Regional panels and targeted surveys are also conducted annually to verify and reinforce the continuous feedback. The practice analysis process ultimately defines the Candidate Body of Knowledge (CBOK™) an inventory of knowledge and responsibilities expected of the investment management professional at the level of a new CFA charterholder. The process also determines how much emphasis each of the major topic areas receives on the CFA examinations.

A committee made up of practicing charterholders, in conjunction with CFA Institute staff, designs the CFA Program curriculum to deliver the CBOK to candidates. The examinations, also written by practicing charterholders, are designed to allow you to demonstrate your mastery of the CBOK as set forth in the CFA Program curriculum. As you structure your personal study program, you should emphasize mastery of the CBOK and the practical application of that knowledge. For more information on the practice analysis, CBOK, and development of the CFA Program curriculum, please visit www.cfainstitute.org/toolkit.

Organization

The Level I CFA Program curriculum is organized into 10 topic areas. Each topic area begins with a brief statement of the material and the depth of knowledge expected.

Each topic area is then divided into one or more study sessions. These study sessions—18 sessions in the Level I curriculum—should form the basic structure of your reading and preparation.

Each study session includes a statement of its structure and objective, and is further divided into specific reading assignments. The outline on the inside front cover of each volume illustrates the organization of these 18 study sessions.

The reading assignments are the basis for all examination questions, and are selected or developed specifically to teach the CBOK. These readings are drawn from CFA Program-commissioned content, textbook chapters, professional journal articles, research analyst reports, and cases. Many readings include problems and solutions as well as appendices to help you learn.

Reading-specific Learning Outcome Statements (LOS) are listed in the pages introducing each study session as well as at the beginning of each reading. These LOS indicate what you should be able to accomplish after studying the reading. We encourage you to review how to properly use LOS, and the descriptions of commonly used LOS "command words," at www.cfainstitute.org/toolkit. The command words signal the depth of learning you are expected to achieve from the reading. You should use the LOS to guide and focus your study, as each examination question is based on an assigned reading and one or more LOS. However, the readings provide context for the LOS and enable you to apply a principle or concept in a variety of scenarios. The candidate is responsible for the entirety of all of the required material in a study session, the assigned readings as well as the end-of-reading questions and problems.

Features of the Curriculum

- ▶ **Required vs. Optional Segments** - You should read all of the pages for an assigned reading. In some cases, however, we have reprinted an entire chapter or article and marked those parts of the reading that are not required as "optional." The CFA examination is based only on the required segments, and the optional segments are included only when they might help you to better understand the required segments (by seeing the required material in its full context). When an optional segment begins, you will see an icon and a solid vertical bar in the outside margin that will continue until the optional segment ends, accompanied by another icon. *Unless the material is specifically marked as optional, you should assume it is required.* Keep in mind that the optional material is provided strictly for your convenience and will not be tested. You should rely on the required segments and the reading-specific LOS in preparing for the examination.

- ▶ **Problems/Solutions** - *All questions and problems in the readings as well as their solutions (which are provided directly following the problems) are required material.* When appropriate, we have included problems within and after the readings to demonstrate practical application and reinforce your understanding of the concepts presented. The questions and problems are designed to help you learn these concepts and may serve as a basis for exam questions. Many of the questions are adapted from past CFA examinations.

- ▶ **Margins** - The wide margins in each volume provide space for your note-taking.

- ▶ **Two-Color Format** - To enrich the visual appeal and clarity of the exhibits, tables, and text, the curriculum is printed in a two-color format.

- ▶ **Six-Volume Structure** - For portability of the curriculum, the material is spread over six volumes.

- ▶ **Glossary and Index** - For your convenience, we have printed a comprehensive glossary and index in each volume. Throughout the curriculum, a **bolded blue** word in a reading denotes a term defined in the glossary.

▶ **Source Material** - The authorship, publisher, and copyright owners are given for each reading for your reference. We recommend that you use this CFA Institute curriculum rather than the original source materials because the curriculum may include only selected pages from outside readings, updated sections within the readings, and may have problems and solutions tailored to the CFA Program.

▶ **LOS Self-Check** - We have inserted checkboxes next to each LOS that you can use to track your progress in mastering the concepts in each reading.

Designing Your Personal Study Program

Create a Schedule - An orderly, systematic approach to examination preparation is critical. You should dedicate a consistent block of time every week to reading and studying. Complete all reading assignments and the associated problems and solutions in each study session. Review the LOS both before and after you study each reading to ensure that you have mastered the applicable content and can demonstrate the knowledge, skill, or ability described by the LOS and the assigned reading. Use the new LOS self-check to track your progress and highlight areas of weakness for later review.

You will receive periodic e-mail communications that contain important study tips and preparation strategies. Be sure to read these carefully.

CFA Institute estimates that you will need to devote a minimum of 10–15 hours per week for 18 weeks to study the assigned readings. Allow a minimum of one week for each study session, and plan to complete them all at least 30–45 days prior to the examination. This schedule will allow you to spend the final four to six weeks before the examination reviewing the assigned material and taking online sample and mock examinations.

At CFA Institute, we believe that candidates need to commit to a *minimum* of 270–300 hours reading and reviewing the curriculum and end-of-reading questions and problems. Many candidates have also incorporated the online sample examinations into their preparations during the final weeks before the exam. This recommendation, however, may substantially underestimate the hours needed for appropriate examination preparation depending on your individual circumstances, relevant experience, and academic background. You will undoubtedly adjust your study time to conform to your own strengths and weaknesses, and your educational and professional background.

You will probably spend more time on some study sessions than on others, but on average you should plan on devoting 15 hours per study session. You should allow ample time for both in-depth study of all topic areas and additional concentration on those topic areas for which you feel least prepared.

Preliminary Readings - The reading assignments in Economics assume candidates already have a basic mastery of the concepts typically presented in introductory university-level economics courses. Information on suggested readings to improve your knowledge of these topics precedes the relevant study sessions.

Candidate Preparation Toolkit - We have created the online toolkit to provide a single comprehensive location with resources and guidance for candidate preparation. In addition to in-depth information on study program planning, the CFA Program curriculum, and the online sample and mock examinations, the toolkit also contains curriculum errata, printable study session outlines, sample examination questions, and more. Errata that we have identified in the curriculum are corrected and listed periodically in the errata listing in the toolkit. We encourage you to use the toolkit as your central preparation resource during your tenure as a candidate. Visit the toolkit at www.cfainstitute.org/toolkit.

Online Sample Examinations - As part of your study of the assigned curriculum, use the CFA Institute online sample examinations to assess your exam preparation as you progress toward the end of your study. After each question, you will receive immediate feedback noting the correct response and indicating the relevant assigned reading, so you'll be able to identify areas of weakness for further study. The 120-minute sample examinations reflect the question formats, topics, and level of difficulty of the actual CFA examinations. Aggregate data indicate that the CFA examination pass rate was higher among candidates who took one or more online sample examinations than among candidates who did not take the online sample examinations. For more information on the online sample examinations, please visit www.cfainstitute.org/toolkit.

Online Mock Examinations - In response to candidate requests, CFA Institute has developed mock examinations that mimic the actual CFA examinations not only in question format and level of difficulty, but also in length. The three-hour online mock exams simulate the morning and afternoon sessions of the actual CFA exam, and are intended to be taken after you complete your study of the full curriculum, so you can test your understanding of the CBOK and your readiness for the exam. To further differentiate, feedback is provided at the end of the exam, rather than after each question as with the sample exams. CFA Institute recommends that you take these mock exams at the final stage of your preparation toward the actual CFA examination. For more information on the online mock examinations, please visit www.cfainstitute.org/toolkit.

Tools to Measure Your Comprehension of the Curriculum

With the addition of the online mock exams, CFA Institute now provides three distinct ways you can practice for the actual CFA exam. The full descriptions are above, but below is a brief summary of each:

End-of-Reading Questions and Problems - These are found at the end of each reading in the printed curriculum, and should be used to test your understanding of the concepts.

Online Sample Exams - Typically available two months before the CFA exam, online sample exams are designed to assess your exam preparation, and can help you target areas of weakness for further study.

Online Mock Exams - In contrast to the sample exams, mock exams are not available until closer to the actual exam date itself. Mock exams are designed to replicate the exam day experience, and should be taken near the end of your study period to prepare for exam day.

Preparatory Providers - After you enroll in the CFA Program, you may receive numerous solicitations for preparatory courses and review materials. Although preparatory courses and notes may be helpful to some candidates, you should view these resources as *supplements* to the assigned CFA Program curriculum. The CFA examinations reference only the CFA Institute assigned curriculum—no preparatory course or review course materials are consulted or referenced. Before you decide on a supplementary prep course, do some research. Determine the experience and expertise of the instructors, the accuracy and currency of their content, the delivery method for their materials, and the provider's claims of success. Most importantly, make sure the provider is in compliance with the CFA Institute Prep Provider Guidelines Program. Three years of prep course products can be a significant investment, so make sure you're getting a sufficient return. Just remember, there are no shortcuts to success on the CFA examinations. Prep products can enhance your learning experience, but the CFA curriculum is the key to success. For more information on the Prep Provider Guidelines Program, visit www.cfainstitute.org/cfaprog/resources/prepcourse.html.

SUMMARY

Every question on the CFA examination is based on specific pages in the required readings and on one or more LOS. Frequently, an examination question is also tied to a specific example highlighted within a reading or to a specific end-of-reading question and/or problem and its solution. To make effective use of the curriculum, please remember these key points:

1. All pages printed in the Custom Curriculum are required reading for the examination except for occasional sections marked as optional. You may read optional pages as background, but you will not be tested on them.

2. All questions, problems, and their solutions - printed at the end of readings - are required study material for the examination.

3. You should make appropriate use of the CFA Candidate Toolkit, the online sample/mock examinations, and preparatory courses and review materials.

4. You should schedule and commit sufficient study time to cover the 18 study sessions, review the materials, and take sample/mock examinations.

5. **Note:** Some of the concepts in the study sessions may be superseded by updated rulings and/or pronouncements issued after a reading was published. Candidates are expected to be familiar with the overall analytical framework contained in the assigned readings. Candidates are not responsible for changes that occur after the material was written.

Feedback

At CFA Institute, we are committed to delivering a comprehensive and rigorous curriculum for the development of competent, ethically grounded investment professionals. We rely on candidate and member feedback as we work to incorporate content, design, and packaging improvements. You can be assured that we will continue to listen to your suggestions. Please send any comments or feedback to curriculum@cfainstitute.org. Ongoing improvements in the curriculum will help you prepare for success on the upcoming examinations, and for a lifetime of learning as a serious investment professional.

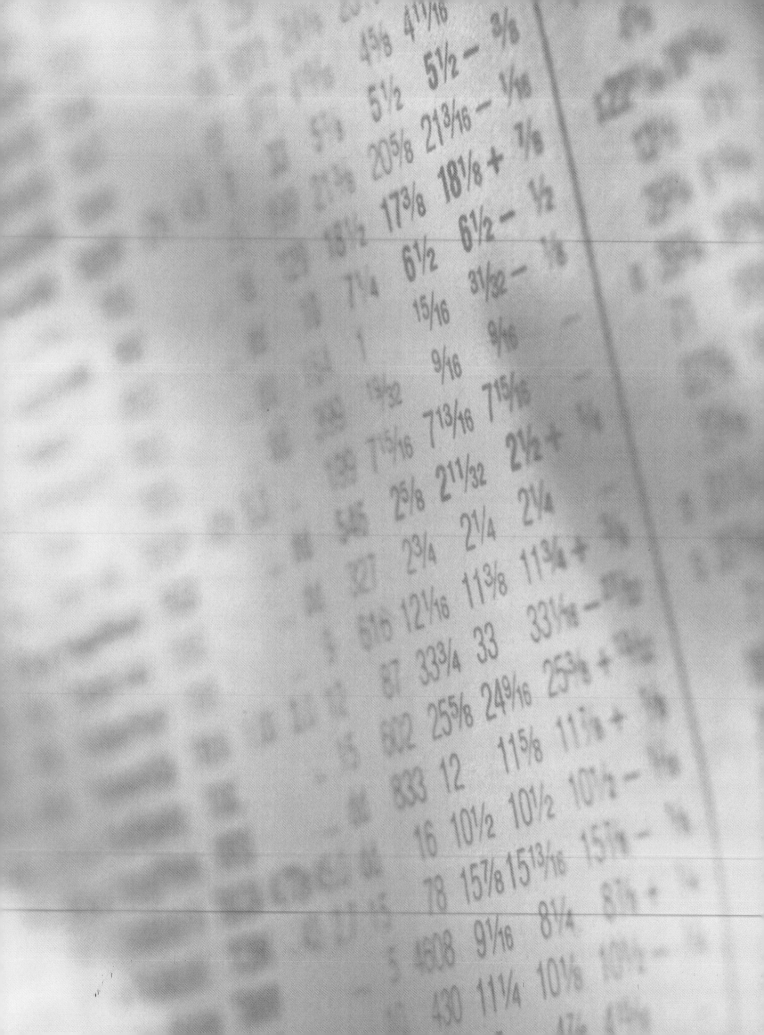

DERIVATIVES

TOPIC LEVEL LEARNING OUTCOME

The candidate should be able to demonstrate a working knowledge of the analysis of derivative investments, including forwards, futures, options, and swaps.

STUDY SESSION 17
DERIVATIVE INVESTMENTS

Derivatives—financial instruments that offer a return based on the return of some underlying asset—have become increasingly important and fundamental in effectively managing financial risk and creating synthetic exposures to asset classes. As in other security markets, arbitrage and market efficiency play a critical role in establishing prices and maintaining parity.

This study session builds the conceptual framework for understanding derivative investments (forwards, futures, options, and swaps), derivative markets, and the use of options in risk management.

READING ASSIGNMENTS

Reading 67   Derivative Markets and Instruments
*Analysis of Derivatives for the Chartered Financial Analyst®
Program*, by Don M. Chance, CFA

Reading 68   Forward Markets and Contracts
*Analysis of Derivatives for the Chartered Financial Analyst®
Program*, by Don M. Chance, CFA

Reading 69   Futures Markets and Contracts
*Analysis of Derivatives for the Chartered Financial Analyst®
Program*, by Don M. Chance, CFA

Reading 70   Option Markets and Contracts
*Analysis of Derivatives for the Chartered Financial Analyst®
Program*, by Don M. Chance, CFA

Reading 71   Swap Markets and Contracts
*Analysis of Derivatives for the Chartered Financial Analyst®
Program*, by Don M. Chance, CFA

Reading 72   Risk Management Applications of Option Strategies
*Analysis of Derivatives for the Chartered Financial Analyst®
Program*, by Don M. Chance, CFA

DERIVATIVE MARKETS AND INSTRUMENTS

by Don M. Chance, CFA

LEARNING OUTCOMES

The candidate should be able to:	Mastery
a. define a derivative and differentiate between exchange-traded and over-the-counter derivatives;	☐
b. define a forward commitment and a contingent claim;	☐
c. differentiate the basic characteristics of forward contracts, futures contracts, options (calls and puts), and swaps;	☐
d. discuss the purposes and criticisms of derivative markets;	☐
e. explain arbitrage and the role it plays in determining prices and promoting market efficiency.	☐

INTRODUCTION   1

The concept of risk is at the heart of investment management. Financial analysts and portfolio managers continually identify, measure, and manage risk. In a simple world where only stocks and bonds exist, the only risks are the fluctuations associated with market values and the potential for a creditor to default. Measuring risk often takes the form of standard deviations, betas, and probabilities of default. In the above simple setting, managing risk is limited to engaging in stock and bond transactions that reduce or increase risk. For example, a portfolio manager may hold a combination of a risky stock portfolio and a risk-free bond, with the relative allocations determined by the investor's tolerance for risk. If for some reason the manager desires a lower level of risk, the only transactions available to adjust the risk downward are to reduce the allocation to the risky stock portfolio and increase the allocation to the risk-free bond.

Analysis of Derivatives for the Chartered Financial Analyst® Program, by Don M. Chance, CFA. Copyright © 2003 by AIMR. Reprinted with permission.

5

But we do not live in a simple world of only stocks and bonds, and in fact investors can adjust the level of risk in a variety of ways. For example, one way to reduce risk is to use insurance, which can be described as the act of paying someone to assume a risk for you. The financial markets have created their own way of offering insurance against financial loss in the form of contracts called **derivatives**. *A derivative is a financial instrument that offers a return based on the return of some other underlying asset.* In this sense, its return is *derived* from another instrument—hence, the name.

As the definition states, a derivative's performance is based on the performance of an underlying asset. This underlying asset is often referred to simply as the **underlying**.[1] It trades in a market in which buyers and sellers meet and decide on a price; the seller then delivers the asset to the buyer and receives payment. The price for immediate purchase of the underlying asset is called the **cash price** or **spot price** (in this volume, we will use the latter term). A derivative also has a defined and limited life: A derivative contract initiates on a certain date and terminates on a later date. Often the derivative's payoff is determined and/or made on the expiration date, although that is not always the case. In accordance with the usual rules of law, a derivative contract is an agreement between two parties in which each does something for the other. In some cases, as in the simple insurance analogy, a derivative contract involves one party paying the other some money and receiving coverage against potential losses. In other cases, the parties simply agree that each will do something for the other at a later date. In other words, no money need change hands up front.

We have alluded to several general characteristics of derivative contracts. Let us now turn to the specific types of derivatives that we will cover in this volume.

2   TYPES OF DERIVATIVES

In this section, we take a brief look at the different types of derivative contracts. This brief treatment serves only as a short introduction to familiarize you with the general ideas behind the contracts. We shall examine these derivatives in considerable detail in later readings.

Let us start by noting that derivative contracts are created on and traded in two distinct but related types of markets: exchange traded and over the counter. Exchange-traded contracts have standard terms and features and are traded on an organized derivatives trading facility, usually referred to as a futures exchange or an options exchange. Over-the-counter contracts are any transactions created by two parties anywhere else. We shall examine the other distinctive features of these two types of contracts as we proceed.

Derivative contracts can be classified into two general categories: forward commitments and contingent claims. In the following section, we examine for-

---

[1] On behalf of the financial world, we apologize to all English teachers. "Underlying" is not a noun, but in the world of derivatives it is commonly used as such. To be consistent with that terminology, we use it in that manner here.

ward commitments, which are contracts in which the two parties enter into an agreement to engage in a transaction at a later date at a price established at the start. Within the category of forward commitments, two major classifications exist: exchanged-traded contracts, specifically futures, and over-the-counter contracts, which consist of forward contracts and swaps.

2.1 Forward Commitments

The **forward contract** is an agreement between two parties in which one party, the buyer, agrees to buy from the other party, the seller, an underlying asset at a future date at a price established at the start. The parties to the transaction specify the forward contract's terms and conditions, such as when and where delivery will take place and the precise identity of the underlying. In this sense, the contract is said to be *customized*. Each party is subject to the possibility that the other party will default.

Many simple, everyday transactions are forms of forward commitments. For example, when you order a pizza for delivery to your home, you are entering into an agreement for a transaction to take place later ("30 minutes or less," as some advertise) at a price agreed on at the outset. Although default is not likely, it could occur—for instance, if the party ordering the pizza decided to go out to eat, leaving the delivery person wondering where the customer went. Or perhaps the delivery person had a wreck on the way to delivery and the pizza was destroyed. But such events are extremely rare.

Forward contracts in the financial world take place in a large and private market consisting of banks, investment banking firms, governments, and corporations. These contracts call for the purchase and sale of an underlying asset at a later date. The underlying asset could be a security (i.e., a stock or bond), a foreign currency, a commodity, or combinations thereof, or sometimes an interest rate. In the case of an interest rate, the contract is not on a bond from which the interest rate is derived but rather on the interest rate itself. Such a contract calls for the exchange of a single interest payment for another at a later date, where at least one of the payments is determined at the later date.[2]

As an example of someone who might use a forward contract in the financial world, consider a pension fund manager. The manager, anticipating a future inflow of cash, could engage in a forward contract to purchase a portfolio equivalent to the S&P 500 at a future date—timed to coincide with the future cash inflow date—at a price agreed on at the start. When that date arrives, the cash is received and used to settle the obligation on the forward contract.[3] In this manner, the pension fund manager commits to the position in the S&P 500 without having to worry about the risk that the market will rise during that period. Other common forward contracts include commitments to buy and sell a foreign currency or a commodity at a future date, locking in the exchange rate or commodity price at the start.

The forward market is a private and largely unregulated market. Any transaction involving a commitment between two parties for the future purchase/sale of an asset is a forward contract. Although pizza deliveries are generally not considered forward contracts, similar transactions occur commonly in the financial world. Yet we cannot simply pick up the *Wall Street Journal* or the *Financial Times* and read

---

[2] These instruments are called forward rate agreements and will be studied in detail in the reading on forward markets and contracts.

[3] The settling of the forward contract can occur through delivery, in which case the buyer pays the agreed-upon price and receives the asset from the seller, or through an equivalent cash settlement. In the latter case, the seller pays the buyer the difference between the market price and the agreed-upon price if the market price is higher. The buyer pays the seller the difference between the agreed-upon price and the market price if the agreed-upon price is higher.

about them or determine how many contracts were created the previous day.[4] They are private transactions for a reason: The parties want to keep them private and want little government interference. This need for privacy and the absence of regulation does not imply anything illegal or corrupt but simply reflects a desire to maintain a prudent level of business secrecy.

Recall that we described a forward contract as an agreement between two parties in which one party, the buyer, agrees to buy from the other party, the seller, an underlying asset at a future date at a price agreed upon at the start. A **futures contract** is a variation of a forward contract that has essentially the same basic definition but some additional features that clearly distinguish it from a forward contract. For one, a futures contract is not a private and customized transaction. Instead, it is a public, standardized transaction that takes place on a futures exchange. A futures exchange, like a stock exchange, is an organization that provides a facility for engaging in futures transactions and establishes a mechanism through which parties can buy and sell these contracts. The contracts are standardized, which means that the exchange determines the expiration dates, the underlying, how many units of the underlying are included in one contract, and various other terms and conditions.

Probably the most important distinction between a futures contract and a forward contract, however, lies in the default risk associated with the contracts. As noted above, in a forward contract, the risk of default is a concern. Specifically, the party with a loss on the contract could default. Although the legal consequences of default are severe, parties nonetheless sometimes fall into financial trouble and are forced to default. For that reason, only solid, creditworthy parties can generally engage in forward contracts. In a futures contract, however, the futures exchange guarantees to each party that if the other fails to pay, the exchange will pay. In fact, the exchange actually writes itself into the middle of the contract so that each party effectively has a contract with the exchange and not with the other party. The exchange collects payment from one party and disburses payment to the other.

The futures exchange implements this performance guarantee through an organization called the clearinghouse. For some futures exchanges, the clearinghouse is a separate corporate entity. For others, it is a division or subsidiary of the exchange. In either case, however, the clearinghouse protects itself by requiring that the parties settle their gains and losses to the exchange on a daily basis. This process, referred to as the daily settlement or marking to market, is a critical distinction between futures and forward contracts. With futures contracts, profits and losses are charged and credited to participants' accounts each day. This practice prevents losses from accumulating without being collected. For forward contracts, losses accumulate until the end of the contract.[5]

One should not get the impression that forward contracts are rife with credit losses and futures contracts never involve default. Credit losses on forward contracts are extremely rare, owing to the excellent risk management practices of participants. In the case of futures contracts, parties do default on occasion. In fact, it is likely that there are more defaults on futures contracts than on forward

---

[4] In Section 4 of this reading, we will look at some ways to measure the amount of this type of trading.

[5] Although this process of losses accumulating on forward contracts until the expiration day is the standard format for a contract, modern risk management procedures include the possibility of forcing a party in debt to periodically pay losses accrued prior to expiration. In addition, a variety of risk-reducing techniques, such as the use of collateral, are used to mitigate the risk of loss. We discuss these points in more detail in the reading on forward markets and contracts.

contracts.[6] Nonetheless, the exchange guarantee has never failed for the party on the other side of the transaction. Although the possibility of the clearinghouse defaulting does exist, the probability of such a default happening is extremely small. Thus, we can generally assume that futures contracts are default-free. In contrast, the possibility of default, although relatively small, exists for forward contracts.

Another important distinction between forward contracts and futures contracts lies in the ability to engage in offsetting transactions. Forward contracts are generally designed to be held until expiration. It is possible, however, for a party to engage in the opposite transaction prior to expiration. For example, a party might commit to purchase one million euros at a future date at an exchange rate of \$0.85/€. Suppose that later the euro has a forward price of \$0.90/€. The party might then choose to engage in a new forward contract to sell the euro at the new price of \$0.90/€. The party then has a commitment to buy the euro at \$0.85 and sell it at \$0.90. The risk associated with changes in exchange rates is eliminated, but both transactions remain in place and are subject to default.[7]

In futures markets, the contracts have standardized terms and trade in a market that provides sufficient liquidity to permit the parties to enter the market and offset transactions previously created. The use of contracts with standardized terms results in relatively widespread acceptance of these terms as homogeneous agreed-upon standards for trading these contracts. For example, a U.S. Treasury bond futures contract covering \$100,000 face value of Treasury bonds, with an expiration date in March, June, September, or December, is a standard contract. In contrast, if a party wanted a contract covering \$120,000 of Treasury bonds, he would not find any such instrument in the futures markets and would have to create a nonstandard instrument in the forward market. The acceptance of standardized terms makes parties more willing to trade futures contracts. Consequently, futures markets offer the parties liquidity, which gives them a means of buying and selling the contracts. Because of this liquidity, a party can enter into a contract and later, before the contract expires, enter into the opposite transaction and offset the position, much the same way one might buy or sell a stock or bond and then reverse the transaction later. This reversal of a futures position completely eliminates any further financial consequences of the original transaction.[8]

A **swap** is a variation of a forward contract that is essentially equivalent to a series of forward contracts. Specifically, a swap is an agreement between two parties to exchange a series of future cash flows. Typically at least one of the two series of cash flows is determined by a later outcome. In other words, one party agrees to pay the other a series of cash flows whose value will be determined by the unknown future course of some underlying factor, such as an interest rate, exchange rate, stock price, or commodity price. The other party promises to make a series of payments that could also be determined by a second unknown factor or, alternatively, could be preset. We commonly refer to swap payments as being "fixed" or "floating" (sometimes "variable").

---

[6] Defaults are more likely for futures contracts than for forward contracts because participants in the forward markets must meet higher credit-worthiness standards than those in the futures markets. Indeed, many individuals participate in the futures markets; forward market participants are usually large, creditworthy companies. But the forward markets have no guarantor of performance, whereas the futures markets do. Therefore, participants in the forward markets have incurred credit losses in the past, while participants in the futures markets have not.

[7] It is possible for the party engaging in the first transaction to engage in the second transaction with the same party. The two parties agree to cancel their transactions, settling the difference in value in cash and thereby eliminating the risk associated with exchange rates as well as the possibility of default.

[8] A common misconception is that, as a result of their standardized terms, futures contracts are liquid but nonstandardized forward contracts are illiquid. This is not always the case; many futures contracts have low liquidity, and many forward contracts have high liquidity.

We noted that a forward contract is an agreement to buy or sell an underlying asset at a future date at a price agreed on today. A swap in which one party makes a single fixed payment and the other makes a single floating payment amounts to a forward contract. One party agrees to make known payments to the other and receive something unknown in return. This type of contract is like an agreement to buy at a future date, paying a fixed amount and receiving something of unknown future value. That the swap is a *series* of such payments distinguishes it from a forward contract, which is only a single payment.[9]

Swaps, like forward contracts, are private transactions and thus not subject to direct regulation.[10] Swaps are arguably the most successful of all derivative transactions. Probably the most common use of a swap is a situation in which a corporation, currently borrowing at a floating rate, enters into a swap that commits it to making a series of interest payments to the swap counterparty at a fixed rate, while receiving payments from the swap counterparty at a rate related to the floating rate at which it is making its loan payments. The floating components cancel, resulting in the effective conversion of the original floating-rate loan to a fixed-rate loan.

Forward commitments (whether forwards, futures, or swaps) are firm and binding agreements to engage in a transaction at a future date. They obligate each party to complete the transaction, or alternatively, to offset the transaction by engaging in another transaction that settles each party's financial obligation to the other. Contingent claims, on the other hand, allow one party the flexibility to not engage in the future transaction, depending on market conditions.

2.2 Contingent Claims

Contingent claims are derivatives in which the payoffs occur if a specific event happens. We generally refer to these types of derivatives as options. Specifically, an **option** is a financial instrument that gives one party the right, but not the obligation, to buy or sell an underlying asset from or to another party at a fixed price over a specific period of time. An option that gives the right to buy is referred to as a call; an option that gives the right to sell is referred to as a put. The fixed price at which the underlying can be bought or sold is called the exercise price, strike price, striking price, or strike, and is determined at the outset of the transaction. In this book, we refer to it as the exercise price, and the action of buying or selling the underlying at the exercise price is called exercising the option. The holder of the option has the right to exercise it and will do so if conditions are advantageous; otherwise, the option will expire unexercised. Thus, the payoff of the option is contingent on an event taking place, so options are sometimes referred to as contingent claims.

In contrast to participating in a forward or futures contract, which represents a *commitment* to buy or sell, owning an option represents the *right* to buy or sell. To acquire this right, the buyer of the option must pay a price at the start to the option seller. This price is called the option premium or sometimes just the option price. In this book, we usually refer to it as the option price.

Because the option buyer has the right to buy or sell an asset, the seller of the option has the potential commitment to sell or buy this asset. If the option

---

[9] A few other distinctions exist between swaps and forward contracts, such as the fact that swaps can involve both parties paying a variable amount.

[10] Like all over-the-counter derivatives transactions, swaps are subject to indirect regulatory oversight in that the companies using them could be regulated by securities or banking authorities. In addition, swaps, like all contracts, are subject to normal contract and civil law.

buyer has the right to buy, the option seller may be obligated to sell. If the option buyer has the right to sell, the option seller may be obligated to buy. As noted above, the option seller receives the amount of the option price from the option buyer for his willingness to bear this risk.

An important distinction we made between forward and futures contracts was that the former are customized private transactions between two parties without a guarantee against losses from default. The latter are standardized contracts that take place on futures exchanges and are guaranteed by the exchange against losses from default. For options, both types of contracts—over-the-counter customized and exchange-listed standardized—exist. In other words, the buyer and seller of an option can arrange their own terms and create an option contract. Alternatively, the buyer and seller can meet directly, or through their brokers, on an options exchange and trade standardized options. In the case of customized options, the buyer is subject to the possibility of the seller defaulting when and if the buyer decides to exercise the option. Because the option buyer is not obligated to do anything beyond paying the original price, the seller of any type of option is not subject to the buyer defaulting. In the case of a standardized option, the buyer does not face the risk of the seller defaulting. The exchange, through its clearinghouse, guarantees the seller's performance to the buyer.

A variety of other instruments contain options and thus are forms of contingent claims. For instance, many corporations issue convertible bonds offering the holder an optionlike feature that enables the holder to participate in gains on the market price of the corporation's stock without having to participate in losses on the stock. Callable bonds are another example of a common financial instrument that contains an option, in this case the option of the issuer to pay off the bond before its maturity. Options themselves are often characterized in terms of standard or fairly basic options and more advanced options, often referred to as exotic options. There are also options that are not even based on assets but rather on futures contracts or other derivatives. A very widely used group of options is based on interest rates.

Another common type of option is contained in asset-backed securities. An asset-backed security is a claim on a pool of securities. The pool, which might be mortgages, loans, or bonds, is a portfolio assembled by a financial institution that then sells claims on the portfolio. Often, the borrowers who issued the mortgages, loans, or bonds have the right to pay off their debts early, and many choose to do so when interest rates fall significantly. They then refinance their loans by taking out a new loan at a lower interest rate. This right, called a prepayment feature, is a valuable option owned by the borrower. Holders of asset-backed securities bear the risk associated with prepayment options and hence are sellers of those options. The holders, or option sellers, receive a higher promised yield on their bond investment than they would have received on an otherwise equivalent bond without the option.

With an understanding of derivatives, there are no limits to the types of financial instruments that can be constructed, analyzed, and applied to achieve investment objectives. What you learn from this book and the CFA Program will help you recognize and understand the variety of derivatives that appear in many forms in the financial world.

Exhibit 1 presents a classification of the types of derivative contracts as we have described them. Note that we have partitioned derivatives into those that are exchange-traded and those that trade in the over-the-counter market. The exhibit also notes some other categories not specifically mentioned above. These instruments are included for completeness, but they are relatively advanced and not covered in this reading.

EXHIBIT 1	A Classification of Derivatives

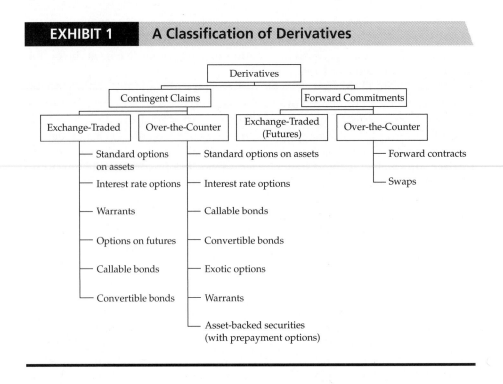

We have now looked at the basic characteristics of derivative contracts. In order to better understand and appreciate derivatives, we should take a quick look at where they came from and where they are now. Accordingly, we take a brief look at the history and current state of derivative markets.

3   DERIVATIVE MARKETS: PAST AND PRESENT

Derivative markets have an exciting and colorful history. Examining that history gives insights that help us understand the structure of these markets as they exist today.

The basic characteristics of derivative contracts can be found throughout the history of humankind. Agreements to engage in a commercial transaction as well as agreements that provide the right to engage in a commercial transaction date back hundreds of years. In medieval times, contracts for the future delivery of an asset with the price fixed at the time of the contract initiation were frequent. Early indications of futures markets were seen in Japan many hundreds of years ago. The futures markets generally trace their roots, however, to the 1848 creation of the Chicago Board of Trade, the first organized futures market. Its origins resulted from the burgeoning grain markets in Chicago, which created a need for a farmer to secure a price at one point in time, store the grain, and deliver it at a later point in time. At around the same time, customized option transactions were being offered, including some by the well-known financier Russell Sage, who found a clever way to offer combinations of customized options that replicated a loan at a rate that exceeded the maximum allowable rate under the then-existing usury laws.[11]

---

[11] Sage was perhaps the first options arbitrageur. Of course, usury laws are rare these days and most investors understand **put–call parity**, so do not expect to make any money copying Sage's scheme.

In the century that followed, the futures industry grew rapidly. Institutions such as the Chicago Board of Trade, the Chicago Mercantile Exchange, and later, the New York Mercantile Exchange and the Chicago Board Options Exchange became the primary forces in the global derivatives industry. These exchanges created and successfully marketed many innovative derivative contracts.[12] Although the first 100 years of futures exchanges were dominated by trading in futures on agricultural commodities, the 1970s saw the introduction of futures on financial instruments such as currencies, bonds, and stock indices. These "financial futures," as well as newly introduced options on individual stocks, currencies, bonds, and stock indices, ushered in a new era in which financial derivatives dominated agricultural derivatives—a situation that continues today. Although the commodity derivatives market includes very active contracts in oil and precious metals, financial derivatives have remained the primary force in the worldwide derivatives market.

Exchange-listed standardized derivatives, however, have hardly been the only instruments in the derivatives world. As noted, customized options have been around since at least the 19th century. The customized-options market flourished until the early 1970s, largely as a retail product. With the introduction of standardized options in 1973, however, the customized options market effectively died. But something else was going on at the time that would later revive this market. In the early 1970s, foreign exchange rates were deregulated and allowed to float freely. This deregulation led not only to the development of a futures, and later options, market for currencies but also to a market for customized forward contracts in foreign currencies. This market became known as the interbank market because it was largely operated within the global banking community, and it grew rapidly. Most importantly, it set the stage for the banking industry to engage in other customized derivative transactions.

Spurred by deregulation of their permitted activities during the 1980s, banks discovered that they could create derivatives of all forms and sell them to corporations and institutions that had risks that could best be managed with products specifically tailored for a given situation. These banks make markets in derivative products by assuming the risks that the corporations want to eliminate. But banks are not in the business of assuming unwanted risks. They use their vast resources and global networks to transfer or lay off the risk elsewhere, often in the futures markets. If they successfully lay off these risks, they can profit by buying and selling the derivatives at a suitable bid–ask spread. In addition to banks, investment banking firms also engage in derivatives transactions of this sort. The commercial and investment banks that make markets in derivatives are called **derivatives dealers**. Buying and selling derivatives is a natural extension of the activity these banks normally undertake in financial markets. This market for customized derivatives is what we refer to as the over-the-counter derivatives market.

By the end of the 20th century, the derivatives market reached a mature stage, growing at only a slow pace but providing a steady offering of existing products and a continuing slate of new products. Derivatives exchanges underwent numerous changes, often spurred by growing competition from the over-the-counter market. Some merged; others that were formerly nonprofit corporations have since become profit making. Some derivatives exchanges have even experimented with offering somewhat customized transactions. Nearly all have lobbied heavily for a reduction in the level or structure of the regulations imposed on them. Some derivatives exchanges have altered the manner in which trading takes place, from the old system of face-to-face on a trading floor (in sections called pits) to off-floor electronic trading in which participants communicate

---

[12] It is probably also important to note that the futures and options exchanges have introduced many unsuccessful contracts as well.

through computer screens. This type of transacting, called electronic trading, has even been extended to the internet and, not surprisingly, is called e-trading. Pit trading is still the primary format for derivatives exchanges in the United States, but electronic trading is clearly the wave of the future. As the dominant form of trading outside the United States, it will likely replace pit trading in the United States in coming years.

Exhibit 2 lists all global derivatives exchanges as of January 2002. Note that almost every country with a reasonably advanced financial market system has a derivatives exchange.

EXHIBIT 2	Global Derivatives Exchanges

North America
American Stock Exchange
Bourse de Montreal
BrokerTec Futures Exchange
Chicago Board Options Exchange
Chicago Board of Trade
Chicago Mercantile Exchange
International Securities Exchange (New York)
Kansas City Board of Trade
Minneapolis Grain Exchange
New York Board of Trade
New York Mercantile Exchange
Pacific Exchange (San Francisco)
Philadelphia Stock Exchange
Winnipeg Commodity Exchange

Asia
Central Japan Commodity Exchange
Dalian Commodity Exchange
Hong Kong Exchanges & Clearing
Kansai Commodities Exchange (Osaka)
Korea Futures Exchange
Korea Stock Exchange
Malaysia Derivatives Exchange
New Zealand Futures & Options Exchange
Osaka Mercantile Exchange
Shanghai Futures Exchange
Singapore Commodity Exchange
Singapore Exchange
Tokyo Commodity Exchange
Tokyo Grain Exchange
Tokyo International Financial Futures Exchange
Tokyo Stock Exchange
Zhengzhou Commodity Exchange

Europe
Bolsa de Valores de Lisboa e Porto
Borsa Italiana
Budapest Commodity Exchange
Eurex Frankfurt
Eurex Zurich
Euronext Amsterdam
Euronext Brussels
Euronext Paris
FUTOP Market (Copenhagen)
Helsinki Exchanges Group
International Petroleum Exchange of London
London International Financial Futures and Options Exchange
London Metal Exchange
MEFF Renta Fija (Barcelona)
MEFF Renta Variable (Madrid)
OM London Exchange
OM Stockholm Exchange
Romanian Commodity Exchange
Sibiu Monetary–Financial and Commodities Exchange (Romania)
Tel Aviv Stock Exchange
Wiener Borse AG (Vienna)

South America
Bolsa de Mercadorias & Futuros (Sao Paulo)
Mercado a Termino de Buenos Aires
Santiago Stock Exchange

Africa
South African Futures Exchange

Australia
Australian Stock Exchange
Sydney Futures Exchange

Source: Futures [magazine] *2002 Sourcebook.*

We cannot technically identify where over-the-counter derivatives markets exist. These types of transactions can conceivably occur anywhere two parties can agree to engage in a transaction. It is generally conceded, however, that London and New York are the primary markets for over-the-counter derivatives; considerable activity also takes place in Tokyo, Paris, Frankfurt, Chicago, Amsterdam, and many other major world cities.

Now we know where the derivative markets are, but are they big enough for us to care about? We examine this question in Section 4.

HOW BIG IS THE DERIVATIVES MARKET?
4

Good question. And the answer is: We really do not know. Because trading in exchange-listed contracts, such as futures and some options, is recorded, volume figures for those types of contracts are available. Exhibit 3 presents summary statistics for contract volume of global futures and options for 2000 and 2001. Note that in 2001, the largest category is equity indices. In 2000, the largest category was individual equities, followed by interest rates. In prior years, the largest category had been interest rates.

Currently, the United States accounts for approximately 35 percent of global futures and options volume. The largest exchange in the world, however, is the Korea Stock Exchange, which trades an exceptionally large volume of options on a Korean stock index. The second-largest exchange (and the largest exchange in terms of futures volume only) is the combined German–Swiss exchange called Eurex. The other largest exchanges (in order of 2001 volume) are the Chicago Mercantile Exchange, the Chicago Board of Trade, the London International Financial Futures and Options Exchange, the Paris Bourse, the New York Mercantile Exchange, the Bolsa de Mercadorias & Futuros of Brazil, and the Chicago Board Options Exchange. All of these exchanges traded at least 70 million contracts in 2001.[13]

EXHIBIT 3	Global Exchange-Traded Futures and Options Contract Volume (in Millions of Contracts)	
Contract Type	**2000**	**2001**
Equity indices	674.8	1,470.3
Interest rates	844.3	1,216.1
Individual equities	969.7	1,112.7
Energy	154.8	166.9
Agricultural	185.7	156.5
Nonprecious metals	75.7	70.2
Currencies	47.0	49.2
Precious metals	36.2	39.1
Other	1.3	0.8
Overall Total	2,989.5	4,281.8

Source: Futures Industry (January/February 2002).

---

[13] *Futures Industry* (January/February 2002).

One important factor that must be considered, however, in looking at trading volume as a measure of activity is that the futures and options exchanges influence their own volume by designating a contract's size. For example, a standard option in the United States covers 100 shares of the underlying stock. If an investor takes a position in options on 1,000 shares of stock, the investor would trade 10 options. If the options exchange had designated that the contract size be 200 shares, then the investor would trade only five contracts. Although there are often good reasons for setting a contract size at a certain level, volume comparisons must be taken with a degree of skepticism.[14]

The over-the-counter derivatives market is much more difficult to measure. Because the transactions are private, unregulated, and can take place virtually anywhere two parties can enter into an agreement, no official tabulation exists that allows us to identify the size of the market. Information is available, however, from semiannual surveys conducted by the Bank for International Settlements (BIS) of Basel, Switzerland, an international organization of central banks. The BIS publishes this data in its semiannual report "Regular OTC Derivatives Market Statistics," available on its website at www.bis.org/publ/regpubl.htm.

Exhibit 4 presents two charts constructed from the 30 June 2001 BIS survey and shows figures for foreign exchange, interest rate, equity, and commodity derivatives transactions. The "other" category, however, does include transactions of these types and reflects the BIS's estimates of positions taken by parties that do not report in this survey. It is used primarily to obtain an estimate for the overall size of the market and is not broken down by category.

For over-the-counter derivatives, notional principal is the most widely used measure of market size. Notional principal measures the amount of the underlying asset covered by a derivative contract. For example, a swap involving interest payments on ¥500 million has a notional principal of ¥500 million. The actual payments made in the swap, however, are merely interest payments on ¥500 million and do not come close to ¥500 million.[15] Thus, although notional principal is a commonly used measure of the size of the market, it can give a misleading impression by suggesting that it reflects the amount of money involved.[16]

Nonetheless, we would be remiss if we failed to note the market size as measured by notional principal. Based on Exhibit 4A, the total notional principal summing over these five categories is almost $100 trillion. Also note that interest rate derivatives are the most widely used category by far.

Exhibit 4B gives another picture of the size of the market by indicating the market value of over-the-counter derivatives. Market value indicates the

---

[14] For example, in 1999 the volume of Treasury bond futures on the Chicago Board of Trade was about 90 million contracts while the volume of Eurodollar futures on the Chicago Mercantile Exchange was about 93 million contracts. Consequently, at that time these two contracts appeared to have about the same amount of activity. But the Treasury bond contract covers Treasury bonds with a face value of $100,000, while the Eurodollar contract covers Eurodollars with a face value of $1,000,000. Thus, the Eurodollar futures market was arguably 10 times the size of the Treasury bond futures market. In 2002, about three Eurodollar futures contracts were traded for every Treasury bond futures contract traded.

[15] In fact, the payments on a swap are even smaller than the interest payments on the notional principal. Swap interest payments usually equal only the difference between the interest payments owed by the two parties.

[16] The over-the-counter derivatives industry originally began the practice of measuring its size by notional principal. This was a deliberate tactic designed to make the industry look larger so it would be more noticed and viewed as a significant and legitimate force. As it turns out, this tactic backfired, resulting in fears that more money was involved and at risk of loss than really was. Calls for increased scrutiny of the industry by government authorities resulted in the industry backpedaling on its use of notional principal and focusing more on market value as a measure of its size. Nonetheless, notional principal continues to be used as one, if not the primary, measure of the industry's size.

EXHIBIT 4A	Outstanding Notional Principal of Global Over-the-Counter Derivatives, 30 June 2001 (Billions)

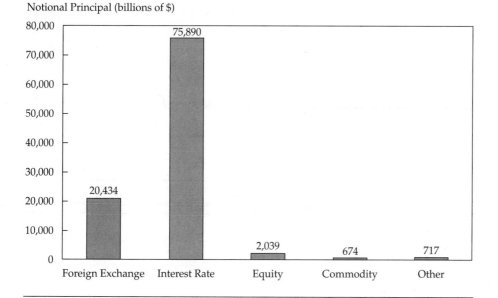

Notional Principal (billions of $)

Source: Bank for International Settlements, www.bis.org/publ/regpubl.htm.

EXHIBIT 4B	Outstanding Market Value of Global Over-the-Counter Derivatives, 30 June 2001 (Billions)

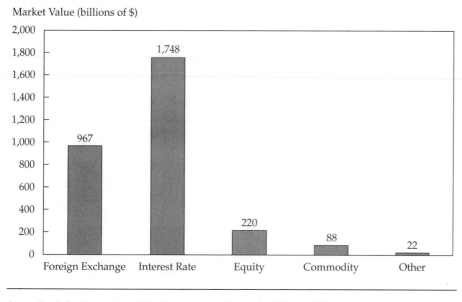

Market Value (billions of $)

Source: Bank for International Settlements, www.bis.org/publ/regpubl.htm.

economic worth of a derivative contract and represents the amount of money that would change hands if these transactions were terminated at the time of the report. The total market value for all categories is about $3 trillion. Market value is a better indication of the size of the market because it more accurately represents the actual money involved. Nonetheless, market value is subject to greater errors in estimation and thus is a less reliable measure than notional principal.

Although it is impossible to determine where these contracts originate, dollar-denominated derivatives represented about 34 percent of the global interest rate derivatives market in 2001, with euro-denominated derivatives accounting for about 27 percent and yen-denominated derivatives representing 17 percent.

Whether notional principal or market value is used, it is clear that the derivatives industry is large by any standard. Derivatives are widely available in global asset markets, and consequently, understanding derivatives is essential to operating in these markets, whether one chooses to use them or not.

Because derivative markets have been created around the world, there must be a reason for their continued existence. Let us now look at why derivative markets exist.

5   THE PURPOSES OF DERIVATIVE MARKETS

Derivative markets serve a variety of purposes in global social and economic systems. One of the primary functions of futures markets is **price discovery**. Futures markets provide valuable information about the prices of the underlying assets on which futures contracts are based. They provide this information in two ways. First, many of these assets are traded in geographically dispersed markets. Recall that the current price of the underlying asset is called the spot price. With geographically dispersed markets, many different spot prices could exist. In the futures markets, the price of the contract with the shortest time to expiration often serves as a proxy for the price of the underlying asset. Second, the prices of all futures contracts serve as prices that can be accepted by those who trade contracts in lieu of facing the risk of uncertain future prices. For example, a company that mines gold can hedge by selling a futures contract on gold expiring in two months, which locks in the price of gold two months later. In this manner, the two-month futures price substitutes for the uncertainty of the price of gold over the next two months.[17]

Futures contracts are not, however, the only derivatives that serve this purpose. In fact, forward contracts and swaps allow users to substitute a single locked-in price for the uncertainty of future spot prices and thereby permit the same form of price discovery as do futures.

Options work in a slightly different manner. They are used in a different form of hedging, one that permits the holder to protect against loss while allowing participation in gains if prices move favorably. Options do not so much reveal *prices* as they reveal *volatility*. As we shall see in the reading on option markets and contracts, the volatility of the underlying asset is a critical factor in the pricing of options. It is possible, therefore, to infer what investors feel about volatility from the prices of options.

---

[17] Some people view futures prices as revealing expectations of future spot prices of the underlying asset, and in that sense, leading to price discovery. This view, however, is incorrect. Futures prices are not necessarily expectations of future spot prices. As we discussed above, they allow a substitution of the futures price for the uncertainty of future spot prices of the asset. In that sense they permit the acceptance of a sure price and the avoidance of risk.

Perhaps the most important purpose of derivative markets is **risk management**. We define risk management as the process of identifying the desired level of risk, identifying the actual level of risk, and altering the latter to equal the former. Often this process is described as hedging, which generally refers to the reduction, and in some cases the elimination, of risk. On the other side is the process called speculation. Traditional discussions of derivatives refer to hedging and speculation as complementary activities. In general, hedgers seek to eliminate risk and need speculators to assume risk, but such is not always the case. Hedgers often trade with other hedgers, and speculators often trade with other speculators. All one needs to hedge or speculate is a party with opposite beliefs or opposite risk exposure. For example, a corporation that mines gold could hedge the future sale of gold by entering into a derivative transaction with a company that manufactures jewelry. Both of these companies are hedgers, seeking to avoid the uncertainty of future gold prices by locking in a price for a future transaction. The mining corporation has concerns about a price decrease, and the jewelry manufacturer is worried about a price increase.

An unfortunate consequence of the use of the terms "hedging" and "speculating" is that hedgers are somehow seen as on the high moral ground and speculators are sometimes seen as evil—a distortion of the role of speculators. In fact, there need be very little difference between hedgers and speculators. To restate an example we used when discussing swaps, consider a corporation that currently borrows at a floating rate. A common response to a fear of rising interest rates is for the corporation to use an interest rate swap in which it will make payments at a fixed rate and receive payments at a floating rate. The floating-rate payments it receives from the swap offset the floating-rate payments on the loan, thereby effectively converting the loan to a fixed-rate loan. The company is now borrowing at a fixed rate and, in the eyes of many, hedging.

But is the company really hedging? Or is it simply making a bet that interest rates will increase? If interest rates decrease, the company will be losing money in the sense of the lost opportunity to borrow at a lower rate. From a budgeting and cash flow standpoint, however, its fixed interest payments are set in stone. Moreover, the market value of a fixed-rate loan is considerably more volatile than that of a floating-rate loan. Thus, our "hedging" corporation can be viewed as taking more risk than it originally had.

The more modern view of the reason for using derivatives does not refer to hedging or speculation. Although we shall sometimes use those terms, we shall use them carefully and make our intentions clear. In the grander scheme of things, derivatives are tools that enable companies to more easily practice risk management. In the context of our corporation borrowing at the floating rate, it made a conscious decision to borrow at a fixed rate. Engaging in the swap is simply an activity designed to align its risk with the risk it wants, given its outlook for interest rates. Whether one calls this activity hedging or speculation is not even very important. The company is simply managing risk.

Derivative markets serve several other useful purposes. As we show later when exploring the pricing of derivative contracts, they improve market efficiency for the underlying assets. Efficient markets are fair and competitive and do not allow one party to easily take money from another. As a simple example, buying a stock index fund can be replicated by buying a futures on the fund and investing in risk-free bonds with the money that otherwise would have been spent on the fund. In other words, the fund and the combination of the futures and risk-free bond will have the same performance. But if the fund costs more than the combination of the futures and risk-free bond, investors have the opportunity to avoid the overpriced fund and take the combination.[18] This decreased demand for the fund will lower its price. The benefits to investors who do not even use derivatives should be clear: They can now invest in the fund at a more attractive price, because the derivatives market forced the price back to its appropriate level.

Derivative markets are also characterized by relatively low transaction costs. For example, the cost of investing in a stock index portfolio is as much as 20 times the cost of buying a futures contract on the index and a risk-free bond as described above. One might reasonably ask why derivatives are so much less expensive in terms of transaction costs. The answer is that derivatives are designed to provide a means of managing risk. As we have previously described, they serve as a form of insurance. Insurance cannot be a viable product if its cost is too high relative to the value of the insured asset. In other words, derivatives must have low transaction costs; otherwise, they would not exist.

It would be remiss to overlook the fact that derivative markets have been subject to many criticisms. We next present some of these complaints and the reasons behind them.

6   CRITICISMS OF DERIVATIVE MARKETS

Derivatives have been highly controversial for a number of reasons. For one, they are very complex. Much of the criticism has stemmed from a failure to understand derivatives. When derivatives fail to do their job, it is often the derivatives themselves, rather than the users of derivatives, that take the blame. Yet, in many cases, the critics of derivatives simply do not understand them well enough. As described in Section 2, when homeowners take out mortgages, they usually receive a valuable option: the right to prepay their mortgages. When interest rates fall, homeowners often pay off their mortgages, refinancing them at lower rates. The holders of these mortgages usually sell them to other parties, which can include small organizations and individuals. Thus, we often find unsophisticated investors holding securities based on the payments from mortgages. When homeowners refinance, they capture huge interest savings. Where does this money come from? It comes from the pockets of the holders of mortgage securities. When these unsophisticated investors lose a lot of money, derivatives usually get the blame. Yet these losses went into the pockets of homeowners in the form of interest savings. Who is to blame? Probably the brokers, who sold the securities to investors who did not know what they were buying—which leads us to the next common criticism of derivatives.

The complexity of derivatives means that sometimes the parties that use them do not understand them well. As a result, they are often used improperly, leading to potentially large losses. Such an argument can, however, be used to describe fire, electricity, and chemicals. Used improperly, perhaps in the hands of a child or someone who does not know how to use them, all of these can be extremely dangerous. Yet, we know that sufficient knowledge of fire, electricity, and chemicals to use them properly is not very difficult to obtain. The same is true for derivatives; treat them with respect and healthy doses of knowledge.

Derivatives are also mistakenly characterized as a form of legalized gambling. Although gambling is certainly legal in many parts of the world, derivatives

---

[18] Some investors, called arbitrageurs, will even find ways to sell the fund short to eliminate the risk of holding the futures and the bond, earning a profit from any discrepancy in their prices. We shall cover this type of transaction later in this reading.

are often viewed as a government's sanction of gambling via the financial markets. But there is an important distinction between gambling and derivatives: The benefits of derivatives extend much further across society. By providing a means of managing risk along with the other benefits discussed above, derivatives make financial markets work better. The organized gambling industry affects the participants, the owners of casinos, and perhaps some citizens who benefit from state lotteries. Organized gambling does not, however, make society function better, and it arguably incurs social costs.

We have taken a look at what derivatives are, where they come from, where they are now, why we have them, and what people think of them. Understanding derivatives, however, requires a basic understanding of the market forces that govern derivative prices. Although we shall cover derivative pricing in more detail in later readings, here we take a brief look at the process of pricing derivatives by examining some important fundamental principles.

ELEMENTARY PRINCIPLES OF DERIVATIVE PRICING

7

In this section, we take a preliminary glance at how derivative contracts are priced. First, we introduce the concept of **arbitrage**. Arbitrage occurs when equivalent assets or combinations of assets sell for two different prices. This situation creates an opportunity to profit at no risk with no commitment of money. Let us start with the simplest (and least likely) opportunity for arbitrage: the case of a stock selling for more than one price at a given time. Assume that a stock is trading in two markets simultaneously. Suppose the stock is trading at $100 in one market and $98 in the other market. We simply buy a share for $98 in one market and immediately sell it for $100 in the other. We have no net position in the stock, so it does not matter what price the stock moves to. We make an easy $2 at no risk and we did not have to put up any funds of our own. The sale of the stock at $100 was more than adequate to finance the purchase of the stock at $98. Naturally, many market participants would do this, which would create downward pressure on the price of the stock in the market where it trades for $100 and upward pressure on the price of the stock in the market where it trades for $98. Eventually the two prices must come together so that there is but a single price for the stock. Accordingly, the principle that no arbitrage opportunities should be available is often referred to as the **law of one price**.

Recall that we mentioned in Section 5 that an asset can potentially trade in different geographic markets and, therefore, have several spot prices. This potential would appear to violate the law of one price, but in reality, the law is still upheld. A given asset selling in two different locations is not necessarily the same asset. If a buyer in one location discovered that it is possible to buy the asset more cheaply in another location, the buyer would still have to incur the cost of moving the asset to the buyer's location. Transportation costs could offset any such price differences.[19]

Now suppose we face the situation illustrated in Exhibit 5. In Exhibit 5A, observe that we have one stock, AXE Electronics, which today is worth $50 and which, one period later, will be worth either $75 or $40. We shall denote these

---

[19] One might reasonably wonder if finding a consumer article selling in Wal-Mart at a lower price than in Target is not a violation of the law of one price. It certainly is, but we make no claim that the market for consumer products is efficient. Our focus is on the financial markets where, for example, Goldman Sachs can hardly offer shares of IBM at one price while Merrill Lynch offers them at another.

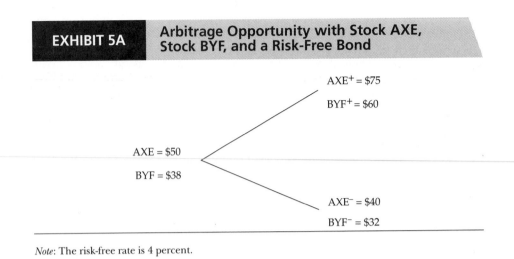

| EXHIBIT 5A | Arbitrage Opportunity with Stock AXE, Stock BYF, and a Risk-Free Bond |

AXE = $50
BYF = $38

AXE$^+$ = $75
BYF$^+$ = $60

AXE$^-$ = $40
BYF$^-$ = $32

Note: The risk-free rate is 4 percent.

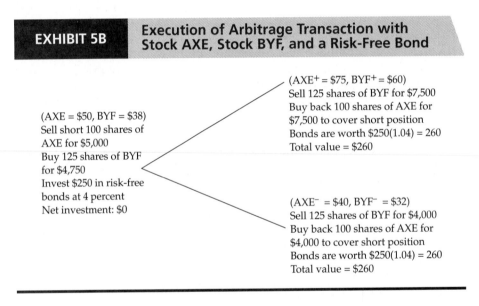

| EXHIBIT 5B | Execution of Arbitrage Transaction with Stock AXE, Stock BYF, and a Risk-Free Bond |

(AXE = $50, BYF = $38)
Sell short 100 shares of
AXE for $5,000
Buy 125 shares of BYF
for $4,750
Invest $250 in risk-free
bonds at 4 percent
Net investment: $0

(AXE$^+$ = $75, BYF$^+$ = $60)
Sell 125 shares of BYF for $7,500
Buy back 100 shares of AXE for
$7,500 to cover short position
Bonds are worth $250(1.04) = 260
Total value = $260

(AXE$^-$ = $40, BYF$^-$ = $32)
Sell 125 shares of BYF for $4,000
Buy back 100 shares of AXE for
$4,000 to cover short position
Bonds are worth $250(1.04) = 260
Total value = $260

prices as AXE = 50, AXE$^+$ = 75, and AXE$^-$ = 40. Another stock, BYF Technology, is today worth $38 and one period later will be worth $60 or $32. Thus, BYF = 38, BYF$^+$ = 60, and BYF$^-$ = 32. Let us assume the risk-free borrowing and lending rate is 4 percent. We assume no dividends on either stock during the period covered by this example.

The opportunity exists to make a profit at no risk without committing any of our funds, as demonstrated in Exhibit 5B. Suppose we borrow 100 shares of stock AXE, which is selling for $50, and sell short, thereby receiving $5,000. We take $4,750 and purchase 125 shares of stock BYF. We invest the remaining $250 in risk-free bonds at 4 percent. This transaction will not require us to put up any funds of our own: The short sale will be sufficient to fund the investment in BYF and leave money to invest in risk-free bonds.

If the top outcome in Exhibit 5 occurs, we sell the 125 shares of BYF for 125 × $60 = $7,500. This amount is sufficient to buy back the 100 shares of AXE, which is selling for $75. But we will also have the bonds, which are worth

$250 \times 1.04 = \$260$. If the bottom outcome occurs, we sell the 125 shares of BYF for $125 \times \$32 = \$4,000$—enough money to buy back the 100 shares of AXE, which is selling for \$40. Again, we will have the risk-free bonds, worth \$260. Regardless of the outcome, we end up with \$260.

Recall that we put up no money of our own and ended up with a sure \$260. It should be apparent that this is an extremely attractive transaction, so everyone would do it. The combined actions of multiple investors would drive down the price of AXE and/or drive up the price of BYF until an equilibrium was reached at which this transaction would not be profitable. Assuming stock BYF's price remained constant, stock AXE would fall to \$47.50. Or assuming stock AXE's price remained constant, stock BYF would rise to \$40.

Of course, this example is extremely simplified. Clearly a stock price can change to more than two other prices. Also, if a given stock is at one price, another stock may be at any other price. We have created a simple case here to illustrate a point. When derivatives are involved, the simplification here is relatively safe. In fact, it is quite appropriate.

Now we look at another type of arbitrage opportunity, which involves a forward contract and will establish an appropriate price for the forward contract. Let stock AXE sell for \$50. We borrow \$50 at 4 percent interest by issuing a risk-free bond, use the money to buy one share of stock AXE, and simultaneously enter into a forward contract to sell this share at a price of \$54 one period later. The stock will then move to either \$75 or \$40 in the next period; the forward contract will require that we deliver the stock and accept \$54 for it; and we shall owe $\$50 \times 1.04 = \$52$ on the loan.

Let us look at the two outcomes. Suppose stock AXE goes to \$75. We deliver the stock to settle the obligation on the forward contract and receive \$54 for it. We use \$52 of the \$54 to pay back the loan, leaving a gain of \$2. Now suppose AXE goes to \$40. We deliver the stock, fulfilling the obligation of the forward contract, and receive \$54. Again, we use \$52 of the \$54 to pay back the loan, leaving a gain of \$2.

In either case we made \$2, free and clear. In fact, we can even accommodate the possibility of more than two future prices for AXE. The key point is that we faced no risk and did not have to put up any of our own money, but we ended up with \$2—clearly a good deal. In fact, this is what we would call an arbitrage profit. But from where did it originate?

It turns out that the forward price we received, \$54, was an inappropriate price given current market conditions. In fact, it was just an arbitrary price, made up to illustrate the point. To eliminate the opportunity to earn the \$2 profit, the forward price should be \$52—equal, not coincidentally, to the amount owed on the loan. It is also no coincidence that \$52 is the price of the asset increased by the rate of interest.

In this example, many market participants would do this transaction as long as it generates an arbitrage profit. These forces of arbitrage would either force the forward price down or force the price of the stock up until an equilibrium is reached that eliminates the opportunity to profit at no risk with no commitment of one's own funds.

We have just had a taste of not only the powerful forces of arbitrage but also a pricing model for one derivative, the forward contract. In this simple example, according to the pricing model, the forward price should be the spot price increased by the interest rate. Although there is a lot more to derivative pricing than shown here, the basic principle remains the same regardless of the type of instrument or the complexity of the setting: *Prices are set to eliminate the opportunity to profit at no risk with no commitment of one's own funds.* There are no opportunities for arbitrage profits.

Lest we be too naive, however, we must acknowledge that there is a large industry of arbitrageurs. So how can such an industry exist if there are no opportunities for riskless profit? One explanation is that most of the arbitrage transactions are more complex than this simple example and involve estimating information, which can result in differing opinions. Arbitrage involving options, for example, usually requires estimates of a stock's volatility. Different participants have different opinions about this volatility. It is quite possible that two counterparties trading with each other can believe that each is arbitraging against the other.

But more importantly, the absence of arbitrage opportunities is upheld, ironically, only if participants believe that arbitrage opportunities *do* exist. If market traders believe that no opportunities exist to earn arbitrage profits, then they will not follow market prices and compare these prices with what they ought to be, as in the forward contract example given above. Without participants watching closely, prices would surely get out of line and offer arbitrage opportunities. Thus, eliminating arbitrage opportunities requires that participants be vigilant to arbitrage opportunities. In other words, strange as it may sound, disbelief and skepticism concerning the absence of arbitrage opportunities are required in order that it hold as a legitimate principle.

Markets in which arbitrage opportunities are either nonexistent or are quickly eliminated are relatively efficient markets. Recall from your study of portfolio theory and investment analysis that efficient markets are those in which it is not possible, except by chance, to earn returns in excess of those that would be fair compensation for the risk assumed. Although abnormal returns can be earned in a variety of ways, arbitrage profits are definitely examples of abnormal returns, relatively obvious to identify and easy to capture. Thus, they are the most egregious violations of the principle of market efficiency. A market in which arbitrage profits do not exist is one in which the most obvious violations of market efficiency have been eliminated.

Throughout this study session, we shall study derivatives by using the principle of arbitrage as a guide. We will assume that arbitrage opportunities cannot exist for any significant length of time. Thus, prices must conform to models that assume no arbitrage. On the other hand, we do not want to take the absence of arbitrage opportunities so seriously that we give up and believe that arbitrage opportunities never exist. Otherwise, they will arise, and someone else will take them from us.

SUMMARY

▶ A derivative contract is a financial instrument with a return that is obtained from or "derived" from the return of another underlying financial instrument.

▶ Exchange-traded derivatives are created, authorized, and traded on a derivatives exchange, an organized facility for trading derivatives. Exchange-traded derivatives are standardized instruments with respect to certain terms and conditions of the contract. They trade in accordance with rules and specifications prescribed by the derivatives exchange and are usually subject to governmental regulation. Exchange-traded derivatives are guaranteed by the exchange against loss resulting from the default of one of the parties. Over-the-counter derivatives are transactions created by any two parties off of a derivatives exchange. The parties set all of their own terms and conditions, and each assumes the credit risk of the other party.

▶ A forward commitment is an agreement between two parties in which one party agrees to buy and the other agrees to sell an asset at a future date at a price agreed on today. The three types of forward commitments are forward contracts, futures contracts, and swaps.

▶ A forward contract is a forward commitment created in the over-the-counter market. A futures contract is a forward commitment created and traded on a futures exchange. A swap is an over-the-counter transaction consisting of a series of forward commitments.

▶ A contingent claim is a derivative contract with a payoff dependent on the occurrence of a future event. The primary types of contingent claims are options, but other types involve variations of options, often combined with other financial instruments or derivatives.

▶ An option is a derivative contract giving one party the right to buy or sell an underlying asset at a fixed price over a period of time or at a specific point in time. The party obtaining the right pays a premium (the option price) at the start and receives the right to buy or sell, as prescribed by the contract. The two types of options are a call (the right to buy) and a put (the right to sell).

▶ The size of the global derivatives market can be measured by notional principal, which is the amount of the underlying on which a derivative is based, and by market value, which is the economic worth of the derivative.

▶ Derivative markets serve many useful purposes such as providing price discovery, facilitating risk management, making markets more efficient, and lowering transaction costs. Derivatives are often criticized as being excessively dangerous for unknowledgeable investors and have been inappropriately likened to gambling.

▶ Arbitrage is a process through which an investor can buy an asset or combination of assets at one price and concurrently sell at a higher price, thereby earning a profit without investing any money or being exposed to any risk. The combined actions of many investors engaging in arbitrage results in rapid price adjustments that eliminate these opportunities, thereby bringing prices back in line and making markets more efficient.

PRACTICE PROBLEMS FOR READING 67

1. For all parties involved, which of the following financial instruments is *not* an example of a forward commitment?

   A. Swap.

   B. Call option.

   C. Futures contract.

2. The main risk faced by an individual who enters into a forward contract to buy the S&P 500 Index is that:

   A. the market may rise.

   B. the market may fall.

   C. market volatility may rise.

3. Which of the following statements is *most* accurate?

   A. Forward contracts are marked to market daily.

   B. Futures contracts have more default risk than forward contracts.

   C. Forward contracts require that both parties to the transaction have a high degree of credit-worthiness.

4. Which of the following statements is *least* accurate?

   A. Futures contracts are easier to offset than forward contracts.

   B. Forward contracts are generally more liquid than futures contracts.

   C. Forward contracts are easier to tailor to specific needs than futures contracts.

5. A swap is *best* characterized as a:

   A. series of forward contracts.

   B. derivative contract that has not gained widespread popularity.

   C. single fixed payment in exchange for a single floating payment.

6. Which of the following is *most* representative of forward contracts and contingent claims?

	Forward Contracts	Contingent Claims
A.	Premium paid at inception	Premium paid at inception
B.	Premium paid at inception	No premium paid at inception
C.	No premium paid at inception	Premium paid at inception

7. For the long position, the *most likely* advantage of contingent claims over forward commitments is that contingent claims:

   A. are easier to offset than forward commitments.

   B. have lower default risk than forward commitments.

   C. permit gains while protecting against losses.

8. For derivative contracts, the notional principal is *best* described as:

   A. the amount of the underlying asset covered by the contract.

   B. a measure of the actual payments made and received in the contract.

   C. tending to underestimate the actual payments made and received in the contract.

9. By volume, the most widely used group of derivatives is the one with contracts written on which of the following types of underlying assets?

   A. Financial.

   B. Commodities.

   C. Energy-related.

10. Which of the following is *least* likely to be a purpose served by derivative markets?

    A. Arbitrage.

    B. Price discovery.

    C. Risk management.

11. The *most likely* reason derivative markets have flourished is that:

    A. derivatives are easy to understand and use.

    B. derivatives have relatively low transaction costs.

    C. the pricing of derivatives is relatively straightforward.

12. A private transaction in which one party agrees to make a single fixed payment in the future and another party agrees to make a single floating payment in the future is *best* characterized as a(n):

    A. futures contract.

    B. forward contract.

    C. over-the-counter contingent claim.

13. A public, standardized transaction that constitutes a commitment between two parties to transfer the underlying asset at a future date at a price agreed upon now is *best* characterized as a(n):

    A. swap.

    B. futures contract.

    C. exchange-traded contingent claim.

SOLUTIONS FOR READING 67

1. B is correct. A call option is not binding on *both* parties in the same sense that the other financial instruments are. The call option gives the holder a right but does not impose an obligation.

2. B is correct. If the market falls, the buyer of a forward contract could pay more for the index, as determined by the price that was contracted for at the inception of the contract, than the index is worth when the contract matures.

3. C is correct. Forward contracts are usually private transactions that do not have an intermediary such as a clearinghouse to guarantee performance by both parties. This type of transaction requires a high degree of credit-worthiness for both parties.

4. B is correct. Forward contracts are usually less liquid than futures contracts because they are typically private transactions tailored to suit both parties, unlike futures contracts, which are usually for standardized amounts and are exchange traded.

5. A is correct. A swap is most like a series of forward contracts. An example is a swap in which one party makes a set of fixed-rate payments over time in exchange for a set of floating-rate payments based on some notional amount.

6. C is correct. Unlike a contingent claim, a forward commitment typically requires no premium to be paid up front. An intuitive way to look at this is to realize that a forward commitment is binding on both parties, so any up-front fees would cancel, while a contingent claim is binding only on the party in the short position. For this, the party in the short position demands (and receives) compensation.

7. C is correct. Because the holder of a contingent claim (the party in the long position) has a right but not an obligation, she will only exercise when it is in her best interest to do so and not otherwise. This will happen only when she stands to gain and never when she stands to lose.

8. A is correct. The notional principal is the amount of the underlying asset covered by the derivative contract.

9. A is correct. The most widely used derivative contracts are written on underlying assets that are financial, such as Treasury instruments and stock indices.

10. A is correct. Arbitrage, or the absence of it, is the basis for pricing most derivative contracts. Consequently, it is relatively unusual, although certainly not impossible, for derivative markets to be used to generate arbitrage profits.

11. B is correct. One reason derivative markets have flourished is that they have relatively low transaction costs. For example, buying a risk-free Treasury security and a futures contract on the S&P 500 Index to replicate payoffs to the index is cheaper than buying the 500 stocks in the index in their proper proportions to get the same payoff.

12. B is correct. The clues that guide the response are 1) the transaction is private, which eliminates the futures contract answer, and 2) the transaction is a commitment ("agrees to make") thus eliminating the contingent claims answers. A swap with a single payment is equivalent to a forward contract.

13. B is correct. The transaction is a commitment, which eliminates the contingent claim answer; the transaction is standardized, which is a characteristic of futures contracts; and the transaction is for single delivery at a future date, which is, in general, not a characteristic of a newly-initiated swap contract.

FORWARD MARKETS AND CONTRACTS
by Don M. Chance, CFA

LEARNING OUTCOMES

The candidate should be able to:	Mastery
a. explain delivery/settlement and default risk for both long and short positions in a forward contract;	☐
b. describe the procedures for settling a forward contract at expiration and discuss how termination alternatives prior to expiration can affect credit risk;	☐
c. differentiate between a dealer and an end user of a forward contract;	☐
d. describe the characteristics of equity forward contracts and forward contracts on zero-coupon and coupon bonds;	☐
e. describe the characteristics of the Eurodollar time deposit market and define LIBOR and Euribor;	☐
f. describe the characteristics and calculate the gain/loss of forward rate agreements (FRAs);	☐
g. calculate and interpret the payoff of an FRA, and explain each of the component terms;	☐
h. describe the characteristics of currency forward contracts.	☐

INTRODUCTION 1

In the reading on derivative markets and instruments, we gave a general overview of global derivative markets. We identified those markets as forward markets, futures markets, options markets, and swap markets. The following series of readings focuses individually on those markets. We begin with forward markets.

First recall our definition of a forward contract: *A forward contract is an agreement between two parties in which one party, the buyer, agrees to buy from the other party, the seller, an underlying asset or other derivative, at a*

Analysis of Derivatives for the Chartered Financial Analyst® Program, by Don M. Chance, CFA. Copyright © 2003 by AIMR. Reprinted with permission.

future date at a price established at the start of the contract. Therefore, it is a commitment by two parties to engage in a transaction at a later date with the price set in advance. The buyer is often called the **long** and the seller is often called the **short**.[1] Although any two parties can agree on such a contract, in this book we are interested only in forward contracts that involve large corporations, financial institutions, nonprofit organizations, or governments.

Recalling an example from the reading on derivative markets and instruments, a pension fund manager, anticipating the receipt of cash at a future date, might enter into a commitment to purchase a stock portfolio at a later date at a price agreed on today. By doing so, the manager's position is unaffected by any changes in the value of the stock portfolio between today and the date of the actual investment in the stock portfolio. In this sense, the manager is hedged against an increase in stock prices until the cash is received and invested. The disadvantage of such a transaction is that the manager is also hedged against any decreases in stock prices. If stock prices fall between the time the commitment is established and the time the cash is received, the manager will regret having entered into the forward contract because the stock could have been acquired at a lower price. But that is the nature of a forward contract hedge: It locks in a price.

An important feature of a forward contract is that neither party pays any money at the start. The parties might require some collateral to minimize the risk of default, but for most of this book, we shall ignore this point. So keep in mind this very important aspect of forward contracts: *No money changes hands at the start.*

1.1 Delivery and Settlement of a Forward Contract

When a forward contract expires, there are two possible arrangements that can be used to settle the obligations of the parties. A deliverable forward contract stipulates that the long will pay the agreed-upon price to the short, who in turn will deliver the underlying asset to the long, a process called **delivery**. An alternative procedure, called **cash settlement**, permits the long and short to pay the net cash value of the position on the delivery date. For example, suppose two parties agree to a forward contract to deliver a zero-coupon bond at a price of $98 per $100 par. At the contract's expiration, suppose the underlying zero-coupon bond is selling at a price of $98.25. The long is due to receive from the short an asset worth $98.25, for which a payment to the short of $98.00 is required. In a cash-settled forward contract, the short simply pays the long $0.25. If the zero-coupon bond were selling for $97.50, the long would pay the short $0.50. Delivery of a zero-coupon bond is not a difficult thing to do, however, and cash-settled contracts are more commonly used in situations where delivery is impractical.[2]

---

[1] As pointed out in the reading on derivative markets and instruments with respect to the word *underlying*, the derivatives industry often uses nouns, verbs, adjectives, and adverbs as parts of speech other than what they are. Hence, words like *long* and *short* are used not as adjectives but as nouns.

[2] Be aware, however, that the choice of delivery or cash settlement is not an option available at expiration. It is negotiated between the parties at the start.

For example, if the underlying is the Russell 3000 Index, the short would have to deliver to the long a portfolio containing each of the Russell 3000 stocks proportionate to its weighting in the index. Consequently, cash settlement is much more practical. Cash-settled forward contracts are sometimes called **NDFs**, for **nondeliverable forwards**, although this term is used predominately with respect to foreign exchange forwards.

1.2 Default Risk and Forward Contracts

An important characteristic of forward contracts is that they are subject to default. Regardless of whether the contract is for delivery or cash settlement, the potential exists for a party to default. In the zero-coupon bond example above, the long might be unable to pay the $98 or the short might be unable to buy the zero-coupon bond and make delivery of the bond to the long. Generally speaking, however, forward contracts are structured so that only the party owing the greater amount can default. In other words, if the short is obligated to deliver a zero-coupon bond selling for more than $98, then the long would not be obligated to make payment unless the short makes delivery. Likewise, in a cash settled contract, only one party—the one owing the greater amount—can default. We discuss the nature of this credit risk in the following section and in Section 5 after we have determined how to value forward contracts.

1.3 Termination of a Forward Contract

Let us note that a forward contract is nearly always constructed with the idea that the participants will hold on to their positions until the contract expires and either engage in delivery of the asset or settle the cash equivalent, as required in the specific contract. The possibility exists, however, that at least one of the participants might wish to terminate the position prior to expiration. For example, suppose a party goes long, meaning that she agrees to buy the asset at the expiration date at the price agreed on at the start, but she subsequently decides to terminate the contract before expiration. We shall assume that the contract calls for delivery rather than cash settlement at expiration.

To see the details of the contract termination, suppose it is part of the way through the life of the contract, and the long decides that she no longer wishes to buy the asset at expiration. She can then re-enter the market and create a new forward contract expiring at the same time as the original forward contract, taking the position of the seller instead. Because of price changes in the market during the period since the original contract was created, this new contract would likely have a different price at which she would have to commit to sell. She would then be long a contract to buy the asset at expiration at one price and short a contract to sell the asset at expiration at a different price. It should be apparent that she has no further exposure to the price of the asset.

For example, suppose she is long to buy at $40 and short to deliver at $42. Depending on the characteristics of the contract, one of several possibilities could occur at expiration. Everything could go as planned—the party holding the short position of the contract on which she is long at $40 delivers the asset to her, and she pays him $40. She then delivers the asset to the party who is long the contract on which she is short at $42. That party pays her $42. She nets $2. The transaction is over.

There is always a possibility that her counterparty on the long contract could default. She is still obligated to deliver the asset on the short contract, for which she will receive $42. But if her counterparty on the long contract defaults, she has to buy the asset in the market and could suffer a significant loss. There is also a possibility that the counterparty on her short contract could fail to pay her the $42. Of course, she would then not deliver the asset but would be exposed to the risk of changes in the asset's price. This type of problem illustrates the credit risk in a forward contract.

To avoid the credit risk, when she re-enters the market to go short the forward contract, she could contact the same counterparty with whom she engaged in the long forward contract. They could agree to cancel both contracts. Because she would be owed $2 at expiration, cancellation of the contract would result in the counterparty paying her the present value of $2. This termination or offset of the original forward position is clearly desirable for both counterparties because it eliminates the credit risk.[3] It is always possible, however, that she might receive a better price from another counterparty. If that price is sufficiently attractive and she does not perceive the credit risk to be too high, she may choose to deal with the other counterparty and leave the credit risk in the picture.

2 THE STRUCTURE OF GLOBAL FORWARD MARKETS

The global market for forward contracts is part of a vast network of financial institutions that make markets in these instruments as well as in other related derivatives, such as swaps and options. Some dealers specialize in certain markets and contracts, such as forward contracts on the euro or forward contracts on Japanese equity products. These dealers are mainly large global banking institutions, but many large non-banking institutions, such as Goldman Sachs and Merrill Lynch, are also big players in this market.

Dealers engage in transactions with two types of parties: end users and other dealers. An end user is typically a corporation, nonprofit organization, or government.[4] An end user is generally a party with a risk management problem that is searching for a dealer to provide it with a financial transaction to solve that problem. Although the problem could simply be that the party wants to take a position in anticipation of a market move, more commonly the end user has a risk it wants to reduce or eliminate.

As an example, Hoffman-LaRoche, the large Swiss pharmaceutical company, sells its products globally. Anticipating the receipt of a large amount of cash in U.S. dollars and worried about a decrease in the value of the dollar relative to the Swiss franc, it could buy a forward contract to sell the dollar and buy Swiss francs. It might seek out a dealer such as UBS Warburg, the investment firm affiliated with the large Swiss bank UBS, or it might approach any of the other large multinational banks with which it does business. Or it might end up dealing with a nonbank entity, like Merrill Lynch. Assume that Hoffman-LaRoche enters into this contract with UBS Warburg. Hoffman-LaRoche is the end user; UBS Warburg is the dealer.

---

[3] This statement is made under the assumption that the parties do not want the credit risk. Credit risk, like other risks, however, can be a risk that some parties want because of the potential for earning attractive returns by using their expertise in measuring the actual credit risk relative to the credit risk as perceived by the market. In addition, credit risk offers diversification benefits.

[4] The U.S. government does not transact in forward contracts or other derivatives, but some foreign governments and central banks do. Within the United States, however, some state and local governments do engage in forward contracts and other derivatives.

Transactions in forward contracts typically are conducted over the phone. Each dealer has a quote desk, whose phone number is well known to the major participants in the market. If a party wishes to conduct a transaction, it simply phones the dealer for a quote. The dealer stands ready to take either side of the transaction, quoting a bid and an ask price or rate. The bid is the price at which the dealer is willing to pay for the future purchase of the asset, and the ask is the price at which the dealer is willing to sell. When a dealer engages in a forward transaction, it has then taken on risk from the other party. For example, in the aforementioned transaction of Hoffman-LaRoche and UBS Warburg, by entering into the contract, UBS Warburg takes on a risk that Hoffman-LaRoche has eliminated. Specifically, UBS Warburg has now committed to buying dollars and selling Swiss francs at a future date. Thus, UBS Warburg is effectively long the dollar and stands to gain from a strengthening dollar/weakening Swiss franc. Typically dealers do not want to hold this exposure. Rather, they find another party to offset the exposure with another derivative or spot transaction. Thus, UBS Warburg is a wholesaler of risk—buying it, selling it, and trying to earn a profit off the spread between its buying price and selling price.

One might reasonably wonder why Hoffman-LaRoche could not avoid the cost of dealing with UBS Warburg. In some cases, it might be able to. It might be aware of another party with the exact opposite needs, but such a situation is rare. The market for financial products such as forward contracts is made up of wholesalers of risk management products who use their technical expertise, their vast network of contacts, and their access to critical financial market information to provide a more efficient means for end users to engage in such risk management transactions.

Dealers such as UBS Warburg lay off the risk they do not wish to assume by transacting with other dealers and potentially other end users. If they do this carefully, quickly, and at accurate prices, they can earn a profit from this market-making activity. One should not get the impression, however, that market making is a highly profitable activity. The competition is fierce, which keeps bid–ask spreads very low and makes it difficult to earn much money on a given transaction. Indeed, many market makers do not make much money on individual transactions—they typically make a small amount of money on each transaction and do a large number of transactions. They may even lose money on some standard transactions, hoping to make up losses on more-complicated, nonstandard transactions, which occur less frequently but have higher bid–ask spreads.

Risk magazine conducts annual surveys to identify the top dealers in various derivative products. Exhibit 1 presents the results of those surveys for two of the forward products we cover here, currency and interest rate forwards. Interest rate forwards are called forward rate agreements (FRAs). In the next section, we shall study the different types of forward contracts and note that there are some others not covered in the *Risk* surveys.

One of these surveys was sent to banks and investment banks that are active dealers in over-the-counter derivatives. The other survey was sent to end users. The tabulations are based on respondents' simple rankings of who they think are the best dealers. Although the identities of the specific dealer firms are not critical, it is interesting and helpful to be aware of the major players in these types of contracts. Most of the world's leading global financial institutions are listed, but many other big names are not. It is also interesting to observe that the perceptions of the users of these dealer firms' services differ somewhat from the dealers' self-perceptions. Be aware, however, that the rankings change, sometimes drastically, each year.

EXHIBIT 1	*Risk* Magazine Surveys of Banks, Investment Banks, and Corporate End Users to Determine the Top Three Dealers in Currency and Interest Rate Forwards

| | Respondents | |
Currencies	Banks and Investment Banks	Corporate End Users
Currency Forwards		
$/€	UBS Warburg	Citigroup
	Deutsche Bank	Royal Bank of Scotland
	JP Morgan Chase	JP Morgan Chase/Bank of America
$/¥	UBS Warburg	Citigroup
	Citigroup	Bank of America
	JP Morgan Chase	JP Morgan Chase/UBS Warburg
$/£	UBS Warburg	Royal Bank of Scotland
	Royal Bank of Scotland	Citigroup
	Hong Kong Shanghai Banking Corporation	UBS Warburg
$/SF	UBS Warburg	UBS Warburg
	Credit Suisse First Boston	Citigroup
	BNP Paribas	Credit Suisse First Boston
Interest Rate Forwards (FRAs)		
$	JP Morgan Chase	JP Morgan Chase
	Bank of America	Royal Bank of Scotland
	Deutsche Bank	Bank of America
€	Deutsche Bank	Royal Bank of Scotland
	Intesa BCI	JP Morgan Chase
	Royal Bank of Scotland	Deutsche Bank
¥	Mizuho Securities	Citigroup
	JP Morgan Chase	Merrill Lynch
	BNP Paribas	Hong Kong Shanghai Banking Corporation
£	Royal Bank of Scotland	Royal Bank of Scotland
	Commerzbank	Bank of America/ING Barings
	Deutsche Bank	
SF	Credit Suisse First Boston	UBS Warburg
	UBS Warburg	Credit Suisse First Boston
	Deutsche Bank	Citigroup/ING Barings

Note: $ = U.S. dollar, € = euro, ¥ = Japanese yen, £ = U.K. pound sterling, SF = Swiss franc.

Source: *Risk*, September 2002, pp. 30–67 for banks and investment banking dealer respondents, and June 2002, pp. 24–34 for end user respondents. The end user survey provides responses from corporations and asset managers. The above results are for corporate respondents only.

TYPES OF FORWARD CONTRACTS   3

In this section, we examine the types of forward contracts that fall within the scope of this book. By the word "types," we mean the underlying asset groups on which these forward contracts are created. Because the CFA Program focuses on the asset management industry, our primary interest is in equity, interest rate and fixed-income, and currency forwards.

3.1 Equity Forwards

An **equity forward** is a contract calling for the purchase of an individual stock, a stock portfolio, or a stock index at a later date. For the most part, the differences in types of equity forward contracts are only slight, depending on whether the contract is on an individual stock, a portfolio of stocks, or a stock index.

3.1.1 Forward Contracts on Individual Stocks

Consider an asset manager responsible for the portfolio of a high-net-worth individual. As is sometimes the case, such portfolios may be concentrated in a small number of stocks, sometimes stocks that have been in the family for years. In many cases, the individual may be part of the founding family of a particular company. Let us say that the stock is called Gregorian Industries, Inc., or GII, and the client is so heavily invested in this stock that her portfolio is not diversified. The client notifies the portfolio manager of her need for $2 million in cash in six months. This cash can be raised by selling 16,000 shares at the current price of $125 per share. Thus, the risk exposure concerns the market value of $2 million of stock. For whatever reason, it is considered best not to sell the stock any earlier than necessary. The portfolio manager realizes that a forward contract to sell GII in six months will accomplish the client's desired objective. The manager contacts a forward contract dealer and obtains a quote of $128.13 as the price at which a forward contract to sell the stock in six months could be constructed. In other words, the portfolio manager could enter into a contract to sell the stock to the dealer in six months at $128.13. We assume that this contract is deliverable, meaning that when the sale is actually made, the shares will be delivered to the dealer. Assuming that the client has some flexibility in the amount of money needed, let us say that the contract is signed for the sale of 15,600 shares at $128.13, which will raise $1,998,828. Of course when the contract expires, the stock could be selling for any price. The client can gain or lose on the transaction. If the stock rises to a price above $128.13 during the six-month period, the client will still have to deliver the stock for $128.13. But if the price falls, the client will still get $128.13 per share for the stock.

3.1.2 Forward Contracts on Stock Portfolios

Because modern portfolio theory and good common sense dictate that investors should hold diversified portfolios, it is reasonable to assume that forward contracts on specific stock portfolios would be useful. Suppose a pension fund manager knows that in three months he will need to sell about $20 million of stock to make payments to retirees. The manager has analyzed the portfolio and determined the precise identities of the stocks he wants to sell and the number of shares of each that he would like to sell. Thus the manager has designated a specific subportfolio to be sold. The problem is that the prices of these stocks in three months are uncertain. The manager can, however, lock in the sale prices by entering into a forward contract to sell the portfolio. This can be done one of two ways.

The manager can enter into a forward contract on each stock that he wants to sell. Alternatively, he can enter into a forward contract on the overall portfolio. The first way would be more costly, as each contract would incur administrative costs, whereas the second way would incur only one set of costs.[5] Assume that the manager chooses the second method. He provides a list of the stocks and number of shares of each he wishes to sell to the dealer and obtains a quote. The dealer gives him a quote of $20,200,000. So, in three months, the manager will sell the stock to the dealer and receive $20,200,000. The transaction can be structured to call for either actual delivery or cash settlement, but in either case, the client will effectively receive $20,200,000 for the stock.[6]

3.1.3 Forward Contracts on Stock Indices

Many equity forward contracts are based on a stock index. For example, consider a U.K. asset manager who wants to protect the value of her portfolio that is a Financial Times Stock Exchange 100 index fund, or who wants to eliminate a risk for which the FTSE 100 Index is a sufficiently accurate representation of the risk she wishes to eliminate. For example, the manager may be anticipating the sale of a number of U.K. blue chip shares at a future date. The manager could, as in our stock portfolio example, take a specific portfolio of stocks to a forward contract dealer and obtain a forward contract on that portfolio. She realizes, however, that a forward contract on a widely accepted benchmark would result in a better price quote, because the dealer can more easily hedge the risk with other transactions. Moreover, the manager is not even sure which stocks she will still be holding at the later date. She simply knows that she will sell a certain amount of stock at a later date and believes that the FTSE 100 is representative of the stock that she will sell. The manager is concerned with the systematic risk associated with the U.K. stock market, and accordingly, she decides that selling a forward contract on the FTSE 100 would be a good way to manage the risk.

Assume that the portfolio manager decides to protect £15,000,000 of stock. The dealer quotes a price of £6,000 on a forward contract covering £15,000,000. We assume that the contract will be cash settled because such index contracts are nearly always done that way. When the contract expiration date arrives, let us say that the index is at £5,925—a decrease of 1.25 percent from the forward price. Because the manager is short the contract and its price went down, the transaction makes money. But how much did it make on a notional principal of £15,000,000?

---

[5] Ignoring those costs, there would be no difference in doing forward contracts on individual stocks or a single forward contract on a portfolio. Because of the non-linearity of their payoffs, this is not true for options. A portfolio of options is not the same as an option on a portfolio, but a portfolio of forward contracts is the same as a forward contract on a portfolio, ignoring the aforementioned costs.

[6] If, for example, the stock is worth $20,500,000 and the transaction calls for delivery, the manager will transfer the stocks to the dealer and receive $20,200,000. The client effectively takes an opportunity loss of $300,000. If the transaction is structured as a cash settlement, the client will pay the dealer $300,000. The client would then sell the stock in the market, receiving $20,500,000 and netting $20,200,000 after settling the forward contract with the dealer. Similarly, if the stock is selling for less than the amount guaranteed by the forward contract, the client will deliver the stock and receive $20,200,000 or, if the transaction is cash settled, the client will sell the stock in the market and receive a cash payment from the dealer, making the effective sale price still $20,200,000.

The index declined by 1.25 percent. Thus, the transaction should make $0.0125 \times £15,000,000 = £187,500$. In other words, the dealer would have to pay £187,500 in cash. If the portfolio were a FTSE 100 index fund, then it would be viewed as a portfolio initially worth £15,000,000 that declined by 1.25 percent, a loss of £187,500. The forward contract offsets this loss. Of course, in reality, the portfolio is not an index fund and such a hedge is not perfect, but as noted above, there are sometimes reasons for preferring that the forward contract be based on an index.

3.1.4 The Effect of Dividends

It is important to note the effect of dividends in equity forward contracts. Any equity portfolio nearly always has at least a few stocks that pay dividends, and it is inconceivable that any well-known equity index would not have some component stocks that pay dividends. Equity forward contracts typically have payoffs based only on the price of the equity, value of the portfolio, or level of the index. They do not ordinarily pay off any dividends paid by the component stocks. An exception, however, is that some equity forwards on stock indices are based on total return indices. For example, there are two versions of the well-known S&P 500 Index. One represents only the market value of the stocks. The other, called the S&P 500 Total Return Index, is structured so that daily dividends paid by the stocks are reinvested in additional units of the index, as though it were a portfolio. In this manner, the rate of return on the index, and the payoff of any forward contract based on it, reflects the payment and reinvestment of dividends into the underlying index. Although this feature might appear attractive, it is not necessarily of much importance in risk management problems. The variability of prices is so much greater than the variability of dividends that managing price risk is considered much more important than worrying about the uncertainty of dividends.

In summary, equity forwards can be based on individual stocks, specific stock portfolios, or stock indices. Moreover, these underlying equities often pay dividends, which can affect forward contracts on equities. Let us now look at bond and **interest rate forward** contracts.

3.2 Bond and Interest Rate Forward Contracts

Forward contracts on bonds are similar to forward contracts on interest rates, but the two are different instruments. Forward contracts on bonds, in fact, are no more difficult to understand than those on equities. Drawing on our experience of Section 3.1, we simply extend the notion of a forward contract on an individual stock, a specific stock portfolio, or a stock index to that of a forward contract on an individual bond, a specific bond portfolio, or a bond index.[7]

3.2.1 Forward Contracts on Individual Bonds and Bond Portfolios

Although a forward contract on a bond and one on a stock are similar, some basic differences nonetheless exist between the two. For example, the bond may pay a coupon, which corresponds somewhat to the dividend that a stock might pay. But unlike a stock, a bond matures, and a forward contract on a bond must

---

[7] It may be useful to review Chapters 1 and 3 of *Fixed Income Analysis for the Chartered Financial Analyst Program* by Frank J. Fabozzi, New Hope, PA: Frank J. Fabozzi Associates (2000).

expire prior to the bond's maturity date. In addition, bonds often have many special features such as calls and convertibility. Finally, we should note that unlike a stock, a bond carries the risk of default. A forward contract written on a bond must contain a provision to recognize how default is defined, what it means for the bond to default, and how default would affect the parties to the contract.

In addition to forward contracts on individual bonds, there are also forward contracts on portfolios of bonds as well as on bond indices. The technical distinctions between forward contracts on individual bonds and collections of bonds, however, are relatively minor.

The primary bonds for which we shall consider forward contracts are default-free zero-coupon bonds, typically called Treasury bills or T-bills in the United States, which serve as a proxy for the risk-free rate.[8] In a forward contract on a T-bill, one party agrees to buy the T-bill at a later date, prior to the bill's maturity, at a price agreed on today. T-bills are typically sold at a discount from par value and the price is quoted in terms of the discount rate. Thus, if a 180-day T-bill is selling at a discount of 4 percent, its price per $1 par will be $1 − 0.04(180/360) = $0.98. The use of 360 days is the convention in calculating the discount. So the bill will sell for $0.98. If purchased and held to maturity, it will pay off $1. This procedure means that the interest is deducted from the face value in advance, which is called **discount interest**.

The T-bill is usually traded by quoting the discount rate, not the price. It is understood that the discount rate can be easily converted to the price by the above procedure. A forward contract might be constructed that would call for delivery of a 90-day T-bill in 60 days. Such a contract might sell for $0.9895, which would imply a discount rate of 4.2 percent because $1 − 0.042(90/360) = $0.9895.

In addition to forward contracts on zero-coupon bonds/T-bills, there are also forward contracts on default-free coupon-bearing bonds, also called Treasury bonds in the United States. These instruments pay interest, typically in semi-annual installments, and can sell for more (less) than par value if the yield is lower (higher) than the coupon rate. Prices are typically quoted without the interest that has accrued since the last coupon date, but with a few exceptions, we shall always work with the full price—that is, the price including accrued interest. Prices are often quoted by stating the yield. Forward contracts call for delivery of such a bond at a date prior to the bond's maturity, for which the long pays the short the agreed-upon price.

3.2.2 Forward Contracts on Interest Rates: Forward Rate Agreements

So far in Section 3.2 we have discussed forward contracts on actual fixed-income securities. Fixed-income security prices are driven by interest rates. A more common type of forward contract is the interest rate forward contract, more commonly called a **forward rate agreement** or **FRA**. Before we can begin to understand FRAs, however, we must examine the instruments on which they are based.

There is a large global market for time deposits in various currencies issued by large creditworthy banks. This market is primarily centered in London but also exists elsewhere, though not in the United States. The primary time deposit instrument is called the **Eurodollar**, which is a dollar deposited outside the

---

[8] A government-issued zero-coupon bond is typically used as a proxy for a risk-free asset because it is assumed to be free of default risk. It can be purchased and held to maturity, thereby eliminating any market value risk, and it has no reinvestment risk because it has no coupons. If the bond is liquidated before maturity, however, some market value risk exists in addition to the risk associated with reinvesting the market price.

United States. Banks borrow dollars from other banks by issuing Eurodollar time deposits, which are essentially short-term unsecured loans. In London, the rate on such dollar loans is called the London Interbank Rate. Although there are rates for both borrowing and lending, in the financial markets the lending rate, called the **London Interbank Offer Rate** or **LIBOR**, is more commonly used in derivative contracts. LIBOR is the rate at which London banks lend dollars to other London banks. Even though it represents a loan outside of the United States, LIBOR is considered to be the best representative rate on a dollar borrowed by a private, i.e., nongovernmental, high-quality borrower. It should be noted, however, that the London market includes many branches of banks from outside the United Kingdom, and these banks are also active participants in the Eurodollar market.

A Eurodollar time deposit is structured as follows. Let us say a London bank such as NatWest needs to borrow $10 million for 30 days. It obtains a quote from the Royal Bank of Scotland for a rate of 5.25 percent. Thus, 30-day LIBOR is 5.25 percent. If NatWest takes the deal, it will owe $10,000,000 \times [1 + 0.0525(30/360)] = $10,043,750$ in 30 days. Note that, like the Treasury bill market, the convention in the Eurodollar market is to prorate the quoted interest rate over 360 days. In contrast to the Treasury bill market, the interest is not deducted from the principal. Rather, it is added on to the face value, a procedure appropriately called **add-on interest**. The market for Eurodollar time deposits is quite large, and the rates on these instruments are assembled by a central organization and quoted in financial newspapers. The British Bankers Association publishes a semi-official Eurodollar rate, compiled from an average of the quotes of London banks.

The U.S. dollar is not the only instrument for which such time deposits exist. Eurosterling, for example, trades in Tokyo, and Euroyen trades in London. You may be wondering about Euroeuro. Actually, there is no such entity as Euroeuro, at least not by that name. The Eurodollar instrument described here has nothing to do with the European currency known as the euro. Eurodollars, Euroyen, Eurosterling, etc. have been around longer than the euro currency and, despite the confusion, have retained their nomenclature. An analogous instrument does exist, however—a euro-denominated loan in which one bank borrows euros from another. Trading in euros and euro deposits occurs in most major world cities, and two similar rates on such euro deposits are commonly quoted. One, called EuroLIBOR, is compiled in London by the British Bankers Association, and the other, called Euribor, is compiled in Frankfurt and published by the European Central Bank. Euribor is more widely used and is the rate we shall refer to in this book.

Now let us return to the world of FRAs. FRAs are contracts in which the underlying is neither a bond nor a Eurodollar or Euribor deposit but simply an interest payment made in dollars, Euribor, or any other currency at a rate appropriate for that currency. Our primary focus will be on dollar LIBOR and Euribor, so we shall henceforth adopt the terminology LIBOR to represent dollar LIBOR and Euribor to represent the euro deposit rate.

Because the mechanics of FRAs are the same for all currencies, for illustrative purposes we shall use LIBOR. Consider an FRA expiring in 90 days for which the underlying is 180-day LIBOR. Suppose the dealer quotes this instrument at a rate of 5.5 percent. Suppose the end user goes long and the dealer goes short. The end user is essentially long the rate and will benefit if rates increase. The dealer is essentially short the rate and will benefit if rates decrease. The contract covers a given notional principal, which we shall assume is $10 million.

The contract stipulates that at expiration, the parties identify the rate on new 180-day LIBOR time deposits. This rate is called 180-day LIBOR. It is, thus, the underlying rate on which the contract is based. Suppose that at expiration in

90 days, the rate on 180-day LIBOR is 6 percent. That 6 percent interest will be paid 180 days later. Therefore, the present value of a Eurodollar time deposit at that point in time would be

$$\frac{\$10,000,000}{1 + 0.06\left(\dfrac{180}{360}\right)}$$

At expiration, then, the end user, the party going long the FRA in our example, receives the following payment from the dealer, which is the party going short:

$$\$10,000,000\left[\frac{(0.06 - 0.055)\left(\dfrac{180}{360}\right)}{1 + 0.06\left(\dfrac{180}{360}\right)}\right] = \$24,272$$

If the underlying rate is less than 5.5 percent, the payment is calculated based on the difference between the 5.5 percent rate and the underlying rate and is paid by the long to the short. It is important to note that even though the contract expires in 90 days, the rate is on a 180-day LIBOR instrument; therefore, the rate calculation adjusts by the factor 180/360. The fact that 90 days have elapsed at expiration is not relevant to the calculation of the payoff.

Before presenting the general formula, let us review the calculations in the numerator and denominator. In the numerator, we see that the contract is obviously paying the difference between the actual rate that exists in the market on the contract expiration date and the agreed-upon rate, adjusted for the fact that the rate applies to a 180-day instrument, multiplied by the notional principal. The divisor appears because when Eurodollar rates are quoted in the market, they are based on the assumption that the rate applies to an instrument that accrues interest at that rate with the interest paid a certain number of days (here 180) later. When participants determine this rate in the London Eurodollar market, it is understood to apply to a Eurodollar time deposit that begins now and matures 180 days later. So the interest on an actual Eurodollar deposit would not be paid until 180 days later. Thus, it is necessary to adjust the FRA payoff to reflect the fact that the rate implies a payment that would occur 180 days later on a standard Eurodollar deposit. This adjustment is easily done by simply discounting the payment at the current LIBOR, which here is 6 percent, prorated over 180 days. These conventions are also followed in the market for FRAs with other underlying rates.

In general, the FRA payoff formula (from the perspective of the party going long) is

$$\text{Notional principal}\left[\frac{(\text{Underlying rate at expiration} - \text{Forward contract rate})\left(\dfrac{\text{Days in underlying rate}}{360}\right)}{1 + \text{Underlying rate at expiration}\left(\dfrac{\text{Days in underlying rate}}{360}\right)}\right]$$

where *forward contract rate* represents the rate the two parties agree will be paid and *days in underlying rate* refers to the number of days to maturity of the instrument on which the underlying rate is based.

One somewhat confusing feature of FRAs is the fact that they mature in a certain number of days and are based on a rate that applies to an instrument maturing in a certain number of days measured from the maturity of the FRA.

EXHIBIT 2	FRA Descriptive Notation and Interpretation	
Notation	**Contract Expires in**	**Underlying Rate**
1 × 3	1 month	60-day LIBOR
1 × 4	1 month	90-day LIBOR
1 × 7	1 month	180-day LIBOR
3 × 6	3 months	90-day LIBOR
3 × 9	3 months	180-day LIBOR
6 × 12	6 months	180-day LIBOR
12 × 18	12 months	180-day LIBOR

Note: This list is not exhaustive and represents only the most commonly traded FRAs.

Thus, there are two day figures associated with each contract. Our example was a 90-day contract on 180-day LIBOR. To avoid confusion, the FRA markets use a special type of terminology that converts the number of days to months. Specifically, our example FRA is referred to as a 3 × 9, reflecting the fact that the contract expires in three months and that six months later, or nine months from the contract initiation date, the interest is paid on the underlying Eurodollar time deposit on whose rate the contract is based.[9]

FRAs are available in the market for a variety of maturities that are considered somewhat standard. Exhibit 2 presents the most common maturities. Most dealers follow the convention that contracts should expire in a given number of exact months and should be on the most commonly traded Eurodollar rates such as 30-day LIBOR, 60-day LIBOR, 90-day LIBOR, 180-day LIBOR, and so on. If a party wants a contract expiring in 37 days on 122-day LIBOR, it would be considered an exception to the standard, but most dealers would be willing to make a market in such an instrument. Such nonstandard instruments are called *off the run*. Of course, FRAs are available in all of the leading currencies.

The FRA market is large, but not as large as the swaps market. It is important, however, to understand FRAs before trying to understand swaps. As we will show in the reading on swap markets and contracts, a swap is a special combination of FRAs. But let us now turn to another large forward market, the market for currency forwards.

3.3 Currency Forward Contracts

Spurred by the relaxation of government controls over the exchange rates of most major currencies in the early 1970s, a currency forward market developed and grew extremely large. Currency forwards are widely used by banks and corporations to manage foreign exchange risk. For example, suppose Microsoft has a European subsidiary that expects to send it €12 million in three months. When Microsoft receives the euros, it will then convert them to dollars. Thus, Microsoft is essentially long euros because it will have to sell euros, or equivalently, it is short dollars because it will have to buy dollars. A currency forward contract is especially useful in this situation, because it enables Microsoft to lock in the rate

---

[9] The notation "3 × 9" is pronounced "three by nine."

at which it will sell euros and buy dollars in three months. It can do this by going short the forward contract, meaning that it goes short the euro and long the dollar. This arrangement serves to offset its otherwise long-euro, short-dollar position. In other words, it needs a forward contract to sell euros and buy dollars.

For example, say Microsoft goes to JP Morgan Chase and asks for a quote on a currency forward for €12 million in three months. JP Morgan Chase quotes a rate of $0.925, which would enable Microsoft to sell euros and buy dollars at a rate of $0.925 in three months. Under this contract, Microsoft would know it could convert its €12 million to 12,000,000 × $0.925 = $11,100,000. The contract would also stipulate whether it will settle in cash or will call for Microsoft to actually deliver the euros to the dealer and be paid $11,100,000. This simplified example is a currency forward hedge.

Now let us say that three months later, the spot rate for euros is $0.920. Microsoft is quite pleased that it locked in a rate of $0.925. It simply delivers the euros and receives $11,100,000 at an exchange rate of $0.925.[10] Had rates risen, however, Microsoft would still have had to deliver the euros and accept a rate of $0.925.

A few variations of currency forward contracts exist, but most of them are somewhat specialized and beyond the objectives of this book. Let us now take a very brief look at a few other types of forward contracts.

3.4 Other Types of Forward Contracts

Although this book focuses primarily on the financial derivatives used by asset managers, we should mention here some of the other types. Commodity forwards—in which the underlying asset is oil, a precious metal, or some other commodity—are widely used. In addition, the derivatives industry has created forward contracts and other derivatives on various sources of energy (electricity, gas, etc.) and even weather, in which the underlying is a measure of the temperature or the amount of disaster damage from hurricanes, earthquakes, or tornados.

Many of these instruments are particularly difficult to understand, price, and trade. Nonetheless, through the use of derivatives and indirect investments, such as hedge funds, they can be useful for managing risk and investing in general. They are not, however, the focus of this book.

In the examples and illustrations used, we have made reference to certain prices. Determining appropriate prices and fair values of financial instruments is a central objective of much of the process of asset management. Accordingly, pricing and valuation occupies a major portion of the CFA Program.

---

[10] Had the contract been structured to settle in cash, the dealer would have paid Microsoft 12,000,000 × ($0.925 − $0.920) = $60,000. Microsoft would have converted the euros to dollars at the current spot exchange rate of $0.920, receiving 12,000,000 × $0.920 = $11,040,000. Adding the $60,000 payment from the dealer, Microsoft would have received $11,100,000, an effective rate of $0.925.

SUMMARY

▶ The holder of a long forward contract (the "long") is obligated to take delivery of the underlying asset and pay the forward price at expiration. The holder of a short forward contract (the "short") is obligated to deliver the underlying asset and accept payment of the forward price at expiration.

▶ At expiration, a forward contract can be terminated by having the short make delivery of the underlying asset to the long or having the long and short exchange the equivalent cash value. If the asset is worth more (less) than the forward price, the short (long) pays the long (short) the cash difference between the market price or rate and the price or rate agreed on in the contract.

▶ A party can terminate a forward contract prior to expiration by entering into an opposite transaction with the same or a different counterparty. It is possible to leave both the original and new transactions in place, thereby leaving both transactions subject to credit risk, or to have the two transactions cancel each other. In the latter case, the party owing the greater amount pays the market value to the other party, resulting in the elimination of the remaining credit risk. This elimination can be achieved, however, only if the counterparty to the second transaction is the same counterparty as in the first.

▶ A dealer is a financial institution that makes a market in forward contracts and other derivatives. A dealer stands ready to take either side of a transaction. An end user is a party that comes to a dealer needing a transaction, usually for the purpose of managing a particular risk.

▶ Equity forward contracts can be written on individual stocks, specific stock portfolios, or stock indices. Equity forward contract prices and values must take into account the fact that the underlying stock, portfolio, or index could pay dividends.

▶ Forward contracts on bonds can be based on zero-coupon bonds or on coupon bonds, as well as portfolios or indices based on zero-coupon bonds or coupon bonds. Zero-coupon bonds pay their return by discounting the face value, often using a 360-day year assumption. Forward contracts on bonds must expire before the bond's maturity. In addition, a forward contract on a bond can be affected by special features of bonds, such as callability and convertibility.

▶ Eurodollar time deposits are dollar loans made by one bank to another. Although the term "Eurodollars" refers to dollar-denominated loans, similar loans exist in other currencies. Eurodollar deposits accrue interest by adding it on to the principal, using a 360-day year assumption. The primary Eurodollar rate is called LIBOR.

▶ LIBOR stands for London Interbank Offer Rate, the rate at which London banks are willing to lend to other London banks. Euribor is the rate on a euro time deposit, a loan made by banks to other banks in Frankfurt in which the currency is the euro.

▶ An FRA is a forward contract in which one party, the long, agrees to pay a fixed interest payment at a future date and receive an interest payment at a rate to be determined at expiration. FRAs are described by a special notation. For example, a 3×6 FRA expires in three months; the underlying is a Eurodollar deposit that begins in three months and ends three months later, or six months from now.

▶ The payment of an FRA at expiration is based on the net difference between the underlying rate and the agreed-upon rate, adjusted by the notional principal and the number of days in the instrument on which the underlying rate is based. The payoff is also discounted, however, to reflect the fact that the underlying rate on which the instrument is based assumes that payment will occur at a later date.

▶ A currency forward contract is a commitment for one party, the long, to buy a currency at a fixed price from the other party, the short, at a specific date. The contract can be settled by actual delivery, or the two parties can choose to settle in cash on the expiration day.

PRACTICE PROBLEMS FOR READING 68

1. The treasurer of Company A expects to receive a cash inflow of $15,000,000 in 90 days. The treasurer expects short-term interest rates to fall during the next 90 days. In order to hedge against this risk, the treasurer decides to use an FRA that expires in 90 days and is based on 90-day LIBOR. The FRA is quoted at 5 percent. At expiration, LIBOR is 4.5 percent. Assume that the notional principal on the contract is $15,000,000.

   A. Indicate whether the treasurer should take a long or short position to hedge interest rate risk.

   B. Using the appropriate terminology, identify the type of FRA used here.

   C. Calculate the gain or loss to Company A as a consequence of entering the FRA.

2. Suppose that a party wanted to enter into an FRA that expires in 42 days and is based on 137-day LIBOR. The dealer quotes a rate of 4.75 percent on this FRA. Assume that at expiration, the 137-day LIBOR is 4 percent and the notional principal is $20,000,000.

   A. What is the term used to describe such nonstandard instruments?

   B. Calculate the FRA payoff on a long position.

3. Assume Sun Microsystems expects to receive €20,000,000 in 90 days. A dealer provides a quote of $0.875 for a currency forward contract to expire in 90 days. Suppose that at the end of 90 days, the rate is $0.90. Assume that settlement is in cash. Calculate the cash flow at expiration if Sun Microsystems enters into a forward contract expiring in 90 days to buy dollars at $0.875.

SOLUTIONS FOR READING 68

1. A. Taking a short position will hedge the interest rate risk for Company A. The gain on the contract will offset the reduced interest rate that can be earned when rates fall.

B. This is a 3×6 FRA.

C. $\$15,000,000 \left[\dfrac{(0.045 - 0.05)(90/360)}{1 + 0.045(90/360)} \right] = -\$18,541.41$

The negative sign indicates a gain to the short position, which Company A holds.

2. A. These instruments are called off-the-run FRAs.

B. $\$20,000,000 \left[\dfrac{(0.04 - 0.0475)(137/360)}{1 + 0.04(137/360)} \right] = -\$56,227.43$

Because the party is long, this amount represents a loss.

3. The contract is settled in cash, so the settlement would be €20,000,000(0.875 − 0.90) = −$500,000. This amount would be paid by Sun Microsystems to the dealer. Sun would convert euros to dollars at the spot rate of $0.90, receiving €20,000,000 × (0.90) = $18,000,000. The net cash receipt is $17,500,000, which results in an effective rate of $0.875.

FUTURES MARKETS AND CONTRACTS
by Don M. Chance, CFA

LEARNING OUTCOMES

The candidate should be able to:	Mastery
a. describe the characteristics of futures contracts;	☐
b. distinguish between futures contracts and forward contracts;	☐
c. differentiate between margin in the securities markets and margin in the futures markets, and explain the role of initial margin, maintenance margin, variation margin, and settlement in futures trading;	☐
d. describe price limits and the process of marking to market and compute and interpret the margin balance, given the previous day's balance and the change in the futures price;	☐
e. describe how a futures contract can be terminated at or prior to expiration;	☐
f. describe the characteristics of the following types of futures contracts: Eurodollar, Treasury bond, stock index, and currency.	☐

INTRODUCTION   1

In the reading on derivative markets and instruments, we undertook a general overview of derivative markets. In the reading on forward markets and contracts, we focused on forward markets. Now we explore futures markets in a similar fashion. Although we shall see a clear similarity between forward and futures contracts, critical distinctions nonetheless exist between the two.

In the reading on derivative markets and instruments we learned that, like a forward contract, *a futures contract is an agreement between two parties in which one party, the buyer, agrees to buy from the other party, the seller, an*

Analysis of Derivatives for the Chartered Financial Analyst® Program, by Don M. Chance, CFA. Copyright © 2003 by AIMR. Reprinted with permission.

underlying asset or other derivative, at a future date at a price agreed on today. Unlike a forward contract, however, a futures contract is not a private and customized transaction but rather a public transaction that takes place on an organized futures exchange. In addition, a futures contract is standardized—the exchange, rather than the individual parties, sets the terms and conditions, with the exception of price. As a result, futures contracts have a secondary market, meaning that previously created contracts can be traded. Also, parties to futures contracts are guaranteed against credit losses resulting from the counterparty's inability to pay. A clearinghouse provides this guarantee via a procedure in which it converts gains and losses that accrue on a daily basis into actual cash gains and losses. Futures contracts are regulated at the federal government level; as we noted in the reading on forward markets and contracts, forward contracts are essentially unregulated. Futures contracts are created on organized trading facilities referred to as futures exchanges, whereas forward contracts are not created in any specific location but rather initiated between any two parties who wish to enter into such a contract. Finally, each futures exchange has a division or subsidiary called a clearinghouse that performs the specific responsibilities of paying and collecting daily gains and losses as well as guaranteeing to each party the performance of the other.

In a futures transaction, one party, the long, is the buyer and the other party, the short, is the seller. The buyer agrees to buy the underlying at a later date, the expiration, at a price agreed on at the start of the contract. The seller agrees to sell the underlying to the buyer at the expiration, at the price agreed on at the start of the contract. Every day, the futures contract trades in the market and its price changes in response to new information. Buyers benefit from price increases, and sellers benefit from price decreases. On the expiration day, the contract terminates and no further trading takes place. Then, either the buyer takes delivery of the underlying from the seller, or the two parties make an equivalent cash settlement. We shall explore each of these characteristics of futures contracts in more detail. First, however, it is important to take a brief look at how futures markets came into being.

1.1 A Brief History of Futures Markets

Although vestiges of futures markets appear in the Japanese rice markets of the 18th century and perhaps even earlier, the mid-1800s marked the first clear origins of modern futures markets. For example, in the United States in the 1840s, Chicago was becoming a major transportation and distribution center for agricultural commodities. Its central location and access to the Great Lakes gave Chicago a competitive advantage over other U.S. cities. Farmers from the Midwest would harvest their grain and take it to Chicago for sale. Grain production, however, is seasonal. As a result, grain prices would rise sharply just prior to the harvest but then plunge when the grain was brought to the market. Too much grain at one time and too little at another resulted in severe problems. Grain storage facilities in Chicago were inadequate to accommodate the oversupply. Some farmers even dumped their grain in the Chicago River because prices were so low that they could not afford to take their grain to another city to sell.

To address this problem, in 1848 a group of businessmen formed an organization later named the Chicago Board of Trade (CBOT) and created an arrangement called a "to-arrive" contract. These contracts permitted farmers to sell their grain before delivering it. In other words, farmers could harvest the grain and enter into a contract to deliver it at a much later date at a price already agreed on. This transaction allowed the farmer to hold the grain in storage at some other location besides Chicago. On the other side of these contracts were the businessmen who had formed the Chicago Board of Trade.

It soon became apparent that trading in these to-arrive contracts was more important and useful than trading in the grain itself. Soon the contracts began trading in a type of secondary market, which allowed buyers and sellers to discharge their obligations by passing them on, for a price, to other parties. With the addition of the clearinghouse in the 1920s, which provided a guarantee against default, modern futures markets firmly established their place in the financial world. It was left to other exchanges, such as today's Chicago Mercantile Exchange, the New York Mercantile Exchange, Eurex, and the London International Financial Futures Exchange, to develop and become, along with the Chicago Board of Trade, the global leaders in futures markets.

We shall now explore the important features of futures contracts in more detail.

1.2 Public Standardized Transactions

A private transaction is not generally reported in the news or to any price-reporting service. Forward contracts are private contracts. Just as in most legal contracts, the parties do not publicly report that they have engaged in a contract. In contrast, a futures transaction is reported to the futures exchange, the clearinghouse, and at least one regulatory agency. The price is recorded and available from price reporting services and even on the internet.[1]

We noted that a futures transaction is not customized. Recall from the reading on forward markets and contracts that in a forward contract, the two parties establish all of the terms of the contract, including the identity of the underlying, the expiration date, and the manner in which the contract is settled (cash or actual delivery) as well as the price. The terms are customized to meet the needs of both parties. In a futures contract, the price is the only term established by the two parties; the exchange establishes all other terms. Moreover, the terms that are established by the exchange are standardized, meaning that the exchange selects a number of choices for underlyings, expiration dates, and a variety of other contract-specific items. These standardized terms are well known to all parties. If a party wishes to trade a futures contract, it must accept these terms. The only alternative would be to create a similar but customized contract on the forward market.

With respect to the underlying, for example, a given asset has a variety of specifications and grades. Consider a futures contract on U.S. Treasury bonds. There are many different Treasury bonds with a variety of characteristics. The futures exchange must decide which Treasury bond or group of bonds the contract covers. One of the most actively traded commodity futures contracts is oil, but there are many different types of oil.[2] To which type of oil does the contract apply? The exchange decides at the time it designs the contract.

The parties to a forward contract set its expiration at whatever date they want. For a futures contract, the exchange establishes a set of expiration dates.

---

[1] The information reported to the general public does not disclose the identity of the parties to transactions but only that a transaction took place at a particular price.

[2] Some of the main types are Saudi Arabian light crude, Brent crude, and West Texas intermediate crude.

The first specification of the expiration is the month. An exchange might establish that a given futures contract expires only in the months of March, June, September, and December. The second specification determines how far the expirations go out into the future. For example, in January of a given year, there may be expirations of March, June, September, and December. Expirations might also be available for March, June, September, and December of the following year, and perhaps some months of the year after that. The exchange decides which expiration months are appropriate for trading, based on which expirations they believe would be actively traded. Treasury bond futures have expirations going out only about a year. Eurodollar futures, however, have expirations that go out about 10 years.[3] The third specification of the expiration is the specific day of expiration. Many, but not all, contracts expire some time during the third week of the expiration month.

The exchange determines a number of other contract characteristics, including the contract size. For example, one Eurodollar futures contract covers $1 million of a Eurodollar time deposit. One U.S. Treasury bond futures contract covers $100,000 face value of Treasury bonds. One futures contract on crude oil covers 1,000 barrels. The exchange also decides on the price quotation unit. For example, Treasury bond futures are quoted in points and 32nds of par of 100. Hence, you will see a price like 104 21/32, which means 104.65625. With a contract size of $100,000, the actual price is $104,656.25.

The exchange also determines what hours of the day trading takes place and at what physical location on the exchange the contract will be traded. Many futures exchanges have a trading floor, which contains octagonal-shaped pits. A contract is assigned to a certain pit. Traders enter the pits and express their willingness to buy and sell by calling out and/or indicating by hand signals their bids and offers. Some exchanges have electronic trading, which means that trading takes place on computer terminals, generally located in companies' offices. Some exchanges have both floor trading and electronic trading; some have only one or the other.

1.3 Homogenization and Liquidity

By creating contracts with generally accepted terms, the exchange standardizes the instrument. In contrast, forward contracts are quite heterogeneous because they are customized. Standardizing the instrument makes it more acceptable to a broader group of participants, with the advantage being that the instrument can then more easily trade in a type of secondary market. Indeed, the ability to sell a previously purchased contract or purchase a previously sold contract is one of the important features of futures contracts. A futures contract is therefore said to have liquidity in contrast to a forward contract, which does not generally trade after it has been created.[4] This ability to trade a previously opened contract allows participants in this market to offset the position before expiration, thereby obtaining exposure to price movements in the underlying without the actual requirement of holding the position to expiration. We shall discuss this characteristic further when we describe futures trading in Section 2.

---

[3] You may be wondering why some Eurodollar futures contracts have such long expirations. Dealers in swaps and forward rate agreements use Eurodollar futures to hedge their positions. Many of those over-the-counter contracts have very long expirations.

[4] The notion of liquidity here is only that a market exists for futures contracts, but this does not imply a high degree of liquidity. There may be little trading in a given contract, and the bid–ask spread can be high. In contrast, some forward markets can be very liquid, allowing forward contracts to be offset.

1.4 The Clearinghouse, Daily Settlement, and Performance Guarantee

Another important distinction between futures and forwards is that the futures exchange guarantees to each party the performance of the other party, through a mechanism known as the clearinghouse. This guarantee means that if one party makes money on the transaction, it does not have to worry about whether it will collect the money from the other party because the clearinghouse ensures it will be paid. In contrast, each party to a forward contract assumes the risk that the other party will default.

An important and distinguishing feature of futures contracts is that the gains and losses on each party's position are credited and charged on a daily basis. This procedure, called **daily settlement** or **marking to market**, essentially results in paper gains and losses being converted to cash gains and losses each day. It is also equivalent to terminating a contract at the end of each day and reopening it the next day at that settlement price. In some sense, a futures contract is like a strategy of opening up a forward contract, closing it one day later, opening up a new contract, closing it one day later, and continuing in that manner until expiration. The exact manner in which the daily settlement works will be covered in more detail later in Section 3.

1.5 Regulation

In most countries, futures contracts are regulated at the federal government level. State and regional laws may also apply. In the United States, the Commodity Futures Trading Commission regulates the futures market. In the United Kingdom, the Financial Services Authority regulates both the securities and futures markets.

Federal regulation of futures markets generally arises out of a concern to protect the general public and other futures market participants, as well as through a recognition that futures markets affect all financial markets and the economy. Regulations cover such matters as ensuring that prices are reported accurately and in a timely manner, that markets are not manipulated, that professionals who offer their services to the public are qualified and honest, and that disputes are resolved. In the United States, the government has delegated some of these responsibilities to an organization called the National Futures Association (NFA). An industry self-regulatory body, the NFA was created with the objective of having the industry regulate itself and reduce the federal government's burden.

FUTURES TRADING   2

In this section, we look more closely at how futures contracts are traded. As noted above, futures contracts trade on a futures exchange either in a pit or on a screen or electronic terminal.

We briefly mentioned pit trading, also known as floor-based trading, in Section 1.2. Pit trading is a very physical activity. Traders stand in the pit and shout out their orders in the form of prices they are willing to pay or accept. They also use hand signals to indicate their bids and offers.[5] They engage in

---

[5] Hand signals facilitate trading with someone who is too far away in the pit for verbal communication.

transactions with other traders in the pits by simply agreeing on a price and number of contracts to trade. The activity is fast, furious, exciting, and stressful. The average pit trader is quite young, owing to the physical demands of the job and the toll it takes on body and mind. In recent years, more trading has come off of the exchange floor to electronic screens or terminals. In electronic or screen-based trading, exchange members enter their bids and offers into a computer system, which then displays this information and allows a trader to consummate a trade electronically. In the United States, pit trading is dominant, owing to its long history and tradition. Exchange members who trade on the floor enjoy pit trading and have resisted heavily the advent of electronic trading. Nonetheless, the exchanges have had to respond to market demands to offer electronic trading. In the United States, both pit trading and electronic trading are used, but in other countries, electronic trading is beginning to drive pit trading out of business.[6]

A person who enters into a futures contract establishes either a long position or a short position. Similar to forward contracts, long positions are agreements to buy the underlying at the expiration at a price agreed on at the start. Short positions are agreements to sell the underlying at a future date at a price agreed on at the start. When the position is established, each party deposits a small amount of money, typically called the margin, with the clearinghouse. Then, as briefly described in Section 1.4, the contract is marked to market, whereby the gains are distributed to and the losses collected from each party. We cover this marking-to-market process in more detail in the next section. For now, however, we focus only on the opening and closing of the position.

A party that has opened a long position collects profits or incurs losses on a daily basis. At some point in the life of the contract prior to expiration, that party may wish to re-enter the market and close out the position. This process, called **offsetting**, is the same as selling a previously purchased stock or buying back a stock to close a short position. The holder of a long futures position simply goes back into the market and offers the identical contract for sale. The holder of a short position goes back into the market and offers to buy the identical contract. It should be noted that when a party offsets a position, it does not necessarily do so with the same counterparty to the original contract. In fact, rarely would a contract be offset with the same counterparty. Because of the ability to offset, futures contracts are said to be fungible, which means that any futures contract with any counterparty can be offset by an equivalent futures contract with another counterparty. Fungibility is assured by the fact that the clearinghouse inserts itself in the middle of each contract and, therefore, becomes the counterparty to each party.

For example, suppose in early January a futures trader purchases an S&P 500 stock index futures contract expiring in March. Through 15 February, the trader has incurred some gains and losses from the daily settlement and decides that she wants to close the position out. She then goes back into the market and offers for sale the March S&P 500 futures. Once she finds a buyer to take the position, she has a long and short position in the same contract. The clearinghouse considers that she no longer has a position in that contract and has no remaining exposure, nor any obligation to make or take delivery at expiration. Had she initially gone short the March futures, she might re-enter the market in February offering to buy it. Once she finds a seller to take the opposite position, she becomes long and short the same contract and is considered to have offset the contract and therefore have no net position.

---

[6] For example, in France electronic trading was introduced while pit trading continued. Within two weeks, all of the volume had migrated to electronic trading and pit trading was terminated.

THE CLEARINGHOUSE, MARGINS, AND PRICE LIMITS

As briefly noted in the previous section, when a trader takes a long or short position in a futures, he must first deposit sufficient funds in a margin account. This amount of money is traditionally called the margin, a term derived from the stock market practice in which an investor borrows a portion of the money required to purchase a certain amount of stock.

Margin in the stock market is quite different from margin in the futures market. In the stock market, "margin" means that a loan is made. The loan enables the investor to reduce the amount of his own money required to purchase the securities, thereby generating leverage or gearing, as it is sometimes known. If the stock goes up, the percentage gain to the investor is amplified. If the stock goes down, however, the percentage loss is also amplified. The borrowed money must eventually be repaid with interest. The margin percentage equals the market value of the stock minus the market value of the debt divided by the market value of the stock—in other words, the investor's own equity as a percentage of the value of the stock. For example, in the United States, regulations permit an investor to borrow up to 50 percent of the initial value of the stock. This percentage is called the initial margin requirement. On any day thereafter, the equity or percentage ownership in the account, measured as the market value of the securities minus the amount borrowed, can be less than 50 percent but must be at least a percentage known as the maintenance margin requirement. A typical maintenance margin requirement is 25 to 30 percent.

In the futures market, by contrast, the word **margin** is commonly used to describe the amount of money that must be put into an account by a party opening up a futures position, but the term is misleading. When a transaction is initiated, a futures trader puts up a certain amount of money to meet the **initial margin requirement**; however, the remaining money is not borrowed. The amount of money deposited is more like a down payment for the commitment to purchase the underlying at a later date. Alternatively, one can view this deposit as a form of good faith money, collateral, or a performance bond: The money helps ensure that the party fulfills his or her obligation.[7] Moreover, both the buyer and the seller of a futures contract must deposit margin.

In securities markets, margin requirements are normally set by federal regulators. In the United States, maintenance margin requirements are set by the securities exchanges and the NASD. In futures markets, margin requirements are set by the clearinghouses. In further contrast to margin practices in securities markets, futures margins are traditionally expressed in dollar terms and not as a percentage of the futures price. For ease of comparison, however, we often speak of the futures margin in terms of its relationship to the futures price. In futures markets, the initial margin requirement is typically much lower than the initial margin requirement in the stock market. In fact, futures margins are usually less than 10 percent of the futures price.[8] Futures clearinghouses set their margin requirements by studying historical price movements. They then establish minimum margin levels by taking into account normal price movements and the fact that accounts are marked to market daily. The clearinghouses thus collect and

---

[7] In fact, the Chicago Mercantile Exchange uses the term "performance bond" instead of "margin." Most other exchanges use the term "margin."

[8] For example, the margin requirement of the Eurodollar futures contract at the Chicago Mercantile Exchange has been less than one-tenth of one percent of the futures price. An exception to this requirement, however, is individual stock futures, which in the United States have margin requirements comparable to those of the stock market.

disburse margin money every day. Moreover, they are permitted to do so more often than daily, and on some occasions they have used that privilege. By carefully setting margin requirements and collecting margin money every day, clearinghouses are able to control the risk of default.

In spite of the differences in margin practices for futures and securities markets, the effect of leverage is similar for both. By putting up a small amount of money, the trader's gains and losses are magnified. Given the tremendously low margin requirements of futures markets, however, the magnitude of the leverage effect is much greater in futures markets. We shall see how this works as we examine the process of the daily settlement.

As previously noted, each day the clearinghouse conducts an activity known as the daily settlement, also called marking to market. This practice results in the conversion of gains and losses on paper into actual gains and losses. As margin account balances change, holders of futures positions must maintain balances above a level called the **maintenance margin requirement**. The maintenance margin requirement is lower than the initial margin requirement. On any day in which the amount of money in the margin account at the end of the day falls below the maintenance margin requirement, the trader must deposit sufficient funds to bring the balance back up to the initial margin requirement. Alternatively, the trader can simply close out the position but is responsible for any further losses incurred if the price changes before a closing transaction can be made.

To provide a fair mark-to-market process, the clearinghouse must designate the official price for determining daily gains and losses. This price is called the **settlement price** and represents an average of the final few trades of the day. It would appear that the closing price of the day would serve as the settlement price, but the closing price is a single value that can potentially be biased high or low or perhaps even manipulated by an unscrupulous trader. Hence, the clearinghouse takes an average of all trades during the closing period (as defined by each exchange).

Exhibit 1 provides an example of the marking-to-market process that occurs over a period of six trading days. We start with the assumption that the futures price is $100 when the transaction opens, the initial margin requirement is $5, and the maintenance margin requirement is $3. In Panel A, the trader takes a long position of 10 contracts on Day 0, depositing $50 ($5 times 10 contracts) as indicated in Column 3. At the end of the day, his ending balance is $50.[9] Although the trader can withdraw any funds in excess of the initial margin requirement, we shall assume that he does not do so.[10]

The ending balance on Day 0 is then carried forward to the beginning balance on Day 1. On Day 1, the futures price moves down to 99.20, as indicated in Column 4 of Panel A. The futures price change, Column 5, is −0.80 (99.20 − 100). This amount is then multiplied by the number of contracts to obtain the number in Column 6 of −0.80 × 10 = −$8. The ending balance, Column 7, is the beginning balance plus the gain or loss. The ending balance on Day 1 of $42 is above the maintenance margin requirement of $30, so no funds need to be deposited on Day 2.

---

[9] Technically, we are assuming that the position was opened at the settlement price on Day 0. If the position is opened earlier during the day, it would be marked to the settlement price at the end of the day.

[10] Virtually all professional traders are able to deposit interest-earning assets, although many other account holders are required to deposit cash. If the deposit earns interest, there is no opportunity cost and no obvious necessity to withdraw the money to invest elsewhere.

EXHIBIT 1	Mark-to-Market Example

Initial futures price = \$100, Initial margin requirement = \$5, Maintenance margin requirement = \$3

Panel A. Holder of Long Position of 10 Contracts

Day (1)	Beginning Balance (2)	Funds Deposited (3)	Settlement Price (4)	Futures Price Change (5)	Gain/ Loss (6)	Ending Balance (7)
0	0	50	100.00			50
1	50	0	99.20	−0.80	−8	42
2	42	0	96.00	−3.20	−32	10
3	10	40	101.00	5.00	50	100
4	100	0	103.50	2.50	25	125
5	125	0	103.00	−0.50	−5	120
6	120	0	104.00	1.00	10	130

Panel B. Holder of Short Position of 10 Contracts

Day (1)	Beginning Balance (2)	Funds Deposited (3)	Settlement Price (4)	Futures Price Change (5)	Gain/ Loss (6)	Ending Balance (7)
0	0	50	100.00			50
1	50	0	99.20	−0.80	8	58
2	58	0	96.00	−3.20	32	90
3	90	0	101.00	5.00	−50	40
4	40	0	103.50	2.50	−25	15
5	15	35	103.00	−0.50	5	55
6	55	0	104.00	1.00	−10	45

On Day 2 the settlement price goes down to \$96. Based on a price decrease of \$3.20 per contract and 10 contracts, the loss is \$32, lowering the ending balance to \$10. This amount is \$20 below the maintenance margin requirement. Thus, the trader will get a margin call the following morning and must deposit \$40 to bring the balance up to the initial margin level of \$50. This deposit is shown in Column 3 on Day 3.

Here, we must emphasize two important points. First, additional margin that must be deposited is the amount sufficient to bring the ending balance up to the initial margin requirement, not the maintenance margin requirement.[11] This additional margin is called the **variation margin**. In addition, the amount that must be deposited the following day is determined regardless of the price change the following day, which might bring the ending balance well above the initial margin requirement, as it does here, or even well below the maintenance margin requirement. Thus, another margin call could occur. Also note that

---

[11] In the stock market, one must deposit only the amount necessary to bring the balance up to the maintenance margin requirement.

when the trader closes the position, the account is marked to market to the final price at which the transaction occurs, not the settlement price that day.

Over the six-day period, the trader in this example deposited $90. The account balance at the end of the sixth day is $130—nearly a 50 percent return over six days; not bad. But look at Panel B, which shows the position of a holder of 10 short contracts over that same period. Note that the short gains when prices decrease and loses when prices increase. Here the ending balance falls below the maintenance margin requirement on Day 4, and the short must deposit $35 on Day 5. At the end of Day 6, the short has deposited $85 and the balance is $45, a loss of $40 or nearly 50 percent, which is the same $40 the long made. Both cases illustrate the leverage effect that magnifies gains and losses.

When establishing a futures position, it is important to know the price level that would trigger a margin call. In this case, it does not matter how many contracts one has. The price change would need to fall for a long position (or rise for a short position) by the difference between the initial and maintenance margin requirements. In this example, the difference between the initial and maintenance margin requirements is $5 - $3 = $2. Thus, the price would need to fall from $100 to $98 for a long position (or rise from $100 to $102 for a short position) to trigger a margin call.

As described here, when a trader receives a margin call, he is required to deposit funds sufficient to bring the account balance back up to the initial margin level. Alternatively, the trader can choose to simply close out the position as soon as possible. For example, consider the position of the long at the end of the second day when the margin balance is $10. This amount is $20 below the maintenance level, and he is required to deposit $40 to bring the balance up to the initial margin level. If he would prefer not to deposit the additional funds, he can close out the position as soon as possible the following day. Suppose, however, that the price is moving quickly at the opening on Day 3. If the price falls from $96 to $95, he has lost $10 more, wiping out the margin account balance. In fact, if it fell any further, he would have a negative margin account balance. He is still responsible for these losses. Thus, the trader could lose more than the amount of money he has placed in the margin account. The total amount of money he could lose is limited to the price per contract at which he bought, $100, times the number of contracts, 10, or $1,000. Such a loss would occur if the price fell to zero, although this is not likely. This potential loss may not seem like a lot, but it is certainly large relative to the initial margin requirement of $50. For the holder of the short position, there is no upper limit on the price and the potential loss is theoretically infinite.

EXAMPLE 1

Consider a futures contract in which the current futures price is $82. The initial margin requirement is $5, and the maintenance margin requirement is $2. You go long 20 contracts and meet all margin calls but do not withdraw any excess margin. Assume that on the first day, the contract is established at the settlement price, so there is no mark-to-market gain or loss on that day.

A. Complete the table below and provide an explanation of any funds deposited.

Day	Beginning Balance	Funds Deposited	Futures Price	Price Change	Gain/Loss	Ending Balance
0			82			
1			84			
2			78			
3			73			
4			79			
5			82			
6			84			

B. Determine the price level that would trigger a margin call.

Solution to A:

Day	Beginning Balance	Funds Deposited	Futures Price	Price Change	Gain/Loss	Ending Balance
0	0	100	82			100
1	100	0	84	2	40	140
2	140	0	78	−6	−120	20
3	20	80	73	−5	−100	0
4	0	100	79	6	120	220
5	220	0	82	3	60	280
6	280	0	84	2	40	320

On Day 0, you deposit $100 because the initial margin requirement is $5 per contract and you go long 20 contracts. At the end of Day 2, the balance is down to $20, which is $20 below the $40 maintenance margin requirement ($2 per contract times 20 contracts). You must deposit enough money to bring the balance up to the initial margin requirement of $100 ($5 per contract times 20 contracts). So on Day 3, you deposit $80. The price change on Day 3 causes a gain/loss of −$100, leaving you with a balance of $0 at the end of Day 3. On Day 4, you must deposit $100 to return the balance to the initial margin level.

Solution to B: A price decrease to $79 would trigger a margin call. This calculation is based on the fact that the difference between the initial margin requirement and the maintenance margin requirement is $3. If the futures price starts at $82, it can fall by $3 to $79 before it triggers a margin call.

Some futures contracts impose limits on the price change that can occur from one day to the next. Appropriately, these are called **price limits**. These limits are usually set as an absolute change over the previous day. Using the example above, suppose the price limit was $4. This would mean that each day, no transaction could take place higher than the previous settlement price plus $4 or lower than the previous settlement price minus $4. So the next day's settlement price cannot go beyond the price limit and thus no transaction can take place beyond the limits.

If the price at which a transaction would be made exceeds the limits, then price essentially freezes at one of the limits, which is called a **limit move**. If the price is stuck at the upper limit, it is called **limit up**; if stuck at the lower limit, it is called **limit down**. If a transaction cannot take place because the price would be beyond the limits, this situation is called **locked limit**. By the end of the day, unless the price has moved back within the limits, the settlement price will then be at one of the limits. The following day, the new range of acceptable prices is based on the settlement price plus or minus limits. The exchanges have different rules that provide for expansion or contraction of price limits under some circumstances. In addition, not all contracts have price limits.

Finally, we note that the exchanges have the power to mark contracts to market whenever they deem it necessary. Thus, they can do so during the trading day rather than wait until the end of the day. They sometimes do so when abnormally large market moves occur.

The daily settlement procedure is designed to collect losses and distribute gains in such a manner that losses are paid before becoming large enough to impose a serious risk of default. Recall that the clearinghouse guarantees to each party that it need not worry about collecting from the counterparty. The clearinghouse essentially positions itself in the middle of each contract, becoming the short counterparty to the long and the long counterparty to the short. The clearinghouse collects funds from the parties incurring losses in this daily settlement procedure and distributes them to the parties incurring gains. By doing so each day, the clearinghouse ensures that losses cannot build up. Of course, this process offers no guarantee that counterparties will not default. Some defaults do occur, but the counterparty is defaulting to the clearinghouse, which has never failed to pay off the opposite party. In the unlikely event that the clearinghouse were unable to pay, it would turn to a reserve fund or to the exchange, or it would levy a tax on exchange members to cover losses.

4   DELIVERY AND CASH SETTLEMENT

As previously described, a futures trader can close out a position before expiration. If the trader holds a long position, she can simply enter into a position to go short the same futures contract. From the clearinghouse's perspective, the trader holds both a long and short position in the same contract. These positions are considered to offset and, therefore, there is no open position in place. Most futures contracts are offset before expiration. Those that remain in place are subject to either delivery or a final cash settlement. Here we explore this process, which determines how a futures contract terminates at expiration.

When the exchange designs a futures contract, it specifies whether the contract will terminate with delivery or cash settlement. If the contract terminates in delivery, the clearinghouse selects a counterparty, usually the holder of the oldest long contract, to accept delivery. The holder of the short position then delivers the underlying to the holder of the long position, who pays the short the necessary cash for the underlying. Suppose, for example, that two days before expiration, a party goes long one futures contract at a price of $50. The following day (the day before expiration), the settlement price is $52. The trader's margin account is then marked to market by crediting it with a gain of $2. Then suppose that the next day the contract expires with the settlement price at $53. As the end of the trading day draws near, the trader has two choices. She can attempt to close out the position by selling the futures contract. The margin account would then be marked to market at the price at which she sells. If she sells close enough to the expiration, the price she sold at would be very close to the final settlement price of $53. Doing so would add $1 to her margin account balance.

The other choice is to leave the position open at the end of the trading day. Then she would have to take delivery. If that occurred, she would be required to take possession of the asset and pay the short the settlement price of the previous day. Doing so would be equivalent to paying $52 and receiving the asset. She could then sell the asset for its price of $53, netting a $1 gain, which is equivalent to the final $1 credited to her margin account if she had terminated the position at the settlement price of $53, as described above.[12]

An alternative settlement procedure, which we described in the reading on forward markets and contracts, is cash settlement. The exchange designates certain futures contracts as cash-settled contracts. If the contract used in this example were cash settled, then the trader would not need to close out the position close to the end of the expiration day. She could simply leave the position open. When the contract expires, her margin account would be marked to market for a gain on the final day of $1. Cash settlement contracts have some advantages over delivery contracts, particularly with respect to significant savings in transaction costs.[13]

Exhibit 2 illustrates the equivalence of these three forms of delivery. Note, however, that because of the transaction costs of delivery, parties clearly prefer a

EXHIBIT 2	Closeout versus Physical Delivery versus Cash Settlement

Closeout:
Sell contract at 53
Mark to market profit/loss:
53 − 52 = 1
or
Physical Delivery:
Pay 52, receive asset worth 53
or

Mark to market
profit/loss:
52 − 50 = 2

Cash Settlement:
Receive 53 − 52 = 1

Buy futures at 50:
Pay nothing

|————————————|————————————|————————————|

2 days before expiration
(futures price = 50)

1 day before expiration
(settlement price = 52)

Expiration
(settlement price = 53)

[12] The reason she pays the settlement price of the previous day is because on the previous day when her account was marked to market, she essentially created a new futures position at a price of $52. Thus, she committed to purchase the asset at expiration, just one day later, at a price of $52. The next day when the contract expires, it is then appropriate that she buy the underlying for $52.

[13] Nonetheless, cash settlement has been somewhat controversial in the United States. If a contract is designated as cash settlement, it implies that the buyer of the contract never intended to actually take possession of the underlying asset. Some legislators and regulators feel that this design is against the spirit of the law, which views a futures contract as a commitment to buy the asset at a later date. Even though parties often offset futures contracts prior to expiration, the possibility of actual delivery is still present in contracts other than those settled by cash. This controversy, however, is relatively minor and has caused no serious problems or debates in recent years.

closeout or cash settlement over physical delivery, particularly when the underlying asset is a physical commodity.

Contracts designated for delivery have a variety of features that can complicate delivery. In most cases, delivery does not occur immediately after expiration but takes place over several days. In addition, many contracts permit the short to choose when delivery takes place. For many contracts, delivery can be made any business day of the month. The delivery period usually includes the days following the last trading day of the month, which is usually in the third week of the month.

In addition, the short often has other choices regarding delivery, a major one being exactly which underlying asset is delivered. For example, a futures contract on U.S. Treasury bonds trading at the Chicago Board of Trade permits the short to deliver any of a number of U.S. Treasury bonds.[14] The wheat futures contract at the Chicago Board of Trade permits delivery of any of several types of wheat. Futures contracts calling for physical delivery of commodities often permit delivery at different locations. A given commodity delivered to one location is not the same as that commodity delivered to another because of the costs involved in transporting the commodity. The short holds the sole right to make decisions about what, when, and where to deliver, and the right to make these decisions can be extremely valuable. The right to make a decision concerning these aspects of delivery is called a **delivery option**.

Some futures contracts that call for delivery require delivery of the actual asset, and some use only a book entry. For example, in this day and age, no one physically handles U.S. Treasury bonds in the form of pieces of paper. Bonds are transferred electronically over the Federal Reserve's wire system. Other contracts, such as oil or wheat, do actually involve the physical transfer of the asset. Physical delivery is more common when the underlying is a physical commodity, whereas book entry is more common when the underlying is a financial asset.

Futures market participants use one additional delivery procedure, which is called **exchange for physicals (EFP)**. In an EFP transaction, the long and short arrange an alternative delivery procedure. For example, the Chicago Board of Trade's wheat futures contracts require delivery on certain dates at certain locations either in Chicago or in a few other specified locations in the Midwest. If the long and short agree, they could effect delivery by having the short deliver the wheat to the long in, for example, Omaha. The two parties would then report to the Chicago Board of Trade that they had settled their contract outside of the exchange's normal delivery procedures, which would be satisfactory to the exchange.

5   FUTURES EXCHANGES

A futures exchange is a legal corporate entity whose shareholders are its members. The members own memberships, more commonly called **seats**. Exchange members have the privilege of executing transactions on the exchange. Each member acts as either a **floor trader** or a **broker**. Floor traders are typically called **locals**; brokers are typically called **futures commission merchants (FCMs)**. Locals are market makers, standing ready to buy and sell by quoting a bid and an ask

---

[14] We shall cover this feature in more detail in Section 6.2.

price. They are the primary providers of liquidity to the market. FCMs execute transactions for other parties off the exchange.

The locals on the exchange floor typically trade according to one of several distinct styles. The most common is called scalping. A **scalper** offers to buy or sell futures contracts, holding the position for only a brief period of time, perhaps just seconds. Scalpers attempt to profit by buying at the bid price and selling at the higher ask price. A **day trader** holds a position open somewhat longer but closes all positions at the end of the day.[15] A **position trader** holds positions open overnight. Day traders and position traders are quite distinct from scalpers in that they attempt to profit from the anticipated direction of the market; scalpers are trying simply to buy at the bid and sell at the ask.

Recall that futures exchanges have trading either on the floor or off the floor on electronic terminals, or in some cases, both. As previously described, floor trading in the United States takes place in pits, which are octagonal, multitiered areas where floor traders stand and conduct transactions. Traders wear jackets of specific colors and badges to indicate such information as what type of trader (FCM or local) they are and whom they represent.[16] As noted, to indicate a willingness to trade, a trader shouts and uses a set of standard hand signals. A trade is consummated by two traders agreeing on a price and a number of contracts. These traders might not actually say anything to each other; they may simply use a combination of hand signals and/or eye contact to agree on a transaction. When a transaction is agreed on, the traders fill out small paper forms and turn them over to clerks, who then see that the transactions are entered into the system and reported.

Each trader is required to have an account at a clearing firm. The clearing firms are the actual members of the clearinghouse. The clearinghouse deals only with the clearing firms, which then deal with their individual and institutional customers.

In electronic trading, the principles remain essentially the same but the traders do not stand in the pits. In fact, they do not see each other at all. They sit at computer terminals, which enable them to see the bids and offers of other traders. Transactions are executed by the click of a computer mouse or an entry from a keyboard.

Exhibit 3 lists the world's 20 leading futures exchanges in 2001, ranked by trading volume. Recall from the reading on derivative markets and instruments that trading volume can be a misleading measure of the size of futures markets; nonetheless, it is the measure primarily used. The structure of global futures exchanges has changed considerably in recent years. Exchanges in the United States, primarily the Chicago Board of Trade and the Chicago Mercantile Exchange, were clearly the world leaders in the past. Note that the volume leader now, however, is Eurex, the combined German–Swiss exchange. Eurex has been so successful partly because of its decision to be an all-electronic futures exchange, whereas the Chicago exchanges are still primarily pit-trading exchanges. Note the popularity of futures trading in Japan; four of the 20 leading exchanges are Japanese.

---

[15] The term "day trader" has been around the futures market for a long time but has recently acquired a new meaning in the broader financial markets. The term is now used to describe individual investors who trade stocks, often over the internet, during the day for a living or as a hobby. In fact, the term has even been used in a somewhat pejorative manner, in that day traders are often thought of as naïve investors speculating wildly with money they can ill afford to lose.

[16] For example, an FCM or local could be trading for himself or could represent a company.

EXHIBIT 3	The World's 20 Leading Futures Exchanges

Exchange and Location	Volume in 2001 (Number of Contracts)
Eurex (Germany and Switzerland)	435,141,707
Chicago Mercantile Exchange (United States)	315,971,885
Chicago Board of Trade (United States)	209,988,002
London International Financial Futures and Options Exchange (United Kingdom)	161,522,775
Bolsa de Mercadorias & Futuros (Brazil)	94,174,452
New York Mercantile Exchange (United States)	85,039,984
Tokyo Commodity Exchange (Japan)	56,538,245
London Metal Exchange (United Kingdom)	56,224,495
Paris Bourse SA (France)	42,042,673
Sydney Futures Exchange (Australia)	34,075,508
Korea Stock Exchange (Korea)	31,502,184
Singapore Exchange (Singapore)	30,606,546
Central Japan Commodity Exchange (Japan)	27,846,712
International Petroleum Exchange (United Kingdom)	26,098,207
OM Stockholm Exchange (Sweden)	23,408,198
Tokyo Grain Exchange (Japan)	22,707,808
New York Board of Trade (United States)	14,034,168
MEFF Renta Variable (Spain)	13,108,293
Tokyo Stock Exchange (Japan)	12,465,433
South African Futures Exchange (South Africa)	11,868,242

Source: *Futures Industry*, January/February 2002.

6   TYPES OF FUTURES CONTRACTS

The different types of futures contracts are generally divided into two main groups: commodity futures and financial futures. Commodity futures cover traditional agricultural, metal, and petroleum products. Financial futures include stocks, bonds, and currencies. Exhibit 4 gives a broad overview of the most active types of futures contracts traded on global futures exchanges. These contracts are those covered by the *Wall Street Journal* on the date indicated.

Our primary focus in this book is on financial and currency futures contracts. Within the financials group, our main interest is on interest rate and bond futures, stock index futures, and currency futures. We may occasionally make reference to a commodity futures contract, but that will primarily be for illustrative purposes. In the following subsections, we introduce the primary contracts we shall focus on. These are U.S. contracts, but they resemble most types of futures contracts found on exchanges throughout the world. Full contract specifications for these and other contracts are available on the websites of the futures exchanges, which are easy to locate with most internet search engines.

EXHIBIT 4	Most-Active Global Futures Contracts as Covered by the *Wall Street Journal*, 18 June 2002

Commodity Futures   ## Financial Futures

Commodity Futures	Financial Futures	
Corn (CBOT)	Treasury Bonds (CBOT)	Euro (CME)
Oats (CBOT)	Treasury Notes (CBOT)	Euro–Sterling (NYBOT)
Soybeans (CBOT)	10-Year Agency Notes (CBOT)	Euro–U.S. Dollar (NYBOT)
Soybean Meal (CBOT)	10-Year Interest Rate Swaps (CBOT)	Euro–Yen (NYBOT)
Soybean Oil (CBOT)	2-Year Agency Notes (CBOT)	Dow Jones Industrial Average (CBOT)
Wheat (CBOT, KCBT, MGE)	5-Year Treasury Notes (CBOT)	Mini Dow Jones Industrial Average (CBOT)
Canola (WPG)	2-Year Treasury Notes (CBOT)	S&P 500 Index (CME)
Barley (WPG)	Federal Funds (CBOT)	Mini S&P 500 Index (CME)
Feeder Cattle (CME)	Municipal Bond Index (CBOT)	S&P Midcap 400 Index (CME)
Live Cattle (CME)	Treasury Bills (CME)	Nikkei 225 (CME)
Lean Hogs (CME)	1-Month LIBOR (CME)	Nasdaq 100 Index (CME)
Pork Bellies (CME)	Eurodollar (CME)	Mini Nasdaq Index (CME)
Milk (CME)	Euroyen (CME, SGX)	Goldman Sachs Commodity Index (CME)
Lumber (CME)	Short Sterling (LIFFE)	Russell 1000 Index (CME)
Cocoa (NYBOT)	Long Gilt (LIFFE)	Russell 2000 Index (CME)
Coffee (NYBOT)	3-Month Euribor (LIFFE)	NYSE Composite Index (NYBOT)
World Sugar (NYBOT)	3-Month Euroswiss (LIFFE)	U.S. Dollar Index (NYBOT)
Domestic Sugar (NYBOT)	Canadian Bankers Acceptance (ME)	Share Price Index (SFE)
Cotton (NYBOT)	10-Year Canadian Government Bond (ME)	CAC 40 Stock Index (MATIF)
Orange Juice (NYBOT)	10-Year Euro Notional Bond (MATIF)	Xetra Dax (EUREX)
Copper (NYMEX)	3-Month Euribor (MATIF)	FTSE 200 Index (LIFFE)
Gold (NYMEX)	3-Year Commonwealth T-Bonds (SFE)	Dow Jones Euro Stoxx 50 Index (EUREX)
Platinum (NYMEX)	5-Year German Euro Government Bond (EUREX)	Dow Jones Stoxx 50 Index (EUREX)
Palladium (NYMEX)	10-Year German Euro Government Bond (EUREX)	
Silver (NYMEX)	2-Year German Euro Government Bond (EUREX)	
Crude Oil (NYMEX)	Japanese Yen (CME)	
No. 2 Heating Oil (NYMEX)	Canadian Dollar (CME)	
Unleaded Gasoline (NYMEX)	British Pound (CME)	
Natural Gas (NYMEX)	Swiss Franc (CME)	
Brent Crude Oil (IPEX)	Australian Dollar (CME)	
Gas Oil (IPEX)	Mexican Peso (CME)	

Exchange codes: CBOT (Chicago Board of Trade), CME (Chicago Mercantile Exchange), LIFFE (London International Financial Futures Exchange), WPG (Winnipeg Grain Exchange), EUREX (Eurex), NYBOT (New York Board of Trade), IPEX (International Petroleum Exchange), MATIF (Marché a Terme International de France), ME (Montreal Exchange), MGE (Minneapolis Grain Exchange), SFE (Sydney Futures Exchange), SGX (Singapore Exchange), KCBT (Kansas City Board of Trade), NYMEX (New York Mercantile Exchange).
Note: These are not the only global futures contracts but are those covered in the *Wall Street Journal* on the date given and represent the most active contracts at that time.

6.1 Short-Term Interest Rate Futures Contracts

The primary short-term interest rate futures contracts are those on U.S. Treasury bills and Eurodollars on the Chicago Mercantile Exchange.

6.1.1 Treasury Bill Futures

The Treasury bill contract, launched in 1976, was the first interest rate futures contract. It is based on a 90-day U.S. Treasury bill, one of the most important U.S. government debt instruments (described in Section 3.2.1 of the reading on forward markets and contracts). The Treasury bill, or T-bill, is a discount instrument, meaning that its price equals the face value minus a discount representing interest. The discount equals the face value multiplied by the quoted rate times the days to maturity divided by 360. Thus, using the example from the reading on forward markets and contracts, if a 180-day T-bill is selling at a discount of 4 percent, its price per $1 par is $1 - 0.04(180/360) = \$0.98$. An investor who buys the bill and holds it to maturity would receive $1 at maturity, netting a gain of $0.02.

The futures contract is based on a 90-day $1,000,000 U.S. Treasury bill. Thus, on any given day, the contract trades with the understanding that a 90-day T-bill will be delivered at expiration. While the contract is trading, its price is quoted as 100 minus the rate quoted as a percent priced into the contract by the futures market. This value, $100 - \text{Rate}$, is known as the IMM Index; IMM stands for International Monetary Market, a division of the Chicago Mercantile Exchange. The IMM Index is a reported and publicly available price; however, it is not the actual futures price, which is

$$100[1 - (\text{Rate}/100)(90/360)]$$

For example, suppose on a given day the rate priced into the contract is 6.25 percent. Then the quoted price will be $100 - 6.25 = 93.75$. The actual futures price would be

$$\$1,000,000[1 - 0.0625(90/360)] = \$984,375$$

Recall, however, that except for the small margin deposit, a futures transaction does not require any cash to be paid up front. As trading takes place, the rate fluctuates with market interest rates and the associated IMM Index price changes accordingly. The actual futures price, as calculated above, also fluctuates according to the above formula, but interestingly, that price is not very important. The same information can be captured more easily by referencing the IMM Index than by calculating the actual price.

Suppose, for example, that a trader had his account marked to market to the above price, 6.25 in terms of the rate, 93.75 in terms of the IMM Index, and $984,375 in terms of the actual futures price. Now suppose the rate goes to 6.50, an increase of 0.25 or 25 basis points. The IMM Index declines to 93.50, and the actual futures price drops to

$$\$1,000,000[1 - 0.065(90/360)] = \$983,750$$

Thus, the actual futures price decreased by $\$984,375 - \$983,750 = \$625$. A trader who is long would have a loss of $625; a trader who is short would have a gain of $625.

This $625 gain or loss can be arrived at more directly, however, by simply noting that each basis point move is equivalent to $25.[17] This special design of the contract makes it easy for floor traders to do the necessary arithmetic in their heads. For example, if floor traders observe the IMM Index move from 93.75 to 93.50, they immediately know that it has moved down 25 basis points and that 25 basis points times $25 per basis point is a loss of $625. The minimum tick size is one-half basis point or $12.50.

T-bill futures contracts have expirations of the current month, the next month, and the next four months of March, June, September, and December. Because of the small trading volume, however, only the closest expiration has much trading volume, and even that one is only lightly traded. T-bill futures expire specifically on the Monday of the week of the third Wednesday each month and settle in cash rather than physical delivery of the T-bill, as described in Section 4.

As important as Treasury bills are in U.S. financial markets, however, today this futures contract is barely active. The Eurodollar contract is considered much more important because it reflects the interest rate on a dollar borrowed by a high-quality private borrower. The rates on T-bills are considered too heavily influenced by U.S. government policies, budget deficits, government funding plans, politics, and Federal Reserve monetary policy. Although unquestionably Eurodollar rates are affected by those factors, market participants consider them much less directly influenced. But in spite of this relative inactivity, T-bill futures are useful instruments for illustrating certain principles of futures market pricing and trading. Accordingly, we shall use them on some occasions. For now, however, we turn to the Eurodollar futures contract.

6.1.2 Eurodollar Futures

Recall that in the reading on forward markets and contracts, we devoted a good bit of effort to understanding Eurodollar forward contracts, known as FRAs. These contracts pay off based on LIBOR on a given day. The Eurodollar futures contract of the Chicago Mercantile Exchange is based on $1 million notional principal of 90-day Eurodollars. Specifically, the underlying is the rate on a 90-day dollar-denominated time deposit issued by a bank in London. As we described in the reading on forward markets and contracts, this deposit is called a Eurodollar time deposit, and the rate is referred to as LIBOR (London Interbank Offer Rate). On a given day, the futures contract trades based on the understanding that at expiration, the official Eurodollar rate, as compiled by the British Bankers Association (BBA), will be the rate at which the final settlement of the contract is made. While the contract is trading, its price is quoted as 100 minus the rate priced into the contract by futures traders. Like its counterpart in the T-bill futures market, this value, $100 - \text{Rate}$, is also known as the IMM Index.

As in the T-bill futures market, on a given day, if the rate priced into the contract is 5.25 percent, the quoted price will be $100 - 5.25 = 94.75$. With each contract based on $1 million notional principal of Eurodollars, the actual futures price is

$$\$1,000,000[1 - 0.0525(90/360)] = \$986,875$$

Like the T-bill contract, the actual futures price moves $25 for every basis point move in the rate or IMM Index price.

---

[17] Expressed mathematically, $\$1,000,000[0.0001(90/360)] = \$25$. In other words, any move in the last digit of the rate (a basis point) affects the actual futures price by $25.

As with all futures contracts, the price fluctuates on a daily basis and margin accounts are marked to market according to the exchange's official settlement price. At expiration, the final settlement price is the official rate quoted on a 90-day Eurodollar time deposit by the BBA. That rate determines the final settlement. Eurodollar futures contracts do not permit actual delivery of a Eurodollar time deposit; rather, they settle in cash, as described in Section 4.

The Eurodollar futures contract is one of the most active in the world. Because its rate is based on LIBOR, it is widely used by dealers in swaps, FRAs, and interest rate options to hedge their positions taken in dollar-denominated over-the-counter interest rate derivatives. Such derivatives usually use LIBOR as the underlying rate.

It is important to note, however, that there is a critical distinction between the manner in which the interest calculation is built into the Eurodollar futures contract and the manner in which interest is imputed on actual Eurodollar time deposits. Recall from the reading on forward markets and contracts that when a bank borrows $1 million at a rate of 5 percent for 90 days, the amount it will owe in 90 days is

$$\$1,000,000[1 + 0.05(90/360)] = \$1,012,500$$

Interest on Eurodollar time deposits is computed on an add-on basis to the principal. As described in this section, however, it appears that in computing the futures price, interest is deducted from the principal so that a bank borrowing $1,000,000 at a rate of 5 percent would receive

$$\$1,000,000[1 - 0.05(90/360)] = \$987,500$$

and would pay back $1,000,000. This procedure is referred to as discount interest and is used in the T-bill market.

The discount interest computation associated with Eurodollar futures is merely a convenience contrived by the futures exchange to facilitate quoting prices in a manner already familiar to its traders, who were previously trading T-bill futures.

The minimum tick size for Eurodollar futures is 1 basis point or $25. The available expirations are the next two months plus March, June, September, and December. The expirations go out about 10 years, a reflection of their use by over-the-counter derivatives dealers to hedge their positions in long-term interest rate derivatives. Eurodollar futures expire on the second business day on which London banks are open before the third Wednesday of the month and terminate with a cash settlement.

6.2 Intermediate- and Long-Term Interest Rate Futures Contracts

In U.S. markets, the primary interest-rate-related instruments of intermediate and long maturities are U.S. Treasury notes and bonds. The U.S. government issues both instruments: Treasury notes have an original maturity of 2 to 10 years, and Treasury bonds have an original maturity of more than 10 years. Futures contracts on these instruments are very actively traded on the Chicago Board of Trade. For the most part, there are no real differences in the contract characteristics for Treasury note and Treasury bond futures; the underlying bonds differ slightly, but the futures contracts are qualitatively the same. We shall focus here on one of the most active instruments, the U.S. Treasury bond futures contract.

The contract is based on the delivery of a U.S. Treasury bond with any coupon but with a maturity of at least 15 years. If the deliverable bond is callable, it cannot be callable for at least 15 years from the delivery date.[18] These specifications mean that there are potentially a large number of deliverable bonds, which is exactly the way the Chicago Board of Trade, the Federal Reserve, and the U.S. Treasury want it. They do not want a potential run on a single issue that might distort prices. By having multiple deliverable issues, however, the contract must be structured with some fairly complicated procedures to adjust for the fact that the short can deliver whatever bond he chooses from among the eligible bonds. This choice gives the short a potentially valuable option and puts the long at a disadvantage. Moreover, it complicates pricing the contract, because the identity of the underlying bond is not clear. Although when referring to a futures contract on a 90-day Eurodollar time deposit we are relatively clear about the underlying instrument, a futures contract on a long-term Treasury bond does not allow us the same clarity.

To reduce the confusion, the exchange declares a standard or hypothetical version of the deliverable bond. This hypothetical deliverable bond has a 6 percent coupon. When a trader holding a short position at expiration delivers a bond with a coupon greater (less) than 6 percent, she receives an upward (a downward) adjustment to the price paid for the bond by the long. The adjustment is done by means of a device called the **conversion factor**. In brief, the conversion factor is the price of a $1.00 par bond with a coupon and maturity equal to those of the deliverable bond and a yield of 6 percent. Thus, if the short delivers a bond with a coupon greater (less) than 6 percent, the conversion factor exceeds (is less than) 1.0.[19] The amount the long pays the short is the futures price at expiration multiplied by the conversion factor. Thus, delivery of a bond with coupon greater (less) than the standard amount, 6 percent, results in the short receiving an upward (a downward) adjustment to the amount received. A number of other technical considerations are also involved in determining the delivery price.[20]

The conversion factor system is designed to put all bonds on equal footing. Ideally, application of the conversion factor would result in the short finding no preference for delivery of any one bond over any other. That is not the case, however, because the complex relationships between bond prices cannot be reduced to a simple linear adjustment, such as the conversion factor method. As a result, some bonds are cheaper to deliver than others. When making the delivery decision, the short compares the cost of buying a given bond on the open market with the amount she would receive upon delivery of that bond. The former will always exceed the latter; otherwise, a clear arbitrage opportunity would be available. The most attractive bond for delivery would be the one in which the amount received for delivering the bond is largest relative to the amount paid on the open market for the bond. The bond that minimizes this loss is referred to as the **cheapest-to-deliver** bond.

At any time during the life of a Treasury bond futures contract, traders can identify the cheapest-to-deliver bond. Determining the amount received at delivery is straightforward; it equals the current futures price times the conversion

---

[18] The U.S. government no longer issues callable bonds but has done so in the past.

[19] This statement is true regardless of the maturity of the deliverable bond. Any bond with a coupon in excess of its yield is worth more than its par value.

[20] For example, the actual procedure for delivery of U.S. Treasury bonds is a three-day process starting with the short notifying the exchange of intention to make delivery. Delivery actually occurs several days later. In addition, as is the custom in U.S. bond markets, the quoted price does not include the accrued interest. Accordingly, an adjustment must be made.

factor for a given bond. To determine the amount the bond would cost at expiration, one calculates the forward price of the bond, positioned at the delivery date. Of course, this is just a forward computation; circumstances could change by the expiration date. But this forward calculation gives a picture of circumstances as they currently stand and identifies which bond is currently the cheapest to deliver. That bond is then considered the bond most likely to be delivered. Recall that one problem with this futures contract is that the identity of the underlying bond is unclear. Traders traditionally treat the cheapest to deliver as the bond that underlies the contract. As time passes and interest rates change, however, the cheapest-to-deliver bond can change. Thus, the bond underlying the futures contract can change, adding an element of uncertainty to the pricing and trading of this contract.

With this complexity associated with the U.S. Treasury bond futures contract, one might suspect that it is less actively traded. In fact, the opposite is true: Complexity creates extraordinary opportunities for gain for those who understand what is going on and can identify the cheapest bond to deliver.

The Chicago Board of Trade's U.S. Treasury bond futures contract covers $100,000 par value of U.S. Treasury bonds. The expiration months are March, June, September, and December. They expire on the seventh business day preceding the last business day of the month and call for actual delivery, through the Federal Reserve's wire system, of the Treasury bond. Prices are quoted in points and 32nds, meaning that you will see prices like 98 18/32, which equals 98.5625. For a contract covering $100,000 par value, for example, the price is $98,562.50. The minimum tick size is 1/32, which is $31.25.

In addition to the futures contract on the long-term government bond, there are also very similar futures contracts on intermediate-term government bonds. The Chicago Board of Trade's contracts on 2-, 5-, and 10-year Treasury notes are very actively traded and are almost identical to its long-term bond contract, except for the exact specification of the underlying instrument. Intermediate and long-term government bonds are important instruments in every country's financial markets. They give the best indication of the long-term default-free interest rate and are often viewed as a benchmark bond for various comparisons in financial markets.[21] Accordingly, futures contracts on such bonds play an important role in a country's financial markets and are almost always among the most actively traded contracts in futures markets around the world.

If the underlying instrument is not widely available and not actively traded, the viability of a futures contract on it becomes questionable. The reduction seen in U.S. government debt in the late 1990s has led to a reduction in the supply of intermediate and long-term government bonds, and some concern has arisen over this fact. In the United States, some efforts have been made to promote the long-term debt of Fannie Mae and Freddie Mac as substitute benchmark bonds.[22] It remains to be seen whether such efforts will be necessary and, if so, whether they will succeed.

---

[21] For example, the default risk of a corporate bond is often measured as the difference between the corporate bond yield and the yield on a Treasury bond or note of comparable maturity. Fixed rates on interest rate swaps are usually quoted as a spread over the rate on a Treasury bond or note of comparable maturity.

[22] Fannie Mae is the Federal National Mortgage Association, and Freddie Mac is the Federal Home Loan Mortgage Corporation. These institutions were formerly U.S. government agencies that issued debt to raise funds to buy and sell mortgages and mortgage-backed securities. These institutions are now publicly traded corporations but are considered to have extremely low default risk because of their critical importance in U.S. mortgage markets. It is believed that an implicit Federal government guarantee is associated with their debt. Nonetheless, it seems unlikely that the debt of these institutions could take over that of the U.S. government as a benchmark. The Chicago Board of Trade has offered futures contracts on the bonds of these organizations, but the contracts have not traded actively.

6.3 Stock Index Futures Contracts

One of the most successful types of futures contracts of all time is the class of futures on stock indices. Probably the most successful has been the Chicago Mercantile Exchange's contract on the Standard and Poor's 500 Stock Index. Called the S&P 500 Stock Index futures, this contract premiered in 1982 and has benefited from the widespread acceptance of the S&P 500 Index as a stock market benchmark. The contract is quoted in terms of a price on the same order of magnitude as the S&P 500 itself. For example, if the S&P 500 Index is at 1183, a two-month futures contract might be quoted at a price of, say, 1187.

The contract implicitly contains a multiplier, which is (appropriately) multiplied by the quoted futures price to produce the actual futures price. The multiplier for the S&P 500 futures is $250. Thus, when you hear of a futures price of 1187, the actual price is 1187($250) = $296,750.

S&P 500 futures expirations are March, June, September, and December and go out about two years, although trading is active only in the nearest two to three expirations. With occasional exceptions, the contracts expire on the Thursday preceding the third Friday of the month. Given the impracticality of delivering a portfolio of the 500 stocks in the index combined according to their relative weights in the index, the contract is structured to provide for cash settlement at expiration.

The S&P 500 is not the only active stock index futures contract. In fact, the Chicago Mercantile Exchange has a smaller version of the S&P 500 contract, called the Mini S&P 500, which has a multiplier of $50 and trades only electronically. Other widely traded contracts in the United States are on the Dow Jones Industrials, the S&P Midcap 400, and the Nasdaq 100. Virtually every developed country has a stock index futures contract based on the leading equities of that country. Well-known stock index futures contracts around the world include the United Kingdom's FTSE 100 (pronounced "Footsie 100"), Japan's Nikkei 225, France's CAC 40, and Germany's DAX 30.

6.4 Currency Futures Contracts

In the reading on forward markets and contracts, we described forward contracts on foreign currencies. There are also futures contracts on foreign currencies. Although the forward market for foreign currencies is much more widely used, the futures market is still quite active. In fact, currency futures were the first futures contracts not based on physical commodities. Thus, they are sometimes referred to as the first financial futures contracts, and their initial success paved the way for the later introduction of interest rate and stock index futures.

Compared with forward contracts on currencies, currency futures contracts are much smaller in size. In the United States, these contracts trade at the Chicago Mercantile Exchange with a small amount of trading at the New York Board of Trade. In addition there is some trading on exchanges outside the United States. The characteristics we describe below refer to the Chicago Mercantile Exchange's contract.

In the United States, the primary currencies on which trading occurs are the euro, Canadian dollar, Swiss franc, Japanese yen, British pound, Mexican peso, and Australian dollar. Each contract has a designated size and a quotation unit. For example, the euro contract covers €125,000 and is quoted in dollars per euro. A futures price such as $0.8555 is stated in dollars and converts to a contract price of

$$125,000(\$0.8555) = \$106,937.50$$

The Japanese yen futures price is structured somewhat differently. Because of the large number of yen per dollar, the contract covers ¥12,500,000 and is quoted without two zeroes that ordinarily precede the price. For example, a price might be stated as 0.8205, but this actually represents a price of 0.008205, which converts to a contract price of

$$12,500,000(0.008205) = \$102,562.50$$

Alternatively, a quoted price of 0.8205 can be viewed as $1/0.008205 = ¥121.88$ per dollar.

Currency futures contracts expire in the months of March, June, September, and December. The specific expiration is the second business day before the third Wednesday of the month. Currency futures contracts call for actual delivery, through book entry, of the underlying currency.

We have briefly examined the different types of futures contracts of interest to us. Of course there are a variety of similar instruments trading on futures exchanges around the world. The purpose of this book, however, is not to provide institutional details, which can be obtained at the websites of the world's futures exchanges, but rather to enhance your understanding of the important principles necessary to function in the world of derivatives.

SUMMARY

- Futures contracts are standardized instruments that trade on a futures exchange, have a secondary market, and are guaranteed against default by means of a daily settling of gains and losses. Forward contracts are customized instruments that are not guaranteed against default and are created anywhere off of an exchange.

- Modern futures markets primarily originated in Chicago out of a need for grain farmers and buyers to be able to transact for delivery at future dates for grain that would, in the interim, be placed in storage.

- Futures transactions are standardized and conducted in a public market, are homogeneous, have a secondary market giving them an element of liquidity, and have a clearinghouse, which collects margins and settles gains and losses daily to provide a guarantee against default. Futures markets are also regulated at the federal government level.

- Margin in the securities markets is the deposit of money, the margin, and a loan for the remainder of the funds required to purchase a stock or bond. Margin in the futures markets is much smaller and does not involve a loan. Futures margin is more like a performance bond or down payment.

- Futures trading occurs on a futures exchange, which involves trading either in a physical location called a pit or via a computer terminal off of the floor of the futures exchange as part of an electronic trading system. In either case, a party to a futures contract goes long, committing to buy the underlying asset at an agreed-upon price, or short, committing to sell the underlying asset at an agreed-upon price.

- A futures trader who has established a position can re-enter the market and close out the position by doing the opposite transaction (sell if the original position was long or buy if the original position was short). The party has offset the position, no longer has a contract outstanding, and has no further obligation.

- Initial margin is the amount of money in a margin account on the day of a transaction or when a margin call is made. Maintenance margin is the amount of money in a margin account on any day other than when the initial margin applies. Minimum requirements exist for the initial and maintenance margins, with the initial margin requirement normally being less than 10 percent of the futures price and the maintenance margin requirement being smaller than the initial margin requirement. Variation margin is the amount of money that must be deposited into the account to bring the balance up to the required level. The settlement price is an average of the last few trades of the day and is used to determine the gains and losses marked to the parties' accounts.

- The futures clearinghouse engages in a practice called marking to market, also known as the daily settlement, in which gains and losses on a futures position are credited and charged to the trader's margin account on a daily basis. Thus, profits are available for withdrawal and losses must be paid quickly before they build up and pose a risk that the party will be unable to cover large losses.

- The margin balance at the end of the day is determined by taking the previous balance and accounting for any gains or losses from the day's activity, based on the settlement price, as well as any money added or withdrawn.

▶ Price limits are restrictions on the price of a futures trade and are based on a range relative to the previous day's settlement price. No trade can take place outside of the price limits. A limit move is when the price at which two parties would like to trade is at or beyond the price limit. Limit up is when the market price would be at or above the upper limit. Limit down is when the market price would be at or below the lower limit. Locked limit occurs when a trade cannot take place because the price would be above the limit up or below the limit down prices.

▶ A futures contract can be terminated by entering into an offsetting position very shortly before the end of the expiration day. If the position is still open when the contract expires, the trader must take delivery (if long) or make delivery (if short), unless the contract requires that an equivalent cash settlement be used in lieu of delivery. In addition, two participants can agree to alternative delivery terms, an arrangement called exchange for physicals.

▶ Delivery options are features associated with a futures contract that permit the short some flexibility in what to deliver, where to deliver it, and when in the expiration month to make delivery.

▶ Scalpers are futures traders who take positions for very short periods of time and attempt to profit by buying at the bid price and selling at the ask price. Day traders close out all positions by the end of the day. Position traders leave their positions open overnight and potentially longer.

▶ Treasury bill futures are contracts in which the underlying is $1,000,000 of a U.S. Treasury bill. Eurodollar futures are contracts in which the underlying is $1,000,000 of a Eurodollar time deposit. Treasury bond futures are contracts in which the underlying is $100,000 of a U.S. Treasury bond with a minimum 15-year maturity. Stock index futures are contracts in which the underlying is a well-known stock index, such as the S&P 500 or FTSE 100. Currency futures are contracts in which the underlying is a foreign currency.

PRACTICE PROBLEMS FOR READING 69

1. A. In February, Dave Parsons purchased a June futures contract on the Nasdaq 100 Index. He decides to close out his position in April. Describe how he would do so.

  B. Peggy Smith is a futures trader. In early August, she took a short position in an S&P 500 Index futures contract expiring in September. After a week, she decides to close out her position. Describe how she would do so.

2. A gold futures contract requires the long trader to buy 100 troy ounces of gold. The initial margin requirement is $2,000, and the maintenance margin requirement is $1,500.

  A. Matthew Evans goes long one June gold futures contract at the futures price of $320 per troy ounce. When could Evans receive a maintenance margin call? *Price falls below $315*

  B. Chris Tosca sells one August gold futures contract at a futures price of $323 per ounce. When could Tosca receive a maintenance margin call? *323+5=$328*

[handwritten margin notes: 2000 ; 1500 ; 500 – per 100 troy ounces ; 700 $5 per ounce]

3. A copper futures contract requires the long trader to buy 25,000 lbs of copper. A trader buys one November copper futures contract at a price of $0.75/lb. Theoretically, what is the maximum loss this trader could have? *$18,750* Another trader sells one November copper futures contract. Theoretically, what is the maximum loss this trader with a short position could have?

4. Consider a hypothetical futures contract in which the current price is $212. The initial margin requirement is $10, and the maintenance margin requirement is $8. You go long 20 contracts and meet all margin calls but do not withdraw any excess margin.

  A. When could there be a margin call? *10−8=2   212−2=(210)*

  B. Complete the table below and explain any funds deposited. Assume that the contract is purchased at the settlement price of that day so there is no mark-to-market profit or loss on the day of purchase.

Day	Beginning Balance	Funds Deposited	Futures Price	Price Change	Gain/Loss	Ending Balance
0	0	200	212	0	0	200
1	200	200	211	−1	−20	180
2	180		214	+3	+60	240
3	240		209	−5	−100	+140
4	140	60	210	+1	20	220
5	220		204	−6	−120	100
6	100	100	202	−2	−40	160

  C. How much are your total gains or losses by the end of day 6? *(212 − 202) = 10×20 = 20)*

5. Sarah Moore has taken a short position in one Chicago Board of Trade Treasury bond futures contract with a face value of $100,000 at the price of 96 6/32. The initial margin requirement is $2,700, and the maintenance margin requirement is $2,000. Moore would meet all margin calls but would not withdraw any excess margin.

A. Complete the table below and provide an explanation of any funds deposited. Assume that the contract is purchased at the settlement price of that day, so there is no mark-to-market profit or loss on the day of purchase.

Day	Beginning Balance	Funds Deposited	Futures Price	Price Change	Gain/Loss	Ending Balance
0	0	2700	96–06	0	0	2700
1	2700	0	96–31	+25/32	−781.25	1918.75
2	1918.75	781.25	97–22	23/32	−718.75	1981.25
3	1981.25	718.75	97–18	−4/32	+125	2825
4			97–24			
5			98–04			
6			97–31			

B. How much are Moore's total gains or losses by the end of day 6?

6. A. The IMM index price in yesterday's newspaper for a September Eurodollar futures contract is 95.23. What is the actual price of this contract?

$100 - 95.23 \quad 4.77 \qquad 100\left(1 - .0477\ \frac{90}{360}\right) =$

988075

B. The IMM index price in today's newspaper for the contract mentioned above is 95.25. How much is the change in the actual futures price of the contract since the previous day?

$\$50 \quad 100\left(1 - .0475\ \frac{90}{360}\right)$

$988,125$

7. Consider the following statements about a futures clearinghouse:

Statement 1: "A clearinghouse in futures contracts allows for the offsetting of contracts prior to delivery."

Statement 2: "A clearinghouse in futures contracts collects initial margin (performance bonds) from both the long and short sides in the contract."

Are the statements *most likely* correct or incorrect?

A. Both statements are correct.

B. Statement 1 is incorrect, but Statement 2 is correct.

C. Statement 1 is correct, but Statement 2 is incorrect.

8. A trader enters into a short position of 20 futures contracts at an initial futures price of $85.00. Initial margin, per contract, is $7.50. Maintenance margin, per contract, is $7.00. Each contract is for one unit of the underlying asset. Over the next three days, the contact settles at $86.00, $84.25, and $85.50, respectively. Assuming the trader does not withdraw any funds from his/her margin account during the period, but does post variation margin sufficient to meet any maintenance margin calls, the balance in the margin account will be:

   A. $140.00 at initiation and $150.00 at settlement on day three.

   B. $150.00 at initiation and $150.00 at settlement on day three.

   C. $150.00 at initiation and $160.00 at settlement on day three.

9. Consider the following statements regarding futures contracts that may be settled by delivery:

   Statement 1:   "The long initiates the delivery process."

   Statement 2:   "For many such contracts, delivery can take place any business day during the delivery month."

   Are the statements *most likely* correct or incorrect?

   A. Both statements are correct.

   B. Statement 1 is incorrect, but Statement 2 is correct.

   C. Statement 1 is correct, but Statement 2 is incorrect.

SOLUTIONS FOR READING 69

1. A. Parsons would close out his position in April by offsetting his long position with a short position. To do so, he would re-enter the market and offer for sale a June futures contract on the Nasdaq 100 index. When he has a buyer, he has both a long and a short position in the June futures contract on the Nasdaq 100 index. From the point of view of the clearinghouse, he no longer has a position in the contract.

B. Smith would close out her position in August by offsetting her short position with a long position. To do so, she would re-enter the market and purchase a September futures contract on the S&P 500. She then has both a short and a long position in the September futures contract on the S&P 500. From the point of view of the clearinghouse, she no longer has a position in the contract.

2. The difference between initial and maintenance margin requirements for one gold futures contract is $2,000 − $1,500 = $500. Because one gold futures contract is for 100 troy ounces, the difference between initial and maintenance margin requirements per troy ounce is $500/100, or $5.

A. Because Evans has a long position, he would receive a maintenance margin call if the price were to *fall* below $320 − $5, or $315 per troy ounce.

B. Because Tosca has a short position, he would receive a maintenance margin call if the price were to *rise* above $323 + $5, or $328 per troy ounce.

3. *Trader with a long position*: This trader loses if the price falls. The maximum loss would be incurred if the futures price falls to zero, and this loss would be $0.75/lb × 25,000 lbs, or $18,750. Of course, this scenario is only theoretical, not realistic.

Trader with a short position: This trader loses if the price increases. Because there is no limit on the price increase, there is no theoretical upper limit on the loss that the trader with a short position could incur.

4. A. The difference between the initial margin requirement and the maintenance margin requirement is $2. Because the initial futures price was $212, a margin call would be triggered if the price falls below $210.

B.

Day	Beginning Balance	Funds Deposited	Futures Price	Price Change	Gain/Loss	Ending Balance
0	0	200	212			200
1	200	0	211	−1	−20	180
2	180	0	214	3	60	240
3	240	0	209	−5	−100	140
4	140	60	210	1	20	220
5	220	0	204	−6	−120	100
6	100	100	202	−2	−40	160

Solutions to 1–6 taken from *Analysis of Derivatives for the Chartered Financial Analyst® Program*, by Don M. Chance, CFA. Copyright © 2003 by AIMR. Reprinted with permission. All other solutions copyright © CFA Institute.

On day 0, you deposit $200 because the initial margin requirement is $10 per contract and you go long 20 contracts ($10 per contract times 20 contracts equals $200). At the end of day 3, the balance is down to $140, $20 below the $160 maintenance margin requirement ($8 per contract times 20 contracts). You must deposit enough money to bring the balance up to the initial margin requirement of $200. So, the next day (day 4), you deposit $60. The price change on day 5 causes a gain/loss of −$120, leaving you with a balance of $100 at the end of day 5. Again, this amount is less than the $160 maintenance margin requirement. You must deposit enough money to bring the balance up to the initial margin requirement of $200. So on day 6, you deposit $100.

C. By the end of day 6, the price is $202, a decrease of $10 from your purchase price of $212. Your loss so far is $10 per contract times 20 contracts, or $200.

You could also look at your loss so far as follows. You initially deposited $200, followed by margin calls of $60 and $100. Thus, you have deposited a total of $360 so far and have not withdrawn any excess margin. The ending balance, however, is only $160. Thus, the total loss incurred by you so far is $360 − $160, or $200.

5. A.

Day	Beginning Balance	Funds Deposited	Futures Price	Price Change	Gain/Loss	Ending Balance
0	0	2,700.00	96-06			2,700.00
1	2,700.00	0	96-31	25/32	−781.25	1,918.75
2	1,918.75	781.25	97-22	23/32	−718.75	1,981.25
3	1,981.25	718.75	97-18	−4/32	125.00	2,825.00
4	2,825.00	0	97-24	6/32	−187.50	2,637.50
5	2,637.50	0	98-04	12/32	−375.00	2,262.50
6	2,262.50	0	97-31	−5/32	156.25	2,418.75

On day 0, Moore deposits $2,700 because the initial margin requirement is $2,700 per contract and she has gone short one contract. At the end of day 1, the price has increased from 96-06 to 96-31—that is, the price has increased from $96,187.50 to $96,968.75. Because Moore has taken a short position, this increase of $781.25 is an adverse price movement for her, and the balance is down by $781.25 to $1,918.75. Because this amount is less than the $2,000 maintenance margin requirement, she must deposit additional funds to bring her account back to the initial margin requirement of $2,700. So, the next day (day 2), she deposits $781.25. Another adverse price movement takes place on day 2 as the price further increases by $718.75 to $97,687.50. Her ending balance is again below the maintenance margin requirement of $2,000, and she must deposit enough money to bring her account back to the initial margin requirement of $2,700. So, the next day (day 3), she deposits $718.75. Subsequently, even though her balance falls below the initial margin requirement, it does not go below the maintenance margin requirement, and she does not need to deposit any more funds.

B. Moore bought the contract at a futures price of 96-06. By the end of day 6, the price is 97-31, an increase of 1 25/32. Therefore, her loss so far is 1.78125 percent of $100,000, which is $1,781.25.

You could also look at her loss so far as follows: She initially deposited $2,700, followed by margin calls of $781.25 and $718.75. Thus, she has deposited a total of $4,200 so far, and has not withdrawn any excess margin. Her ending balance is $2,418.75. Thus, the total loss so far is $4,200 − $2,418.75, or $1,781.25.

6. A. Because the IMM index price is 95.23, the annualized LIBOR rate priced into the contract is 100 − 95.23 = 4.77 percent. With each contract based on $1 million notional principal of 90-day Eurodollars, the actual futures price is $1,000,000[1 − 0.0477(90/360)] = $988,075.

B. Because the IMM index price is 95.25, the annualized LIBOR rate priced into the contract is 100 − 95.25 = 4.75 percent. The actual futures price is $1,000,000[1 − 0.0475(90/360)] = $988,125. So, the change in actual futures price is $988,125 − $988,075 = $50.

You could also compute the change in price directly by noting that the IMM index price increased by 2 basis points. Because each basis point move in the rate moves the actual futures price by $25, the increase in the actual futures price is 2 × $25, or $50.

7. A is correct. Both statements describe functions of a clearinghouse.

8. C is correct. Initial margin is 20 contracts × $7.50 margin per contract = $150. At the end of day one, the short position has lost $20 ((85 − 86) × 20 contracts) leaving a margin balance of $130. Because this violates the required maintenance margin of $140, the short must deposit $20 variation margin to bring the margin account back to the initial margin balance of $150. On day two, the short position has a daily gain of $35 ((86 − 84.25) × 20) bringing the margin account to a balance of $185. The short position loses $25 on day three ((84.25 − 85.50) × 20) leaving a margin balance of $160.

9. B is correct. The short initiates the delivery process and actual delivery typically can occur on any business day of the delivery month.

OPTION MARKETS AND CONTRACTS

by Don M. Chance, CFA

LEARNING OUTCOMES

The candidate should be able to:	Mastery
a. define European option, American option, and the concept of moneyness of an option;	☐
b. differentiate between exchange-traded options and over-the-counter options;	☐
c. identify the types of options in terms of the underlying instruments;	☐
d. compare and contrast interest rate options with forward rate agreements (FRAs);	☐
e. define interest rate caps, floors, and collars;	☐
f. compute and interpret option payoffs, and explain how interest rate option payoffs differ from the payoffs of other types of options;	☐
g. define intrinsic value and time value and explain their relationship;	☐
h. determine the minimum and maximum values of European options and American options;	☐
i. calculate and interpret the lowest prices of European and American calls and puts based on the rules for minimum values and lower bounds;	☐
j. explain how option prices are affected by the exercise price and the time to expiration;	☐
k. explain put–call parity for European options, and relate put–call parity to arbitrage and the construction of synthetic options;	☐
l. contrast American options with European options in terms of the lower bounds on option prices and the possibility of early exercise;	☐
m. explain how cash flows on the underlying asset affect put–call parity and the lower bounds of option prices;	☐
n. indicate the directional effect of an interest rate change or volatility change on an option's price.	☐

Analysis of Derivatives for the Chartered Financial Analyst® Program, by Don M. Chance, CFA. Copyright © 2003 by AIMR. Reprinted with permission.

1 INTRODUCTION

Prior readings provided a general introduction to derivative markets and examined forward contracts and futures contracts. We noted how similar forward and futures contracts are: Both are commitments to buy an underlying asset at a fixed price at a later date. Forward contracts, however, are privately created, over-the-counter customized instruments that carry credit risk. Futures contracts are publicly traded, exchange-listed standardized instruments that effectively have no credit risk. Now we turn to options. Like forwards and futures, they are derivative instruments that provide the opportunity to buy or sell an underlying asset with a specific expiration date. But in contrast, buying an option gives the *right,* not the obligation, to buy or sell an underlying asset. And whereas forward and futures contracts involve no exchange of cash up front, options require a cash payment from the option buyer to the option seller.

Yet options contain several features common to forward and futures contracts. For one, options can be created by any two parties with any set of terms they desire. In this sense, options can be privately created, over-the-counter, customized instruments that are subject to credit risk. In addition, however, there is a large market for publicly traded, exchange-listed, standardized options, for which credit risk is essentially eliminated by the clearinghouse.

Just as we examined the pricing of forwards and futures in the last two readings, we shall examine option pricing in this reading. We shall also see that options can be created out of forward contracts, and that forward contracts can be created out of options. With some simplifying assumptions, options can be created out of futures contracts and futures contracts can be created out of options.

Finally, note that options also exist that have a futures or forward contract as the underlying. These instruments blend some of the features of both options and forwards/futures.

As background, we discuss the definitions and characteristics of options.

2 BASIC DEFINITIONS AND ILLUSTRATIONS OF OPTIONS CONTRACTS

In the reading on derivative markets and instruments, we defined an option as a financial derivative contract that provides a party the right to buy or sell an underlying at a fixed price by a certain time in the future. The party holding the right is the option buyer; the party granting the right is the option seller. There are two types of options, a **call** and a **put**. A call is an option granting the right to buy the underlying; a put is an option granting the right to sell the underlying. With the exception of some advanced types of options, a given option contract is either a call, granting the right to buy, or a put, granting the right to sell, but not both.[1] We emphasize that this right to buy or sell is held by the option buyer, also called the long or option holder, and granted by the option seller, also called the short or option writer.

To obtain this right, the option buyer pays the seller a sum of money, commonly referred to as the **option price**. On occasion, this option price is called the **option premium** or just the **premium**. This money is paid when the option contract is initiated.

2.1 Basic Characteristics of Options

The fixed price at which the option holder can buy or sell the underlying is called the **exercise price**, **strike price**, **striking price**, or **strike**. The use of this right to buy or sell the underlying is referred to as **exercise** or **exercising the option**. Like all derivative contracts, an option has an expiration date, giving rise to the notion of an option's **time to expiration**. When the expiration date arrives, an option that is not exercised simply expires.

What happens at exercise depends on whether the option is a call or a put. If the buyer is exercising a call, she pays the exercise price and receives either the underlying or an equivalent cash settlement. On the opposite side of the transaction is the seller, who receives the exercise price from the buyer and delivers the underlying, or alternatively, pays an equivalent cash settlement. If the buyer is exercising a put, she delivers the stock and receives the exercise price or an equivalent cash settlement. The seller, therefore, receives the underlying and must pay the exercise price or the equivalent cash settlement.

As noted in the above paragraph, cash settlement is possible. In that case, the option holder exercising a call receives the difference between the market value of the underlying and the exercise price from the seller in cash. If the option holder exercises a put, she receives the difference between the exercise price and the market value of the underlying in cash.

There are two primary exercise styles associated with options. One type of option has European-style exercise, which means that the option can be exercised only on its expiration day. In some cases, exercise could occur during that day; in others, exercise can occur only when the option has expired. In either case, such an option is called a **European option**. The other style of exercise is American-style exercise. Such an option can be exercised on any day through the expiration day and is generally called an **American option**.[2]

Option contracts specify a designated number of units of the underlying. For exchange-listed, standardized options, the exchange establishes each term, with the exception of the price. The price is negotiated by the two parties. For an over-the-counter option, the two parties decide each of the terms through negotiation.

In an over-the-counter option—one created off of an exchange by any two parties who agree to trade—the buyer is subject to the possibility of the writer defaulting. When the buyer exercises, the writer must either deliver the stock or cash if a call, or pay for the stock or pay cash if a put. If the writer cannot do so for financial reasons, the option holder faces a credit loss. Because the option holder paid the price up front and is not required to do anything else, the seller does not face any credit risk. Thus, although credit risk is bilateral in forward contracts—the long assumes the risk of the short defaulting, and the short assumes the risk of

---

[1] Of course, a party could buy both a call and a put, thereby holding the right to buy *and* sell the underlying.

[2] It is worthwhile to be aware that these terms have nothing to do with Europe or America. Both types of options are found in Europe and America. The names are part of the folklore of options markets, and there is no definitive history to explain how they came into use.

the long defaulting—the credit risk in an option is unilateral. Only the buyer faces credit risk because only the seller can default. As we discuss later, in exchange-listed options, the clearinghouse guarantees payment to the buyer.

2.2 Some Examples of Options

Consider some call and put options on Sun Microsystems (SUNW). The date is 13 June and Sun is selling for $16.25. Exhibit 1 gives information on the closing prices of four options, ones expiring in July and October and ones with exercise prices of 15.00 and 17.50. The July options expire on 20 July and the October options expire on 18 October. In the parlance of the profession, these are referred to as the July 15 calls, July 17.50 calls, October 15 calls, and October 17.50 calls, with similar terminology for the puts. These particular options are American style.

EXHIBIT 1	Closing Prices of Selected Options on SUNW, 13 June			
Exercise Price	July Calls	October Calls	July Puts	October Puts
15.00	2.35	3.30	0.90	1.85
17.50	1.00	2.15	2.15	3.20

Note: Stock price is $16.25; July options expire on 20 July; October options expire on 18 October.

Consider the July 15 call. This option permits the holder to buy SUNW at a price of $15 a share any time through 20 July. To obtain this option, one would pay a price of $2.35. Therefore, a writer received $2.35 on 13 June and must be ready to sell SUNW to the buyer for $15 during the period through 20 July. Currently, SUNW trades above $15 a share, but as we shall see in more detail later, the option holder has no reason to exercise the option right now.[3] To justify purchase of the call, the buyer must be anticipating that SUNW will increase in price before the option expires. The seller of the call must be anticipating that SUNW will not rise sufficiently in price before the option expires.

Note that the option buyer could purchase a call expiring in July but permitting the purchase of SUNW at a price of $17.50. This price is more than the $15.00 exercise price, but as a result, the option, which sells for $1.00, is considerably cheaper. The cheaper price comes from the fact that the July 17.50 call is less likely to be exercised, because the stock has a higher hurdle to clear. A buyer is not willing to pay as much and a seller is more willing to take less for an option that is less likely to be exercised.

Alternatively, the option buyer could choose to purchase an October call instead of a July call. For any exercise price, however, the October calls would be more expensive than the July calls because they allow a longer period for the stock to make the move that the buyer wants. October options are more likely to

---

[3] The buyer paid $2.35 for the option. If he exercised it right now, he would pay $15.00 for the stock, which is worth only $16.25. Thus, he would have effectively paid $17.35 (the cost of the option of $2.35 plus the exercise price of $15) for a stock worth $16.25. Even if he had purchased the option previously at a much lower price, the current option price of $2.35 is the opportunity cost of exercising the option—that is, he can always sell the option for $2.35. Therefore, if he exercised the option, he would be throwing away the $2.35 he could receive if he sold it.

be exercised than July options; therefore, a buyer would be willing to pay more and the seller would demand more for the October calls.

Suppose the buyer expects the stock price to go down. In that case, he might buy a put. Consider the October 17.50 put, which would cost the buyer $3.20. This option would allow the holder to sell SUNW at a price of $17.50 any time up through 18 October.[4] He has no reason to exercise the option right now, because it would mean he would be buying the option for $3.20 and selling a stock worth $16.25 for $17.50. In effect, the option holder would part with $19.45 (the cost of the option of $3.20 plus the value of the stock of $16.25) and obtain only $17.50.[5] The buyer of a put obviously must be anticipating that the stock will fall before the expiration day.

If he wanted a cheaper option than the October 17.50 put, he could buy the October 15 put, which would cost only $1.85 but would allow him to sell the stock for only $15.00 a share. The October 15 put is less likely to be exercised than the October 17.50, because the stock price must fall below a lower hurdle. Thus, the buyer is not willing to pay as much and the seller is willing to take less.

For either exercise price, purchase of a July put instead of an October put would be much cheaper but would allow less time for the stock to make the downward move necessary for the transaction to be worthwhile. The July put is cheaper than the October put; the buyer is not willing to pay as much and the seller is willing to take less because the option is less likely to be exercised.

In observing these option prices, we have obtained our first taste of some principles involved in pricing options.

> *Call options have a lower premium the higher the exercise price.*
> *Put options have a lower premium the lower the exercise price.*
> *Both call and put options are cheaper the shorter the time to expiration.*[6]

These results should be intuitive, but later in this reading we show unequivocally why they must be true.

2.3 The Concept of Moneyness of an Option

An important concept in the study of options is the notion of an option's **moneyness**, which refers to the relationship between the price of the underlying and the exercise price.

We use the terms **in-the-money**, **out-of-the-money**, and **at-the-money**. We explain the concept in Exhibit 2 with examples from the SUNW options. Note that in-the-money options are those in which exercising the option would produce a cash inflow that exceeds the cash outflow. Thus, calls are in-the-money when the value of the underlying exceeds the exercise price. Puts are in-the-money when the exercise price exceeds the value of the underlying. In our example, there are no at-the-money SUNW options, which would require that the stock value equal the exercise price; however, an at-the-money option can effectively be viewed as an out-of-the-money option, because its exercise would not bring in more money than is paid out.

---

[4] Even if the option holder did not own the stock, he could use the option to sell the stock short.

[5] Again, even if the option were purchased in the past at a much lower price, the $3.20 current value of the option is an opportunity cost. Exercise of the option is equivalent to throwing away the opportunity cost.

[6] There is an exception to the rule that put options are cheaper the shorter the time to expiration. This statement is always true for American options but not always for European options. We explore this point later.

EXHIBIT 2	Moneyness of an Option		
In-the-Money		**Out-of-the-Money**	
Option	Justification	Option	Justification
July 15 call	16.25 > 15.00	July 17.50 call	16.25 < 17.50
October 15 call	16.25 > 15.00	October 17.50 call	16.25 < 17.50
July 17.50 put	17.50 > 16.25	July 15 put	15.00 < 16.25
October 17.50 put	17.50 > 16.25	October 15 put	15.00 < 16.25

Notes: Sun Microsystems options on 13 June; stock price is 16.25. See Exhibit 1 for more details. There are no options with an exercise price of 16.25, so no options are at-the-money.

As explained above, *one would not necessarily exercise an in-the-money option, but one would never exercise an out-of-the-money option.*

We now move on to explore how options markets are organized.

THE STRUCTURE OF GLOBAL OPTIONS MARKETS

Although no one knows exactly how options first got started, contracts similar to options have been around for thousands of years. In fact, insurance is a form of an option. The insurance buyer pays the insurance writer a premium and receives a type of guarantee that covers losses. This transaction is similar to a put option, which provides coverage of a portion of losses on the underlying and is often used by holders of the underlying. The first true options markets were over-the-counter options markets in the United States in the 19th century.

3.1 Over-the-Counter Options Markets

In the United States, customized over-the-counter options markets were in existence in the early part of the 20th century and lasted well into the 1970s. An organization called the Put and Call Brokers and Dealers Association consisted of a group of firms that served as brokers and dealers. As brokers, they attempted to match buyers of options with sellers, thereby earning a commission. As dealers, they offered to take either side of the option transaction, usually laying off (hedging) the risk in another transaction. Most of these transactions were retail, meaning that the general public were their customers.

As we discuss in Section 3.2, the creation of the Chicago Board Options Exchange was a revolutionary event, but it effectively killed the Put and Call Brokers and Dealers Association. Subsequently, the increasing use of swaps facilitated a rebirth of the customized over-the-counter options market. Currency options, a natural extension to currency swaps, were in much demand. Later, interest rate options emerged as a natural outgrowth of interest rate swaps. Soon bond, equity, and index options were trading in a vibrant over-the-counter market. In contrast to the previous over-the-counter options market, however, the current one emerged as a largely wholesale market. Transactions are usually made with institutions and corporations and are rarely conducted directly with individuals. This market is much like the forward market described in the reading on forward markets and contracts, with dealers offering to take either the long or short position in options and hedging that risk with transactions in other options or derivatives. There are no guarantees that the seller will perform; hence, the buyer faces credit risk. As such, option buyers must scrutinize sellers' credit risk and may require some risk reduction measures, such as collateral.

As previously noted, customized options have *all* of their terms—such as price, exercise price, time to expiration, identification of the underlying, settlement or delivery terms, size of the contract, and so on—determined by the two parties.

Like forward markets, over-the-counter options markets are essentially unregulated. In most countries, participating firms, such as banks and securities firms, are regulated by the appropriate authorities, but there is usually no particular regulatory body for the over-the-counter options markets. In some countries, however, there are regulatory bodies for these markets.

Exhibit 3 provides information on the leading dealers in over-the-counter currency and interest rate options as determined by *Risk* magazine in its annual surveys of banks and investment banks and also end users.

EXHIBIT 3	*Risk* Magazine Surveys of Banks, Investment Banks, and Corporate End Users to Determine the Top Three Dealers in Over-the-Counter Currency and Interest Rate Options

	Respondents	
Currencies	**Banks and Investment Banks**	**Corporate End Users**
Currency Options		
$/€	UBS Warburg	Citigroup
	Citigroup/Deutsche Bank	Royal Bank of Scotland
		Deutsche Bank
$/¥	UBS Warburg	Citigroup
	Credit Suisse First Boston	JP Morgan Chase
	JP Morgan Chase/Royal Bank of Scotland	UBS Warburg
$/£	Royal Bank of Scotland	Royal Bank of Scotland
	UBS Warburg	Citigroup
	Citigroup	Hong Kong Shanghai Banking Corp.
$/SF	UBS Warburg	UBS Warburg
	Credit Suisse First Boston	Credit Suisse First Boston
	Citigroup	Citigroup
Interest Rate Options		
$	JP Morgan Chase	JP Morgan Chase
	Deutsche Bank	Citigroup

(Exhibit continued on next page ...)

EXHIBIT 3	(continued)

	Respondents	
Currencies	**Banks and Investment Banks**	**Corporate End Users**
Interest Rate Options		
	Bank of America	Deutsche Bank/ Lehman Brothers*
€	JP Morgan Chase	JP Morgan Chase
	Credit Suisse First Boston/ Morgan Stanley	Citigroup UBS Warburg
¥	JP Morgan Chase/ Deutsche Bank	UBS Warburg
	Bank of America	Barclays Capital Citigroup
£	Barclays Capital	Royal Bank of Scotland
	Societe Generale Groupe	Citigroup
	Bank of America/Royal Bank of Scotland	Hong Kong Shanghai Banking Corp.
SF	UBS Warburg	UBS Warburg
	JP Morgan Chase	JP Morgan Chase
	Credit Suisse First Boston	Goldman Sachs

Notes: $ = U.S. dollar, € = euro, ¥ = Japanese yen, £ = U.K. pound sterling, SF = Swiss franc.

Source: *Risk*, September 2002, pp. 30–67 for Banks and Investment Banking dealer respondents, and June 2002, pp. 24–34 for Corporate End User respondents.

Results for Corporate End Users for Interest Rate Options are from *Risk*, July 2001, pp. 38–46. *Risk* omitted this category from its 2002 survey.

*Barclays has acquired Lehman Brothers and will maintain the family of Lehman Brothers indices and the associated index calculation, publication, and analytical infrastructure and tools.

3.2 Exchange Listed Options Markets

As briefly noted above, the Chicago Board Options Exchange was formed in 1973. Created as an extension of the Chicago Board of Trade, it became the first organization to offer a market for standardized options. In the United States, standardized options also trade on the Amex–Nasdaq, the Philadelphia Stock Exchange, and the Pacific Stock Exchange.[7] On a worldwide basis, standardized options are widely traded on such exchanges as LIFFE (the London International Financial Futures and Options Exchange) in London, Eurex in Frankfurt, and most other foreign exchanges. Exhibit 4 shows the 20 largest options exchanges in the world. Note, perhaps surprisingly, that the leading options exchange is in Korea.

[7]You may wonder why the New York Stock Exchange is not mentioned. Standardized options did trade on the NYSE at one time but were not successful, and the right to trade these options was sold to another exchange.

EXHIBIT 4	World's 20 Largest Options Exchanges

Exchange and Location	Volume in 2001
Korea Stock Exchange (Korea)	854,791,792
Chicago Board Options Exchange (United States)	306,667,851
MONEP (France)	285,667,686
Eurex (Germany and Switzerland)	239,016,516
American Stock Exchange (United States)	205,103,884
Pacific Stock Exchange (United States)	102,701,752
Philadelphia Stock Exchange (United States)	101,373,433
Chicago Mercantile Exchange (United States)	95,740,352
Amsterdam Exchange (Netherlands)	66,400,654
LIFFE (United Kingdom)	54,225,652
Chicago Board of Trade (United States)	50,345,068
OM Stockholm (Sweden)	39,327,619
South African Futures Exchange (South Africa)	24,307,477
MEFF Renta Variable (Spain)	23,628,446
New York Mercantile Exchange (United States)	17,985,109
Korea Futures Exchange (Korea)	11,468,991
Italian Derivatives Exchange (Italy)	11,045,804
Osaka Securities Exchange (Japan)	6,991,908
Bourse de Montreal (Canada)	5,372,930
Hong Kong Futures Exchange (China)	4,718,880

Note: Volume given is in number of contracts.
Source: Data supplied by *Futures Industry* magazine.

As described in the reading on futures markets and contracts, the exchange fixes all terms of standardized instruments except the price. Thus, the exchange establishes the expiration dates and exercise prices as well as the minimum price quotation unit. The exchange also determines whether the option is European or American, whether the exercise is cash settlement or delivery of the underlying, and the contract size. In the United States, an option contract on an individual stock covers 100 shares of stock. Terminology such as "one option" is often used to refer to one option contract, which is really a set of options on 100 shares of stock. Index option sizes are stated in terms of a multiplier, indicating that the contract covers a hypothetical number of shares, as though the index were an individual stock. Similar specifications apply for options on other types of underlyings.

The exchange generally allows trading in exercise prices that surround the current stock price. As the stock price moves, options with exercise prices around the new stock price are usually added. The majority of trading occurs in options that are close to being at-the-money. Options that are far in-the-money or far out-of-the-money, called **deep-in-the-money** and **deep-out-of-the-money** options, are usually not very actively traded and are often not even listed for trading.

Most exchange-listed options have fairly short-term expirations, usually the current month, the next month, and perhaps one or two other months. Most of the trading takes place for the two shortest expirations. Some exchanges list options with expirations of several years, which have come to be called LEAPS, for **long-term equity anticipatory securities**. These options are fairly actively purchased, but most investors tend to buy and hold them and do not trade them as often as they do the shorter-term options.

The exchanges also determine on which companies they will list options for trading. Although specific requirements do exist, generally the exchange will list the options of any company for which it feels the options would be actively traded. The company has no voice in the matter. Options of a company can be listed on more than one exchange in a given country.

In the reading on futures markets and contracts, we described the manner in which futures are traded. The procedure is very similar for exchange-listed options. Some exchanges have pit trading, whereby parties meet in the pit and arrange a transaction. Some exchanges use electronic trading, in which transactions are conducted through computers. In either case, the transactions are guaranteed by the clearinghouse. In the United States, the clearinghouse is an independent company called the Options Clearing Corporation or OCC. The OCC guarantees to the buyer that the clearinghouse will step in and fulfill the obligation if the seller reneges at exercise.

When the buyer purchases the option, the premium, which one might think would go to the seller, instead goes to the clearinghouse, which maintains it in a margin account. In addition, the seller must post some margin money, which is based on a formula that reflects whether the seller has a position that hedges the risk and whether the option is in- or out-of-the-money. If the price moves against the seller, the clearinghouse will force the seller to put up additional margin money. Although defaults are rare, the clearinghouse has always been successful in paying when the seller defaults. Thus, exchange-listed options are effectively free of credit risk.

Because of the standardization of option terms and participants' general acceptance of these terms, exchange-listed options can be bought and sold at any time prior to expiration. Thus, a party who buys or sells an option can re-enter the market before the option expires and offset the position with a sale or a purchase of the identical option. From the clearinghouse's perspective, the positions cancel.

As in futures markets, traders on the options exchange are generally either market makers or brokers. Some slight technical distinctions exist between different types of market makers in different options markets, but the differences are minor and do not concern us here. Like futures traders, option market makers attempt to profit by scalping (holding positions very short term) to earn the bid–ask spread and sometimes holding positions longer, perhaps closing them overnight or leaving them open for days or more.

When an option expires, the holder decides whether or not to exercise it. When the option is expiring, there are no further gains to waiting, so in-the-money options are always exercised, assuming they are in-the-money by more than the transaction cost of buying or selling the underlying or arranging a cash settlement when exercising. Using our example of the SUNW options, if at expiration the stock is at 16, the calls with an exercise price of 15 would be exercised. Most exchange-listed stock options call for actual delivery of the stock. Thus, the seller delivers the stock and the buyer pays the seller, through the clearinghouse, $15 per share. If the exchange specifies that the contract is cash settled, the seller simply pays the buyer $1. For puts requiring delivery, the buyer tenders the stock and receives the exercise price from the seller. If the option is out-of-the-money, it simply expires unexercised and is removed from the books. If the put is cash settled, the writer pays the buyer the equivalent cash amount.

Some nonstandardized exchange-traded options exist in the United States. In an attempt to compete with the over-the-counter options market, some exchanges permit some options to be individually customized and traded on the exchange, thereby benefiting from the advantages of the clearinghouse's credit guarantee. These options are primarily available only in large sizes and tend to be traded only by large institutional investors.

Like futures markets, exchange-listed options markets are typically regulated at the federal level. In the United States, federal regulation of options markets is the responsibility of the Securities and Exchange Commission; similar regulatory structures exist in other countries.

TYPES OF OPTIONS   4

Almost anything with a random outcome can have an option on it. Note that by using the word *anything*, we are implying that the underlying does not even need to be an asset. In this section, we shall discover the different types of options, identified by the nature of the underlying. Our focus in this book is on financial options, but it is important, nonetheless, to gain some awareness of other types of options.

4.1 Financial Options

Financial options are options in which the underlying is a financial asset, interest rate, or a currency.

4.1.1 Stock Options

Options on individual stocks, also called **equity options**, are among the most popular. Exchange-listed options are available on most widely traded stocks and an option on any stock can potentially be created on the over-the-counter market. We have already given examples of stock options in an earlier section; we now move on to index options.

4.1.2 Index Options

Stock market indices are well known, not only in the investment community but also among many individuals who are not even directly investing in the market. Because a stock index is just an artificial portfolio of stocks, it is reasonable to expect that one could create an option on a stock index. Indeed, we have already covered forward and futures contracts on stock indices; options are no more difficult in structure.

For example, consider options on the S&P 500 Index, which trade on the Chicago Board Options Exchange and have a designated index contract multiplier of 100. On 13 June of a given year, the S&P 500 closed at 1241.60. A call option with an exercise price of $1,250 expiring on 20 July was selling for $28. The option is European style and settles in cash. The underlying, the S&P 500, is treated as though it were a share of stock worth $1,241.60, which can be bought, using the call option, for $1,250 on 20 July. At expiration, if the option is in-the-money, the buyer exercises it and the writer pays the buyer the $100 contract multiplier times the difference between the index value at expiration and $1,250.

In the United States, there are also options on the Dow Jones Industrial Average, the Nasdaq, and various other indices. There are nearly always options on the best-known stock indices in most countries.

Just as there are options on stocks, there are also options on bonds.

4.1.3 Bond Options

Options on bonds, usually called **bond options**, are primarily traded in the over-the-counter markets. Options exchanges have attempted to generate interest in options on bonds, but have not been very successful. Corporate bonds are not very actively traded; most are purchased and held to expiration. Government bonds, however, are very actively traded; nevertheless, options on them have not gained widespread acceptance on options exchanges. Options exchanges generate much of their trading volume from individual investors, who have far more interest in and understanding of stocks than bonds.

Thus, bond options are found almost exclusively in the over-the-counter market and are almost always options on government bonds. Consider, for example, a U.S. Treasury bond maturing in 27 years. The bond has a coupon of 5.50 percent, a yield of 5.75 percent, and is selling for $0.9659 per $1 par. An over-the-counter options dealer might sell a put or call option on the bond with an exercise price of $0.98 per $1.00 par. The option could be European or American. Its expiration day must be significantly before the maturity date of the bond. Otherwise, as the bond approaches maturity, its price will move toward par, thereby removing much of the uncertainty in its price. The option could be specified to settle with actual delivery of the bond or with a cash settlement. The parties would also specify that the contract cover a given notional principal, expressed in terms of a face value of the underlying bond.

Continuing our example, let us assume that the contract covers $5 million face value of bonds and is cash settled. Suppose the buyer exercises a call option when the bond price is at $0.995. Then the option is in-the-money by $0.995 − $0.98 = $0.015 per $1 par. The seller pays the buyer 0.015($5,000,000) = $75,000. If instead the contract called for delivery, the seller would deliver $5 million face value of bonds, which would be worth $5,000,000($0.995) = $4,975,000. The buyer would pay $5,000,000($0.98) = $4,900,000. Because the option is created in the over-the-counter market, the option buyer would assume the risk of the seller defaulting.

Even though bond options are not very widely traded, another type of related option is widely used, especially by corporations. This family of options is called **interest rate options**. These are quite different from the options we have previously discussed, because the underlying is not a particular financial instrument.

4.1.4 Interest Rate Options

In the reading on futures markets and contracts, we devoted considerable effort to understanding the Eurodollar spot market and forward contracts on the Eurodollar rate or LIBOR, called FRAs. In this reading, we cover options on LIBOR. Although these are not the only interest rate options, their characteristics are sufficiently general to capture most of what we need to know about options on other interest rates. First recall that a Eurodollar is a dollar deposited outside of the United States. The primary Eurodollar rate is LIBOR, and it is considered the best measure of an interest rate paid in dollars on a nongovernmental borrower. These Eurodollars represent dollar-denominated time deposits issued by banks in London borrowing from other banks in London.

Before looking at the characteristics of interest rate options, let us set the perspective by recalling that FRAs are forward contracts that pay off based on the difference between the underlying rate and the fixed rate embedded in the contract when it is constructed. For example, consider a 3 × 9 FRA. This contract expires in three months. The underlying rate is six-month LIBOR. Hence, when the contract is constructed, the underlying Eurodollar instrument matures in nine months. *When the contract expires, the payoff is made immediately,* but the rate on which it is based, 180-day LIBOR, is set in the spot market, where it is assumed that interest will be paid 180 days later. Hence, the payoff on an FRA is discounted by the spot rate on 180-day LIBOR to give a present value for the payoff as of the expiration date.

Just as an FRA is a forward contract in which the underlying is an interest rate, an **interest rate option** is an option in which the underlying is an interest rate. Instead of an exercise price, it has an **exercise rate** (or **strike rate**), which is expressed on an order of magnitude of an interest rate. At expiration, the option payoff is based on the difference between the underlying rate in the market and the exercise rate. Whereas an FRA is a *commitment* to make one interest payment and receive another at a future date, an interest rate option is the *right* to make one interest payment and receive another. And just as there are call and put options, there is also an **interest rate call** and an **interest rate put**.

An interest rate call is an option in which the holder has the right to make a known interest payment and receive an unknown interest payment. The underlying is the unknown interest rate. If the unknown underlying rate turns out to be higher than the exercise rate at expiration, the option is in-the-money and is exercised; otherwise, the option simply expires. *An interest rate put is an option in which the holder has the right to make an unknown interest payment and receive a known interest payment.* If the unknown underlying rate turns out to be lower than the exercise rate at expiration, the option is in-the-money and is exercised; otherwise, the option simply expires. All interest rate option contracts have a specified size, which, as in FRAs, is called the notional principal. An interest rate option can be European or American style, but most tend to be European style. Interest rate options are settled in cash.

As with FRAs, these options are offered for purchase and sale by dealers, which are financial institutions, usually the same ones who offer FRAs. These dealers quote rates for options of various exercise prices and expirations. When a dealer takes an option position, it usually then offsets the risk with other transactions, often Eurodollar futures.

To use the same example we used in introducing FRAs, consider options expiring in 90 days on 180-day LIBOR. The option buyer specifies whatever exercise rate he desires. Let us say he chooses an exercise rate of 5.5 percent and a notional principal of $10 million.

Now let us move to the expiration day. Suppose that 180-day LIBOR is 6 percent. Then the call option is in-the-money. The payoff to the holder of the option is

$$(\$10,000,000)(0.06 - 0.055)\left(\frac{180}{360}\right) = \$25,000$$

This money is not paid at expiration, however; it is paid 180 days later. There is no reason why the payoff could not be made at expiration, as is done with an FRA. The delay of payment associated with interest rate options actually makes more sense, because these instruments are commonly used to hedge floating-rate loans in which the rate is set on a given day but the interest is paid later. We shall see examples of the convenience of this type of structure in the reading on risk management applications of option strategies.

Note that the difference between the underlying rate and the exercise rate is multiplied by 180/360 to reflect the fact that the rate quoted is a 180-day rate but is stated as an annual rate. Also, the interest calculation is multiplied by the notional principal.

In general, the payoff of an interest rate call is

$$\text{(Notional Principal)}\text{Max}\left(0, \text{Underlying rate at expiration} - \text{Exercise rate}\right)\left(\frac{\text{Days in underlying rate}}{360}\right) \tag{1}$$

The expression Max(0,Underlying rate at expiration − Exercise rate) is similar to a form that we shall commonly see throughout this reading for all options. The payoff of a call option at expiration is based on the maximum of zero or the underlying minus the exercise rate. If the option expires out-of-the-money, then "Underlying rate at expiration − Exercise rate" is negative; consequently, zero is greater. Thus, the option expires with no value. If the option expires in-the-money, "Underlying rate at expiration − Exercise rate" is positive. Thus, the option expires worth this difference (multiplied by the notional principal and the Days/360 adjustment). The expression "Days in underlying rate," which we used in the reading on forward markets and contracts, refers to the fact that the rate is specified as the rate on an instrument of a specific number of days to maturity, such as a 90-day or 180-day rate, thereby requiring that we multiply by 90/360 or 180/360 or some similar adjustment.

For an interest rate put option, the general formula is

$$\text{(Notional Principal)}\text{Max}\left(0, \text{Exercise rate} - \text{Underlying rate at expiration}\right)\left(\frac{\text{Days in underlying rate}}{360}\right) \tag{2}$$

For an exercise rate of 5.5 percent and an underlying rate at expiration of 6 percent, an interest rate put expires out-of-the-money. Only if the underlying rate is less than the exercise rate does the put option expire in-the-money.

As noted above, borrowers often use interest rate call options to hedge the risk of rising rates on floating-rate loans. Lenders often use interest rate put options to hedge the risk of falling rates on floating-rate loans. The form we have seen here, in which the option expires with a single payoff, is not the more commonly used variety of interest rate option. Floating-rate loans usually involve multiple interest payments. Each of those payments is set on a given date. To hedge the risk of interest rates increasing, the borrower would need options expiring on each rate reset date. Thus, the borrower would require a combination of interest rate call options. Likewise, a lender needing to hedge the risk of falling rates on a multiple-payment floating-rate loan would need a combination of interest rate put options.

A combination of interest rate calls is referred to as an **interest rate cap** or sometimes just a **cap**. A combination of interest rate puts is called an **interest rate floor** or sometimes just a **floor**.[8] Specifically, *an interest rate cap is a series of call options on an interest rate, with each option expiring at the date on which the floating loan rate will be reset, and with each option having the same exercise rate.*[9] Each option is independent of the others; thus, exercise of one option does not affect the right to exercise any of the others. Each component call option is called a **caplet**. *An interest rate floor is a series of put options on an interest rate, with each option expiring at the date on which the floating loan rate will be reset, and with each option having the same exercise rate.* Each component put option is called a **floorlet**. The price of an interest rate cap or floor is the sum of the prices of the options that make up the cap or floor.

A special combination of caps and floors is called an **interest rate collar**. *An interest rate collar is a combination of a long cap and a short floor or a short cap and a long*

---

[8] It is possible to construct caps and floors with options on any other type of underlying, but they are very often used when the underlying is an interest rate.

[9] Technically, each option need not have the same exercise rate, but they generally do.

floor. Consider a borrower in a floating rate loan who wants to hedge the risk of rising interest rates but is concerned about the requirement that this hedge must have a cash outlay up front: the option premium. A collar, which adds a short floor to a long cap, is a way of reducing and even eliminating the up-front cost of the cap. The sale of the floor brings in cash that reduces the cost of the cap. It is possible to set the exercise rates such that the price received for the sale of the floor precisely offsets the price paid for the cap, thereby completely eliminating the up-front cost. This transaction is sometimes called a **zero-cost collar**. The term is a bit misleading, however, and brings to mind the importance of noting the true cost of a collar. Although the cap allows the borrower to be paid from the call options when rates are high, the sale of the floor requires the borrower to pay the counterparty when rates are low. Thus, the cost of protection against rising rates is the loss of the advantage of falling rates. Caps, floors, and collars are popular instruments in the interest rate markets. We shall explore strategies using them in the reading on risk management applications of option strategies.

Although interest rate options are primarily written on such rates as LIBOR, Euribor, and Euroyen, the underlying can be any interest rate.

4.1.5 Currency Options

As we noted in the reading on forward markets and contracts, the currency forward market is quite large. The same is true for the currency options market. A **currency option** allows the holder to buy (if a call) or sell (if a put) an underlying currency at a fixed exercise rate, expressed as an exchange rate. Many companies, knowing that they will need to convert a currency X at a future date into a currency Y, will buy a call option on currency Y specified in terms of currency X. For example, say that a U.S. company will be needing €50 million for an expansion project in three months. Thus, it will be buying euros and is exposed to the risk of the euro rising against the dollar. Even though it has that concern, it would also like to benefit if the euro weakens against the dollar. Thus, it might buy a call option on the euro. Let us say it specifies an exercise rate of $0.90. So it pays cash up front for the right to buy €50 million at a rate of $0.90 per euro. If the option expires with the euro above $0.90, it can buy euros at $0.90 and avoid any additional cost over $0.90. If the option expires with the euro below $0.90, it does not exercise the option and buys euros at the market rate.

Note closely these two cases:

Euro expires above $0.90
　　Company buys €50 million at $0.90

Euro expires at or below $0.90
　　Company buys €50 million at the market rate

These outcomes can also be viewed in the following manner:

Dollar expires below €1.1111, that is, €1 > $0.90
　　Company sells $45 million (€50 million × $0.90) at €1.1111, equivalent to buying €50 million

Dollar expires above €1.1111, that is, €1 < $0.90
　　Company sells sufficient dollars to buy €50 million at the market rate

This transaction looks more like a put in which the underlying is the dollar and the exercise rate is expressed as €1.1111. Thus, the call on the euro can be viewed as a put on the dollar. Specifically, a call to buy €50 million at an exercise price of $0.90 is also a put to sell €50 million × $0.90 = $45 million at an exercise price of 1/$0.90, or €1.1111.

Most foreign currency options activity occurs on the customized over-the-counter markets. Some exchange-listed currency options trade on a few exchanges, but activity is fairly low.

4.2 Options on Futures

In the reading on forward markets and contracts we covered futures markets. One of the important innovations of futures markets is options on futures. These contracts originated in the United States as a result of a regulatory structure that separated exchange-listed options and futures markets. The former are regulated by the Securities and Exchange Commission, and the latter are regulated by the Commodity Futures Trading Commission (CFTC). SEC regulations forbid the trading of options side by side with their underlying instruments. Options on stocks trade on one exchange, and the underlying trades on another or on Nasdaq.

The futures exchanges got the idea that they could offer options in which the underlying is a futures contract; no such prohibitions for side-by-side trading existed under CFTC rules. As a result, the futures exchanges were able to add an attractive instrument to their product lines. The side-by-side trading of the option and its underlying futures made for excellent arbitrage linkages between these instruments. Moreover, some of the options on futures are designed to expire on the same day the underlying futures expires. Thus, the options on the futures are effectively options on the spot asset that underlies the futures.

A call option on a futures gives the holder the right to enter into a long futures contract at a fixed futures price. A put option on a futures gives the holder the right to enter into a short futures contract at a fixed futures price. The fixed futures price is, of course, the exercise price. Consider an option on the Eurodollar futures contract trading at the Chicago Mercantile Exchange. On 13 June of a particular year, an option expiring on 13 July was based on the July Eurodollar futures contract. That futures contract expires on 16 July, a few days after the option expires.[10] The call option with exercise price of 95.75 had a price of $4.60. The underlying futures price was 96.21. Recall that this price is the IMM index value, which means that the price is based on a discount rate of $100 - 96.21 = 3.79$. The contract size is $1 million.

The buyer of this call option on a futures would pay $0.046(\$1,000,000) = \$46,000$ and would obtain the right to buy the July futures contract at a price of 95.75. Thus, at that time, the option was in the money by $96.21 - 95.75 = 0.46$ per $100 face value. Suppose that when the option expires, the futures price is 96.00. Then the holder of the call would exercise it and obtain a long futures position at a price of 95.75. The price of the underlying futures is 96.00, so the margin account is immediately marked to market with a credit of 0.25 or $625.[11] The party on the short side of the contract is immediately set up with a short futures contract at the price of 95.75. That party will be charged the $625 gain that the long made. If the option is a put, exercise of it establishes a short position. The exchange assigns the put writer a long futures position.

---

[10] Some options on futures expire a month or so before the futures expires. Others expire very close to, if not at, the futures expiration.

[11] If the contract is in-the-money by $96 - 95.75 = 0.25$ per $100 par, it is in-the-money by $0.25/100 = 0.0025$, or 0.25 percent of the face value. Because the face value is $1 million, the contract is in the money by $(0.0025)(90/360)(\$1,000,000) = \$625$. (Note the adjustment by 90/360.) Another way to look at this calculation is that the futures price at 95.75 is $1 - (0.0425)(90/360) = \$0.989375$ per $1 par, or $989,375. At 96, the futures price is $1 - 0.04(90/360) = \$0.99$ per $1 par or $990,000. The difference is $625. So, exercising this option is like entering into a futures contract at a price of $989,375 and having the price immediately go to $990,000, a gain of $625. The call holder must deposit money to meet the Eurodollar futures margin, but the exercise of the option gives him $625. In other words, assuming he meets the minimum initial margin requirement, he is immediately credited with $625 more.

4.3 Commodity Options

Options in which the asset underlying the futures is a commodity, such as oil, gold, wheat, or soybeans, are also widely traded. There are exchange-traded as well as over-the-counter versions. Over-the-counter options on oil are widely used.

Our focus in this book is on financial instruments so we will not spend any time on commodity options, but readers should be aware of the existence and use of these instruments by companies whose business involves the buying and selling of these commodities.

4.4 Other Types of Options

As derivative markets develop, options (and even some other types of derivatives) have begun to emerge on such underlyings as electricity, various sources of energy, and even weather. These instruments are almost exclusively customized over-the-counter instruments. Perhaps the most notable feature of these instruments is how the underlyings are often instruments that cannot actually be held. For example, electricity is not considered a storable asset because it is produced and almost immediately consumed, but it is nonetheless an asset and certainly has a volatile price. Consequently, it is ideally suited for options and other derivatives trading.

Consider weather. It is hardly an asset at all but simply a random factor that exerts an enormous influence on economic activity. The need to hedge against and speculate on the weather has created a market in which measures of weather activity, such as economic losses from storms or average temperature or rainfall, are structured into a derivative instrument. Option versions of these derivatives are growing in importance and use. For example, consider a company that generates considerable revenue from outdoor summer activities, provided that it does not rain. Obviously a certain amount of rain will occur, but the more rain, the greater the losses for the company. It could buy a call option on the amount of rainfall with the exercise price stated as a quantity of rainfall. If actual rainfall exceeds the exercise price, the company exercises the option and receives an amount of money related to the excess of the rainfall amount over the exercise price.

Another type of option, which is not at all new but is increasingly recognized in practice, is the real option. A real option is an option associated with the flexibility inherent in capital investment projects. For example, companies may invest in new projects that have the option to defer the full investment, expand or contract the project at a later date, or even terminate the project. In fact, most capital investment projects have numerous elements of flexibility that can be viewed as options. Of course, these options do not trade in markets the same way as financial and commodity options, and they must be evaluated much more carefully. They are, nonetheless, options and thus have the potential for generating enormous value.

Again, our emphasis is on financial options, but readers should be aware of the growing role of these other types of options in our economy. Investors who buy shares in companies that have real options are, in effect, buying real options. In addition, commodity and other types of options are sometimes found in investment portfolios in the form of "alternative investments" and can provide significant diversification benefits.

To this point, we have examined characteristics of options markets and contracts. Now we move forward to the all-important topic of how options are priced.

PRINCIPLES OF OPTION PRICING   5

In the readings on forward markets and contracts and on futures markets and contracts, we discussed the pricing and valuation of forward and futures contracts. Recall that the value of a contract is what someone must pay to buy into it or what someone would receive to sell out of it. A forward or futures contract has zero value at the start of the contract, but the value turns positive or negative as prices or rates change. A contract that has positive value to one party and negative value to the counterparty can turn around and have negative value to the former and positive value to the latter as prices or rates change. The forward or futures price is the price that the parties agree will be paid on the future date to buy and sell the underlying.

With options, these concepts are different. An option has a positive value at the start. The buyer must pay money and the seller receives money to initiate the contract. Prior to expiration, the option always has positive value to the buyer and negative value to the seller. In a forward or futures contract, the two parties agree on the fixed price the buyer will pay the seller. This fixed price is set such that the buyer and seller do not exchange any money. The corresponding fixed price at which a call holder can buy the underlying or a put holder can sell the underlying is the exercise price. It, too, is negotiated between buyer and seller but still results in the buyer paying the seller money up front in the form of an option premium or price.[12]

Thus, what we called the forward or futures price corresponds more to the exercise price of an option. The option price *is* the option value: With a few exceptions that will be clearly noted, in this reading we do not distinguish between the option price and value.

In this section of the reading, we examine the principles of option pricing. These principles are characteristics of option prices that are governed by the rationality of investors.

Before we begin, it is important to remind the reader that we assume all participants in the market behave in a rational manner such that they do not throw away money and that they take advantage of arbitrage opportunities. As such, we assume that markets are sufficiently competitive that no arbitrage opportunities exist.

Let us start by developing the notation, which is very similar to what we have used previously. Note that time 0 is today and time T is the expiration.

S_0, S_T = price of the underlying asset at time 0 (today) and time T (expiration)

X = exercise price

r = risk-free rate

T = time to expiration, equal to number of days to expiration divided by 365

c_0, c_T = price of European call today and at expiration

C_0, C_T = price of American call today and at expiration

p_0, p_T = price of European put today and at expiration

P_0, P_T = price of American put today and at expiration

On occasion, we will introduce some variations of the above as well as some new notation. For example, we start off with no cash flows on the underlying, but we shall discuss the effects of cash flows on the underlying in Section 5.7.

5.1 Payoff Values

The easiest time to determine an option's value is at expiration. At that point, there is no future. Only the present matters. An option's value at expiration is called its **payoff**. We introduced this material briefly in our basic descriptions of types of options; now we cover it in more depth.

---

[12] For a call, there is no finite exercise price that drives the option price to zero. For a put, the unrealistic example of a zero exercise price would make the put price be zero.

At expiration, a call option is worth either zero or the difference between the underlying price and the exercise price, whichever is greater:

$$c_T = \text{Max}(0, S_T - X)$$
$$C_T = \text{Max}(0, S_T - X)$$

(3)

Note that at expiration, a European option and an American option have the same payoff because they are equivalent instruments at that point.

The expression $\text{Max}(0, S_T - X)$ means to take the greater of zero or $S_T - X$. Suppose the underlying price exceeds the exercise price, $S_T > X$. In this case, the option is expiring in-the-money and the option is worth $S_T - X$. Suppose that at the instant of expiration, it is possible to buy the option for less than $S_T - X$. Then one could buy the option, immediately exercise it, and immediately sell the underlying. Doing so would cost c_T (or C_T) for the option and X to buy the underlying but would bring in S_T for the sale of the underlying. If c_T (or C_T) < $S_T - X$, this transaction would net an immediate risk-free profit. The collective actions of all investors doing this would force the option price up to $S_T - X$. The price could not go higher than $S_T - X$, because all that the option holder would end up with an instant later when the option expires is $S_T - X$. If $S_T < X$, meaning that the call is expiring out-of-the-money, the formula says the option should be worth zero. It cannot sell for less than zero because that would mean that the option seller would have to pay the option buyer. A buyer would not pay more than zero, because the option will expire an instant later with no value.

At expiration, a put option is worth either zero or the difference between the exercise price and the underlying price, whichever is greater:

$$p_T = \text{Max}(0, X - S_T)$$
$$P_T = \text{Max}(0, X - S_T)$$

(4)

Suppose $S_T < X$, meaning that the put is expiring in-the-money. At the instant of expiration, suppose the put is selling for less than $X - S_T$. Then an investor buys the put for p_T (or P_T) and the underlying for S_T and exercises the put, receiving X. If p_T (or P_T) < $X - S_T$, this transaction will net an immediate risk-free profit. The combined actions of participants doing this will force the put price up to $X - S_T$. It cannot go any higher, because the put buyer will end up an instant later with only $X - S_T$ and would not pay more than this. If $S_T > X$, meaning that the put is expiring out-of the-money, it is worth zero. It cannot be worth less than zero because the option seller would have to pay the option buyer. It cannot be worth more than zero because the buyer would not pay for a position that, an instant later, will be worth nothing.

These important results are summarized along with an example in Exhibit 5. The payoff diagrams for the short positions are also shown and are obtained as the negative of the long positions. For the special case of $S_T = X$, meaning that both call and put are expiring at-the-money, we can effectively treat the option as out-of-the-money because it is worth zero at expiration.

The value $\text{Max}(0, S_T - X)$ for calls or $\text{Max}(0, X - S_T)$ for puts is also called the option's **intrinsic value** or **exercise value**. We shall use the former terminology. Intrinsic value is what the option is worth to exercise it based on current conditions. In this section, we have talked only about the option at expiration. Prior to expiration, an option will normally sell for more than its intrinsic value.[13] The difference between the market price of the option and its intrinsic value is called its **time value** or **speculative value**. We shall use the former terminology. The time value reflects

---

[13] We shall later see an exception to this statement for European puts, but for now take it as the truth.

the potential for the option's intrinsic value at expiration to be greater than its current intrinsic value. At expiration, of course, the time value is zero.

There is no question that everyone agrees on the option's intrinsic value; after all, it is based on the current stock price and exercise price. It is the time value that we have more difficulty estimating. So remembering that Option price = Intrinsic value + Time value, let us move forward and attempt to determine the value of an option today, prior to expiration.

EXHIBIT 5	Option Values at Expiration (Payoffs)		

Option	Value	Example (X = 50)	
		$S_T = 52$	$S_T = 48$
European call	$c_T = \text{Max}(0, S_T - X)$	$c_T = \text{Max}(0, 52 - 50) = 2$	$c_T = \text{Max}(0, 48 - 50) = 0$
American call	$C_T = \text{Max}(0, S_T - X)$	$C_T = \text{Max}(0, 52 - 50) = 2$	$C_T = \text{Max}(0, 48 - 50) = 0$
European put	$p_T = \text{Max}(0, X - S_T)$	$p_T = \text{Max}(0, 50 - 52) = 0$	$p_T = \text{Max}(0, 50 - 48) = 2$
American put	$P_T = \text{Max}(0, X - S_T)$	$P_T = \text{Max}(0, 50 - 52) = 0$	$P_T = \text{Max}(0, 50 - 48) = 2$

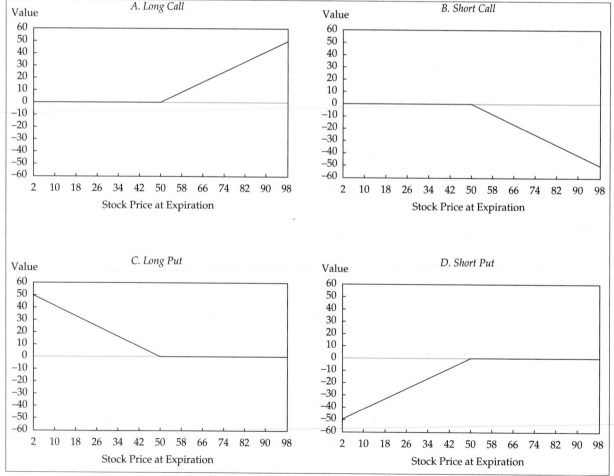

Notes: Results for the European and American calls correspond to Graph A. Results for Graph B are the negative of Graph A. Results for the European and American puts correspond to Graph C, and results for Graph D are the negative of Graph C.

EXAMPLE 1

For Parts A through E, determine the payoffs of calls and puts under the conditions given.

A. The underlying is a stock index and is at 5,601.19 when the options expire. The multiplier is 500. The exercise price is:

   i. 5,500.
   ii. 6,000.

B. The underlying is a bond and is at $1.035 per $1 par when the options expire. The contract is on $100,000 face value of bonds. The exercise price is:

   i. $1.00.
   ii. $1.05.

C. The underlying is a 90-day interest rate and is at 9 percent when the options expire. The notional principal is $50 million. The exercise rate is:

   i. 8 percent.
   ii. 10.5 percent.

D. The underlying is the Swiss franc and is at $0.775 when the options expire. The options are on SF500,000. The exercise price is:

   i. $0.75.
   ii. $0.81.

E. The underlying is a futures contract and is at 110.5 when the options expire. The options are on a futures contract covering $1 million of the underlying. These prices are percentages of par. The exercise price is:

   i. 110.
   ii. 115.

For Parts F and G, determine the payoffs of the strategies indicated and describe the payoff graph.

F. The underlying is a stock priced at $40. A call option with an exercise price of $40 is selling for $7. You buy the stock and sell the call. At expiration, the stock price is:

   i. $52.
   ii. $38.

G. The underlying is a stock priced at $60. A put option with an exercise price of $60 is priced at $5. You buy the stock and buy the put. At expiration, the stock price is:

   i. $68.
   ii. $50.

Solutions:

A. i. Calls: $\text{Max}(0, 5601.19 - 5500) \times 500 = 50,595$
     Puts: $\text{Max}(0, 5500 - 5601.19) \times 500 = 0$
  ii. Calls: $\text{Max}(0, 5601.19 - 6000) \times 500 = 0$
     Puts: $\text{Max}(0, 6000 - 5601.19) \times 500 = 199,405$

B. i. Calls: $\text{Max}(0, 1.035 - 1.00) \times \$100,000 = \$3,500$
     Puts: $\text{Max}(0, 1.00 - 1.035) \times \$100,000 = \$0$

    ii. Calls: $\text{Max}(0, 1.035 - 1.05) \times \$100{,}000 = \$0$
       Puts: $\text{Max}(0, 1.05 - 1.035) \times \$100{,}000 = \$1{,}500$

C. **i.** Calls: $\text{Max}(0, 0.09 - 0.08) \times (90/360) \times \$50{,}000{,}000 = \$125{,}000$
      Puts: $\text{Max}(0, 0.08 - 0.09) \times (90/360) \times \$50{,}000{,}000 = \$0$

   ii. Calls: $\text{Max}(0, 0.09 - 0.105) \times (90/360) \times \$50{,}000{,}000 = \$0$
      Puts: $\text{Max}(0, 0.105 - 0.09) \times (90/360) \times \$50{,}000{,}000 = \$187{,}500$

D. **i.** Calls: $\text{Max}(0, 0.775 - 0.75) \times \text{SF}500{,}000 = \$12{,}500$
      Puts: $\text{Max}(0, 0.75 - 0.775) \times \text{SF}500{,}000 = \$0$

   ii. Calls: $\text{Max}(0, 0.775 - 0.81) \times \text{SF}500{,}000 = \$0$
      Puts: $\text{Max}(0, 0.81 - 0.775) \times \text{SF}500{,}000 = \$17{,}500$

E. **i.** Calls: $\text{Max}(0, 110.5 - 110) \times (1/100) \times \$1{,}000{,}000 = \$5{,}000$
      Puts: $\text{Max}(0, 110 - 110.5) \times (1/100) \times \$1{,}000{,}000 = \$0$

   ii. Calls: $\text{Max}(0, 110.5 - 115) \times (1/100) \times \$1{,}000{,}000 = \$0$
      Puts: $\text{Max}(0, 115 - 110.5) \times (1/100) \times \$1{,}000{,}000 = \$45{,}000$

F. **i.** $52 - \text{Max}(0, 52 - 40) = 40$
   ii. $38 - \text{Max}(0, 38 - 40) = 38$

For any value of the stock price at expiration of 40 or above, the payoff is constant at 40. For stock price values below 40 at expiration, the payoff declines with the stock price. The graph would look similar to the short put in Panel D of Exhibit 5. This strategy is known as a covered call and is discussed in the reading on risk management applications of option strategies.

G. **i.** $68 + \text{Max}(0, 60 - 68) = 68$
   ii. $50 + \text{Max}(0, 60 - 50) = 60$

For any value of the stock price at expiration of 60 or below, the payoff is constant at 60. For stock price values above 60 at expiration, the payoff increases with the stock price at expiration. The graph will look similar to the long call in Panel A of Exhibit 5. This strategy is known as a protective put and is covered later in this reading and in the reading on risk management applications of option strategies.

5.2 Boundary Conditions

We start by examining some simple results that establish minimum and maximum values for options prior to expiration.

5.2.1 Minimum and Maximum Values

The first and perhaps most obvious result is one we have already alluded to: *The minimum value of any option is zero*. We state this formally as

$$c_0 \geq 0, C_0 \geq 0$$
$$p_0 \geq 0, P_0 \geq 0 \qquad (5)$$

No option can sell for less than zero, for in that case the writer would have to pay the buyer.

    Now consider the maximum value of an option. It differs somewhat depending on whether the option is a call or a put and whether it is European or American. *The maximum value of a call is the current value of the underlying:*

$$c_0 \leq S_0, C_0 \leq S_0 \qquad (6)$$

A call is a means of buying the underlying. It would not make sense to pay more for the right to buy the underlying than the value of the underlying itself.

For a put, it makes a difference whether the put is European or American. One way to see the maximum value for puts is to consider the best possible outcome for the put holder. The best outcome is that the underlying goes to a value of zero. Then the put holder could sell a worthless asset for X. For an American put, the holder could sell it immediately and capture a value of X. For a European put, the holder would have to wait until expiration; consequently, we must discount X from the expiration day to the present. Thus, *the maximum value of a European put is the present value of the exercise price. The maximum value of an American put is the exercise price,*

$$p_0 \le X/(1 + r)^T, P_0 \le X \qquad \text{(7)}$$

where r is the risk-free interest rate and T is the time to expiration. These results for the maximums and minimums for calls and puts are summarized in Exhibit 6, which also includes a numerical example.

EXHIBIT 6	Minimum and Maximum Values of Options		
Option	**Minimum Value**	**Maximum Value**	**Example ($S_0 = 52$, $X = 50$, $r = 5\%$, $T = 1/2$ year)**
European call	$c_0 \ge 0$	$c_0 \le S_0$	$0 \le c_0 \le 52$
American call	$C_0 \ge 0$	$C_0 \le S_0$	$0 \le C_0 \le 52$
European put	$p_0 \ge 0$	$p_0 \le X/(1 + r)^T$	$0 \le p_0 \le 48.80$ $[48.80 = 50/(1.05)^{0.5}]$
American put	$P_0 \ge 0$	$P_0 \le X$	$0 \le P_0 \le 50$

5.2.2 Lower Bounds

The results we established in Section 5.2.1 do not put much in the way of restrictions on the option price. They tell us that the price is somewhere between zero and the maximum, which is either the underlying price, the exercise price, or the present value of the exercise price—a fairly wide range of possibilities. Fortunately, we can tighten the range up a little on the low side: We can establish a **lower bound** on the option price.

For American options, which are exercisable immediately, we can state that the lower bound of an American option price is its current intrinsic value:[14]

$$C_0 \ge \text{Max}(0, S_0 - X)$$
$$P_0 \ge \text{Max}(0, X - S_0) \qquad \text{(8)}$$

The reason these results hold today is the same reason we have already shown for why they must hold at expiration. If the option is in-the-money and is selling for less than its intrinsic value, it can be bought and exercised to net an immediate

---

[14] Normally we have italicized sentences containing important results. This one, however, is a little different: We are stating it temporarily. We shall soon show that we can override one of these results with a lower bound that is higher and, therefore, is a better lower bound.

risk-free profit.[15] The collective actions of market participants doing this will force the American option price up to at least the intrinsic value.

Unfortunately, we cannot make such a statement about European options—but we can show that the lower bound is either zero or the current underlying price minus the present value of the exercise price, whichever is greater. They cannot be exercised early; thus, there is no way for market participants to exercise an option selling for too little with respect to its intrinsic value. Fortunately, however, there is a way to establish a lower bound for European options. We can combine options with risk-free bonds and the underlying in such a way that a lower bound for the option price emerges.

First, we need the ability to buy and sell a risk-free bond with a face value equal to the exercise price and current value equal to the present value of the exercise price. This procedure is simple but perhaps not obvious. If the exercise price is X (say, 100), we buy a bond with a face value of X (100) maturing on the option expiration day. The current value of that bond is the present value of X, which is $X/(1 + r)^T$. So we buy the bond today for $X/(1 + r)^T$ and hold it until it matures on the option expiration day, at which time it will pay off X. We assume that we can buy or sell (issue) this type of bond. Note that this transaction involves borrowing or lending an amount of money equal to the present value of the exercise price with repayment of the full exercise price.

Exhibit 7 illustrates the construction of a special combination of instruments. We buy the European call and the risk-free bond and sell short the underlying asset. Recall that short selling involves borrowing the asset and selling it. At expiration, we shall buy back the asset. In order to illustrate the logic behind the lower bound for a European call in the simplest way, we assume that we can sell short without any restrictions.

EXHIBIT 7	A Lower Bound Combination for European Calls		
		Value at Expiration	
Transaction	**Current Value**	$S_T \leq X$	$S_T > X$
Buy call	c_0	0	$S_T - X$
Sell short underlying	$-S_0$	$-S_T$	$-S_T$
Buy bond	$X/(1 + r)^T$	X	X
Total	$c_0 - S_0 + X/(1 + r)^T$	$X - S_T \geq 0$	0

In Exhibit 7 the two right-hand columns contain the value of each instrument when the option expires. The rightmost column is the case of the call expiring in-the-money, in which case it is worth $S_T - X$. In the other column, the out-of-the-money case, the call is worth zero. The underlying is worth $-S_T$ (the negative of its current value) in either case, reflecting the fact that we buy it back

---

[15] Consider, for example, an in-the-money call selling for less than $S_0 - X$. One can buy the call for C_0, exercise it, paying X, and sell the underlying netting a gain of $S_0 - X - C_0$. This value is positive and represents an immediate risk-free gain. If the option is an in-the-money put selling for less than $X - S_0$, one can buy the put for P_0, buy the underlying for S_0, and exercise the put to receive X, thereby netting an immediate risk-free gain of $X - S_0 - P_0$.

to cover the short position. The bond is worth X in both cases. The sum of all the positions is positive when the option expires out-of-the-money and zero when the option expires in-the-money. Therefore, in no case does this combination of instruments have a negative value. That means that we never have to pay out any money at expiration. We are guaranteed at least no loss at expiration and possibly something positive.

If there is a possibility of a positive outcome from the combination and if we know we shall never have to pay anything out from holding a combination of instruments, the cost of that combination must be positive—it must cost us something to enter into the position. We cannot take in money to enter into the position. In that case, we would be receiving money up front and never having to pay anything out. The cost of entering the position is shown in the second column, labeled the "Current Value." Because that value must be positive, we therefore require that $c_0 - S_0 + X/(1 + r)^T \geq 0$. Rearranging this equation, we obtain $c_0 \geq S_0 - X/(1 + r)^T$. Now we have a statement about the minimum value of the option, which can serve as a lower bound. This result is solid, because if the call is selling for less than $S_0 - X/(1 + r)^T$, an investor can buy the call, sell short the underlying, and buy the bond. Doing so would bring in money up front and, as we see in Exhibit 7, an investor would not have to pay out any money at expiration and might even get a little more money. Because other investors would do the same, the call price would be forced up until it is at least $S_0 - X/(1 + r)^T$.

But we can improve on this result. Suppose $S_0 - X/(1 + r)^T$ is negative. Then we are stating that the call price is greater than a negative number. But we already know that the call price cannot be negative. So we can now say that

$$c_0 \geq Max[0, S_0 - X/(1 + r)^T]$$

In other words, *the lower bound on a European call price is either zero or the underlying price minus the present value of the exercise price, whichever is greater.* Notice how this lower bound differs from the minimum value for the American call, $Max(0, S_0 - X)$. For the European call, we must wait to pay the exercise price and obtain the underlying. Therefore, the expression contains the current underlying value—the present value of its future value—as well as the present value of the exercise price. For the American call, we do not have to wait until expiration; therefore, the expression reflects the potential to immediately receive the underlying price minus the exercise price. We shall have more to say, however, about the relationship between these two values.

To illustrate the lower bound, let X = 50, r = 0.05, and T = 0.5. If the current underlying price is 45, then the lower bound for the European call is

$$Max[0, 45 - 50/(1.05)^{0.5}] = Max(0, 45 - 48.80) = Max(0, -3.80) = 0$$

All this calculation tells us is that the call must be worth no less than zero, which we already knew. If the current underlying price is 54, however, the lower bound for the European call is

$$Max(0, 54 - 48.80) = Max(0, 5.20) = 5.20$$

which tells us that the call must be worth no less than 5.20. With European puts, we can also see that the lower bound differs from the lower bound on American puts in this same use of the present value of the exercise price.

Exhibit 8 constructs a similar type of portfolio for European puts. Here, however, we buy the put and the underlying and borrow by issuing the zero-coupon bond. The payoff of each instrument is indicated in the two rightmost columns.

		Value at Expiration	
Transaction	**Current Value**	$S_T < X$	$S_T \geq X$
Buy put	p_0	$X - S_T$	0
Buy underlying	S_0	S_T	S_T
Issue bond	$-X/(1 + r)^T$	$-X$	$-X$
Total	$p_0 + S_0 - X/(1 + r)^T$	0	$S_T - X \geq 0$

EXHIBIT 8   A Lower Bound Combination for European Puts

Note that the total payoff is never less than zero. Consequently, the initial value of the combination must not be less than zero. Therefore, $p_0 + S_0 - X/(1 + r)^T \geq 0$. Isolating the put price gives us $p_0 \geq X/(1 + r)^T - S_0$. But suppose that $X/(1 + r)^T - S_0$ is negative. Then, the put price must be greater than a negative number. We know that the put price must be no less than zero. So we can now formally say that

$$p_0 \geq \text{Max}[0, X/(1 + r)^T - S_0]$$

In other words, *the lower bound of a European put is the greater of either zero or the present value of the exercise price minus the underlying price.* For the American put, recall that the expression was $\text{Max}(0, X - S_0)$. So for the European put, we adjust this value to the present value of the exercise price. The present value of the asset price is already adjusted to S_0.

Using the same example we did for calls, let $X = 50$, $r = 0.05$, and $T = 0.5$. If the current underlying price is 45, then the lower bound for the European put is

$$\text{Max}(0, 50/(1.05)^{0.5} - 45) = \text{Max}(0, 48.80 - 45) = \text{Max}(0, 3.80) = 3.80$$

If the current underlying price is 54, however, the lower bound is

$$\text{Max}(0, 48.80 - 54) = \text{Max}(0, -5.20) = 0$$

At this point let us reconsider what we have found. The lower bound for a European call is $\text{Max}[0, S_0 - X/(1 + r)^T]$. We also observed that an American call must be worth at least $\text{Max}(0, S_0 - X)$. But except at expiration, the European lower bound is greater than the minimum value of the American call.[16] We could not, however, expect an American call to be worth less than a European call. Thus the lower bound of the European call holds for American calls as well. Hence, we can conclude that

$$c_0 \geq \text{Max}[0, S_0 - X/(1 + r)^T]$$
$$C_0 \geq \text{Max}[0, S_0 - X/(1 + r)^T]$$

(9)

For European puts, the lower bound is $\text{Max}[0, X/(1 + r)^T - S_0]$. For American puts, the minimum price is $\text{Max}(0, X - S_0)$. The European lower bound is lower than the minimum price of the American put, so the American put lower bound is not changed to the European lower bound, the way we did for calls. Hence,

---

[16] We discuss this point more formally and in the context of whether it is ever worthwhile to exercise an American call early in Section 5.6.

$$p_0 \geq \text{Max}[0, X/(1 + r)^T - S_0]$$
$$P_0 \geq \text{Max}(0, X - S_0)$$

(10)

These results tell us the lowest possible price for European and American options.

Recall that we previously referred to an option price as having an intrinsic value and a time value. For American options, the intrinsic value is the value if exercised, $\text{Max}(0, S_0 - X)$ for calls and $\text{Max}(0, X - S_0)$ for puts. The remainder of the option price is the time value. For European options, the notion of a time value is somewhat murky, because it first requires recognition of an intrinsic value. Because a European option cannot be exercised until expiration, in a sense, all of the value of a European option is time value. The notion of an intrinsic value and its complement, a time value, is therefore inappropriate for European options, though the concepts are commonly applied to European options. Fortunately, understanding European options does not require that we separate intrinsic value from time value. We shall include them together as they make up the option price.

EXAMPLE 2

Consider call and put options expiring in 42 days, in which the underlying is at 72 and the risk-free rate is 4.5 percent. The underlying makes no cash payments during the life of the options.

A. Find the lower bounds for European calls and puts with exercise prices of 70 and 75.

B. Find the lower bounds for American calls and puts with exercise prices of 70 and 75.

Solutions:

A. 70 call: $\text{Max}[0, 72 - 70/(1.045)^{0.1151}] = \text{Max}(0, 2.35) = 2.35$
75 call: $\text{Max}[0, 72 - 75/(1.045)^{0.1151}] = \text{Max}(0, -2.62) = 0$
70 put: $\text{Max}[0, 70/(1.045)^{0.1151} - 72] = \text{Max}(0, -2.35) = 0$
75 put: $\text{Max}[0, 75/(1.045)^{0.1151} - 72] = \text{Max}(0, 2.62) = 2.62$

B. 70 call: $\text{Max}[0, 72 - 70/(1.045)^{0.1151}] = \text{Max}(0, 2.35) = 2.35$
75 call: $\text{Max}[0, 72 - 75/(1.045)^{0.1151}] = \text{Max}(0, -2.62) = 0$
70 put: $\text{Max}(0, 70 - 72) = 0$
75 put: $\text{Max}(0, 75 - 72) = 3$

5.3 The Effect of a Difference in Exercise Price

Now consider two options on the same underlying with the same expiration day but different exercise prices. Generally, the higher the exercise price, the lower the value of a call and the higher the price of a put. To see this, let the two exercise prices be X_1 and X_2, with X_1 being the smaller. Let $c_0(X_1)$ be the price of a European call with exercise price X_1 and $c_0(X_2)$ be the price of a European call with exercise price X_2. We refer to these as the X_1 call and the X_2 call. In Exhibit 9, we construct a combination in which we buy the X_1 call and sell the X_2 call.

EXHIBIT 9	Portfolio Combination for European Calls Illustrating the Effect of Differences in Exercise Prices

Transaction	Current Value	Value at Expiration $S_T \leq X_1$	$X_1 < S_T < X_2$	$S_T \geq X_2$
Buy call $(X = X_1)$	$c_0(X_1)$	0	$S_T - X_1$	$S_T - X_1$
Sell call $(X = X_2)$	$-c_0(X_2)$	0	0	$-(S_T - X_2)$
Total	$c_0(X_1) - c_0(X_2)$	0	$S_T - X_1 > 0$	$X_2 - X_1 > 0$

Note first that the three outcomes are all non-negative. This fact establishes that the current value of the combination, $c_0(X_1) - c_0(X_2)$ has to be non-negative. We have to pay out at least as much for the X_1 call as we take in for the X_2 call; otherwise, we would get money up front, have the possibility of a positive value at expiration, and never have to pay any money out. Thus, because $c_0(X_1) - c_0(X_2) \geq 0$, we restate this result as

$$c_0(X_1) \geq c_0(X_2)$$

This expression is equivalent to the statement that *a call option with a higher exercise price cannot have a higher value than one with a lower exercise price.* The option with the higher exercise price has a higher hurdle to get over; therefore, the buyer is not willing to pay as much for it. Even though we demonstrated this result with European calls, it is also true for American calls. Thus,[17]

$$C_0(X_1) \geq C_0(X_2)$$

In Exhibit 10 we construct a similar portfolio for puts, except that we buy the X_2 put (the one with the higher exercise price) and sell the X_1 put (the one with the lower exercise price).

EXHIBIT 10	Portfolio Combination for European Puts Illustrating the Effect of Differences in Exercise Prices

Transaction	Current Value	Value at Expiration $S_T \leq X_1$	$X_1 < S_T < X_2$	$S_T \geq X_2$
Buy put $(X = X_2)$	$p_0(X_2)$	$X_2 - S_T$	$X_2 - S_T$	0
Sell put $(X = X_1)$	$-p_0(X_1)$	$-(X_1 - S_T)$	0	0
Total	$p_0(X_2) - p_0(X_1)$	$X_2 - X_1 > 0$	$X_2 - S_T > 0$	0

---

[17] It is possible to use the results from this table to establish a limit on the difference between the prices of these two options, but we shall not do so here.

Observe that the value of this combination is never negative at expiration; therefore, it must be non-negative today. Hence, $p_0(X_2) - p_0(X_1) \geq 0$. We restate this result as

$$p_0(X_2) \geq p_0(X_1)$$

Thus, *the value of a European put with a higher exercise price must be at least as great as the value of a European put with a lower exercise price.* These results also hold for American puts. Therefore,

$$P_0(X_2) \geq P_0(X_1)$$

Even though it is technically possible for calls and puts with different exercise prices to have the same price, *generally we can say that the higher the exercise price, the lower the price of a call and the higher the price of a put.* For example, refer back to Exhibit 1 and observe how the most expensive calls and least expensive puts have the lower exercise prices.

5.4 The Effect of a Difference in Time to Expiration

Option prices are also affected by the time to expiration of the option. Intuitively, one might expect that the longer the time to expiration, the more valuable the option. A longer-term option has more time for the underlying to make a favorable move. In addition, if the option is in-the-money by the end of a given period of time, it has a better chance of moving even further in-the-money over a longer period of time. If the additional time gives it a better chance of moving out-of-the-money or further out-of-the-money, the limitation of losses to the amount of the option premium means that the disadvantage of the longer time is no greater. In most cases, a longer time to expiration is beneficial for an option. We will see that longer-term American and European calls and longer-term American puts are worth no less than their shorter-term counterparts.

First let us consider each of the four types of options: European calls, American calls, European puts, and American puts. We shall introduce options otherwise identical except that one has a longer time to expiration than the other. The one expiring earlier has an expiration of T_1 and the one expiring later has an expiration of T_2. The prices of the options are $c_0(T_1)$ and $c_0(T_2)$ for the European calls, $C_0(T_1)$ and $C_0(T_2)$ for the American calls, $p_0(T_1)$ and $p_0(T_2)$ for the European puts, and $P_0(T_1)$ and $P_0(T_2)$ for the American puts.

When the shorter-term call expires, the European call is worth $\text{Max}(0, S_{T_1} - X)$, but we have already shown that the longer-term European call is worth *at least* $\text{Max}(0, S_{T_1} - X/(1 + r)^{(T_2 - T_1)})$, which is at least as great as this amount.[18] Thus, the longer-term European call is worth at least the value of the shorter-term European call. These results are not altered if the call is American. When the shorter-term American call expires, it is worth $\text{Max}(0, S_{T_1} - X)$. The longer-term American call must be worth at least the value of the European call, so it is worth *at least* $\text{Max}[0, S - X/(1 + r)^{T_2 - T_1}]$. Thus, the longer-term call, European or American, is worth no less than the shorter-term call when the shorter-term call expires. Because this statement is always true, the longer-term call, European or American, is worth no less than the shorter-term call at any time prior to expiration. Thus,

$$c_0(T_2) \geq c_0(T_1)$$
$$C_0(T_2) \geq C_0(T_1)$$

(11)

---

[18] Technically, we showed this calculation using a time to expiration of T, but here the time to expiration is $T_2 - T_1$.

Notice that these statements do not mean that the longer-term call is always worth more; it means that the longer-term call can be worth no less. With the exception of the rare case in which both calls are so far out-of-the-money or in-the-money that the additional time is of no value, the longer-term call will be worth more.

For European puts, we have a slight problem. For calls, the longer term gives additional time for a favorable move in the underlying to occur. For puts, this is also true, but there is one disadvantage to waiting the additional time. When a put is exercised, the holder receives money. The lost interest on the money is a disadvantage of the additional time. For calls, there is no lost interest. In fact, a call holder earns additional interest on the money by paying out the exercise price later. Therefore, it is not always true that additional time is beneficial to the holder of a European put. It is true, however, that the additional time is beneficial to the holder of an American put. An American put can always be exercised; there is no penalty for waiting. Thus, we have

$$p_0(T_2) \text{ can be either greater or less than } p_0(T_1)$$
$$P_0(T_2) \geq P_0(T_1)$$

(12)

So for European puts, either the longer-term or the shorter-term option can be worth more. The longer-term European put will tend to be worth more when volatility is greater and interest rates are lower.

Referring back to Exhibit 1, observe that the longer-term put and call options are more expensive than the shorter-term ones. As noted, we might observe an exception to this rule for European puts, but these are all American options.

5.5 Put–Call Parity

So far we have been working with puts and calls separately. To see how their prices must be consistent with each other and to explore common option strategies, let us combine puts and calls with each other or with a risk-free bond. We shall put together some combinations that produce equivalent results.

5.5.1 Fiduciary Calls and Protective Puts

First we consider an option strategy referred to as a **fiduciary call**. It consists of a European call and a risk-free bond, just like the ones we have been using, that matures on the option expiration day and has a face value equal to the exercise price of the call. The upper part of the table in Exhibit 11 shows the payoffs at expiration of the fiduciary call. We see that if the price of the underlying is below X at expiration, the call expires worthless and the bond is worth X. If the price of the underlying is above X at expiration, the call expires and is worth S_T (the underlying price) $- X$. So at expiration, the fiduciary call will end up worth X or S_T, whichever is greater.

EXHIBIT 11	Portfolio Combinations for Equivalent Packages of Puts and Calls		
		Value at Expiration	
Transaction	Current Value	$S_T \leq X$	$S_T > X$
Fiduciary Call			
Buy call	c_0	0	$S_T - X$

(Exhibit continued on next page ...)

EXHIBIT 11   (continued)

Transaction	Current Value	Value at Expiration $S_T \leq X$	$S_T > X$
Buy bond	$X/(1 + r)^T$	X	X
Total	$c_0 + X/(1 + r)^T$	X	S_T
Protective Put			
Buy put	p_0	$X - S_T$	0
Buy underlying asset	S_0	S_T	S_T
Total	$p_0 + S_0$	X	S_T

Value of Fiduciary Call and
Protective Put at Expiration

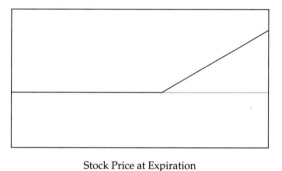

Stock Price at Expiration

This type of combination is called a fiduciary call because it allows protection against downside losses and is thus faithful to the notion of preserving capital.

Now we construct a strategy known as a **protective put**, which consists of a European put and the underlying asset. If the price of the underlying is below X at expiration, the put expires and is worth $X - S_T$ and the underlying is worth S_T. If the price of the underlying is above X at expiration, the put expires with no value and the underlying is worth S_T. So at expiration, the protective put is worth X or S_T, whichever is greater. The lower part of the table in Exhibit 11 shows the payoffs at expiration of the protective put.

Thus, the fiduciary call and protective put end up with the same value. They are, therefore, identical combinations. To avoid arbitrage, their values today must be the same. The value of the fiduciary call is the cost of the call, c_0, and the cost of the bond, $X/(1 + r)^T$. The value of the protective put is the cost of the put, p_0, and the cost of the underlying, S_0. Thus,

$$c_0 + X/(1 + r)^T = p_0 + S_0 \qquad (13)$$

This equation is called **put–call parity** and is one of the most important results in options. It does not say that puts and calls are equivalent, but it does show an equivalence (parity) of a call/bond portfolio and a put/underlying portfolio.

Put–call parity can be written in a number of other ways. By rearranging the four terms to isolate one term, we can obtain some interesting and important results. For example,

$$c_0 = p_0 + S_0 - X/(1 + r)^T$$

means that a call is equivalent to a long position in the put, a long position in the asset, and a short position in the risk-free bond. The short bond position simply means to borrow by issuing the bond, rather than lend by buying the bond as we did in the fiduciary call portfolio. We can tell from the sign whether we should go long or short. Positive signs mean to go long; negative signs mean to go short.

5.5.2 Synthetics

Because the right-hand side of the above equation is equivalent to a call, we often refer to it as a **synthetic call**. To see that the synthetic call is equivalent to the actual call, look at Exhibit 12:

		Value at Expiration	
Transaction	Current Value	$S_T \leq X$	$S_T > X$
Call			
Buy call	c_0	0	$S_T - X$
Synthetic Call			
Buy put	p_0	$X - S_T$	0
Buy underlying asset	S_0	S_T	S_T
Issue bond	$-X/(1 + r)^T$	$-X$	$-X$
Total	$p_0 + S_0 - X/(1 + r)^T$	0	$S_T - X$

EXHIBIT 12   Call and Synthetic Call

The call produces the value of the underlying minus the exercise price or zero, whichever is greater. The synthetic call does the same thing, but in a different way. When the call expires in-the-money, the synthetic call produces the underlying value minus the payoff on the bond, which is X. When the call expires out-of-the-money, the put covers the loss on the underlying and the exercise price on the put matches the amount of money needed to pay off the bond.

Similarly, we can isolate the put as follows:

$$p_0 = c_0 - S_0 + X/(1 + r)^T$$

which says that a put is equivalent to a long call, a short position in the underlying, and a long position in the bond. Because the left-hand side is a put, it follows that the right-hand side is a **synthetic put**. The equivalence of the put and synthetic put is shown in Exhibit 13.

As you can well imagine, there are numerous other combinations that can be constructed. Exhibit 14 shows a number of the more important combinations. There are two primary reasons that it is important to understand synthetic positions in option pricing. Synthetic positions enable us to price options, because they produce the same results as options and have known prices. Synthetic positions also tell how to exploit mispricing of options relative to their underlying assets. Note that we

EXHIBIT 13	Put and Synthetic Put

| | | Value at Expiration | |
Transaction	**Current Value**	$S_T \leq X$	$S_T > X$
Put			
Buy put	p_0	$X - S_T$	0
Synthetic Put			
Buy call	c_0	0	$S_T - X$
Short underlying asset	$-S_0$	$-S_T$	$-S_T$
Buy bond	$X/(1 + r)^T$	X	X
Total	$c_0 - S_0 + X/(1 + r)^T$	$X - S_T$	0

EXHIBIT 14	Alternative Equivalent Combinations of Calls, Puts, the Underlying, and Risk-Free Bonds

Strategy	Consisting of	Worth	Equates to	Strategy	Consisting of	Worth
Fiduciary call	Long call + Long bond	$c_0 + X/(1 + r)^T$	=	Protective put	Long put + Long underlying	$p_0 + S_0$
Long call	Long call	c_0	=	Synthetic call	Long put + Long underlying + Short bond	$p_0 + S_0 - X/(1 + r)^T$
Long put	Long put	p_0	=	Synthetic put	Long call + Short underlying + Long bond	$c_0 - S_0 + X/(1 + r)^T$
Long underlying	Long underlying	S_0	=	Synthetic underlying	Long call + Long bond + Short put	$c_0 + X/(1 + r)^T - p_0$
Long bond	Long bond	$X/(1 + r)^T$	=	Synthetic bond	Long put + Long underlying + Short call	$p_0 + S_0 - c_0$

cannot only synthesize a call or a put, but we can also synthesize the underlying or the bond. As complex as it might seem to do this, it is really quite easy. First, we learn that *a fiduciary call is a call plus a risk-free bond maturing on the option expiration day with a face value equal to the exercise price of the option.* Then we learn that *a protective put is the underlying plus a put.* Then we learn the basic put–call parity equation: *A fiduciary call is equivalent to a protective put:*

$$c_0 + X/(1 + r)^T = p_0 + S_0$$

Learn the put–call parity equation this way, because it is the easiest form to remember and has no minus signs.

Next, we decide which instrument we want to synthesize. We use simple algebra to isolate that instrument, with a plus sign, on one side of the equation, moving all other instruments to the other side. We then see what instruments are on the other side, taking plus signs as long positions and minus signs as short positions. Finally, to check our results, we should construct a table like Exhibits 11 or 12, with the expiration payoffs of the instrument we wish to synthesize compared with the expiration payoffs of the equivalent combination of instruments. We then check to determine that the expiration payoffs are the same.

5.5.3 An Arbitrage Opportunity

In this section we examine the arbitrage strategies that will push prices to put–call parity. Suppose that in the market, prices do not conform to put–call parity. This is a situation in which price does not equal value. Recalling our basic equation, $c_0 + X/(1 + r)^T = p_0 + S_0$, we should insert values into the equation and see if the equality holds. If it does not, then obviously one side is greater than the other. We can view one side as overpriced and the other as underpriced, which suggests an arbitrage opportunity. To exploit this mispricing, we buy the underpriced combination and sell the overpriced combination.

Consider the following example involving call options with an exercise price of $100 expiring in half a year (T = 0.5). The risk-free rate is 10 percent. The call is priced at $7.50, and the put is priced at $4.25. The underlying price is $99.

The left-hand side of the basic put–call parity equation is $c_0 + X/(1 + r)^T = 7.50 + 100/(1.10)^{0.5} = 7.50 + 95.35 = 102.85$. The right-hand side is $p_0 + S_0 = 4.25 + 99 = 103.25$. So the right-hand side is greater than the left-hand side. This means that the protective put is overpriced. Equivalently, we could view this as the fiduciary call being underpriced. Either way will lead us to the correct strategy to exploit the mispricing.

We sell the overpriced combination, the protective put. This means that we sell the put and sell short the underlying. Doing so will generate a cash inflow of $103.25. We buy the fiduciary call, paying out $102.85. This series of transactions nets a cash inflow of $103.25 − $102.85 = $0.40. Now, let us see what happens at expiration.

> *The options expire with the underlying above 100:*
>   The bond matures, paying $100.
>   Use the $100 to exercise the call, receiving the underlying.
>   Deliver the underlying to cover the short sale.
>   The put expires with no value.
>   Net effect: No money in or out.
> *The options expire with the underlying below 100:*
>   The bond matures, paying $100.
>   The put expires in-the-money; use the $100 to buy the underlying.
>   Use the underlying to cover the short sale.
>   The call expires with no value.
>   Net effect: No money in or out.

So we receive $0.40 up front and do not have to pay anything out. The position is perfectly hedged and represents an arbitrage profit. The combined effects of other investors performing this transaction will result in the value of the protective put going down and/or the value of the covered call going up until the two strategies are equivalent in value. Of course, it is possible that transaction costs might consume any profit, so small discrepancies will not be exploited.

It is important to note that regardless of which put–call parity equation we use, we will arrive at the same strategy. For example, in the above problem, the synthetic put (a long call, a short position in the underlying, and a long bond) is worth $7.50 − $99 + $95.35 = $3.85. The actual put is worth $4.25. Thus, we would conclude that we should sell the actual put and buy the synthetic put. To buy the synthetic put, we would buy the call, short the underlying, and buy the bond—precisely the strategy we used to exploit this price discrepancy.

In all of these examples based on put–call parity, we used only European options. Put–call parity using American options is considerably more complicated. The resulting parity equation is a complex combination of inequalities. Thus, we cannot say that a given combination exactly equals another; we can say only that one combination is more valuable than another. Exploitation of any such mispricing is somewhat more complicated, and we shall not explore it here.

EXAMPLE 3

European put and call options with an exercise price of 45 expire in 115 days. The underlying is priced at 48 and makes no cash payments during the life of the options. The risk-free rate is 4.5 percent. The put is selling for 3.75, and the call is selling for 8.00.

A. Identify the mispricing by comparing the price of the actual call with the price of the synthetic call.

B. Based on your answer in Part A, demonstrate how an arbitrage transaction is executed.

Solution to A: Using put–call parity, the following formula applies:

$$c_0 = p_0 + S_0 - X/(1 + r)^T$$

The time to expiration is $T = 115/365 = 0.3151$. Substituting values into the right-hand side:

$$c_0 = 3.75 + 48 - 45/(1.045)^{0.3151} = 7.37$$

Hence, the synthetic call is worth 7.37, but the actual call is selling for 8.00 and is, therefore, overpriced.

Solution to B: Sell the call for 8.00 and buy the synthetic call for 7.37. To buy the synthetic call, buy the put for 3.75, buy the underlying for 48.00, and issue a zero-coupon bond paying 45.00 at expiration. The bond will bring in $45.00/(1.045)^{0.3151} = 44.38$ today. This transaction will bring in 8.00 − 7.37 = 0.63.

At expiration, the following payoffs will occur:

	$S_T < 45$	$S_T \geq 45$
Short call	0	$-(S_T - 45)$
Long put	$45 - S_T$	0
Underlying	S_T	S_T
Bond	−45	−45
Total	0	0

Thus there will be no cash in or out at expiration. The transaction will net a risk-free gain of 8.00 − 7.37 = 0.63 up front.

5.6 American Options, Lower Bounds, and Early Exercise

As we have noted, American options can be exercised early and in this section we specify cases in which early exercise can have value. Because early exercise is never mandatory, the right to exercise early may be worth something but could never hurt the option holder. Consequently, the prices of American options must be no less than the prices of European options:

$$C_0 \geq c_0$$
$$P_0 \geq p_0$$

(14)

Recall that we already used this result in establishing the minimum price from the lower bounds and intrinsic value results in Section 5.2.2. Now, however, our concern is understanding the conditions under which early exercise of an American option might occur.

Suppose today, time 0, we are considering exercising early an in-the-money American call. If we exercise, we pay X and receive an asset worth S_0. But we already determined that a European call is worth at least $S_0 - X/(1 + r)^T$—that is, the underlying price minus the present value of the exercise price, which is more than $S_0 - X$. Because we just argued that the American call must be worth no less than the European call, it therefore must also be worth at least $S_0 - X/(1 + r)^T$. This means that the value we could obtain by selling it to someone else is more than the value we could obtain by exercising it. Thus, there is no reason to exercise the call early.

Some people fail to see the logic behind not exercising early. Exercising a call early simply gives the money to the call writer and throws away the right to decide at expiration if you want the underlying. It is like renewing a magazine subscription before the current subscription expires. Not only do you lose the interest on the money, you also lose the right to decide later if you want to renew. Without offering an early exercise incentive, the American call would have a price equal to the European call price. Thus, we must look at another case to see the value of the early exercise option.

If the underlying makes a cash payment, there may be reason to exercise early. If the underlying is a stock and pays a dividend, there may be sufficient reason to exercise just before the stock goes ex-dividend. By exercising, the option holder throws away the time value but captures the dividend. We shall skip the technical details of how this decision is made and conclude by stating that

▶ *When the underlying makes no cash payments, $C_0 = c_0$.*

▶ *When the underlying makes cash payments during the life of the option, early exercise can be worthwhile and C_0 can thus be higher than c_0.*

We emphasize the word *can*. It is possible that the dividend is not high enough to justify early exercise.

For puts, there is nearly always a possibility of early exercise. Consider the most obvious case, an investor holding an American put on a bankrupt company. The stock is worth zero. It cannot go any lower. Thus, the put holder would exercise immediately. As long as there is a possibility of bankruptcy, the American put will be worth more than the European put. But in fact, bankruptcy is not required for early exercise. The stock price must be very low, although we cannot say exactly how low without resorting to an analysis using option pricing models. Suffice it to say that *the American put is nearly always worth more than the European put: $P_0 > p_0$.*

5.7 The Effect of Cash Flows on the Underlying Asset

Both the lower bounds on puts and calls and the put–call parity relationship must be modified to account for cash flows on the underlying asset. In the readings on forward markets and contracts and on futures markets and contracts, we discussed situations in which the underlying has cash flows. Stocks pay dividends, bonds pay interest, foreign currencies pay interest, and commodities have carrying costs. As we have done in the previous readings, we shall assume that these cash flows are either known or can be expressed as a percentage of the asset price. Moreover, as we did previously, we can remove the present value of those cash flows from the price of the underlying and use this adjusted underlying price in the results we have obtained above.

We can specify these cash flows in the form of the accumulated value at T of all cash flows incurred on the underlying over the life of the derivative contract. When the underlying is a stock, we specify these cash flows more precisely in the form of dividends, using the notation $FV(D,0,T)$ as the future value, or alternatively $PV(D,0,T)$ as the present value, of these dividends. When the underlying is a bond, we use the notation $FV(CI,0,T)$ or $PV(CI,0,T)$, where CI stands for "coupon interest." When the cash flows can be specified in terms of a yield or rate, we use the notation δ where $S_0/(1 + \delta)^T$ is the underlying price reduced by the present value of the cash flows. Using continuous compounding, the rate can be specified as δ^c so that $S_0 e^{-\delta^c T}$ is the underlying price reduced by the present value of the dividends. For our purposes in this reading on options, let us just write this specification as $PV(CF,0,T)$, which represents the present value of the cash flows on the underlying over the life of the options. Therefore, we can restate the lower bounds for European options as

$$c_0 \geq Max\{0,[S_0 - PV(CF,0,T)] - X/(1 + r)^T\}$$
$$p_0 \geq Max\{0,X/(1 + r)^T - [S_0 - PV(CF,0,T)]\}$$

and put–call parity as

$$c_0 + X/(1 + r)^T = p_0 + [S_0 - PV(CF,0,T)]$$

which reflects the fact that, as we said, we simply reduce the underlying price by the present value of its cash flows over the life of the option.

5.8 The Effect of Interest Rates and Volatility

It is important to know that interest rates and volatility exert an influence on option prices. *When interest rates are higher, call option prices are higher and put option prices are lower.* This effect is not obvious and strains the intuition somewhat. When investors buy call options instead of the underlying, they are effectively buying an indirect leveraged position in the underlying. When interest rates are higher, buying the call instead of a direct leveraged position in the underlying is more attractive. Moreover, by using call options, investors save more money by not paying for the underlying until a later date. For put options, however, higher interest rates are disadvantageous. When interest rates are higher, investors lose more interest while waiting to sell the underlying when using puts. Thus, the opportunity cost of waiting is higher when interest rates are higher. Although these points may not seem completely clear, fortunately they are not critical. Except when the underlying is a bond or interest rate, interest rates do not have a very strong effect on option prices.

Volatility, however, has an extremely strong effect on option prices. *Higher volatility increases call and put option prices because it increases possible upside values and increases possible downside values of the underlying.* The upside effect helps calls and does not hurt puts. The downside effect does not hurt calls and helps puts. The reason calls are not hurt on the downside and puts are not hurt on the upside is that when options are out-of-the-money, it does not matter if they end up more out-of-the-money. But when options are in-the-money, it does matter if they end up more in-the-money.

Volatility is a critical variable in pricing options. It is the only variable that affects option prices that is not directly observable either in the option contract or in the market. It must be estimated.

5.9 Option Price Sensitivities

Option price sensitivity measures have Greek names:

▶ *Delta* is the sensitivity of the option price to a change in the price of the underlying.

▶ *Gamma* is a measure of how well the delta sensitivity measure will approximate the option price's response to a change in the price of the underlying.

▶ *Rho* is the sensitivity of the option price to the risk-free rate.

▶ *Theta* is the rate at which the time value decays as the option approaches expiration.

▶ *Vega* is the sensitivity of the option price to volatility.

SUMMARY

▶ Options are rights to buy or sell an underlying at a fixed price, the exercise price, for a period of time. The right to buy is a call; the right to sell is a put. Options have a definite expiration date. Using the option to buy or sell is the action of exercising it. The buyer or holder of an option pays a price to the seller or writer for the right to buy (a call) or sell (a put) the underlying instrument. The writer of an option has the corresponding potential obligation to sell or buy the underlying.

▶ European options can be exercised only at expiration; American options can be exercised at any time prior to expiration. Moneyness refers to the characteristic that an option has positive intrinsic value. The payoff is the value of the option at expiration. An option's intrinsic value is the value that can be captured if the option is exercised. Time value is the component of an option's price that reflects the uncertainty of what will happen in the future to the price of the underlying.

▶ Options can be traded as standardized instruments on an options exchange, where they are protected from default on the part of the writer, or as customized instruments on the over-the-counter market, where they are subject to the possibility of the writer defaulting. Because the buyer pays a price at the start and does not have to do anything else, the buyer cannot default.

▶ The underlying instruments for options are individual stocks, stock indices, bonds, interest rates, currencies, futures, commodities, and even such random factors as the weather. In addition, a class of options called real options is associated with the flexibility in capital investment projects.

▶ Like FRAs, which are forward contracts in which the underlying is an interest rate, interest rate options are options in which the underlying is an interest rate. However, FRAs are commitments to make one interest payment and receive another, whereas interest rate options are rights to make one interest payment and receive another.

▶ Option payoffs, which are the values of options when they expire, are determined by the greater of zero or the difference between underlying price and exercise price, if a call, or the greater of zero or the difference between exercise price and underlying price, if a put. For interest rate options, the exercise price is a specified rate and the underlying price is a variable interest rate.

▶ Interest rate options exist in the form of caps, which are call options on interest rates, and floors, which are put options on interest rates. Caps consist of a series of call options, called caplets, on an underlying rate, with each option expiring at a different time. Floors consist of a series of put options, called floorlets, on an underlying rate, with each option expiring at a different time.

▶ The minimum value of European and American calls and puts is zero. The maximum value of European and American calls is the underlying price. The maximum value of a European put is the present value of the exercise price. The maximum value of an American put is the exercise price.

▶ The lower bound of a European call is established by constructing a portfolio consisting of a long call and risk-free bond and a short position in the underlying asset. This combination produces a non-negative value at expiration, so its current value must be non-negative. For this situation to occur, the call price has to be worth at least the underlying price minus the present value of the exercise price. The lower bound of a European put is established by constructing a portfolio consisting of a long put, a long position in the underlying, and the issuance of a zero-coupon bond. This combination produces a non-negative value at expiration so its current value must be non-negative. For this to occur, the put price has to be at least as much as the present value of the exercise price minus the underlying price. For both calls and puts, if this lower bound is negative, we invoke the rule that an option price can be no lower than zero.

▶ The lowest price of a European call is referred to as the lower bound. The lowest price of an American call is also the lower bound of a European call. The lowest price of a European put is also referred to as the lower bound. The lowest price of an American put, however, is its intrinsic value.

▶ Buying a call with a given exercise price and selling an otherwise identical call with a higher exercise price creates a combination that always pays off with a non-negative value. Therefore, its current value must be non-negative. For this to occur, the call with the lower exercise price must be worth at least as much as the other call. A similar argument holds for puts, except that one would buy the put with the higher exercise price. This line of reasoning shows that the put with the higher exercise price must be worth at least as much as the one with the lower exercise price.

▶ A longer-term European or American call must be worth at least as much as a corresponding shorter-term European or American call. A longer-term American put must be worth at least as much as a shorter-term American put. A longer-term European put, however, can be worth more or less than a shorter-term European put.

▶ A fiduciary call, consisting of a European call and a zero-coupon bond, produces the same payoff as a protective put, consisting of the underlying and a European put. Therefore, their current values must be the same. For this equivalence to occur, the call price plus bond price must equal the underlying price plus put price. This relationship is called put–call parity and can be used to identify combinations of instruments that synthesize another instrument by rearranging the equation to isolate the instrument you are trying to create. Long positions are indicated by positive signs, and short positions are indicated by negative signs. One can create a synthetic call, a synthetic put, a synthetic underlying, and a synthetic bond, as well as synthetic short positions in these instruments for the purpose of exploiting mispricing in these instruments.

▶ Put–call parity violations exist when one side of the equation does not equal the other. An arbitrageur buys the lower-priced side and sells the higher-priced side, thereby earning the difference in price, and the positions offset at expiration. The combined actions of many arbitrageurs performing this set of transactions would increase the demand and price for the underpriced instruments and decrease the demand and price for the overpriced instruments, until the put–call parity relationship is upheld.

▶ American option prices must always be no less than those of otherwise equivalent European options. American call options, however, are never exercised early unless there is a cash flow on the underlying, so they can sell for the same as their European counterparts in the absence of such a cash flow. American put options nearly always have a possibility of early exercise, so they ordinarily sell for more than their European counterparts.

▶ Cash flows on the underlying affect an option's boundary conditions and put–call parity by lowering the underlying price by the present value of the cash flows over the life of the option.

▶ A higher interest rate increases a call option's price and decreases a put option's price.

APPENDIX 70A

Cumulative Probabilities for a Standard Normal Distribution
$P(X \leq x) = N(x)$ for $x \geq 0$ or $1 - N(-x)$ for $x < 0$

x	0	0.01	0.02	0.03	0.04	0.05	0.06	0.07	0.08	0.09
0.00	0.5000	0.5040	0.5080	0.5120	0.5160	0.5199	0.5239	0.5279	0.5319	0.5359
0.10	0.5398	0.5438	0.5478	0.5517	0.5557	0.5596	0.5636	0.5675	0.5714	0.5753
0.20	0.5793	0.5832	0.5871	0.5910	0.5948	0.5987	0.6026	0.6064	0.6103	0.6141
0.30	0.6179	0.6217	0.6255	0.6293	0.6331	0.6368	0.6406	0.6443	0.6480	0.6517
0.40	0.6554	0.6591	0.6628	0.6664	0.6700	0.6736	0.6772	0.6808	0.6844	0.6879
0.50	0.6915	0.6950	0.6985	0.7019	0.7054	0.7088	0.7123	0.7157	0.7190	0.7224
0.60	0.7257	0.7291	0.7324	0.7357	0.7389	0.7422	0.7454	0.7486	0.7517	0.7549
0.70	0.7580	0.7611	0.7642	0.7673	0.7704	0.7734	0.7764	0.7794	0.7823	0.7852
0.80	0.7881	0.7910	0.7939	0.7967	0.7995	0.8023	0.8051	0.8078	0.8106	0.8133
0.90	0.8159	0.8186	0.8212	0.8238	0.8264	0.8289	0.8315	0.8340	0.8365	0.8389
1.00	0.8413	0.8438	0.8461	0.8485	0.8508	0.8531	0.8554	0.8577	0.8599	0.8621
1.10	0.8643	0.8665	0.8686	0.8708	0.8729	0.8749	0.8770	0.8790	0.8810	0.8830
1.20	0.8849	0.8869	0.8888	0.8907	0.8925	0.8944	0.8962	0.8980	0.8997	0.9015
1.30	0.9032	0.9049	0.9066	0.9082	0.9099	0.9115	0.9131	0.9147	0.9162	0.9177
1.40	0.9192	0.9207	0.9222	0.9236	0.9251	0.9265	0.9279	0.9292	0.9306	0.9319
1.50	0.9332	0.9345	0.9357	0.9370	0.9382	0.9394	0.9406	0.9418	0.9429	0.9441
1.60	0.9452	0.9463	0.9474	0.9484	0.9495	0.9505	0.9515	0.9525	0.9535	0.9545
1.70	0.9554	0.9564	0.9573	0.9582	0.9591	0.9599	0.9608	0.9616	0.9625	0.9633
1.80	0.9641	0.9649	0.9656	0.9664	0.9671	0.9678	0.9686	0.9693	0.9699	0.9706
1.90	0.9713	0.9719	0.9726	0.9732	0.9738	0.9744	0.9750	0.9756	0.9761	0.9767
2.00	0.9772	0.9778	0.9783	0.9788	0.9793	0.9798	0.9803	0.9808	0.9812	0.9817
2.10	0.9821	0.9826	0.9830	0.9834	0.9838	0.9842	0.9846	0.9850	0.9854	0.9857
2.20	0.9861	0.9864	0.9868	0.9871	0.9875	0.9878	0.9881	0.9884	0.9887	0.9890
2.30	0.9893	0.9896	0.9898	0.9901	0.9904	0.9906	0.9909	0.9911	0.9913	0.9916
2.40	0.9918	0.9920	0.9922	0.9925	0.9927	0.9929	0.9931	0.9932	0.9934	0.9936
2.50	0.9938	0.9940	0.9941	0.9943	0.9945	0.9946	0.9948	0.9949	0.9951	0.9952
2.60	0.9953	0.9955	0.9956	0.9957	0.9959	0.9960	0.9961	0.9962	0.9963	0.9964
2.70	0.9965	0.9966	0.9967	0.9968	0.9969	0.9970	0.9971	0.9972	0.9973	0.9974
2.80	0.9974	0.9975	0.9976	0.9977	0.9977	0.9978	0.9979	0.9979	0.9980	0.9981
2.90	0.9981	0.9982	0.9982	0.9983	0.9984	0.9984	0.9985	0.9985	0.9986	0.9986
3.00	0.9987	0.9987	0.9987	0.9988	0.9988	0.9989	0.9989	0.9989	0.9990	0.9990

PRACTICE PROBLEMS FOR READING 70

1. A. Calculate the payoff at expiration for a call option on the S&P 100 stock index in which the underlying price is 579.32 at expiration, the multiplier is 100, and the exercise price is:

    i. 450. $\text{Max}(0, 579.32 - 450) = 129.32 \times 100 = 12,932$

    ii. 650. $\text{Max}(0, 579.32 - 650) = 0$

  B. Calculate the payoff at expiration for a put option on the S&P 100 in which the underlying is at 579.32 at expiration, the multiplier is 100, and the exercise price is:

    i. 450. $\text{Max}(0, 450 - 579.32) = 0$

    ii. 650. $\text{Max}(0, 650 - 579.32) = 7068$

2. A. Calculate the payoff at expiration for a call option on a bond in which the underlying is at $0.95 per $1 par at expiration, the contract is on $100,000 face value bonds, and the exercise price is:

    i. $0.85. $\text{Max}(0, .95 - .85) = 10000$

    ii. $1.15. $\text{Max}(0, .95 - 1.15) = 0$

  B. Calculate the payoff at expiration for a put option on a bond in which the underlying is at $0.95 per $1 par at expiration, the contract is on $100,000 face value bonds, and the exercise price is:

    i. $0.85. $\text{Max}(0, .85 - .95) = 0$

    ii. $1.15. $\text{Max}(0, 1.15 - .95) \approx 20,000$

3. A. Calculate the payoff at expiration for a call option on an interest rate in which the underlying is a 180-day interest rate at 6.53 percent at expiration, the notional principal is $10 million, and the exercise price is:

     $\text{Max}(0, .0653 - .05)\left(\dfrac{180}{360}\right) \cdot 10ml = 76,500$

    i. 5 percent.

    ii. 8 percent. 0

  B. Calculate the payoff at expiration for a put option on an interest rate in which the underlying is a 180-day interest rate at 6.53 percent at expiration, the notional principal is $10 million, and the exercise price is:

    i. 5 percent. 0

    ii. 8 percent. $\text{Max}(0, .08 - .0653) \cdot \dfrac{180}{360} \cdot 10 = 74k$

4. A. Calculate the payoff at expiration for a call option on the British pound in which the underlying is at $1.438 at expiration, the options are on 125,000 British pounds, and the exercise price is:

    i. $1.35. $(1.438 - 1.35) \times 125000 \approx 11000$

    ii. $1.55. 0

  B. Calculate the payoff at expiration for a put option on the British pound where the underlying is at $1.438 at expiration, the options are on 125,000 British pounds, and the exercise price is:

    i. $1.35. 0

    ii. $1.55. $(1.55 - 1.438) \, 125000 = 14000$

5. A. Calculate the payoff at expiration for a call option on a futures contract in which the underlying is at 1136.76 at expiration, the options are on a futures contract for $1,000, and the exercise price is:

    i. 1130. $(1136.76 - 1130) \times 1000 = \underline{6,760}$

    ii. 1140.   ○

B. Calculate the payoff at expiration for a put option on a futures contract in which the underlying is at 1136.76 at expiration, the options are on a futures contract for $1000, and the exercise price is:

    i. 1130.   ○

    ii. 1140. $(1140 - 1136.76) \times 1000 = \quad 3240$

6. Consider a stock index option that expires in 75 days. The stock index is currently at 1240.89 and makes no cash payments during the life of the option. Assume that the stock index has a multiplier of 1. The risk-free rate is 3 percent.

A. Calculate the lowest and highest possible prices for European-style call options on the above stock index with exercise prices of: $Max = 1240.89$

    i. 1225. $Max(0, 1240.89 - 1225/(1.03)^{75/360} = 23_{lu}$

    ii. 1255. $Max = 1240.89 \quad Low = 0$

B. Calculate the lowest and highest possible prices for European-style put options on the above stock index with exercise prices of: $Mex = \dfrac{1225}{(1.03)^{75/360}} = 1217.5$

    i. 1225. $Max(0, 1217.5 - 1240.89) = 0$

    ii. 1255. $Max(0, 1247.3 - 1240.89) = 6.405 \quad 1255/1.03^{75/360}$

7. A. Consider American-style call and put options on a bond. The options expire in 60 days. The bond is currently at $1.05 per $1 par and makes no cash payments during the life of the option. The risk-free rate is 5.5 percent. Assume that the contract is on $1 face value bonds. Calculate the lowest and highest possible prices for the calls and puts with exercise prices of:

    i. $0.95.

    ii. $1.10.

B. Consider European-style call and put options on a bond. The options expire in 60 days. The bond is currently at $1.05 per $1 par and makes no cash payments during the life of the option. The risk-free rate is 5.5 percent. Assume that the contract is on $1 face value bonds. Calculate the lowest and highest possible prices for the calls and puts with exercise prices of:

    i. $0.95.

    ii. $1.10.

8. You are provided with the following information on put and call options on a stock:

    Call price, $c_0 = \$6.64$

    Put price, $p_0 = \$2.75$

    Exercise price, $X = \$30$

    Days to option expiration = 219

    Current stock price, $S_0 = \$33.19$

Put–call parity shows the equivalence of a call/bond portfolio (fiduciary call) and a put/underlying portfolio (protective put). Illustrate put–call parity assuming stock prices at expiration (S_T) of $20 and of $40. Assume that the risk-free rate, r, is 4 percent.

9. With respect to put–call parity, a protective put consists of a European:

    A. put option and the underlying asset.

    B. call option and the underlying asset.

    C. put option and a risk-free bond with a face value equal to the exercise price of a European call option on the underlying asset.

10. Unless far out-of-the-money or far in-the-money, for otherwise identical call options, the longer the term to expiration, the lower the price for:

    A. American call options, but not European call options.

    B. both European call options and American call options.

    C. neither European call options nor American call options.

11. A call option with an exercise price of 65 will expire in 73 days. No cash payments will be made by the underlying asset over the life of the option. If the underlying asset price is at 70 and the risk-free rate of return is 5.0 percent, the lower bounds for an American call option and a European call option, respectively, are *closest* to:

	Lower bound for American call option	Lower bound for European call option
A.	5.00	5.63
B.	5.63	5.00
C.	5.63	5.63

12. A put option with an exercise price of 75 will expire in 73 days. No cash payments will be made by the underlying asset over the life of the option. If the underlying asset is at 70 and the risk-free rate of return is 5.0 percent, the lower bounds for an American put option and a European put option, respectively, are *closest* to:

	Lower bound for American put option	Lower bound for European put option
A.	4.27	4.27
B.	4.27	5.00
C.	5.00	4.27

13. Compare an American call with a strike of 50 which expires in 90 days to an American call on the same underlying asset which has a strike of 60 and expires in 120 days. The underlying asset is selling at 55. Consider the following statements:

    Statement 1: "The 50 strike call is in-the-money and the 60 strike call is out-of-the-money."

    Statement 2: "The time value of the 60 strike call, as a proportion of the 60 strike call's premium, exceeds the time value of the 50 strike call as a proportion of the 50 strike call's premium."

    Are the statements *most likely* correct or incorrect?

    A. Both statements are correct.

    B. Statement 1 is incorrect, but Statement 2 is correct.

    C. Statement 1 is correct, but Statement 2 is incorrect.

14. Marla Johnson priced both a put and a call on Alpha Numero using standard option pricing software. To use the program, Johnson entered the strike price of the options, the price of the underlying asset, an estimate of the risk-free rate, the time to expiration of the option, and an estimate of the volatility of the returns of the underlying asset into her computer. Both prices calculated by the software program were substantially above the actual market values observed in that day's exchange trading. Which of the following is the *most likely* explanation? The value Johnson entered into the program for the:

   A. estimate of volatility was too low.
   B. estimate of volatility was too high.
   C. time to expiration of the options was too low.

15. A call with a strike price of $40 is available on a stock currently trading for $35. The call expires in one year and the risk-free rate of return is 10%. The lower bound on this call's value:

   A. is zero.
   B. is $5 if the call is American-style.
   C. is $1.36 if the call is European-style.

16. An investor writes a call option priced at $3 with an exercise price of $100 on a stock that he owns. The investor paid $85 for the stock. If at expiration of the call option the stock price has risen to $110, the profit for the investor's position would be *closest* to:

   A. $3.
   B. $12.
   C. $18.

17. If an investor paid $5 for a put option with an exercise price of $60 that is in-the-money $2, the price of the underlying is *closest* to:

   A. $53.
   B. $58.
   C. $62.

18. An investor paid $10 for an option that is currently in-the-money $5. If the underlying is priced at $90, which of the following *best* describes that option?

   A. Call option with an exercise price of $80.
   B. Put option with an exercise price of $95.
   C. Call option with an exercise price of $95.

19. Assume the probability of bankruptcy for the underlying asset is high. Compared to the price of an American put option on the same underlying asset, the price of an equivalent European put option will *most likely* be:

   A. lower.
   B. higher.
   C. the same because the probability of bankruptcy does not affect pricing.

SOLUTIONS FOR READING 70

1. A. $S_T = 579.32$
    i. Call payoff, X = 450: Max(0,579.32 − 450) × 100 = $12,932
    ii. Call payoff, X = 650: Max(0,579.32 − 650) × 100 = 0

  B. $S_T = 579.32$
    i. Put payoff, X = 450: Max(0,450 − 579.32) × 100 = 0
    ii. Put payoff, X = 650: Max(0,650 − 579.32) × 100 = $7,068

2. A. $S_T = \$0.95$
    i. Call payoff, X = 0.85: Max(0,0.95 − 0.85) × 100,000 = $10,000
    ii. Call payoff, X = 1.15: Max(0,0.95 − 1.15) × 100,000 = $0

  B. $S_T = \$0.95$
    i. Put payoff, X = 0.85: Max(0,0.85 − 0.95) × 100,000 = $0
    ii. Put payoff, X = 1.15: Max(0,1.15 − 0.95) × 100,000 = $20,000

3. A. $S_T = 0.0653$
    i. Call payoff, X = 0.05: Max(0,0.0653 − 0.05) × (180/360) ×
    10,000,000 = $76,500
    ii. Call payoff, X = 0.08: Max(0,0.0653 − 0.08) × (180/360) ×
    10,000,000 = 0

  B. $S_T = 0.0653$
    i. Put payoff, X = 0.05: Max(0,0.05 − 0.0653) × (180/360) ×
    10,000,000 = 0
    ii. Put payoff, X = 0.08: Max(0,0.08 − 0.0653) × (180/360) ×
    10,000,000 = $73,500

4. A. $S_T = \$1.438$
    i. Call payoff, X = 1.35: Max(0,1.438 − 1.35) × 125,000 = $11,000
    ii. Call payoff, X = 1.55: Max(0,1.438 − 1.55) × 125,000 = $0

  B. $S_T = \$1.438$
    i. Put payoff, X = 1.35: Max(0,1.35 − 1.438) × 125,000 = $0
    ii. Put payoff, X = 1.55: Max(0,1.55 − 1.438) × 125,000 = $14,000

5. A. $S_T = 1136.76$
    i. Call payoff, X = 1130: Max(0,1136.76 − 1130) × 1,000 = $6,760
    ii. Call payoff, X = 1140: Max(0,1136.76 − 1140) × 1,000 = 0

  B. $S_T = 1136.76$
    i. Put payoff, X = 1130: Max(0,1130 − 1136.76) × 1,000 = 0
    ii. Put payoff, X = 1140: Max(0,1140 − 1136.76) × 1,000 = $3,240

6. A. $S_0 = 1240.89$, T = 75/365 = 0.2055, X = 1225 or 1255, call options
    i. X = 1225
    Maximum value for the call: $c_0 = S_0 = 1240.89$
    Lower bound for the call: $c_0 = Max[0,1240.89 − 1225/(1.03)^{0.2055}] =$
    23.31
    ii. X = 1255
    Maximum value for the call: $c_0 = S_0 = 1240.89$
    Lower bound for the call: $c_0 = Max[0,1240.89 − 1255/(1.03)^{0.2055}] = 0$

  B. $S_0 = 1240.89$, T = 75/365 = 0.2055, X = 1225 or 1255, put options
    i. X = 1225
    Maximum value for the put: $p_0 = 1225/(1.03)^{0.2055} = 1217.58$
    Lower bound for the put: $p_0 = Max[0,1225/(1.03)^{0.2055} − 1240.89] = 0$

Solutions to 1–8 taken from *Analysis of Derivatives for the Chartered Financial Analyst® Program*, by Don M. Chance, CFA. Copyright © 2003 by AIMR. Reprinted with permission. All other solutions copyright © CFA Institute.

ii. X = 1255

Maximum value for the put: $p_0 = 1255/(1.03)^{0.2055} = 1247.40$

Lower bound for the put: $p_0 = Max[0,1255/(1.03)^{0.2055} - 1240.89]$
$= 6.51$

7. A. $S_0 = 1.05$, T = 60/365 = 0.1644, X = 0.95 or 1.10, American-style options

i. X = $0.95

Maximum value for the call: $C_0 = S_0 = \$1.05$

Lower bound for the call: $C_0 = Max[0,1.05 - 0.95/(1.055)^{0.1644}]$
$= \$0.11$

Maximum value for the put: $P_0 = X = \$0.95$

Lower bound for the put: $P_0 = Max(0,0.95 - 1.05) = \$0$

ii. X = $1.10

Maximum value for the call: $C_0 = S_0 = \$1.05$

Lower bound for the call: $C_0 = Max[0,1.05 - 1.10/(1.055)^{0.1644}] = \$0$

Maximum value for the put: $P_0 = X = \$1.10$

Lower bound for the put: $P_0 = Max(0,1.10 - 1.05) = \$0.05$

B. $S_0 = 1.05$, T = 60/365 = 0.1644, X = 0.95 or 1.10, European-style options

i. X = $0.95

Maximum value for the call: $c_0 = S_0 = \$1.05$

Lower bound for the call: $c_0 = Max[0,1.05 - 0.95/(1.055)^{0.1644}]$
$= \$0.11$

Maximum value for the put: $p_0 = 0.95/(1.055)^{0.1644} = \$0.94$

Lower bound for the put: $p_0 = Max[0,0.95/(1.055)^{0.1644} - 1.05] = \$0$

ii. X = $1.10

Maximum value for the call: $c_0 = S_0 = \$1.05$

Lower bound for the call: $c_0 = Max[0,1.05 - 1.10/(1.055)^{0.1644}] = \$0$

Maximum value for the put: $p_0 = 1.10/(1.055)^{0.1644} = \$1.09$

Lower bound for the put: $p_0 = Max[0,1.10/(1.055)^{0.1644} - 1.05]$
$= \$0.04$

8. We can illustrate put–call parity by showing that for the fiduciary call and the protective put, the current values and values at expiration are the same.

Call price, $c_0 = \$6.64$

Put price, $p_0 = \$2.75$

Exercise price, X = $30

Risk-free rate, r = 4 percent

Time to expiration = 219/365 = 0.6

Current stock price, $S_0 = \$33.19$

Bond price, $X/(1 + r)^T = 30/(1 + 0.04)^{0.6} = \$29.30$

		Value at Expiration	
Transaction	Current Value	$S_T = 20$	$S_T = 40$
Fiduciary call			
Buy call	6.64	0	40 − 30 = 10
Buy bond	29.30	30	30
Total	35.94	30	40
Protective put			
Buy put	2.75	30 − 20 = 10	0
Buy stock	33.19	20	40
Total	35.94	30	40

The values in the table show that the current values and values at expiration for the fiduciary call and the protective put are the same. That is, $c_0 + X/(1 + r)^T = p_0 + S_0$.

9. A is correct. This is the definition of a protective put.

10. C is correct. Although there are exceptions, in general the longer the time to expiration the more valuable is the option, ceteris paribus. With the exception of the rare case in which [options] are so far out-of-the-money or in-the-money that the additional time is of no value, the longer term [options] will be worth more. In addition, it is not always true that a longer-term is beneficial to the holder of a European put.

11. C is correct. Because time remains until expiration and the problem deals with calls, the lower bound of the European call will exceed the intrinsic value. In concept, one can invest the strike price amount until it is needed at expiration and earn the risk-free rate on this amount for that period of time. The intrinsic value is $5.00; given the available answers, the lower bound for the European call must be $5.63. This is confirmed by applying the formula $c_0 \geq \text{Max}[0, S_0 - X/(1 + r)^T]$. In this problem, the lower bound is the greater of 0 or $70 - 65/(1.05)^{0.2} = 5.63$. Note that the value of the American call cannot be less than the value of the European call.

12. C is correct. When valuing European puts that have time left until expiration, the lower bound must reflect the fact that exercise is delayed until the expiration date. That is, with a European put one can't recognize the current intrinsic value, but must wait until expiration. This delay in receiving payment for selling (putting) the stock to the writer has a cost. The lower bound will therefore be below the intrinsic value (but never negative). This can be confirmed by applying the formula $p_0 \geq \text{Max}[0, X/(1 + r)^T - S_0]$. In this problem, the lower bound is the greater of 0 or $75/(1.05)^{0.2}$ 70 = 4.27. Regarding the American put, as one can recognize the intrinsic value of an American put immediately if one chooses to, the lower bound of an American put, in the absence of intervening cash payments on the underlying asset, will simply be equal to the intrinsic value.

13. A is correct. A call is in-the-money when the underlying asset price exceeds the strike price. The entire premium of the 60 strike call reflects time value; only a part of the 50 strike call's premium is time value, the rest will be intrinsic value.

14. B is correct. If Johnson entered too high an estimate of volatility into the program, both the put and the call values given by the program would be too high.

15. A is correct. For an American- or European-style call, the lower bound is the greater of zero or the difference between the stock price and the present value of the strike price. In this problem, the difference is 35 minus (40 / 1.10) = negative $1.36. Thus, the lower bound is zero.

16. C is correct. The investor collects $3 from writing the call and makes $15 on the stock before it is called, resulting in a profit of $18.

17. B is correct. A put option is in-the-money if the price of the underlying is less than the exercise price. The difference between the exercise price and the underlying equals the amount the put option is in-the-money. $60 − 58 = $2.

18. B is correct. A put option is in-the-money if the stock price is less than the exercise price. The put option with an exercise price of $95 is in-the-money $5. The call option with an exercise price of $80 is out-of-the-money $10, and the call option with an exercise price of $95 is out-of-the-money $5.

19. A is correct. In bankruptcy, the price of the bankrupt company's stock falls. In the limit it falls to zero. At a price of zero, the price cannot go any lower, and it would be advantageous to exercise the American put at that point in time rather than be forced to wait until the expiration date. Therefore, the American-style put is likely to have a higher price than an equivalent European-style put.

SWAP MARKETS AND CONTRACTS
by Don M. Chance, CFA

LEARNING OUTCOMES

The candidate should be able to:

Mastery

a. describe the characteristics of swap contracts and explain how swaps are terminated; ☐

b. define, calculate, and interpret the payment of currency swaps, plain vanilla interest rate swaps, and equity swaps. ☐

INTRODUCTION

1

This reading completes the survey of the main types of derivative instruments. The three preceding readings covered forward contracts, futures contracts, and options. This reading covers swaps. Although swaps were the last of the main types of derivatives to be invented, they are clearly not the least important. In fact, judging by the size of the swap market, they are probably the most important. In the reading on derivative markets and instruments, we noted that the Bank for International Settlements had estimated the notional principal of the global over-the-counter derivatives market as of 30 June 2001 at $100 trillion. Of that amount, interest rate and currency swaps account for about $61 trillion, with interest rate swaps representing about $57 trillion of that total.[1] Indeed, interest rate swaps have had overwhelming success as a derivative product. They are widely used by corporations, financial institutions, and governments.

In the reading on derivative markets and instruments, we briefly described the characteristics of swaps, but now we explore this subject in more detail. Recall first

---

[1] Equity and commodity swaps account for less than the notional principal of currency swaps.

Analysis of Derivatives for the Chartered Financial Analyst® Program, by Don M. Chance, CFA. Copyright © 2003 by AIMR. Reprinted with permission.

131

that *a swap is an agreement between two parties to exchange a series of future cash flows*. For most types of swaps, one party makes payments that are determined by a random outcome, such as an interest rate, a currency rate, an equity return, or a commodity price. These payments are commonly referred to as variable or *floating*. The other party either makes variable or floating payments determined by some other random factor or makes fixed payments. At least one type of swap involves both parties making fixed payments, but the values of those payments vary due to random factors.

In forwards, futures, and options, the terminology of *long* and *short* has been used to describe buyers and sellers. These terms are not used as often in swaps. The preferred terminology usually designates a party as being the floating- (or variable-) rate payer or the fixed-rate payer. Nonetheless, in swaps in which one party receives a floating rate and the other receives a fixed rate, the former is usually said to be long and the latter is said to be short. This usage is in keeping with the fact that parties who go long in other instruments pay a known amount and receive a claim on an unknown amount. In some swaps, however, both sides are floating or variable, and this terminology breaks down.

1.1 Characteristics of Swap Contracts

Although technically a swap can have a single payment, most swaps involve multiple payments. Thus, we refer to a swap as a *series* of payments. In fact, we have already covered a swap with one payment, which is just a forward contract. Hence, a swap is basically a series of forward contracts. With this idea in mind, we can see that a swap is like an agreement to buy something over a period of time. We might be paying a variable price or a price that has already been fixed; we might be paying an uncertain price, or we might already know the price we shall pay.

When a swap is initiated, neither party pays any amount to the other. Therefore, a swap has zero value at the start of the contract. Although it is not absolutely necessary for this condition to be true, swaps are typically done in this fashion. Neither party pays anything up front. There is, however, a technical exception to this point in regard to currency swaps. Each party pays the notional principal to the other, but the amounts exchanged are equivalent, though denominated in two different currencies.

Each date on which the parties make payments is called a **settlement date**, sometimes called a payment date, and the time between settlement dates is called the **settlement period**. On a given settlement date when payments are due, one party makes a payment to the other, which in turn makes a payment to the first party. With the exception of currency swaps and a few variations associated with other types of swaps, both sets of payments are made in the same currency. Consequently, the parties typically agree to exchange only the net amount owed from one party to the other, a practice called **netting**. In currency swaps and a few other special cases, the payments are not made in the same currency; hence, the parties usually make separate payments without netting. Note the implication that swaps are generally settled in cash. It is quite rare for swaps to call for actual physical delivery of an underlying asset.

A swap always has a **termination date**, the date of the final payment. We can think of this date as its expiration date, as we do with other derivatives. The original time to maturity is sometimes called the **tenor** of a swap.

The swap market is almost exclusively an over-the-counter market, so swaps contracts are customized to the parties' specific needs. Several of the leading futures exchanges have created futures contracts on swaps. These contracts allow participants to hedge and speculate on the rates that will prevail in the swap market at future dates. Of course, these contracts are not swaps themselves but, as derivatives of swaps, they can in some ways serve as substitutes for swaps. These futures contracts have been moderately successful, but their volume is insignificant compared with the over-the-counter market for swaps.

As we have discussed in previous readings, over-the-counter instruments are subject to default risk. Default is possible whenever a payment is due. When a series of payments is made, there is default risk potential throughout the life of the contract, depending on the financial condition of the two parties. But default can be somewhat complicated in swaps. Suppose, for example, that on a settlement date, Party A owes Party B a payment of $50,000 and Party B owes Party A a payment of $12,000. Agreeing to net, Party A owes Party B $38,000 for that particular payment. Party A may be illiquid, or perhaps even bankrupt, and unable to make the payment. But it may be the case that the market value of the swap, which reflects the present value of the remaining payments, could be positive from the perspective of Party A and negative from the perspective of Party B. In that case, Party B owes Party A more for the remaining payments.

The handling of default in swaps can be complicated, depending on the contract specifications and the applicable laws under which the contract was written. In most cases, the above situation would be resolved by having A be in default but possessing an asset, the swap, that can be used to help settle its other liabilities.

1.2 Termination of a Swap

As we noted earlier, a swap has a termination or expiration date. Sometimes, however, a party could want to terminate a swap before its formal expiration. This scenario is much like a party selling a bond before it matures or selling an exchange-traded option or futures contract before its expiration. With swaps, early termination can take place in several ways.

As we mentioned briefly, a swap has a market value that can be calculated during its life. If a party holds a swap with a market value of $125,000, for example, it can settle the swap with the counterparty by having the counterparty pay it $125,000 in cash. This payment terminates the transaction for both parties. From the opposite perspective, a party holding a swap with a negative market value can terminate the swap by paying the market value to the counterparty. Terminating a swap in this manner is possible only if the counterparties specify in advance that such a transaction can be made, or if they reach an agreement to do so without having specified in advance. In other words, this feature is not automatically available and must be agreed to by both parties.

Many swaps are terminated early by entering into a separate and offsetting swap. For example, suppose a corporation is engaged in a swap to make fixed payments of 5 percent and receive floating payments based on LIBOR, with the payments made each 15 January and 15 July. Three years remain on the swap. That corporation can offset the swap by entering into an entirely new swap in which it makes payments based on LIBOR and receives a fixed rate with the payments made each 15 January and 15 July for three years. The swap fixed rate is determined by market conditions at the time the swap is initiated. Thus, the fixed rate on the new swap is not likely to match the fixed rate on the old swap, but the effect of this transaction is simply to have the floating payments offset;

the fixed payments will net out to a known amount. Hence, the risk associated with the floating rate is eliminated. The default risk, however, is not eliminated because both swaps remain in effect.

Another way to terminate a swap early is sell the swap to another counterparty. Suppose a corporation holds a swap worth $75,000. If it can obtain the counterparty's permission, it can find another party to take over its payments. In effect, it sells the swap for $75,000 to that party. This procedure, however, is not commonly used.

A final way to terminate a swap early is by using a **swaption**. This instrument is an option to enter into a swap at terms that are established in advance. Thus, a party could use a swaption to enter into an offsetting swap, as described above.

2   THE STRUCTURE OF GLOBAL SWAP MARKETS

The global swaps market is much like the global forward and over-the-counter options markets, which we covered in some detail in the preceding readings. It is made up of dealers, which are banks and investment banking firms. These dealers make markets in swaps, quoting bid and ask prices and rates, thereby offering to take either side of a swap transaction. Upon taking a position in a swap, the dealer generally offsets the risk by making transactions in other markets. The counterparties to swaps are either end users or other dealers. The end users are often corporations with risk management problems that can be solved by engaging in a swap—a corporation or other end user is usually exposed to or needs an exposure to some type of risk that arises from interest rates, exchange rates, stock prices, or commodity prices. The end user contacts a dealer that makes a market in swaps. The two engage in a transaction, at which point the dealer assumes some risk from the end user. The dealer then usually lays off the risk by engaging in a transaction with another party. That transaction could be something as simple as a futures contract, or it could be an over-the-counter transaction with another dealer.

Risk magazine conducts annual surveys of participants in various derivative products. Exhibit 1 presents the results of those surveys for currency and interest rate swaps. One survey provides opinions of banks and investment banks that are

EXHIBIT 1	*Risk* Magazine Surveys of Banks, Investment Banks, and Corporate End Users to Determine the Top Three Dealers in Currency and Interest Rate Swaps	
	Respondents	
Currencies	**Banks and Investment Banks**	**Corporate End Users**
Currency Swaps		
$/€	UBS Warburg	Citigroup
	JP Morgan Chase	Royal Bank of Scotland
	Deutsche Bank	Bank of America

(Exhibit continued on next page . . .)

EXHIBIT 1   **(continued)**

$/¥	JP Morgan Chase	Citigroup
	UBS Warburg	Bank of America
	Credit Suisse First Boston/ Deutsche Bank	JP Morgan Chase
$/£	Royal Bank of Scotland	Royal Bank of Scotland
	JP Morgan Chase	Citigroup
	Goldman Sachs	Deutsche Bank
$/SF	UBS Warburg	UBS Warburg
	Goldman Sachs	Citigroup
	Credit Suisse First Boston	Credit Suisse First Boston

Interest Rate Swaps (2–10 years)

$	JP Morgan Chase	JP Morgan Chase
	Bank of America	Bank of America
	Morgan Stanley	Royal Bank of Scotland
€	JP Morgan Chase	Royal Bank of Scotland
	Deutsche Bank	Deutsche Bank
	Morgan Stanley	Citigroup
¥	JP Morgan Chase	Royal Bank of Scotland
	Deutsche Bank	Barclays Capital
	Bank of America	Citigroup/JP Morgan Chase
£	Royal Bank of Scotland	Royal Bank of Scotland
	Barclays Capital	Barclays Capital
	UBS Warburg	Deutsche Bank
SF	UBS Warburg	UBS Warburg
	Credit Suisse First Boston	Credit Suisse First Boston
	Zürcher Kantonalbank	Zürcher Kantonalbank

Note: $ = U.S. dollar, € = euro, ¥ = Japanese yen, £ = U.K. pound sterling, SF = Swiss franc.

Source: *Risk*, September 2002, pp. 30–67 for banks and investment banking dealer respondents, and June 2002, pp. 24–34 for corporate end user respondents. Ratings for swaps with maturities less than 2 years and greater than 10 years are also provided in the September 2002 issue of *Risk*.

swaps dealers. In the other survey, the respondents are end users. The results give a good idea of the major players in this market. It is interesting to note the disagreement between how dealers view themselves and how end users view them. Also, note that the rankings change, sometimes drastically, from year to year.

TYPES OF SWAPS   3

We alluded to the fact that the underlying asset in a swap can be a currency, interest rate, stock, or commodity. We now take a look at these types of swaps in more detail.

3.1 Currency Swaps

In a currency swap, each party makes interest payments to the other in different currencies.[2] Consider this example. The U.S. retailer Target Corporation (NYSE: TGT) does not have an established presence in Europe. Let us say that it has decided to begin opening a few stores in Germany and needs €9 million to fund construction and initial operations. TGT would like to issue a fixed-rate euro-denominated bond with face value of €9 million, but the company is not very well known in Europe. European investment bankers have given it a quote for such a bond. Deutsche Bank, AG (NYSE: DB), however, tells TGT that it should issue the bond in dollars and use a swap to convert it into euros.

Suppose TGT issues a five-year US$10 million bond at a rate of 6 percent. It then enters into a swap with DB in which DB will make payments to TGT in U.S. dollars at a fixed rate of 5.5 percent and TGT will make payments to DB in euros at a fixed rate of 4.9 percent each 15 March and 15 September for five years. The payments are based on a notional principal of 10 million in dollars and 9 million in euros. We assume the swap starts on 15 September of the current year. The swap specifies that the two parties exchange the notional principal at the start of the swap and at the end. Because the payments are made in different currencies, netting is not practical, so each party makes its respective payments.[3]

Thus, the swap is composed of the following transactions:
15 September:

▶ DB pays TGT €9 million
▶ TGT pays DB $10 million

Each 15 March and 15 September for five years:

▶ DB pays TGT 0.055(180/360)$10 million = $275,000
▶ TGT pays DB 0.049(180/360) €9 million = €220,500

15 September five years after initiation:

▶ DB pays TGT $10 million
▶ TGT pays DB €9 million

Note that we have simplified the interest calculations a little. In this example, we calculated semiannual interest using the fraction 180/360. Some parties might

---

[2] It is important at this point to clear up some terminology confusion. Foreign currency is often called *foreign exchange* or sometimes *FX*. There is another transaction called an *FX swap*, which sounds as if it might be referring to a currency swap. In fact, an FX swap is just a long position in a forward contract on a foreign currency and a short position in a forward contract on the same currency with a different expiration. Why this transaction is called a swap is not clear, but this transaction existed before currency swaps were created. In futures markets, the analogous transaction is called a *spread*, reflecting as it does the risk associated with the spread between the prices of futures contracts with different expirations.

[3] In this example, we shall assume 180 days between payment dates. In practice, exact day counts are usually used, leading to different fixed payment amounts in one six-month period from those of another. In the example here, we are only illustrating the idea behind swap cash flows, so it is convenient to keep the fixed payments the same. Later in the reading, we shall illustrate situations in which the exact day count is used, leading to fixed payments that vary slightly.

EXHIBIT 2	Cash Flows to TGT on Swap with DB

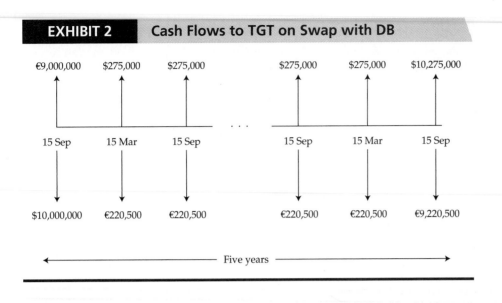

choose to use the exact day count in the six-month period divided by 365 days. LIBOR and Euribor transactions, the predominant rates used in interest rate swaps, nearly always use 360 days, as mentioned in previous readings. Exhibit 2 shows the stream of cash flows from TGT's perspective.

Note that the Target–Deutsche Bank transaction looks just like TGT is issuing a bond with face value of €9 million and that bond is purchased by DB. TGT converts the €9 million to $10 million and buys a dollar-denominated bond issued by DB. Note that TGT, having issued a bond denominated in euros, accordingly makes interest payments to DB in euros. DB, appropriately, makes interest payments in dollars to TGT. At the end, they each pay off the face values of the bonds they have issued. We emphasize that the Target–Deutsche Bank transaction *looks like* what we have just described. In fact, neither TGT nor DB actually issues or purchases a bond. They exchange only a series of cash flows that replicated the issuance and purchase of these bonds.

Exhibit 3 illustrates how such a combined transaction would work. TGT issues a bond in dollars (Exhibit 3, Panel A). It takes the dollars and passes them through to DB, which gives TGT the €9 million it needs. On the interest payment dates, the swap generates $275,000 of the $300,000 in interest TGT needs to pay its bondholders (Panel B). In turn, TGT makes interest payments in euros. Still, small dollar interest payments are necessary because TGT cannot issue a dollar bond at the swap rate. At the end of the transaction, TGT receives $10 million back from DB and passes it through to its bondholders (Panel C). TGT pays DB €9 million, thus effectively paying off a euro-denominated bond.

TGT has effectively issued a dollar-denominated bond and converted it to a euro-denominated bond. In all likelihood, it can save on interest expense by funding its need for euros in this way, because TGT is better known in the United States than in Europe. Its swap dealer, DB, knows TGT well and also obviously has a strong presence in Europe. Thus, DB can pass on its advantage in euro bond markets to TGT. In addition, had TGT issued a euro-denominated bond, it would have assumed no credit risk. By entering into the swap, TGT assumes a remote possibility of DB defaulting. Thus, TGT saves a little money by assuming some credit risk.

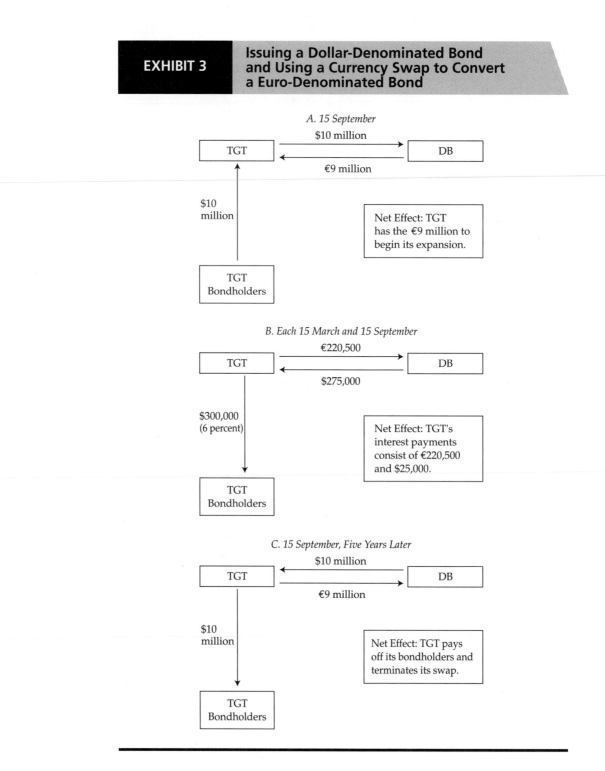

EXHIBIT 3   Issuing a Dollar-Denominated Bond and Using a Currency Swap to Convert a Euro-Denominated Bond

A. 15 September

$10 million → TGT → DB

€9 million

$10 million (from TGT Bondholders)

Net Effect: TGT has the €9 million to begin its expansion.

B. Each 15 March and 15 September

€220,500 → TGT → DB

$275,000

$300,000 (6 percent) to TGT Bondholders

Net Effect: TGT's interest payments consist of €220,500 and $25,000.

C. 15 September, Five Years Later

$10 million → TGT → DB

€9 million

$10 million to TGT Bondholders

Net Effect: TGT pays off its bondholders and terminates its swap.

Returning to the Target swap, recall that Target effectively converted a fixed-rate loan in dollars to a fixed-rate loan in euros. Suppose instead that TGT preferred to borrow in euros at a floating rate. It then would have specified that the swap required it to make payments to DB at a floating rate. Had TGT preferred to issue the dollar-denominated bond at a floating rate, it would have specified that DB pay it dollars at a floating rate.

EXAMPLE 1

Consider a currency swap in which the domestic party pays a fixed rate in the foreign currency, the British pound, and the counterparty pays a fixed rate in U.S. dollars. The notional principals are $50 million and £30 million. The fixed rates are 5.6 percent in dollars and 6.25 percent in pounds. Both sets of payments are made on the basis of 30 days per month and 365 days per year, and the payments are made semiannually.

A. Determine the initial exchange of cash that occurs at the start of the swap.

B. Determine the semiannual payments.

C. Determine the final exchange of cash that occurs at the end of the swap.

D. Give an example of a situation in which this swap might be appropriate.

Solution to A: At the start of the swap:
Domestic party pays counterparty $50 million
Counterparty pays domestic party £30 million

Solution to B: Semiannually:
Domestic party pays counterparty £30,000,000(0.0625)(180/365) = £924,658
Counterparty pays domestic party $50,000,000(0.056)(180/365) = $1,380,822

Solution to C: At the end of the swap:
Domestic party pays counterparty £30,000,000 + £924,658 = £30,924,658
Counterparty pays domestic party $50,000,000 + $1,380,222 = $51,380,222

Solution to D: This swap would be appropriate for a U.S. company that issues a dollar-denominated bond but would prefer to borrow in British pounds.

Although TGT and DB exchanged notional principal, some scenarios exist in which the notional principals are not exchanged. For example, suppose many years later, TGT is generating €10 million in cash semi-annually and converting it back to dollars on 15 January and 15 July. It might then wish to lock in the conversion rate by entering into a currency swap that would require it to pay a dealer €10 million and receive a fixed amount of dollars. If the euro fixed rate were 5 percent, a notional principal of €400 million would generate a payment of 0.05(180/360)€400 million = €10 million. If the exchange rate is, for example, $0.85, the equivalent dollar notional principal would be $340 million. If the dollar fixed rate is 6 percent, TGT would receive 0.06(180/360)$340 million = $10.2 million.[4] These payments would occur twice a year for the life of the swap. TGT might

---

[4] It might appear that TGT has somehow converted cash flows worth €10 million($0.085) = $8.5 million into cash flows worth $10.2 million. Recall, however, that the €10 million cash flows are generated yearly and $0.85 is the *current* exchange rate. We cannot apply the current exchange rate to a series of cash flows over various future dates. We would apply the respective forward exchange rates, not the spot rate, to the series of future euro cash flows.

then lock in the conversion rate by entering into a currency swap with notional principal amounts that would allow it to receive a fixed amount of dollars on 15 January and 15 July. There would be no reason to specify an exchange of notional principal. As we previously described, there are four types of currency swaps. Using the original Target–Deutsche Bank swap as an example, the semi-annual payments would be

    A. TGT pays euros at a fixed rate; DB pays dollars at a fixed rate.

    B. TGT pays euros at a fixed rate; DB pays dollars at a floating rate.

    C. TGT pays euros at a floating rate; DB pays dollars at a floating rate.

    D. TGT pays euros at a floating rate; DB pays dollars at a fixed rate.

Or, reversing the flow, TGT could be the payer of dollars and DB could be the payer of euros:

    E. TGT pays dollars at a fixed rate; DB pays euros at a fixed rate.

    F. TGT pays dollars at a fixed rate; DB pays euros at a floating rate.

    G. TGT pays dollars at a floating rate; DB pays euros at a floating rate.

    H. TGT pays dollars at a floating rate; DB pays euros at a fixed rate.

Suppose we combine Swap A with Swap H. With TGT paying euros at a fixed rate and DB paying euros at a fixed rate, the euro payments wash out and the net effect is

    I. TGT pays dollars at a floating rate; DB pays dollars at a fixed rate.

Suppose we combine Swap B with Swap E. Similarly, the euro payments again wash out, and the net effect is

    J. TGT pays dollars at a fixed rate; DB pays dollars at a floating rate.

Suppose we combine Swap C with Swap F. Likewise, the euro floating payments wash out, and the net effect is

    K. TGT pays dollars at a fixed rate; DB pays dollars at a floating rate.

Lastly, suppose we combine Swap D with Swap G. Again, the euro floating payments wash out, and the net effect is

    L. TGT pays dollars at a floating rate; DB pays dollars at a fixed rate.

Of course, the net results of I and L are equivalent, and the net results of J and K are equivalent. What we have shown here, however, is that combinations of currency swaps eliminate the currency flows and leave us with transactions in only one currency. A swap in which both sets of interest payments are made in the same currency is an interest rate swap.

3.2 Interest Rate Swaps

As we discovered in the above paragraph, an interest rate swap can be created as a combination of currency swaps. Of course, no one would create an interest rate swap that way; doing so would require two transactions when only one would suffice. Interest rate swaps evolved into their own market. In fact, the interest rate swap market is much bigger than the currency swap market, as we have seen in the notional principal statistics.

As previously noted, one way to look at an interest rate swap is that it is a currency swap in which both currencies are the same. Consider a swap to pay Currency A fixed and Currency B floating. Currency A could be dollars, and B could be euros. But what if A and B are both dollars, or A and B are both euros? The first case is a dollar-denominated plain vanilla swap; the second is a euro-denominated plain vanilla swap. *A **plain vanilla swap** is simply an interest rate swap in which one party pays a fixed rate and the other pays a floating rate, with both sets of payments in the same currency.* In fact, the plain vanilla swap is probably the most common derivative transaction in the global financial system.

Note that because we are paying in the same currency, there is no need to exchange notional principals at the beginning and at the end of an interest rate swap. In addition, the interest payments can be, and nearly always are, netted. If one party owes $X and the other owes $Y, the party owing the greater amount pays the net difference, which greatly reduces the credit risk. Finally, we note that there is no reason to have both sides pay a fixed rate. The two streams of payments would be identical in that case. So in an interest rate swap, either one side always pays fixed and the other side pays floating, or both sides pay floating, but never do both sides pay fixed.[5]

Thus, in a plain vanilla interest rate swap, one party makes interest payments at a fixed rate and the other makes interest payments at a floating rate. Both sets of payments are on the same notional principal and occur on regularly scheduled dates. For each payment, the interest rate is multiplied by a fraction representing the number of days in the settlement period over the number of days in a year. In some cases, the settlement period is computed assuming 30 days in each month; in others, an exact day count is used. Some cases assume a 360-day year; others use 365 days.

Let us now illustrate an interest rate swap. Suppose that on 15 December, General Electric Company (NYSE: GE) borrows money for one year from a bank such as Bank of America (NYSE: BAC). The loan is for $25 million and specifies that GE will make interest payments on a quarterly basis on the 15th of March, June, September, and December for one year at the rate of LIBOR plus 25 basis points. At the end of the year, it will pay back the principal. On the 15th of December, March, June, and September, LIBOR is observed and sets the rate for that quarter. The interest is then paid at the end of the quarter.[6]

GE believes that it is getting a good rate, but fearing a rise in interest rates, it would prefer a fixed-rate loan. It can easily convert the floating-rate loan to a fixed-rate loan by engaging in a swap. Suppose it approaches JP Morgan Chase (NYSE: JPM), a large dealer bank, and requests a quote on a swap to pay a fixed rate and receive LIBOR, with payments on the dates of its loan payments. The bank prices the swap and quotes a fixed rate of 6.2 percent.[7] The fixed payments

---

[5] The case of both sides paying floating is called a basis swap.

[6] Again, we assume 90 days in each interest payment period for this example. The exact payment dates are not particularly important for illustrative purposes.

[7] Typically the rate is quoted as a spread over the rate on a U.S. Treasury security with a comparable maturity. Suppose the yield on a two-year Treasury note is 6 percent. Then the swap would be quoted as 20 basis points over the two-year Treasury rate. By quoting the rate in this manner, GE knows what it is paying over the Treasury rate, a differential called the swap spread. In addition, a quote in this form protects the bank from the rate changing drastically either during the phone conversation or shortly thereafter. Thus, the quote can stay in effect for a reasonable period of time while GE checks out quotes from other dealers.

will be made based on a day count of 90/365, and the floating payments will be made based on 90/360. Current LIBOR is 5.9 percent. Therefore, the first fixed payment, which GE makes to JPM, is $25,000,000(0.062)(90/365) = $382,192. This is also the amount of each remaining fixed payment.

The first floating payment, which JPM makes to GE, is $25,000,000(0.059) (90/360) = $368,750. Of course, the remaining floating payments will not be known until later. Exhibit 4 shows the pattern of cash flows on the swap from GE's perspective.

EXHIBIT 4	Cash Flow to GE on Swap with JPM

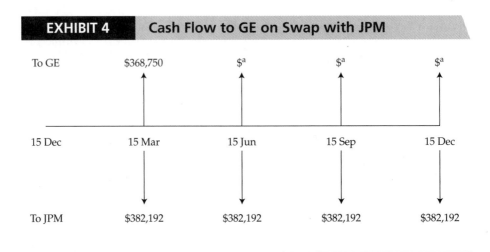

To GE	$368,750	$ᵃ	$ᵃ	$ᵃ
To JPM	$382,192	$382,192	$382,192	$382,192
	15 Mar	15 Jun	15 Sep	15 Dec

15 Dec

ᵃ Computed as $25,000,000(L)90/360, where L is LIBOR on the previous settlement date.

EXAMPLE 2

Determine the upcoming payments in a plain vanilla interest rate swap in which the notional principal is €70 million. The end user makes semiannual fixed payments at the rate of 7 percent, and the dealer makes semiannual floating payments at Euribor, which was 6.25 percent on the last settlement period. The floating payments are made on the basis of 180 days in the settlement period and 360 days in a year. The fixed payments are made on the basis of 180 days in the settlement period and 365 days in a year. Payments are netted, so determine which party pays which and what amount.

Solution:

The fixed payments are €70,000,000(0.07)(180/365) = €2,416,438.

The upcoming floating payment is €70,000,000(0.0625)(180/360) = €2,187,500.

The net payment is that the party paying fixed will pay the party paying floating €2,416,438 − €2,187,500 = €228,938.

Note in Exhibit 4 that we did not show the notional principal, because it was not exchanged. We could implicitly show that GE received $25 million from JPM and paid $25 million to JPM at the start of the swap. We could also show that the same thing happens at the end. If we look at it that way, it appears as if GE has issued a $25 million fixed-rate bond, which was purchased by JPM, which in turn issued a $25 million floating-rate bond, which was in turn purchased by GE. We say that *it appears* as if this is what happened: In fact, neither party actually issued a bond, but they have generated the cash flows that would occur if GE had issued such a fixed-rate bond, JPM had issued such a floating-rate bond, and each purchased the bond of the other. In other words, we could include the principals on both sides to make each set of cash flows look like a bond, yet the overall cash flows would be the same as on the swap.

So let us say that GE enters into this swap. Exhibit 5 shows the net effect of the swap and the loan. GE pays LIBOR plus 25 basis points to Bank of America on its loan, pays 6.2 percent to JPM, and receives LIBOR from JPM. The net effect is that GE pays $6.2 + 0.25 = 6.45$ percent fixed.

EXHIBIT 5   **GE's Conversion of a Floating-Rate Loan to a Fixed-Rate Loan Using an Interest Rate Swap with JPM**

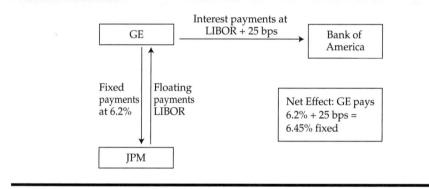

Now, JPM is engaged in a swap to pay LIBOR and receive 6.2 percent. It is exposed to the risk of LIBOR increasing. It would, therefore, probably engage in some other type of transaction to offset this risk. One transaction commonly used in this situation is to sell Eurodollar futures. As discussed in the reading on risk management applications of option strategies, Eurodollar futures prices move $25 in value for each basis point move in LIBOR. JPM will determine how sensitive its position is to a move in LIBOR and sell an appropriate number of futures to offset the risk. Note that Bank of America is exposed to LIBOR as well, but in the banking industry, floating-rate loans are often made because the funding that the bank obtained to make the loan was probably already at LIBOR or a comparable floating rate.

It is possible but unlikely that GE could get a fixed-rate loan at a better rate. The swap involves some credit risk: the possibility, however small, that JPM will default. In return for assuming that risk, GE in all likelihood would get a better rate than it would if it borrowed at a fixed rate. JPM is effectively a wholesaler of risk, using its powerful position as one of the world's leading banks to facilitate the buying and selling of risk for companies such as GE. Dealers profit from the spread between the rates they quote to pay and the rates they quote to receive. The swaps market is, however, extremely competitive and the spreads have been squeezed very tight, which makes it very challenging for dealers to make a profit. Of course, this competition is good for end users, because it gives them more attractive rates.

3.3 Equity Swaps

By now, it should be apparent that a swap requires at least one variable rate or price underlying it. So far, that rate has been an interest rate.[8] In an equity swap, the rate is the return on a stock or stock index. This characteristic gives the equity swap two features that distinguish it from interest rate and currency swaps.

First, the party making the fixed-rate payment could also have to make a variable payment based on the equity return. Suppose the end user pays the equity payment and receives the fixed payment, i.e., it pays the dealer the return on the S&P 500 Index, and the dealer pays the end user a fixed rate. If the S&P 500 increases, the return is positive and the end user pays that return to the dealer. If the S&P 500 goes down, however, its return is obviously negative. In that case, the end user would pay the dealer the *negative return on the S&P 500*, which means that it would receive that return from the dealer. For example, if the S&P 500 falls by 1 percent, the dealer would pay the end user 1 percent, in addition to the fixed payment the dealer makes in any case. So the dealer, or in general the party receiving the equity return, could end up making *both* a fixed-rate payment and an equity payment.

The second distinguishing feature of an equity swap is that the payment is not known until the end of the settlement period, at which time the return on the stock is known. In an interest rate or currency swap, the floating interest rate is set at the beginning of the period.[9] Therefore, one always knows the amount of the upcoming floating interest payment.[10]

Another important feature of some equity swaps is that the rate of return is often structured to include both dividends and capital gains. In interest rate and currency swaps, capital gains are not paid.[11] Finally, we note that in some equity swaps, the notional principal is indexed to change with the level of the stock, although we will not explore such swaps in this volume.[12]

Equity swaps are commonly used by asset managers. Let us consider a situation in which an asset manager might use such a swap. Suppose that the Vanguard Asset Allocation Fund (Nasdaq: VAAPX) is authorized to use swaps. On the last day of December, it would like to sell $100 million in U.S. large-cap equities and invest the proceeds at a fixed rate. It believes that a swap allowing it to pay the total return on the S&P 500, while receiving a fixed rate, would achieve this objective. It would like to hold this position for one year, with payments to be made on the last day of March, June, September, and December. It enters into such a swap with Morgan Stanley (NYSE: MWD).

Specifically, the swap covers a notional principal of $100 million and calls for VAAPX to pay MWD the return on the S&P 500 Total Return Index and for MWD to pay VAAPX a fixed rate on the last day of March, June, September, and December for one year. MWD prices the swap at a fixed rate of 6.5 percent. The

---

[8] Currency swaps also have the element that the exchange rate is variable.

[9] Technically, there are interest rate swaps in which the floating rate is set at the end of the period, at which time the payment is made.

[10] In a currency swap, however, one does not know the exchange rate until the settlement date.

[11] In some kinds of interest rate swaps, the total return on a bond, which includes dividends and capital gains, is paid. This instrument is called a **total return swap** and is a common variety of a credit derivative.

[12] Some interest rate swaps also have a notional principal that changes.

fixed payments will be made using an actual day count/365 days convention. There are 90 days between 31 December and 31 March, 91 days between 31 March and 30 June, 92 days between 30 June and 30 September, and 92 days between 30 September and 31 December. Thus, the fixed payments will be

31 March: $100,000,000(0.065)(90/365) = $1,602,740

30 June: $100,000,000(0.065)(91/365) = $1,620,548

30 September: $100,000,000(0.065)(92/365) = $1,638,356

31 December: $100,000,000(0.065)(92/365) = $1,638,356

Exhibit 6 shows the cash flow stream to VAAPX.

Suppose that on the day the swap is initiated, 31 December, the S&P 500 Total Return Index is at 3,517.76. Now suppose that on 31 March, the index is at 3,579.12. The return on the index is

$$\frac{3,579.12}{3,517.76} - 1 = 0.0174$$

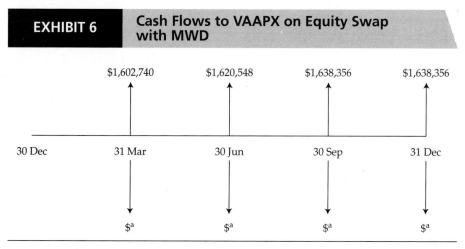

EXHIBIT 6 Cash Flows to VAAPX on Equity Swap with MWD

a Computed as $100,000,000R, where R is the return on the S&P 500 Total Return Index from the previous settlement date.

Thus, the return is 1.74 percent. The equity payment that VAAPX would make to MWD would be $100,000,000(0.0174) = $1,740,000.

Of course, this amount would not be known until 31 March, and only the difference between this amount and the fixed payment would be paid. Then on 31 March, the index value of 3,579.12 would be the base for the following period. Suppose that on 30 June, the index declines to 3,452.78. Then the return for the second quarter would be

$$\frac{3,452.78}{3,579.12} - 1 = -0.0353$$

Therefore, the loss is 3.53 percent, requiring a payment of $100,000,000(0.0353) = $3,530,000.

Because this amount represents a loss on the S&P 500, MWD would make a payment to VAAPX. In addition, MWD would also owe VAAPX the fixed payment of $1,620,548. It is as though VAAPX sold out of its position in stock, thereby avoiding the loss of about $3.5 million, and moved into a fixed-income position, thereby picking up a gain of about $1.6 million.

EXAMPLE 3

A mutual fund has arranged an equity swap with a dealer. The swap's notional principal is $100 million, and payments will be made semi-annually. The mutual fund agrees to pay the dealer the return on a small-cap stock index, and the dealer agrees to pay the mutual fund based on one of the two specifications given below. The small-cap index starts off at 1,805.20; six months later, it is at 1,796.15.

A. The dealer pays a fixed rate of 6.75 percent to the mutual fund, with payments made on the basis of 182 days in the period and 365 days in a year. Determine the first payment for both parties and, under the assumption of netting, determine the net payment and which party makes it.

B. The dealer pays the return on a large-cap index. The index starts off at 1155.14 and six months later is at 1148.91. Determine the first payment for both parties and, under the assumption of netting, determine the net payment and which party makes it.

Solution to A: The fixed payment is $100,000,000(0.0675)182/365 = $3,365,753
The equity payment is

$$\left(\frac{1796.15}{1805.20} - 1\right)\$100,000,000 = -\$501,329$$

Because the fund pays the equity return and the equity return is negative, the dealer must pay the equity return. The dealer also pays the fixed return, so the dealer makes both payments, which add up to $3,365,753 + $501,329 = $3,867,082. The net payment is $3,867,082, paid by the dealer to the mutual fund.

Solution to B: The large-cap equity payment is

$$\left(\frac{1148.91}{1155.14} - 1\right)\$100,000,000 = -\$539,329$$

The fund owes −$501,329, so the dealer owes the fund $501,329. The dealer owes −$539,329, so the fund owes the dealer $539,329. Therefore, the fund pays the dealer the net amount of $539,329 − $501,329 = $38,000.

Exhibit 7 illustrates what VAAPX has accomplished. It is important to note that the conversion of its equity assets into fixed income is not perfect. VAAPX does not hold a portfolio precisely equal to the S&P 500 Total Return Index. To the extent that VAAPX's portfolio generates a return that deviates from the index, some mismatching can occur, which can be a problem. As an alternative, VAAPX can request that MWD give it a swap based on the precise portfolio that VAAPX wishes to sell off. In that case, however, MWD would assess a charge by lowering the fixed rate it pays or raising the rate VAAPX pays to it.[13]

EXHIBIT 7	VAAPX's Conversion of an Equity Position into a Fixed-Income Position

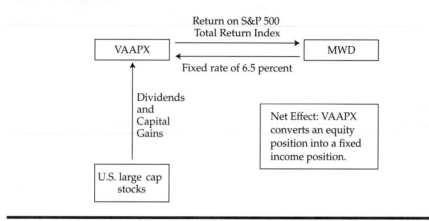

In our previous VAAPX example, the fund wanted to move some money out of a large-cap equity position and invest the proceeds at a fixed rate. Suppose instead that they do not want to move the proceeds into a fixed-rate investment. VAAPX could structure a swap to pay it a floating rate or the return on some other equity index. For example, an asset allocation from U.S. large-cap stocks to U.S. small-cap stocks could be accomplished by having MWD pay the return on the S&P 500 Small Cap 600 Index.

Suppose VAAPX wanted to move out of a position in U.S. stocks and into a position in U.K. large-cap stocks. It could structure the swap to have MWD pay it the return on the FTSE (Financial Times Stock Exchange) 100 Index. Note, however, that this index is based on the prices of U.K. stocks as quoted in pounds sterling. If VAAPX wanted the exposure in pounds—that is, it wanted the currency risk as well as the risk of the U.K. stock market—the payments from MWD to VAAPX would be made in pounds. VAAPX could, however, ask for the payments in dollars. In that case, MWD would hedge the currency risk and make payments in dollars.

Although our focus in this book is on currency, interest rate, and equity products, we shall take a very brief look at some other types of swaps.

3.4 Commodity and Other Types of Swaps

Just as currencies, interest rates, and equities can be used to structure swaps, so too can commodities and just about anything that has a random outcome and to which a corporation, financial institution, or even an individual is exposed.

---

[13] Note, however, that VAAPX is converting not its entire portfolio but simply a $100 million portion of it.

Commodity swaps are very commonly used. For example, airlines enter into swaps to hedge their future purchases of jet fuel. They agree to make fixed payments to a swap dealer on regularly scheduled dates and receive payments determined by the price of jet fuel. Gold mining companies use swaps to hedge future deliveries of gold. Other parties dealing in such commodities as natural gas and precious metals often use swaps to lock in prices for future purchases and sales. In addition, swaps can be based on non-storable commodities, like electricity and the weather. In the case of the weather, payments are made based on a measure of a particular weather factor, such as amounts of rain, snowfall, or weather-related damage.

SUMMARY

▶ Swaps are over-the-counter contracts in which two parties agree to pay a series of cash flows to each other. At least one series is floating or variable and related to an interest rate, exchange rate, equity price, or commodity price; the other can be fixed or floating. Swaps have zero value at the start and have payments made on scheduled payment or settlement dates and a final termination or expiration date. When swap payments are made in the same currency, the payments are usually netted. Swaps are subject to default on the part of either party.

▶ Swaps can be terminated by having one party pay the market value of the swap to the other party, by entering into a swap in which the variable payments offset, by selling the swap to another party, or by exercising a swaption to enter into an offsetting swap.

▶ In a currency swap, each party makes payments to the other in different currencies. A currency swap can have one party pay a fixed rate in one currency and the other pay a fixed rate in the other currency; have both pay a floating rate in their respective currencies; have the first party pay a fixed rate in one currency and the second party pay a floating rate in the other currency; or have the first party pay a floating rate in one currency and the second pay a fixed rate in the other currency. In currency swaps, the notional principal is usually exchanged at the beginning and at the end of the life of the swap, although this exchange is not mandatory.

▶ The payments on a currency swap are calculated by multiplying the notional principal by the fixed or floating interest rate times a day-count adjustment. This procedure is done in each currency, and the respective parties make their separate payments to each other. The payments are not netted.

▶ In a plain vanilla interest rate swap, one party makes payments at a fixed rate and the other makes payments at a floating rate, with no exchange of notional principal. A typical plain vanilla swap involves one party paying a fixed rate and the other paying a floating rate such as LIBOR. Swaps are often done by a party borrowing floating at a rate tied to LIBOR; that party then uses a pay-fixed, receive-floating swap to offset the risk of its exposure to LIBOR and effectively convert its loan to a fixed-rate loan.

▶ The payments on an interest rate swap are calculated by multiplying the notional principal by the fixed or floating interest rate times a day-count adjustment. The respective amounts are netted so that the party owing the greater amount makes a net payment to the other.

▶ The three types of equity swaps involve one party paying a fixed rate, a floating rate, or the return on another equity, while the other party pays an equity return. Therefore, an equity swap is a swap in which at least one party pays the return on a stock or stock index.

▶ The equity payment (or payments, if both sides of the swap are related to an equity return) on an equity swap is calculated by multiplying the return on the stock over the settlement period by the notional principal. If there is a fixed or floating payment, it is calculated in the same manner as in an interest rate swap. With payments in a single currency, the two sets of payments are netted.

PRACTICE PROBLEMS FOR READING 71

1. A U.S. company enters into a currency swap in which it pays a fixed rate of 5.5 percent in euros and the counterparty pays a fixed rate of 6.75 percent in dollars. The notional principals are $100 million and €116.5 million. Payments are made semiannually and on the basis of 30 days per month and 360 days per year.

   A. Calculate the initial exchange of payments that takes place at the beginning of the swap.

   B. Calculate the semiannual payments.

   C. Calculate the final exchange of payments that takes place at the end of the swap.

2. A British company enters into a currency swap in which it pays a fixed rate of 6 percent in dollars and the counterparty pays a fixed rate of 5 percent in pounds. The notional principals are £75 million and $105 million. Payments are made semiannually and on the basis of 30 days per month and 360 days per year.

   A. Calculate the initial exchange of payments that takes place at the beginning of the swap.

   B. Calculate the semiannual payments.

   C. Calculate the final exchange of payments that takes place at the end of the swap.

3. A U.S. company has entered into an interest rate swap with a dealer in which the notional principal is $50 million. The company will pay a floating rate of LIBOR and receive a fixed rate of 5.75 percent. Interest is paid semiannually, and the current LIBOR is 5.15 percent. Calculate the first payment and indicate which party pays which. Assume that floating-rate payments will be made on the basis of 180/360 and fixed-rate payments will be made on the basis of 180/365.

4. A German company that has issued floating-rate notes now believes that interest rates will rise. It decides to protect itself against this possibility by entering into an interest rate swap with a dealer. In this swap, the notional principal is €25 million and the company will pay a fixed rate of 5.5 percent and receive Euribor. The current Euribor is 5 percent. Calculate the first payment and indicate which party pays which. Assume that floating-rate payments will be made on the basis of 90/360 and fixed-rate payments will be made on the basis of 90/365.

5. An asset manager wishes to reduce his exposure to large-cap stocks and increase his exposure to small-cap stocks. He seeks to do so using an equity swap. He agrees to pay a dealer the return on a large-cap index, and the dealer agrees to pay the manager the return on a small-cap index. For each of the scenarios listed below, calculate the first overall payment and indicate which party makes the payment. Assume that payments are made semiannually. The notional principal is $100 million.

   A. The value of the small-cap index starts off at 689.40, and the large-cap index starts at 1130.20. In six months, the small-cap index is at 625.60 and the large-cap index is at 1251.83.

   B. The value of the small-cap index starts off at 689.40 and the large-cap index starts at 1130.20. In six months, the small-cap index is at 703.23 and the large-cap index is at 1143.56.

6. An asset manager wishes to reduce her exposure to small-cap stocks and increase her exposure to fixed-income securities. She seeks to do so using an equity swap. She agrees to pay a dealer the return on a small-cap index and the dealer agrees to pay the manager a fixed rate of 5.5 percent. For each of the scenarios listed below, calculate the overall payment six months later and indicate which party makes the payment. Assume that payments are made semiannually (180 days per period) and there are 365 days in each year. The notional principal is $50 million.

   A. The value of the small-cap index starts off at 234.10 and six months later is at 238.41.

   B. The value of the small-cap index starts off at 234.10 and six months later is at 241.27.

7. An asset manager wishes to reduce his exposure to fixed-income securities and increase his exposure to large-cap stocks. He seeks to do so using an equity swap. He agrees to pay a dealer a fixed rate of 4.5 percent, and the dealer agrees to pay the manager the return on a large-cap index. For each of the scenarios listed below, calculate the overall payment six months later and indicate which party makes it. Assume that payments are made semiannually (180 days per period) and there are 365 days in a year. The notional principal is $25 million.

   A. The value of the large-cap index starts off at 578.50 and six months later is at 622.54.

   B. The value of the large-cap index starts off at 578.50 and six months later is at 581.35.

8. The party agreeing to make the fixed-rate payment might also be required to make the variable payment in:

   A. an equity swap but not an interest rate swap.

   B. an interest rate swap but not an equity swap.

   C. both an equity swap and an interest rate swap.

9. The formula for calculating the payoff at expiration of a forward rate agreement (FRA) is:

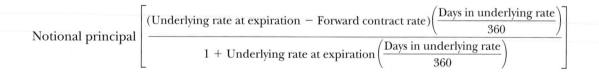

$$\text{Notional principal}\left[\frac{(\text{Underlying rate at expiration} - \text{Forward contract rate})\left(\dfrac{\text{Days in underlying rate}}{360}\right)}{1 + \text{Underlying rate at expiration}\left(\dfrac{\text{Days in underlying rate}}{360}\right)}\right]$$

   Use the above formula to solve for the payment at expiration for an investor who went long a 3 × 9 FRA with a notional principal of $10,000,000 where the 180-day LIBOR rate at expiration is 4.80 percent and the forward contract rate was set at 5.20 percent.

   A. −$588,235.

   B. −$19,531.

   C. $19,493.

10. Agrawal Telecom is considering issuing $10,000,000 of 6.75% fixed coupon bonds to finance an expansion. Alternatively, Agrawal could borrow the funds in the Eurodollar market using a series of six-month LIBOR contracts. A swap contract matching the maturity of the 6.75% coupon bonds is available. The swap uses six-month LIBOR as the floating rate component. Identify the interest rate swap that Agrawal should use to convert the Eurodollar borrowing to the equivalent of issuing fixed income bonds.

   A. Agrawal would use a pay fixed, receive floating interest rate swap.

   B. Agrawal would use a pay floating, receive fixed interest rate swap.

   C. Agrawal would use a total return equity payer swaption to evaluate the two borrowing options.

11. Determine the upcoming payments on a swap with a notional principal of $5,000,000 in which the fixed-rate payer makes semi-annual fixed payments of 8% and the counterparty makes floating rate payments at Euribor. The Euribor rate at the last settlement period was 7.25%.

   The fixed rate payments are made on the basis of 180 days in the settlement period and 365 days in a year. The floating rate payments use a 180/360 day convention.

   A. The net payment is $16,010 from the fixed-rate payer to the floating rate payer.

   B. The net payment is $18,750 from the fixed rate payer to the floating rate payer.

   C. The net payment is $18,750 from the floating rate payer to the fixed rate payer.

12. A portfolio manager entered into a swap with a dealer. The swap's notional principal is $100 million, payments are to be made semiannually, and the swap allows netting of payments. The dealer agrees to pay a fixed annual rate of 4 percent while the asset manager agrees to pay the return on a stock index. The index value at initiation of the swap is 280. If the value of the stock index six months after initiation of the swap is 250, the payment from the dealer to the asset manager would be *closest* to:

   A. $2 million.

   B. $9 million.

   C. $13 million.

SOLUTIONS FOR READING 71

1. A. The payments at the beginning of the swap are as follows:
The U.S. company (domestic party) pays the counterparty $100 million.
The counterparty pays the U.S. company €116.5 million.

B. The semiannual payments are as follows:
The U.S. company (domestic party) pays the counterparty
€116,500,000(0.055)(180/360) = €3,203,750.
The counterparty pays the U.S. company $100,000,000(0.0675) ×
(180/360) = $3,375,000.

C. The payments at the end of the swap are as follows:
The U.S. company (domestic party) pays the counterparty
€116.5 million + €3,203,750.
The counterparty pays the U.S. company $100 million + $3,375,000.

2. A. The payments at the beginning of the swap are as follows:
The British company (domestic party) pays the counterparty £75 million.
The counterparty pays the British company $105 million.

B. The semiannual payments are as follows:
The British company (domestic party) pays the counterparty
$105,000,000(0.06)(180/360) = $3,150,000.
The counterparty pays the British company £75,000,000(0.05) ×
(180/360) = £1,875,000.

C. The payments at the end of the swap are as follows:
The British company (domestic party) pays the counterparty
$105 million + $3,150,000.
The counterparty pays the British company £75 million + £1,875,000.

3. The fixed payments are $50,000,000(0.0575)(180/365) = $1,417,808.
The floating payments are $50,000,000(0.0515)(180/360) = $1,287,500.
The net payment is $130,308, made by the party paying fixed—that is, the
dealer pays the company.

4. The fixed payments are €25,000,000(0.055)(90/365) = €339,041.
The floating payments are €25,000,000(0.05)(90/360) = €312,500.
The net payment is €26,541, made by the party paying fixed—that is, the
company pays the dealer.

5. A. The small-cap equity payment is $\left(\dfrac{625.60}{689.40} - 1\right)(100,000,000) =$
$-\$9,254,424$.
The asset manager owes $9,254,424 to the dealer.

The large-cap equity payment is $\left(\dfrac{1251.83}{1130.20} - 1\right)(100,000,000) =$
$10,761,812.
The asset manager owes this amount to the dealer.
The overall payment made by the asset manager to the dealer is
$9,254,424 + $10,761,812 = $20,016,236.

B. The small-cap equity payment is $\left(\dfrac{703.23}{689.40} - 1\right)(100,000,000) =$
$2,006,092.
The dealer owes the asset manager this amount.

The large-cap equity payment is $\left(\dfrac{1143.56}{1130.20} - 1\right)(100,000,000) =$
$1,182,092.

Solutions to 1–7 taken from *Analysis of Derivatives for the Chartered Financial Analyst® Program*, by Don M. Chance, CFA. Copyright © 2003 by AIMR. Reprinted with permission. All other solutions copyright © CFA Institute.

The asset manager owes this amount to the dealer.
The overall payment made by the dealer to the asset manager is
$2,006,092 − $1,182,092 = $824,000.

6. A. The small-cap equity payment is $\left(\dfrac{238.41}{234.10} - 1\right)(50,000,000) =$
$920,547.
The asset manager owes the dealer this amount.
The fixed interest payment is $(50,000,000)(0.055)(180/365) =$
$1,356,164.
The dealer owes this amount to the asset manager.
So the dealer pays to the asset manager $1,356,164 − $920,547 =
$435,617.

    B. The small-cap equity payment is $\left(\dfrac{241.27}{234.10} - 1\right)(50,000,000) =$
$1,531,397.
The asset manager owes the dealer this amount.
The fixed interest payment is $(50,000,000)(0.055)(180/365) =$
$1,356,164.
The dealer owes this amount to the asset manager.
So the asset manager pays to the dealer $1,531,397 − $1,356,164 =
$175,233.

7. A. The large-cap equity payment is $\left(\dfrac{622.54}{578.50} - 1\right)(25,000,000) =$
$1,903,198.
The dealer owes this amount to the asset manager.
The fixed interest payment is $(25,000,000)(0.045)(180/365) =$
$554,795.
The asset manager owes this amount to the dealer.
So the dealer pays to the asset manager $1,903,198 − $554,795 =
$1,348,403.

    B. The large-cap equity payment is $\left(\dfrac{581.35}{578.50} - 1\right)(25,000,000) =$
$123,163.

The dealer owes this amount to the asset manager.
The fixed interest payment is $(25,000,000)(0.045)(180/365) =$
$554,795.
The asset manager owes this amount to the dealer.
So the asset manager pays to the dealer $554,795 − $123,163 =
$431,632.

8. A is correct. If the equity referenced in the equity swap shows a negative
return for a settlement date, the "receive equity, pay fixed" party would pay
both a variable payment based on the negative equity return and the fixed
rate payment. Given that interest rates will not go negative, an analogous
situation cannot occur in interest rate swaps.

9. B is correct. A 3 × 9 FRA uses the 180-day LIBOR contract as the
underlying rate. Solve $(0.048 − 0.052) \times (180/360) / [1 + 0.048 \times$
$(180/360)] = −0.001953125$. Multiply by $10,000,000. The answer is
approximately −$19,531.

10. A is correct. Agrawal would owe floating rate interest on the LIBOR loans.
The "receive floating" part of the swap would offset those payments, while
the "pay-fixed" side of the swap resembles the fixed coupon payments on
the 6.75 percent coupon bonds.

11. A is correct. The calculation is $5,000,000 × 0.08 × (180/365) − $5,000,000 × 0.0725 × (180/360) = $16,010.

12. C is correct. The loss on the stock index means that the dealer must also pay the negative amount to the asset manager in addition to the fixed rate on the notional principal. The amount that the dealer would pay is approximately $13 million:

($100,000,000)(0.04) / 2 = $2,000,000 for the fixed payment

The negative return on the stock index computed as follows is (250/280) − 1 = −0.1071, for a dollar payment of −0.1071(100,000,000) = $10,714,286 for the stock index.

The asset manager must pay roughly $2 million plus $ 11 million.

RISK MANAGEMENT APPLICATIONS OF OPTION STRATEGIES

by Don M. Chance, CFA

LEARNING OUTCOMES

The candidate should be able to:	Mastery
a. determine the value at expiration, profit, maximum profit, maximum loss, breakeven underlying price at expiration, and general shape of the graph of the strategies of buying and selling calls and puts, and indicate the market outlook of investors using these strategies;	☐
b. determine the value at expiration, profit, maximum profit, maximum loss, breakeven underlying price at expiration, and general shape of the graph of a covered call strategy and a protective put strategy, and explain the risk management application of each strategy.	☐

INTRODUCTION 1

In a previous reading we examined strategies that employ forward and futures contracts. Recall that forward and futures contracts have linear payoffs and do not require an initial outlay. Options, on the other hand, have nonlinear payoffs and require the payment of cash up front. By having nonlinear payoffs, options permit their users to benefit from movements in the underlying in one direction and to not be harmed by movements in the other direction. In many respects, they offer the best of all worlds, a chance to profit if expectations are realized with minimal harm if expectations turn out to be wrong. The price for this opportunity is the cash outlay required to establish the position. From the standpoint of the holder of the short position, options can lead to extremely large losses. Hence, sellers of options must be well compensated in the form of an adequate up-front premium and must skillfully manage the risk they assume.

Analysis of Derivatives for the Chartered Financial Analyst® Program, by Don M. Chance, CFA. Copyright © 2003 by AIMR. Reprinted with permission.

In this reading, we look at option strategies that are typically used in equity investing, which include standard strategies involving single options and strategies that combine options with the underlying.

Let us begin by reviewing the necessary notation. These symbols are the same ones we have previously used. First recall that time 0 is the time at which the strategy is initiated and time T is the time the option expires, stated as a fraction of a year. Accordingly, the amount of time until expiration is simply $T - 0 = T$, which is (Days to expiration)/365. The other symbols are

c_0, c_T = price of the call option at time 0 and time T
p_0, p_T = price of the put option at time 0 and time T[1]
X = exercise price
S_0, S_T = price of the underlying at time 0 and time T
V_0, V_T = value of the position at time 0 and time T
Π = profit from the transaction: $V_T - V_0$
r = risk-free rate

Some additional notation will be introduced when necessary.

Note that we are going to measure the profit from an option transaction, which is simply the final value of the transaction minus the initial value of the transaction. Profit does not take into account the time value of money or the risk. Although a focus on profit is not completely satisfactory from a theoretical point of view, it is nonetheless instructive, simple, and a common approach to examining options. Our primary objective here is to obtain a general picture of the manner in which option strategies perform. With that in mind, discussing profit offers probably the best trade-off in terms of gaining the necessary knowledge with a minimum of complexity.

In this reading, we assume that the option user has a view regarding potential movements of the underlying. In most cases that view is a prediction of the direction of the underlying, but in some cases it is a prediction of the volatility of the underlying. In all cases, we assume this view is specified over a horizon that corresponds to the option's life or that the option expiration can be tailored to the horizon date. Hence, for the most part, these options should be considered customized, over-the-counter options.[2] Every interest rate option is a customized option.

Because the option expiration corresponds to the horizon date for which a particular view is held, there is no reason to use American options. Accordingly, all

---

[1] As in the reading on option markets and contracts, lower case indicates European options, and upper case indicates American options. In this reading, all options are European.

[2] If the options discussed were exchange-listed options, it would not significantly alter the material in this reading.

options in this reading are European options. Moreover, we shall not consider terminating the strategy early. Putting an option in place and closing the position prior to expiration is certainly a legitimate strategy. It could reflect the arrival of new information over the holding period, but it requires an understanding of more complex issues, such as valuation of the option and the rate at which the option loses its time value. Thus, we shall examine the outcome of a particular strategy over a range of possible values of the underlying only on the expiration day.

OPTION STRATEGIES FOR EQUITY PORTFOLIOS   2

Many typical illustrations of option strategies use individual stocks, but we shall use options on a stock index, the Nasdaq 100, referred to simply as the Nasdaq. We shall assume that in addition to buying and selling options on the Nasdaq, we can also buy the index, either through construction of the portfolio itself, through an index mutual fund, or an exchange-traded fund.[3] We shall simply refer to this instrument as a stock. We are given the following numerical data:

$S_0 = 2000$, value of the Nasdaq 100 when the strategy is initiated
$T = 0.0833$, the time to expiration (one month = 1/12)

The options available will be the following:[4]

Exercise Price	Call Price	Put Price
1950	108.43	56.01
2000	81.75	79.25
2050	59.98	107.39

Let us start by examining an initial strategy that is the simplest of all: to buy or sell short the underlying. Panel A of Exhibit 1 illustrates the profit from the transaction of buying a share of stock. We see the obvious result that if you buy the stock and it goes up, you make a profit; if it goes down, you incur a loss. Panel B shows the case of selling short the stock. Recall that this strategy involves borrowing the shares from a broker, selling them at the current price, and then buying them back at a later date. In this case, if you sell short the stock and it goes down, you make a profit. Conversely, if it goes up, you incur a loss. Now we shall move on to strategies involving options, but we shall use the stock strategies again when we combine options with stock.

In this section we examine option strategies in the context of their use in equity portfolios. Although these strategies are perfectly applicable for fixed-income portfolios, corporate borrowing scenarios, or even commodity risk

---

[3] Exchange-traded shares on the Nasdaq 100 are called Nasdaq 100 Trust Shares and QQQs, for their ticker symbol. They are commonly referred to as Qubes, trade on the Amex, and are the most active exchange-traded fund and often the most actively traded of all securities. Options on the Nasdaq 100 are among the most actively traded as well.

[4] These values were obtained using the Black–Scholes–Merton model. By using this model, we know we are working with reasonable values that do not permit arbitrage opportunities.

EXHIBIT 1	Simple Stock Strategies

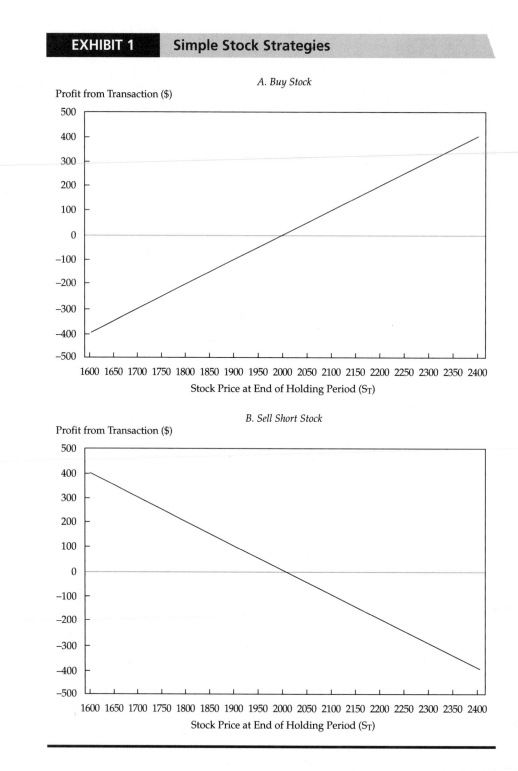

A. Buy Stock

Profit from Transaction ($)

Stock Price at End of Holding Period (S_T)

B. Sell Short Stock

Profit from Transaction ($)

Stock Price at End of Holding Period (S_T)

management situations, they are generally more easily explained and understood in the context of investing in equities or equity indices.

To analyze an equity option strategy, we first assume that we establish the position at the current price. We then determine the value of the option at expiration for a specific value of the index at expiration. We calculate the profit as the value at expiration minus the current price. We then generate a graph to illustrate the value at expiration and profit for a range of index values at expiration. Although the underlying is a stock index, we shall just refer to it as the underlying to keep things as general as possible. We begin by examining the most fundamental option transactions, long and short positions in calls and puts.

2.1 Standard Long and Short Positions

2.1.1 Calls

Consider the purchase of a call option at the price c_0. The value at expiration, c_T, is $c_T = \max(0, S_T - X)$. Broken down into parts,

$$c_T = 0 \qquad \text{if } S_T \leq X$$
$$c_T = S_T - X \qquad \text{if } S_T > X$$

The profit is obtained by subtracting the option premium, which is paid to purchase the option, from the option value at expiration, $\Pi = c_T - c_0$. Broken down into parts,

$$\Pi = -c_0 \qquad \text{if } S_T \leq X$$
$$\Pi = S_T - X - c_0 \qquad \text{if } S_T > X$$

Now consider this example. We buy the call with the exercise price of 2000 for 81.75. Consider values of the index at expiration of 1900 and 2100. For $S_T = 1900$,

$$c_T = \max(0, 1900 - 2000) = 0$$
$$\Pi = 0 - 81.75 = -81.75$$

For $S_T = 2100$,

$$c_T = \max(0, 2100 - 2000) = 100$$
$$\Pi = 100 - 81.75 = 18.25$$

Exhibit 2 illustrates the value at expiration and profit when S_T, the underlying price at expiration, ranges from 1600 to 2400. We see that buying a call results in a limited loss of the premium, 81.75. For an index value at expiration greater than the exercise price of 2000, the value and profit move up one-for-one with the index value, and there is no upper limit.

It is important to identify the breakeven index value at expiration. Recall that the formula for the profit is $\Pi = \max(0, S_T - X) - c_0$. We would like to know the value of S_T for which $\Pi = 0$. We shall call that value S_T^*. It would be nice to be able to solve $\Pi = \max(0, S_T^* - X) - c_0 = 0$ for S_T^*, but that is not directly possible. Instead, we observe that there are two ranges of outcomes, one in which $\Pi = S_T^* - X - c_0$ for $S_T^* > X$, the case of the option expiring in-the-money, and the other in which $\Pi = -c_0$ for $S_T \leq X$, the case of the option expiring out-of-the-money. It is obvious from the equation and by observing Exhibit 2 that in the latter case, there is no possibility of breaking even. In the former case, we see that we can solve for S_T^*. Setting $\Pi = S_T^* - X - c_0 = 0$, we obtain $S_T^* = X + c_0$.

Thus, the breakeven is the exercise price plus the option premium. This result should be intuitive: The value of the underlying at expiration must exceed the exercise price by the amount of the premium to recover the cost of the premium. In this problem, the breakeven is $S_T^* = 2000 + 81.75 = 2081.75$. Observe in Exhibit 2 that the profit line crosses the axis at this value.

In summarizing the strategy, we have the following results for the option buyer:

$c_T = \max(0, S_T - X)$
Value at expiration $= c_T$
Profit: $\Pi = c_T - c_0$
Maximum profit $= \infty$
Maximum loss $= c_0$
Breakeven: $S_T^* = X + c_0$

EXHIBIT 2   **Buy Call**

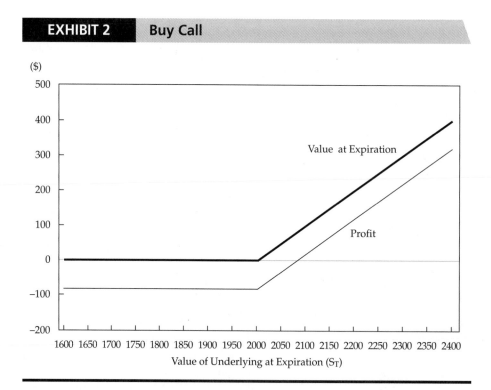

Call options entice naive speculators, but it is important to consider the *likely* gains and losses more than the *potential* gains and losses. For example, in this case, the underlying must go up by about 4.1 percent in one month to cover the cost of the call. This increase equates to an annual rate of almost 50 percent and is an unreasonable expectation by almost any standard. If the underlying does not move at all, the loss is 100 percent of the premium.

For the seller of the call, the results are just the opposite. The sum of the positions of the seller and buyer is zero. Hence, we can take the value and profit results for the buyer and change the signs. The results for the maximum profit and maximum loss are changed accordingly, and the breakeven is the same. Hence, for the option seller,

$c_T = \max(0, S_T - X)$

Value at expiration $= -c_T$

Profit: $\Pi = -c_T + c_0$

Maximum profit $= c_0$

Maximum loss $= \infty$

Breakeven: $S_T^* = X + c_0$

Exhibit 3 shows the results for the seller of the call. Note that the value and profit have a fixed maximum. The worst case is an infinite loss. Just as there is no upper limit to the buyer's potential gain, there is no upper limit to how much the seller can lose.

Call options are purchased by investors who are bullish. We now turn to put options, which are purchased by investors who are bearish.

EXHIBIT 3   Sell Call

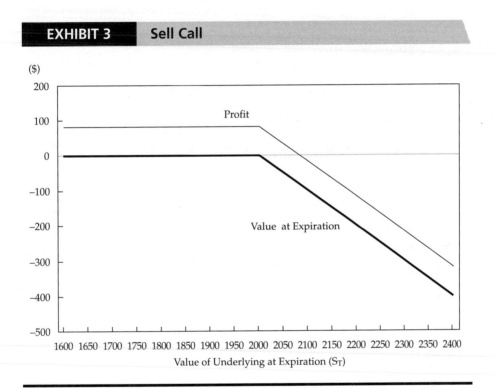

Value of Underlying at Expiration (S_T)

EXAMPLE 1

Consider a call option selling for $7 in which the exercise price is $100 and the price of the underlying is $98.

A. Determine the value at expiration and the profit for a buyer under the following outcomes:

  i. The price of the underlying at expiration is $102.

  ii. The price of the underlying at expiration is $94.

B. Determine the value at expiration and the profit for a seller under the following outcomes:

    i. The price of the underlying at expiration is $91.

    ii. The price of the underlying at expiration is $101.

C. Determine the following:

    i. The maximum profit to the buyer (maximum loss to the seller).

    ii. The maximum loss to the buyer (maximum profit to the seller).

D. Determine the breakeven price of the underlying at expiration.

Solution to A: Call buyer

    i. Value at expiration = $c_T = \max(0, S_T - X) = \max(0, 102 - 100) = 2$
$\Pi = c_T - c_0 = 2 - 7 = -5$

    ii. Value at expiration = $c_T = \max(0, S_T - X) = \max(0, 94 - 100) = 0$
$\Pi = c_T - c_0 = 0 - 7 = -7$

Solution to B: Call seller

    i. Value at expiration = $-c_T = -\max(0, S_T - X) = -\max(0, 91 - 100) = 0$
$\Pi = -c_T + c_0 = -0 + 7 = 7$

    ii. Value at expiration = $-c_T = -\max(0, S_T - X) = -\max(0, 101 - 100) = -1$
$\Pi = -c_T + c_0 = -1 + 7 = 6$

Solution to C: Maximum and minimum

    i. Maximum profit to buyer (loss to seller) = ∞

    ii. Maximum loss to buyer (profit to seller) = $c_0 = 7$

Solution to D: $S_T^* = X + c_0 = 100 + 7 = 107$

2.1.2 Puts

The value of a put at expiration is $p_T = \max(0, X - S_T)$. Broken down into parts,

$$p_T = X - S \qquad \text{if } S_T < X$$
$$p_T = 0 \qquad \text{if } S_T \geq X$$

The profit is obtained by subtracting the premium on the put from the value at expiration:

$$\Pi = p_T - p_0$$

Broken down into parts,

$$\Pi = X - S_T - p_0 \qquad \text{if } S_T < X$$
$$\Pi = -p_0 \qquad \text{if } S_T \geq X$$

For our example and outcomes of S_T = 1900 and 2100, the results are as follows:

S_T = 1900:

$$p_T = \max(0, 2000 - 1900) = 100$$
$$\Pi = 100 - 79.25 = 20.75$$

S_T = 2100:

$$p_T = \max(0, 2000 - 2100) = 0$$
$$\Pi = 0 - 79.25 = -79.25$$

These results are shown in Exhibit 4. We see that the put has a maximum value and profit and a limited loss, the latter of which is the premium. The maximum value is obtained when the underlying goes to zero.[5] In that case, $p_T = X$. So the maximum profit is $X - p_0$. Here that will be $2000 - 79.25 = 1920.75$.

The breakeven is found by breaking up the profit equation into its parts, $\Pi = X - S_T - p_0$ for $S_T < X$ and $\Pi = -p_0$ for $S_T \geq X$. In the latter case, there is no possibility of breaking even. It refers to the range over which the entire premium is lost. In the former case, we denote the breakeven index value as S_T^*, set the equation to zero, and solve for S_T^* to obtain $S_T^* = X - p_0$. In our example, the breakeven is $S_T^* = 2000 - 79.25 = 1920.75$.

EXHIBIT 4	Buy Put

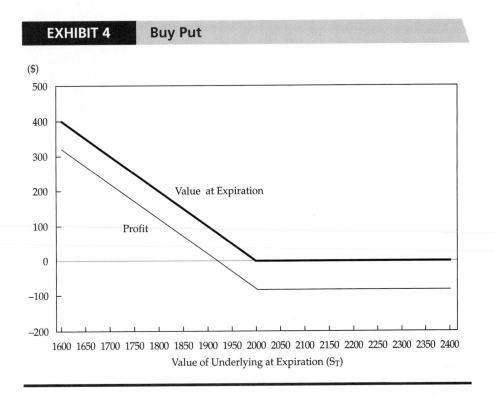

---

[5] The maximum value and profit are not visible on the graph because we do not show S_T all the way down to zero.

In summary, for the strategy of buying a put we have

$p_T = \max(0, X - S_T)$
Value at expiration = p_T
Profit: $\Pi = p_T - p_0$
Maximum profit = $X - p_0$
Maximum loss = p_0
Breakeven: $S_T^* = X - p_0$

Now consider the *likely* outcomes for the holder of the put. In this case, the underlying must move down by almost 4 percent in one month to cover the premium. One would hardly ever expect the underlying to move down at an annual rate of almost 50 percent. Moreover, if the underlying does not move downward at all (a likely outcome given the positive expected return on most assets), the loss is 100 percent of the premium.

For the sale of a put, we simply change the sign on the value at expiration and profit. The maximum profit for the buyer becomes the maximum loss for the seller and the maximum loss for the buyer becomes the maximum profit for the seller. The breakeven for the seller is the same as for the buyer. So, for the seller,

$p_T = \max(0, X - S_T)$
Value at expiration = $-p_T$
Profit: $\Pi = -p_T + p_0$
Maximum profit = p_0
Maximum loss = $X - p_0$
Breakeven: $S_T^* = X - p_0$

Exhibit 5 graphs the value at expiration and the profit for this transaction.

EXHIBIT 5   **Sell Put**

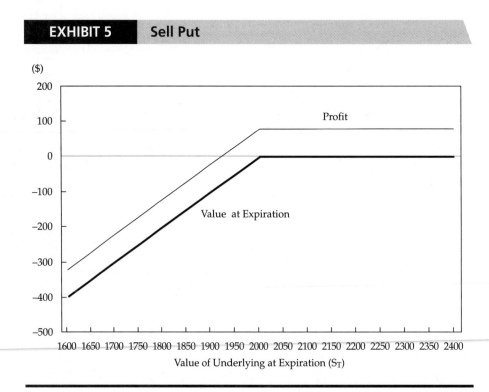

EXAMPLE 2

Consider a put option selling for $4 in which the exercise price is $60 and the price of the underlying is $62.

A. Determine the value at expiration and the profit for a buyer under the following outcomes:
   i. The price of the underlying at expiration is $62.
   ii. The price of the underlying at expiration is $55.

B. Determine the value at expiration and the profit for a seller under the following outcomes:
   i. The price of the underlying at expiration is $51.
   ii. The price of the underlying at expiration is $68.

C. Determine the following:
   i. The maximum profit to the buyer (maximum loss to the seller).
   ii. The maximum loss to the buyer (maximum profit to the seller).

D. Determine the breakeven price of the underlying at expiration.

Solution to A: Put buyer
   i. Value at expiration $= p_T = \max(0, X - S_T) = \max(0, 60 - 62) = 0$
      $\Pi = p_T - p_0 = 0 - 4 = -4$
   ii. Value at expiration $= p_T = \max(0, X - S_T) = \max(0, 60 - 55) = 5$
      $\Pi = p_T - p_0 = 5 - 4 = 1$

Solution to B: Put seller
   i. Value at expiration $= -p_T = -\max(0, X - S_T) = -\max(0, 60 - 51) = -9$
      $\Pi = -p_T + p_0 = -9 + 4 = -5$
   ii. Value at expiration $= -p_T = -\max(0, X - S_T) = -\max(0, 60 - 68) = 0$
      $\Pi = -p_T + p_0 = 0 + 4 = 4$

Solution to C: Maximum and minimum
   i. Maximum profit to buyer (loss to seller) $= X - p_0 = 60 - 4 = 56$
   ii. Maximum loss to buyer (profit to seller) $= p_0 = 4$

Solution to D: $S_T^* = X - p_0 = 60 - 4 = 56$

It may be surprising to find that we have now covered all of the information we need to examine all of the other option strategies. We need to learn only a few basic facts. We must know the formula for the value at expiration of a call and a put. Then we need to know how to calculate the profit for the purchase of a call and a put, but that calculation is simple: the value at expiration minus the initial value. If we know these results, we can calculate the value at expiration of the option and the profit for any value of the underlying at expiration. If we can do that, we can graph the results for a range of possible values of the underlying at expiration. Because graphing can take a long time, however, it is probably helpful to learn the basic shapes of the value and profit graphs for calls and puts. Knowing the profit equation and the shapes of the graphs, it is easy to determine the maximum profit and maximum loss. The breakeven can be determined by setting the profit equation to zero for the case in which the profit equation contains S_T. Once we have these results for the long call and put, it is an easy matter to turn them around and obtain the results for the short call and put. Therefore, little if any memorization is required. From there, we can go on to strategies that combine an option with another option and combine options with the underlying.

2.2 Risk Management Strategies with Options and the Underlying

In this section, we examine two of the most widely used option strategies, particularly for holders of the underlying. One way to reduce exposure without selling the underlying is to sell a call on the underlying; the other way is to buy a put.

2.2.1 Covered Calls

A **covered call** is a relatively conservative strategy, but it is also one of the most misunderstood strategies. A covered call is a position in which you own the underlying and sell a call. The value of the position at expiration is easily found as the value of the underlying plus the value of the short call:

$$V_T = S_T - \max(0, S_T - X)$$

Therefore,

$$V_T = S_T \qquad\qquad \text{if } S_T \leq X$$
$$V_T = S_T - (S_T - X) = X \qquad \text{if } S_T > X$$

We obtain the profit for the covered call by computing the change in the value of the position, $V_T - V_0$. First recognize that V_0, the value of the position at the start of the contract, is the initial value of the underlying minus the call premium. We are long the underlying and short the call, so we must subtract the call premium that was received from the sale of the call. The initial investment in the position is what we pay for the underlying less what we receive for the call. Hence, $V_0 = S_0 - c_0$. The profit is thus

$$\Pi = S_T - \max(0, S_T - X) - (S_0 - c_0)$$
$$= S_T - S_0 - \max(0, S_T - X) + c_0$$

With the equation written in this manner, we see that the profit for the covered call is simply the profit from buying the underlying, $S_T - S_0$, plus the profit from selling the call, $-\max(0, S_T - X) + c_0$. Breaking it down into ranges,

$$\Pi = S_T - S_0 + c_0 \qquad\qquad\qquad \text{if } S_T \leq X$$
$$\Pi = S_T - S_0 - (S_T - X) + c_0 = X - S_0 + c_0 \qquad \text{if } S_T > X$$

In our example, $S_0 = 2000$. In this section we shall use a call option with the exercise price of 2050. Thus $X = 2050$, and the premium, c_0, is 59.98. Let us now examine two outcomes: $S_T = 2100$ and $S_T = 1900$. The value at expiration when $S_T = 2100$ is $V_T = 2100 - (2100 - 2050) = 2050$, and when $S_T = 1900$, the value of the position is $V_T = 1900$.

In the first case, we hold the underlying worth 2100 but are short a call worth 50. Thus, the net value is 2050. In the second case, we hold the underlying worth 1900 and the option expires out-of-the-money.

In the first case, $S_T = 2100$, the profit is $\Pi = 2050 - 2000 + 59.98 = 109.98$. In the second case, $S_T = 1900$, the profit is $\Pi = 1900 - 2000 + 59.98 = -40.02$. These results are graphed for a range of values of S_T in Exhibit 6. Note that for all values of S_T greater than 2050, the value and profit are maximized. Thus, 2050 is the maximum value and 109.98 is the maximum profit.[6]

As evident in Exhibit 6 and the profit equations, the maximum loss would occur when S_T is zero. Hence, the profit would be $S_T - S_0 + c_0$. The profit is $-S_0 + c_0$ when $S_T = 0$. This means that the maximum loss is $S_0 - c_0$. In this example, $-S_0 + c_0$ is $-2000 + 59.98 = -1940.02$. Intuitively, this would mean that you purchased the underlying for 2000 and sold the call for 59.98. The underlying value went to zero, resulting in a loss of 2000, but the call expired with no value, so the gain from the option is the option premium. The total loss is 1940.02.

EXHIBIT 6	Covered Call (Buy Underlying, Sell Call)

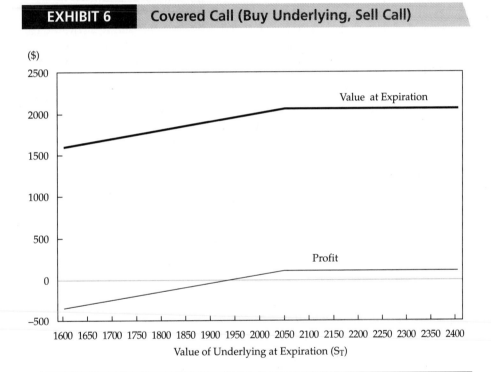

The breakeven underlying price is found by examining the profit equations and focusing on the equation that contains S_T. In equation form, $\Pi = S_T - S_0 + c_0$ when $S_T \leq X$. We let S_T^* denote the breakeven value of S_T, set the equation to zero, and solve for S_T^* to obtain $S_T^* = S_0 - c_0$. The breakeven and the maximum loss are identical. In this example, the breakeven is $S_T^* = 2000 - 59.98 = 1940.02$, which is seen in Exhibit 6.

---

[6] Note in Exhibit 6 that there is a large gap between the value at expiration and profit, especially compared with the graphs of buying and selling calls and puts. This difference occurs because a covered call is mostly a position in the underlying asset. The initial value of the asset, S_0, accounts for most of the difference in the two lines. Note also that because of the put–call parity relationship we covered in the reading on option markets and contracts, a covered call looks very similar to a short put.

To summarize the covered call, we have the following:

Value at expiration: $V_T = S_T - \max(0, S_T - X)$
Profit: $\Pi = V_T - S_0 + c_0$
Maximum profit $= X - S_0 + c_0$
Maximum loss $= S_0 - c_0$
Breakeven: $S_T^* = S_0 - c_0$

Because of the importance and widespread use of covered calls, it is worthwhile to discuss this strategy briefly to dispel some misunderstandings. First of all, some investors who do not believe in using options fail to see that selling a call on a position in the underlying reduces the risk of that position. Options do not automatically increase risk. The option part of this strategy alone, viewed in isolation, seems an extremely risky strategy. We noted in Section 2.1.1 that selling a call without owning the stock exposes the investor to unlimited loss potential. But selling a covered call—adding a short call to a long position in a stock—reduces the overall risk. Thus, any investor who holds a stock cannot say he is too conservative to use options.

Following on that theme, however, one should also view selling a covered call as a strategy that reduces not only the risk but also the expected return compared with simply holding the underlying. Hence, one should not expect to make a lot of money writing calls on the underlying. It should be apparent that in fact the covered call writer could miss out on significant gains in a strong bull market. The compensation for this willingness to give up potential upside gains, however, is that in a bear market the losses on the underlying will be cushioned by the option premium.

It may be disconcerting to some investors to look at the profit profile of a covered call. The immediate response is to think that no one in their right mind would invest in a strategy that has significant downside risk but a limited upside. Just owning the underlying has significant downside risk, but at least there is an upside. But it is important to note that the visual depiction of the strategy, as in Exhibit 6, does not tell the whole story. It says nothing about the likelihood of certain outcomes occurring.

For example, consider the covered call example we looked at here. The underlying starts off at 2000. The maximum profit occurs when the option expires with the underlying at 2050 or above, an increase of 2.5 percent over the life of the option. We noted that this option has a one-month life. Thus, the underlying would have to increase at an approximate annual rate of at least $2.5\%(12) = 30\%$ for the covered call writer to forgo all of the upside gain. There are not many stocks, indices, or other assets in which an investor would expect the equivalent of an annual move of at least 30 percent. Such movements obviously do occur from time to time, but they are not common. Thus, covered call writers do not often give up large gains.

But suppose the underlying did move to 2050 or higher. As we previously showed, the value of the position would be 2050. Because the initial value of the position is $2000 - 59.98 = 1940.02$, the rate of return would be 5.7 percent for one month. Hence, the maximum return is still outstanding by almost anyone's standards.[7]

Many investors believe that the initial value of a covered call should not include the value of the underlying if the underlying had been previously pur-

_____

[7] Of course, we are not saying that the performance reflects a positive alpha. We are saying only that the upside performance given up reflects improbably high returns, and therefore the limits on the upside potential are not too restrictive.

chased. Suppose, for example, that this asset, currently worth 2000, had been bought several months ago at 1900. It is tempting to ignore the current value of the underlying; there is no current outlay. This view, however, misses the notion of opportunity cost. If an investor currently holding an asset chooses to write a call on it, she has made a conscious decision not to sell the asset. Hence, the current value of the asset should be viewed as an opportunity cost that is just as real as the cost to an investor buying the underlying at this time.

Sellers of covered calls must make a decision about the chosen exercise price. For example, one could sell the call with an exercise price of 1950 for 108.43, or sell the call with an exercise price of 2000 for 81.75, or sell the call with an exercise price of 2050 for 59.98. The higher the exercise price, the less one receives for the call but the more room for gain on the upside. There is no clear-cut solution to deciding which call is best; the choice depends on the risk preferences of the investor.

Finally, we should note that anecdotal evidence suggests that writers of call options make small amounts of money, but make it often. The reason for this phenomenon is generally thought to be that buyers of calls tend to be overly optimistic, but that argument is fallacious. The real reason is that the expected profits come from rare but large payoffs. For example, consider the call with exercise price of 2000 and a premium of 81.75. As we learned in Section 2.1, the breakeven underlying price is 2081.75—a gain of about 4.1 percent in a one-month period, which would be an exceptional return for almost any asset. These prices were obtained using the Black–Scholes–Merton model, so they are fair prices. Yet the required underlying price movement to profit on the call is exceptional. Obviously someone buys calls, and naturally, someone must be on the other side of the transaction. Sellers of calls tend to be holders of the underlying or other calls, which reduces the enormous risk they would assume if they sold calls without any other position.[8] Hence, it is reasonable to expect that sellers of calls would make money often, because large underlying price movements occur only rarely. Following this line of reasoning, however, it would appear that sellers of calls can consistently take advantage of buyers of calls. That cannot possibly be the case. What happens is that buyers of calls make money less often than sellers, but when they do make money, the leverage inherent in call options amplifies their returns. Therefore, when call writers lose money, they tend to lose big, but most call writers own the underlying or are long other calls to offset the risk.

EXAMPLE 3

Consider a bond selling for $98 per $100 face value. A call option selling for $8 has an exercise price of $105. Answer the following questions about a covered call.

A. Determine the value of the position at expiration and the profit under the following outcomes:

i. The price of the bond at expiration is $110.

ii. The price of the bond at expiration is $88.

B. Determine the following:

i. The maximum profit.

ii. The maximum loss.

---

[8] Sellers of calls who hold other calls are engaged in transactions called spreads.

C. Determine the breakeven bond price at expiration.

Solutions:

A. i. $V_T = S_T - \max(0, S_T - X) = 110 - \max(0, 110 - 105)$
$= 110 - 110 + 105 = 105$
$\Pi = V_T - V_0 = 105 - (S_0 - c_0) = 105 - (98 - 8) = 15$

ii. $V_T = S_T - \max(0, S_T - X) = 88 - \max(0, 88 - 105) = 88 - 0 = 88$
$\Pi = V_T - V_0 = 88 - (S_0 - c_0) = 88 - (98 - 8) = -2$

B. i. Maximum profit $= X - S_0 + c_0 = 105 - 98 + 8 = 15$

ii. Maximum loss $= S_0 - c_0 = 98 - 8 = 90$

C. $S_T^* = S_0 - c_0 = 98 - 8 = 90$

Covered calls represent one widely used way to protect a position in the underlying. Another popular means of providing protection is to buy a put.

2.2.2 *Protective Puts*

Because selling a call provides some protection to the holder of the underlying against a fall in the price of the underlying, buying a put should also provide protection. A put, after all, is designed to pay off when the price of the underlying moves down. In some ways, buying a put to add to a long stock position is much better than selling a call. As we shall see here, it provides downside protection while retaining the upside potential, but it does so at the expense of requiring the payment of cash up front. In contrast, a covered call generates cash up front but removes some of the upside potential.

Holding an asset and a put on the asset is a strategy known as a **protective put**. The value at expiration and the profit of this strategy are found by combining the value and profit of the two strategies of buying the asset and buying the put. The value is $V_T = S_T + \max(0, X - S_T)$. Thus, the results can be expressed as

$V_T = S_T + (X - S_T) = X$ if $S_T \le X$
$V_T = S_T$ if $S_T > X$

When the underlying price at expiration exceeds the exercise price, the put expires with no value. The position is then worth only the value of the underlying. When the underlying price at expiration is less than the exercise price, the put expires in-the-money and is worth $X - S_T$, while the underlying is worth S_T. The combined value of the two instruments is X. When the underlying is worth less than the exercise price at expiration, the put can be used to sell the underlying for the exercise price.

The initial value of the position is the initial price of the underlying, S_0, plus the premium on the put, p_0. Hence, the profit is $\Pi = S_T + \max(0, X - S_T) - (S_0 + p_0)$. The profit can be broken down as follows:

$\Pi = X - (S_0 + p_0)$ if $S_T \le X$
$\Pi = S_T - (S_0 + p_0)$ if $S_T > X$

In this example, we are going to use the put with an exercise price of 1950. Its premium is 56.01. Recalling that the initial price of the underlying is 2000, the value at expiration and profit for the case of $S_T = 2100$ are

$$V_T = 2100$$
$$\Pi = 2100 - (2000 + 56.01) = 43.99$$

For the case of $S_T = 1900$, the value at expiration and profit are

$$V_T = 1950$$
$$\Pi = 1950 - (2000 + 56.01) = -106.01$$

The results for a range of outcomes are shown in Exhibit 7. Note how the protective put provides a limit on the downside with no limit on the upside.[9] Therefore, we can say that the upper limit is infinite. The lower limit is a loss of 106.01. In the worst possible case, we can sell the underlying for the exercise price, but the up-front cost of the underlying and put are 2056.01, for a maximum loss of 106.01.

Now let us find the breakeven price of the underlying at expiration. Note that the two profit equations are $\Pi = S_T - (S_0 + p_0)$ if $S_T > X$ and $\Pi = X - (S_0 + p_0)$ if $S_T \leq X$. In the latter case, there is no value of the underlying that will allow us to break even. In the former case, $S_T > X$, we change the notation on S_T to S_T^* to denote the breakeven value, set this expression equal to zero, and solve for S_T^*:

$$S_T^* = S_0 + p_0$$

EXHIBIT 7	Protective Put (Buy Underlying, Buy Put)

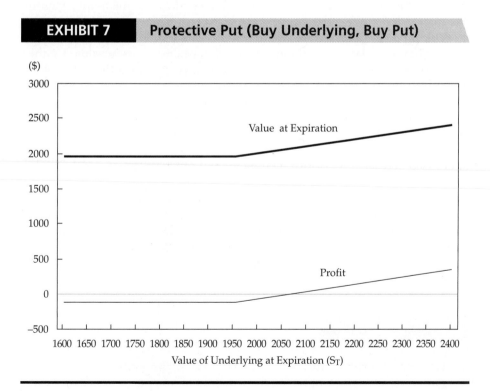

_____

[9] Note that the graph for a protective put looks like the graph for a call. This result is due to put–call parity, as covered in the reading on option markets and contracts.

To break even, the underlying must be at least as high as the amount expended up front to establish the position. In this problem, this amount is $2000 + 56.01 = 2056.01$.

To summarize the protective put, we have the following:

Value at expiration: $V_T = S_T + \max(0, X - S_T)$
Profit: $\Pi = V_T - S_0 - p_0$
Maximum profit $= \infty$
Maximum loss $= S_0 + p_0 - X$
Breakeven: $S_T^* = S_0 + p_0$

A protective put can appear to be a great transaction with no drawbacks. It provides downside protection with upside potential, but let us take a closer look. First recall that this is a one-month transaction and keep in mind that the option has been priced by the Black–Scholes–Merton model and is, therefore, a fair price. The maximum loss of 106.01 is a loss of $106.01/2056.01 = 5.2\%$. The breakeven of 2056.01 requires an upward move of 2.8 percent, which is an annual rate of about 34 percent. From this angle, the protective put strategy does not look quite as good, but in fact, these figures simply confirm that protection against downside loss is expensive. When the protective put is fairly priced, the protection buyer must give up considerable upside potential that may not be particularly evident from just looking at a graph.

The purchase of a protective put also presents the buyer with some choices. In this example, the buyer bought the put with exercise price of 1950 for 56.01. Had he bought the put with exercise price of 2000, he would have paid 79.25. The put with exercise price of 2050 would have cost 107.39. The higher the price for which the investor wants to be able to sell the underlying, the more expensive the put will be.

The protective put is often viewed as a classic example of insurance. The investor holds a risky asset and wants protection against a loss in value. He then buys insurance in the form of the put, paying a premium to the seller of the insurance, the put writer. The exercise price of the put is like the insurance deductible because the magnitude of the exercise price reflects the risk assumed by the party holding the underlying. The higher the exercise price, the less risk assumed by the holder of the underlying and the more risk assumed by the put seller. The lower the exercise price, the more risk assumed by the holder of the underlying and the less risk assumed by the put seller. In insurance, the higher the deductible, the more risk assumed by the insured party and the less risk assumed by the insurer. Thus, a higher exercise price is analogous to a lower insurance deductible.

Like traditional insurance, this form of insurance provides coverage for a period of time. At the end of the period of time, the insurance expires and either pays off or not. The buyer of the insurance may or may not choose to renew the insurance by buying another put.

EXAMPLE 4

Consider a currency selling for $0.875. A put option selling for $0.075 has an exercise price of $0.90. Answer the following questions about a protective put.

A. Determine the value at expiration and the profit under the following outcomes:

   i. The price of the currency at expiration is $0.96.

   ii. The price of the currency at expiration is $0.75.

B. Determine the following:

   i. The maximum profit.

   ii. The maximum loss.

C. Determine the breakeven price of the currency at expiration.

Solutions:

A. **i.** $V_T = S_T + \max(0, X - S_T) = 0.96 + \max(0, 0.90 - 0.96) = 0.96$
$\Pi = V_T - V_0 = 0.96 - (S_0 + p_0) = 0.96 - (0.875 + 0.075) = 0.01$

   ii. $V_T = S_T + \max(0, X - S_T) = 0.75 + \max(0, 0.90 - 0.75) = 0.90$
$\Pi = V_T - V_0 = 0.90 - (S_0 + p_0) = 0.90 - (0.875 + 0.075) = -0.05$

B. **i.** Maximum profit $= \infty$

   ii. Maximum loss $= S_0 + p_0 - X = 0.875 + 0.075 - 0.90 = 0.05$

C. $S_T^* = S_0 + p_0 = 0.875 + 0.075 = 0.95$

Finally, we note that a protective put can be modified in a number of ways. One in particular is to sell a call to generate premium income to pay for the purchase of the put. This strategy is known as a collar.

SUMMARY

▶ The profit from buying a call is the value at expiration, $\max(0, S_T - X)$, minus c_0, the option premium. The maximum profit is infinite, and the maximum loss is the option premium. The breakeven underlying price at expiration is the exercise price plus the option premium. When one sells a call, these results are reversed.

▶ The profit from buying a put is the value at expiration, $\max(0, X - S_T)$, minus p_0, the option premium. The maximum profit is the exercise price minus the option premium, and the maximum loss is the option premium. The breakeven underlying price at expiration is the exercise price minus the option premium. When one sells a put, these results are reversed.

▶ The profit from a covered call—the purchase of the underlying and sale of a call—is the value at expiration, $S_T - \max(0, S_T - X)$, minus $S_0 - c_0$, the cost of the underlying minus the option premium. The maximum profit is the exercise price minus the original underlying price plus the option premium, and the maximum loss is the cost of the underlying less the option premium. The breakeven underlying price at expiration is the original price of the underlying minus the option premium.

▶ The profit from a protective put—the purchase of the underlying and a put—is the value at expiration, $S_T + \max(0, X - S_T)$, minus the cost of the underlying plus the option premium, $S_0 + p_0$. The maximum profit is infinite, and the maximum loss is the cost of the underlying plus the option premium minus the exercise price. The breakeven underlying price at expiration is the original price of the underlying plus the option premium.

PRACTICE PROBLEMS FOR READING 72

1. Consider a call option selling for $4 in which the exercise price is $50.

   A. Determine the value at expiration and the profit for a buyer under the following outcomes:

   i. The price of the underlying at expiration is $55.
   ii. The price of the underlying at expiration is $51.
   iii. The price of the underlying at expiration is $48.

   B. Determine the value at expiration and the profit for a seller under the following outcomes:

   i. The price of the underlying at expiration is $49.
   ii. The price of the underlying at expiration is $52.
   iii. The price of the underlying at expiration is $55.

   C. Determine the following:

   i. The maximum profit to the buyer (maximum loss to the seller).
   ii. The maximum loss to the buyer (maximum profit to the seller).

   D. Determine the breakeven price of the underlying at expiration.

2. Suppose you believe that the price of a particular underlying, currently selling at $99, is going to increase substantially in the next six months. You decide to purchase a call option expiring in six months on this underlying. The call option has an exercise price of $105 and sells for $7.

   A. Determine the profit under the following outcomes for the price of the underlying six months from now.

   i. $99.
   ii. $104.
   iii. $105.
   iv. $109.
   v. $112.
   vi. $115.

   B. Determine the breakeven price of the underlying at expiration. Check that your answer is consistent with the solution to Part A of this problem.

3. Consider a put option on the Nasdaq 100 selling for $106.25 in which the exercise price is 2100.

   A. Determine the value at expiration and the profit for a buyer under the following outcomes:

   i. The price of the underlying at expiration is 2125.
   ii. The price of the underlying at expiration is 2050.
   iii. The price of the underlying at expiration is 1950.

   B. Determine the value at expiration and the profit for a seller under the following outcomes:

   i. The price of the underlying at expiration is 1975.
   ii. The price of the underlying at expiration is 2150.

   C. Determine the following:

   i. The maximum profit to the buyer (maximum loss to the seller).
   ii. The maximum loss to the buyer (maximum profit to the seller).

   D. Determine the breakeven price of the underlying at expiration.

4. Suppose you believe that the price of a particular underlying, currently selling at $99, will decrease considerably in the next six months. You decide to purchase a put option expiring in six months on this underlying. The put option has an exercise price of $95 and sells for $5.

   A. Determine the profit for you under the following outcomes for the price of the underlying six months from now:

      i. $100.
      ii. $95.
      iii. $93.
      iv. $90.
      v. $85.

   B. Determine the breakeven price of the underlying at expiration. Check that your answer is consistent with the solution to Part A of this problem.

   C. i. What is the maximum profit that you can have?

      ii. At what expiration price of the underlying would this profit be realized?

5. You simultaneously purchase an underlying priced at $77 and write a call option on it with an exercise price of $80 and selling at $6.

   A. What is the term commonly used for the position that you have taken?

   B. Determine the value at expiration and the profit for your strategy under the following outcomes:

      i. The price of the underlying at expiration is $70.
      ii. The price of the underlying at expiration is $75.
      iii. The price of the underlying at expiration is $80.
      iv. The price of the underlying at expiration is $85.

   C. Determine the following:

      i. The maximum profit.
      ii. The maximum loss.
      iii. The expiration price of the underlying at which you would realize the maximum profit.
      iv. The expiration price of the underlying at which you would incur the maximum loss.

   D. Determine the breakeven price at expiration.

6. Suppose you simultaneously purchase an underlying priced at $77 and a put option on it, with an exercise price of $75 and selling at $3.

   A. What is the term commonly used for the position that you have taken?

   B. Determine the value at expiration and the profit for your strategy under the following outcomes:

      i. The price of the underlying at expiration is $70.
      ii. The price of the underlying at expiration is $75.
      iii. The price of the underlying at expiration is $80.
      iv. The price of the underlying at expiration is $85.
      v. The price of the underlying at expiration is $90.

   C. Determine the following:

      i. The maximum profit.
      ii. The maximum loss.
      iii. The expiration price of the underlying at which you would incur the maximum loss.

   D. Determine the breakeven price at expiration.

7. The recent price per share of Dragon Vacations Inc. is $50 per share. Calls with exactly six months left to expiration are available on Dragon with strikes of $45, $50, and $55. The prices of the calls are $8.75, $6.00, and $4.00, respectively. Assume that each call contract is for 100 shares of stock and that at initiation of the strategy the investor purchases 100 shares of Dragon at the current market price. Further assume that the investor will close out the strategy in six months when the options expire, including the sale of any stock not delivered against exercise of a call, whether the stock price goes up or goes down. If the closing price of Dragon stock in six months is exactly $60, the profit to a covered call using the $50 strike call is *closest* to:

- **A.** $400.
- **B.** $600.
- **C.** $1,600.

8. The recent price per share of Win Big, Inc., is €50 per share. Verna Hillsborough buys 100 shares at €50. To protect against a fall in price, Hillsborough buys one put, covering 100 shares of Win Big, with a strike price of €40. The put premium is €1 per share. If Win Big closes at €45 per share at the expiration of the put and Hillsborough sells her shares at €45, Hillsborough's profit from the stay/put is *closest* to:

- **A.** −€1,100.
- **B.** −€600.
- **C.** €900.

SOLUTIONS FOR READING 72

1. A. Call buyer

    i. $c_T = \max(0, S_T - X) = \max(0, 55 - 50) = 5$

        $\Pi = c_T - c_0 = 5 - 4 = 1$

    ii. $c_T = \max(0, S_T - X) = \max(0, 51 - 50) = 1$

        $\Pi = c_T - c_0 = 1 - 4 = -3$

    iii. $c_T = \max(0, S_T - X) = \max(0, 48 - 50) = 0$

        $\Pi = c_T - c_0 = 0 - 4 = -4$

B. Call seller

    i. $\text{Value} = -c_T = -\max(0, S_T - X) = -\max(0, 49 - 50) = 0$

        $\Pi = -c_T + c_0 = -0 + 4 = 4$

    ii. $\text{Value} = -c_T = -\max(0, S_T - X) = -\max(0, 52 - 50) = -2$

        $\Pi = -c_T + c_0 = -2 + 4 = 2$

    iii. $\text{Value} = -c_T = -\max(0, S_T - X) = -\max(0, 55 - 50) = -5$

        $\Pi = -c_T + c_0 = -5 + 4 = -1$

C. Maximum and minimum

    i. Maximum profit to buyer (loss to seller) $= \infty$

    ii. Maximum loss to buyer (profit to seller) $= c_0 = 4$

D. $S_T^* = X + c_0 = 50 + 4 = 54$

2. A.   **i.** $c_T = \max(0, S_T - X) = \max(0, 99 - 105) = 0$

        $\Pi = c_T - c_0 = 0 - 7 = -7$

    ii. $c_T = \max(0, S_T - X) = \max(0, 104 - 105) = 0$

        $\Pi = c_T - c_0 = 0 - 7 = -7$

    iii. $c_T = \max(0, S_T - X) = \max(0, 105 - 105) = 0$

        $\Pi = c_T - c_0 = 0 - 7 = -7$

    iv. $c_T = \max(0, S_T - X) = \max(0, 109 - 105) = 4$

        $\Pi = c_T - c_0 = 4 - 7 = -3$

    v. $c_T = \max(0, S_T - X) = \max(0, 112 - 105) = 7$

        $\Pi = c_T - c_0 = 7 - 7 = 0$

    vi. $c_T = \max(0, S_T - X) = \max(0, 115 - 105) = 10$

        $\Pi = c_T - c_0 = 10 - 7 = 3$

B. $S_T^* = X + c_0 = 105 + 7 = 112$

Clearly, this result is consistent with our solution above, where the profit is exactly zero in Part A(v), in which the price at expiration is 112.

3. A. Put buyer

    i. $p_T = \max(0, X - S_T) = \max(0, 2100 - 2125) = 0$

        $\Pi = p_T - p_0 = 0 - 106.25 = -106.25$

    ii. $p_T = \max(0, X - S_T) = \max(0, 2100 - 2050) = 50$

        $\Pi = p_T - p_0 = 50 - 106.25 = -56.25$

       iii. $p_T = \max(0, X - S_T) = \max(0, 2100 - 1950) = 150$

          $\Pi = p_T - p_0 = 150 - 106.25 = 43.75$

  B. Put seller

      i. Value $= -p_T = -\max(0, X - S_T) = -\max(0, 2100 - 1975) = -125$

         $\Pi = -p_T + p_0 = -125 + 106.25 = -18.75$

      ii. Value $= -p_T = -\max(0, X - S_T) = -\max(0, 2100 - 2150) = 0$

         $\Pi = -p_T + p_0 = -0 + 106.25 = 106.25$

  C. Maximum and minimum

      i. Maximum profit to buyer (loss to seller) $= X - p_0 = 2100 - 106.25 = 1993.75$

      ii. Maximum loss to buyer (profit to seller) $= p_0 = 106.25$

  D. $S_T^* = X - p_0 = 2100 - 106.25 = 1993.75$

4. A.   **i.** $p_T = \max(0, X - S_T) = \max(0, 95 - 100) = 0$

        $\Pi = p_T - p_0 = 0 - 5 = -5$

      ii. $p_T = \max(0, X - S_T) = \max(0, 95 - 95) = 0$

        $\Pi = p_T - p_0 = 0 - 5 = -5$

      iii. $p_T = \max(0, X - S_T) = \max(0, 95 - 93) = 2$

        $\Pi = p_T - p_0 = 2 - 5 = -3$

      iv. $p_T = \max(0, X - S_T) = \max(0, 95 - 90) = 5$

        $\Pi = p_T - p_0 = 5 - 5 = 0$

      v. $p_T = \max(0, X - S_T) = \max(0, 95 - 85) = 10$

        $\Pi = p_T - p_0 = 10 - 5 = 5$

  B. $S_T^* = X - p_0 = 95 - 5 = 90$

    Clearly, this result is consistent with our solution above, where the profit is exactly zero in Part A(iv), in which the price at expiration is 90.

  C.   **i.** Maximum profit (to put buyer) $= X - p_0 = 95 - 5 = 90$.

      ii. This profit would be realized in the unlikely scenario of the price of the underlying falling all the way down to zero.

5. A. This position is commonly called a covered call.

  B.   **i.** $V_T = S_T - \max(0, S_T - X) = 70 - \max(0, 70 - 80) = 70 - 0 = 70$

        $\Pi = V_T - V_0 = 70 - (S_0 - c_0) = 70 - (77 - 6) = 70 - 71 = -1$

      ii. $V_T = S_T - \max(0, S_T - X) = 75 - \max(0, 75 - 80) = 75 - 0 = 75$

        $\Pi = V_T - V_0 = 75 - (S_0 - c_0) = 75 - (77 - 6) = 4$

      iii. $V_T = S_T - \max(0, S_T - X) = 80 - \max(0, 80 - 80) = 80 - 0 = 80$

        $\Pi = V_T - V_0 = 80 - (S_0 - c_0) = 80 - (77 - 6) = 9$

      iv. $V_T = S_T - \max(0, S_T - X) = 85 - \max(0, 85 - 80) = 85 - 5 = 80$

        $\Pi = V_T - V_0 = 80 - (S_0 - c_0) = 80 - (77 - 6) = 9$

  C.   **i.** Maximum profit $= X - S_0 + c_0 = 80 - 77 + 6 = 9$

      ii. Maximum loss $= S_0 - c_0 = 77 - 6 = 71$

      iii. The maximum profit would be realized if the expiration price of the underlying is at or above the exercise price of \$80.

      iv. The maximum loss would be incurred if the underlying price drops to zero.

  D. $S_T^* = S_0 - c_0 = 77 - 6 = 71$

6. A. This position is commonly called a protective put.

    B.   **i.** $V_T = S_T + \max(0, X - S_T) = 70 + \max(0, 75 - 70) = 70 + 5 = 75$

          $\Pi = V_T - V_0 = 75 - (S_0 + p_0) = 75 - (77 + 3) = 75 - 80 = -5$

      ii. $V_T = S_T + \max(0, X - S_T) = 75 + \max(0, 75 - 75) = 75 + 0 = 75$

          $\Pi = V_T - V_0 = 75 - (S_0 + p_0) = 75 - (77 + 3) = 75 - 80 = -5$

     iii. $V_T = S_T + \max(0, X - S_T) = 80 + \max(0, 75 - 80) = 80 + 0 = 80$

          $\Pi = V_T - V_0 = 80 - (S_0 + p_0) = 80 - (77 + 3) = 80 - 80 = 0$

     iv. $V_T = S_T + \max(0, X - S_T) = 85 + \max(0, 75 - 85) = 85 + 0 = 85$

          $\Pi = V_T - V_0 = 85 - (S_0 + p_0) = 85 - (77 + 3) = 85 - 80 = 5$

      v. $V_T = S_T + \max(0, X - S_T) = 90 + \max(0, 75 - 90) = 90 + 0 = 90$

          $\Pi = V_T - V_0 = 90 - (S_0 + p_0) = 90 - (77 + 3) = 90 - 80 = 10$

    C.   **i.** Maximum profit $= \infty$

      ii. Maximum loss $= -(X - S_0 - p_0) = -(75 - 77 - 3) = 5$

     iii. The maximum loss would be incurred if the expiration price of the underlying were at or below the exercise price of $75.

    D. $S_T^* = S_0 + p_0 = 77 + 3 = 80$

7. B is correct. Buying the stock at $50 and delivering it against the $50 strike call generates a payoff of zero. The premium is retained by the writer. The net profit is $6.00 per share $\times$ 100 shares or $600.

8. B is correct. The loss on her stock is (€45 − €50) $\times$ 100 = − €500. She also paid €100 for the put. The put expires worthless, making her total loss €600.

ALTERNATIVE INVESTMENTS

STUDY SESSION

Study Session 18   Alternative Investments

TOPIC LEVEL LEARNING OUTCOME

The candidate should be able to demonstrate a working knowledge of the analysis of alternative investments, including mutual funds, exchange-traded funds, real estate, private equity, venture capital, hedge funds, closely held companies, distressed securities, and commodities and commodity derivatives.

STUDY SESSION 18
ALTERNATIVE INVESTMENTS

B ecause of diversification benefits and higher expectations of investment returns, investors are increasingly turning to alternative investments. This study session describes the common types of alternative investments, methods for their valuation, unique risks and opportunities associated with them, and the relation between alternative investments and traditional investments.

Although finding a single definition of an "alternative" investment is difficult, certain features (e.g., limited liquidity, infrequent valuations, and unique legal structures) are typically associated with alternative investments. This study session discusses these features and how to evaluate their impact on expected returns and investment decisions in more detail. The reading provides an overview of the major categories of alternative investments, including real estate, private equity, venture capital, hedge funds, closely held companies, distressed securities, and commodities.

Each of these categories has several unique characteristics, and the readings discuss valuation methods for illiquid assets (such as direct real estate or closely held companies), performance measures for private equity and venture capital investments, differences between various hedge fund strategies, and implementation vehicles for investments in alternative assets.

READING ASSIGNMENTS

Reading 73   Alternative Investments
             Global Investments, Sixth Edition, by Bruno Solnik
             and Dennis McLeavey, CFA

Reading 74   Investing in Commodities
             *Global Perspectives on Investment Management: Learning from
             the Leaders*, edited by Rodney N. Sullivan, CFA

45/8 411/16   3/8
       51/2 —   3/8
51/2 213/16 —   1/8
205/8 181/8 +   7/8
173/8   —   1/2
       61/2   —
61/2   1/8
71/4 331/32 —
       15/16
             9/16   9/8
9/16   715/16
       713/16
715/16   21/2   +
       25/8   211/32
             21/4   21/4
23/4 21/4
      121/16 113/8   113/4 +
      333/4   33   331/4 —
602   255/8 249/16   253/8 +
833   12   115/8   117/8 +
16   101/2 101/2   101/2 —
78   157/8 1513/16 157/8
4608 91/16 81/4   87/8
430   111/4 101/8   101/8

ALTERNATIVE INVESTMENTS
by Bruno Solnik and Dennis McLeavey, CFA

LEARNING OUTCOMES

The candidate should be able to:	Mastery
a. differentiate between an open-end and a closed-end fund, and explain how net asset value of a fund is calculated and the nature of fees charged by investment companies;	☐
b. distinguish among style, sector, index, global, and stable value strategies in equity investment and among exchange traded funds (ETFs), traditional mutual funds, and closed-end funds;	☐
c. explain the advantages and risks of ETFs;	☐
d. describe the forms of real estate investment and explain their characteristics as an investable asset class;	☐
e. describe the various approaches to the valuation of real estate;	☐
f. calculate the net operating income (NOI) from a real estate investment, the value of a property using the sales comparison and income approaches, and the after-tax cash flows, net present value, and yield of a real estate investment;	☐
g. explain the stages in venture capital investing, venture capital investment characteristics and challenges to venture capital valuation and performance measurement;	☐
h. calculate the net present value (NPV) of a venture capital project, given the project's possible payoff and conditional failure probabilities;	☐
i. define hedge fund in terms of objectives, legal structure, and fee structure, and describe the various classifications of hedge funds;	☐
j. explain the benefits and drawbacks to fund of funds investing;	☐
k. discuss the leverage and unique risks of hedge funds;	☐

Jot Yau, CFA, made contributions to the exchange traded and hedge funds sections of this reading.

Global Investments, Sixth Edition, by Bruno Solnik and Dennis McLeavey, CFA. Copyright © 2008 by Pearson Education. Reprinted with permission of Pearson Education, publishing as Pearson Addison Wesley.

l.	discuss the performance of hedge funds, the biases present in hedge fund performance measurement, and explain the effect of survivorship bias on the reported return and risk measures for a hedge fund database;	☐
m.	explain how the legal environment affects the valuation of closely held companies;	☐
n.	describe alternative valuation methods for closely held companies and distinguish among the bases for the discounts and premiums for these companies;	☐
o.	discuss distressed securities investing and compare venture capital investing with distressed securities investing;	☐
p.	discuss the role of commodities as a vehicle for investing in production and consumption;	☐
q.	explain the motivation for investing in commodities, commodities derivatives, and commodity-linked securities;	☐
r.	discuss the sources of return on a collateralized commodity futures position.	☐

Alternative investments complement stocks, bonds, and other traditional financial instruments traded on international financial markets. There is a large variety of alternative investments, and the list evolves over time. Both alternative assets (such as real estate) and alternative strategies (hedge funds) are classified as alternative investments. Alternative investments generally have lower liquidity, sell in less efficient markets, and require a longer time horizon than publicly traded stocks and bonds. Sharpe, Alexander, and Bailey (1999) provide a nice summary of the common features of alternative investments:

► Illiquidity
► Difficulty in determining current market values
► Limited historical risk and return data
► Extensive investment analysis required

When present, liquidity can make alternative investments, such as real estate, attractive; but are there cases in which the general illiquidity of alternative investments can be attractive? Alternative investments beckon investors to areas of the market where alpha[1] is more likely to be found than in more liquid and efficient markets. Illiquidity, limited information, and less efficiency do not suit all investors but can be attractive features to those looking for likely places to add value through investment expertise.

---

[1] *Alpha* is risk-adjusted return in excess of the required rate of return, but, more colloquially, stands for positive excess risk-adjusted return, the goal of active managers.

Terhaar, Staub, and Singer (2003) discuss two additional features of alternative investments:

▶ A liquidity premium compensates the investor for the investor's inability to continuously rebalance the alternative investments in the portfolio.

▶ A segmentation premium compensates investors for the risk of alternative assets that, by nature, are generally not priced in a fully integrated global market.

It is difficult to give a broad characterization of alternative investments, but they are often equity investments in some nonpublicly traded asset. In some cases, however, they may look more like an investment strategy than an asset class. Whatever the nature of alternative investments, specialized intermediaries often link the investor to the investments. Whether the investor invests directly or through an intermediary, he must know the investment's characteristics. In the case of investing through an intermediary, he must make sure that the incentive structure for any intermediary suits his investor needs.

Finally, alternative investments can be characterized as raising unique legal and tax considerations. A financial advisor would coordinate with an attorney and a tax accountant before recommending any specific real estate investment. Also, many forms of alternative investments involve special legal structures that avoid some taxes (exchange traded funds) or avoid some regulations (hedge funds).

Before getting into alternative investments per se, it is useful to first review investment companies.

INVESTMENT COMPANIES

Investment companies are financial intermediaries that earn fees to pool and invest investors' funds, giving the investors rights to a proportional share of the pooled fund performance. Both managed and unmanaged companies pool investor funds in this manner. Unmanaged investment companies (unit investment trusts in the United States) hold a fixed portfolio of investments (often tax-exempt) for the life of the company and usually stand ready to redeem the investor's shares at market value. Managed investment companies are classified according to whether or not they stand ready to redeem investor shares. *Open-end funds* operated by investment companies (mutual funds) offer this redemption feature, but *closed-end funds* do not. Closed-end investment companies issue shares that are then traded in the secondary markets.

Valuing Investment Company Shares

The basis for valuing investment company shares is *net asset value* (*NAV*), the per-share value of the investment company's assets minus its liabilities. Liabilities may come from fees owed to investment managers, for example. Share value equals NAV for unmanaged and open-end investment companies because they stand ready to redeem their shares at NAV. The price of a closed-end investment company's shares is determined in the secondary markets in which they trade, and, consequently, can be at a premium or discount to NAV.

Fund Management Fees

Investment companies charge fees, some as one-time charges and some as annual charges. By setting an initial selling price above the NAV, the unmanaged company charges a fee for the effort of setting up the fund. For managed funds, loads are simply sales commissions charged at purchase (*front-end load*) as a percentage of the investment. A redemption fee (*back-end load*) is a charge to exit the fund. Redemption fees discourage quick trading turnover and are often set up so that the fees decline the longer the shares are held (in this case, the fees are sometimes called *contingent deferred sales charges*). Loads and redemption fees provide sales incentives but not portfolio management performance incentives.

Annual charges are composed of operating expenses including management fees, administrative expenses, and continuing distribution fees (12b-1 fees in the United States). The ratio of operating expenses to average assets is often referred to as the fund's "expense ratio." Distribution fees are fees paid back to the party that arranged the initial sale of the shares and are thus another type of sales incentive fee. Only management fees can be considered a portfolio management incentive fee. Example 1 illustrates the effects of investment company fees on fund performance.

EXAMPLE 1

Investment Company Fees: Effects on Performance

An investor is considering the purchase of TriGroup International Equity Fund (TRIEF) for her portfolio. Like many U.S.-based mutual funds today, TRIEF has more than one class of shares. Although all classes hold the same portfolio of securities, each class has a different expense structure. This particular mutual fund has three classes of shares, A, B, and C. The expenses of these classes are summarized in the following table:

Expense Comparison for Three Classes of TRIEF

	Class A	Class B*	Class C
Sales charge (load) on purchases	3%	None	None
Deferred sales charge (load) on redemptions	None	5% in the first year, declining by 1 percentage point each year thereafter	1% for the initial two years
Annual expenses:			
Distribution fee	0.25%	0.50%	0.50%
Management fee	0.75%	0.75%	0.75%
Other expenses	0.25%	0.25%	0.25%
	1.25%	1.50%	1.50%

* Class B shares automatically convert to Class A shares 72 months (6 years) after purchase, reducing future annual expenses.

The time horizon associated with the investor's objective in purchasing TRIEF is six years. She expects equity investments with risk characteristics similar to TRIEF to earn 8 percent per year, and she decides to make her selection of fund share class based on an assumed 8 percent return each year, gross of any of the expenses given in the preceding table.

A. Based on only the information provided here, determine the class of shares that is most appropriate for this investor. Assume that expense percentages given will be constant at the given values. Assume that the deferred sales charges are computed on the basis of NAV.

B. Suppose that, as a result of an unforeseen liquidity need, the investor needs to liquidate her investment at the end of the first year. Assume an 8 percent rate of return has been earned. Determine the relative performance of the three fund classes, and interpret the results.

C. Based on your answers to A and B, discuss the appropriateness of these share classes as it relates to an investor's time horizon, for example, a one-, six-, and ten-year horizon.

Solution to A: To address this question, we compute the terminal value of $1 invested at the end of year 6. The share class with the highest terminal value, net of all expenses, would be the most appropriate for this investor, as all classes are based on the same portfolio and thus have the same portfolio risk characteristics.

Class A. $1 \times (1 - 0.03) = \$0.97$ is the amount available for investment at $t = 0$, after paying the front-end sales charge. Because this amount grows at 8 percent for six years, reduced by annual expenses of 0.0125, the terminal value per $1 invested after six years is $\$0.97 \times 1.08^6 \times (1 - 0.0125)^6 = \$1.4274$.

Class B. After six years, $1 invested grows to $\$1 \times 1.08^6 \times (1 - 0.015)^6 = \$1.4493$. According to the table, the deferred sales charge disappears after year 5; therefore, the terminal value is $1.4493.

Class C. After six years, $1 invested grows to $\$1 \times 1.08^6 \times (1 - 0.015)^6 = \$1.4493$. There is no deferred sales charge in the sixth year, so $1.4493 is the terminal value.

In summary, the ranking by terminal value after six years is Class B and Class C ($1.4493), followed by Class A ($1.4274). Class B or Class C appears to be the most appropriate for this investor with a six-year horizon.

Solution to B: For Class A shares, the terminal value per $1 invested is $\$0.97 \times 1.08 \times (1 - 0.0125) = \$1.0345$. For Class B shares, it is $\$1 \times 1.08 \times (1 - 0.015) \times (1 - 0.05) = \$1.0106$, reflecting a 5 percent redemption charge; for Class C shares, it is $\$1 \times 1.08 \times (1 - 0.015) \times (1 - 0.01) = \$1.0532$, reflecting a 1 percent redemption charge. Thus, the ranking is Class C ($1.0532), Class A ($1.0345), and Class B ($1.0106).

Solution to C: Although Class B is appropriate given a six-year investment horizon, it is a costly choice if the fund shares need to be liquidated soon after investment. That eventuality would need to be assessed by the investor we are discussing. Class B, like Class A, is more attractive the longer the holding period, in general. Because Class C has higher annual expenses than Class A and Class B (after six years), it becomes less attractive the longer the holding period, in general.

After 10 years Class B shares would return $1 \times 1.08^{10} \times (1 - 0.015)^6 \times (1 - 0.0125)^4 = \$1.8750$, reflecting conversion to Class A after six years. Class C would return $1 \times 1.08^{10} \times (1 - 0.0150)^{10} = \$1.8561$. Class A shares would return the smallest amount, $\$0.97 \times 1.08^{10} \times (1 - 0.0125)^{10} = \$1.8466$. Though Class A underperforms Class C for a ten-year investment horizon, one could verify that Class A outperforms Class C for an investment horizon of 13 years or more. Also, in practice, the sales charge for Class A shares may be lower for purchases over certain sizes, making them more attractive in such comparisons.

Investment Strategies

Investment companies primarily invest in equity. Investment strategies can be characterized as style, sector, index, global, or stable value strategies. Style strategies focus on the underlying characteristics common to certain investments. Growth is a different style than value, and large capitalization investing is a different style than small stock investing. A growth strategy may focus on high price-to-earnings stocks, and a value strategy on low price-to-earnings stocks. Clearly, there are many styles.[2] A sector investment fund focuses on a particular industry. An index fund tracks an index. In the simplest implementation, the fund owns the securities in the index in exactly the same proportion as the market value weights of those securities in the index. A global fund includes securities from around the world and might keep portfolio weights similar to world market capitalization weights. An international fund is one that does not include the home country's securities, whereas a global fund includes the securities from the home country. A stable value fund invests in securities such as short-term fixed income instruments and guaranteed investment contracts which are guaranteed by the issuing insurance company and pay principal and a set rate of interest.

Exchange Traded Funds

Exchange traded funds (ETFs) are index-based investment products that allow investors to buy or sell exposure to an index through a single financial instrument. ETFs are funds that trade on a stock market like shares of any individual companies. Gastineau (2001) gives a good introduction to ETFs. They can be traded at any time during market hours and can be sold short or margined. But they are shares of a portfolio, not of an individual company. They represent shares of ownership in either open-end funds or unit investment trusts that hold portfolios of stocks or bonds in custody, which are designed to track the price and yield performance of their underlying indexes—broad market, sector/industry, single country/region (multiple countries), or fixed income. Although many investors regard ETFs simply as a form of diversified equity investment, their novelty and legal specificity suggested their inclusion in this reading.

---

[2] See, for example, Richard Bernstein, *Style Investing,* Wiley, 1995, and Richard Michaud, *Investment Styles, Market Anomalies, and Global Stock Selection,* The Research Foundation of AIMR, 1999.

Recent Developments of ETFs

ETFs first appeared as TIP 35 (Toronto Index Participation Fund) in Canada in 1989, and they appeared in the United States in 1993 with the introduction of Standard & Poor's 500 (S&P 500) Depositary Receipts (SPDRs or "spiders"). The first Asian ETF, the Hong Kong Tracker Fund, was launched in 1999. The first ETF launched in Europe, Euro STOXX 50, did not appear until 2000. Japan did not trade ETFs until 2001, when eight were listed. Today, most national stock exchanges list some ETFs. Their popularity has grown so quickly that they have become one of the most successful financial products of the decade.

As of 2007, several hundred ETFs were listed in the United States with total assets of around $500 billion. Leading ETF providers are Barclays Global Investors and State Street Global Advisors. Several hundred ETFs are also listed outside the United States. Listings of multiple ETFs on the same underlying index are common in Europe. European ETFs generally are structured according to the European Commission's 2001 Undertakings for Collective Investment in Transferable Securities (UCITS) III directive, which is considered by many managers to be more flexible than the fund guidelines of the U.S. Investment Company Act of 1940. As a result, a number of new strategies in ETF investments—including commodities, long leveraged, short leveraged, and private equity—have been introduced in Europe within the past several years.

ETF Structure

The usual ETF structure adopted worldwide is that of open-end funds with special characteristics, such as the "in-kind" process for creation and redemption of shares described subsequently (see Gastineau, 2001). Details of the legal structure vary depending on the country where the ETF is incorporated. In the United States, ETFs have adopted three different legal structures:

▶ *Managed investment companies* are open-ended investment companies registered under the Investment Company Act of 1940. They offer the most flexible ETF structure. The index can be tracked using various techniques, such as holding only a sample of the underlying securities in the index, lending of securities, and trading in derivatives. Dividends paid on the securities can be immediately reinvested in the fund. Sector SPDRs, iShares, and WEBS (World Equity Benchmark Shares) use this legal structure.

▶ *Unit investment trusts (UITs)* are also registered investment companies, but they operate under more constraints because they do not have a manager per se (but trustees). UITs are required to be fully invested in all underlying securities forming the index and must hold dividends received on securities in cash until the ETF pays a dividend to shareholders. This could result in a slight cash drag on performance. UITs are not permitted to lend securities and do not generally use derivatives. S&P 500 SPDR, Midcap 400 SPDR, and NASDAQ-100 QQQ ("qubes," trading symbol QQQQ) use this legal structure.

▶ *Grantor trusts* are not registered investment companies. Accordingly, owning a grantor trust is substantially similar to holding a basket of securities. A grantor trust often takes the form of an *American Depositary Receipt (ADR)* and trades as such. Because a grantor trust is fully invested in the basket of securities, no investment discretion is exercised by the trust. This is basically an unmanaged (and unregistered) investment company with a limited life. The trust passes all dividends on the underlying securities to shareholders as soon as practicable. Securities lending and use of derivatives are generally not practiced. HOLDRs (Holding Company Depository Receipts) use this legal structure. Grantor trusts

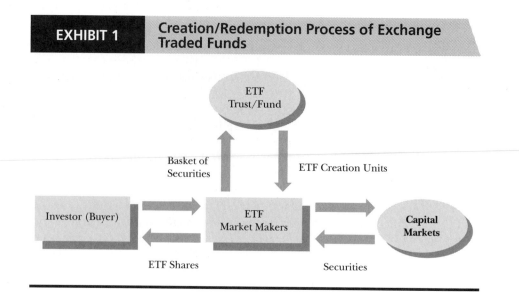

EXHIBIT 1   Creation/Redemption Process of Exchange Traded Funds

are a structure that allows investors to indirectly own an unmanaged basket of stocks rather than tracking an index, and some do not classify them as ETFs.

We will now introduce the unique "in-kind" creation and redemption process used by open-end and UIT ETFs. This in-kind process is a major distinguishing feature of ETFs. Creation/redemption units are created in large multiples of individual ETF shares, for example, 50,000 shares. These units are available to exchange specialists (*authorized participants* or *creation agents*) that are authorized by the fund and who will generally act as market makers on the individual ETF shares. The fund publishes the index tracking portfolio that it is willing to accept for in-kind transactions. When there is excess demand for ETF shares, an authorized participant will create a *creation unit* (a large block of ETF shares) by depositing with the trustee of the fund the specified portfolio of stocks used to track the index. In return, the authorized participant will receive ETF shares that can be sold to investors on the stock market. The redemption process is the same but in reverse. If there is an excess number of ETF shares sold by investors, an authorized participant will decide to redeem ETF shares; it will do so by exchanging with the fund a *redemption unit* (a large block of ETF shares) for a portfolio of stocks held by the fund and used to track the index. Exhibit 1 depicts the ETF structure and the creation/redemption process.

As opposed to traditional open-end funds, the in-kind redemption means that no capital gain will be realized in the fund's portfolio on redemption. If the redemption were in cash, the fund would have to sell stocks held in the fund's portfolio. If their price had appreciated, the fund would realize a capital gain, and the tax burden would have to be passed to all existing fund shareholders. This is not the case with ETFs. This in-kind transfer for redemptions does not create a tax burden for the remaining ETF shareholders under current U.S. tax law, unlike the capital gains distributions on traditional mutual fund shareholders that could result from the sale of securities to meet redemption demand.[3] As in any open-end fund, individual ETF shareholders[4] can require in-cash redemption based on the NAV. Redemption in cash by individual ETF shareholders is discouraged in two ways:

---

[3] There are situations in which capital gains distributions are generated for the ETF, such as capital gains resulting from selling securities directly to the capital markets due to an index reconstitution. Thus, zero capital gains distributions are not guaranteed.

[4] But authorized participants commit to redeem only in kind.

- Redemption is based on the NAV computed a couple of days after the shareholder commits to redemption. So, the redemption value is unknown when the investor decides to redeem. This is a common feature of mutual funds.
- A large fee is assessed on in-cash redemptions.

It is more advantageous for individual shareholders to sell their shares on the market than to redeem them in cash. Arbitrage[5] by authorized participants ensures that the listed price is close to the fund's NAV, and the sale can take place immediately based on observed share prices and at a low transaction cost. Authorized participants maintain a market in the ETF share by posting bid-and-ask prices with a narrow spread, or by entering in an electronic order book buy-and-sell limit orders, which play the same role. The transaction cost of ETFs can be estimated as the sum of the commission charged by the broker plus half this bid–ask spread.

In comparing the ETF structure presented in Exhibit 1 with that of the traditional mutual fund structure, it is clear that market makers in the ETF structure play an instrumental role in the creation and redemption process. In the traditional mutual fund structure, an increase in demand for the shares of the mutual fund is met by the mutual fund, which simply issues new shares to the investor, and the fund manager will take the cash to the capital markets and buy securities appropriate to the fund's objective. When the customer wants to sell the mutual fund shares, the fund manager may need to raise cash by selling securities back to the capital markets. In contrast, when a customer wants to buy ETF shares, the order is not directed to the fund but to the market makers on the exchange. The market maker will exchange ETF shares for cash with the customer (via broker/dealer) and, when necessary, replenish the supply of ETFs through the creation process outlined earlier.

Advantages/Disadvantages of ETFs

ETFs are used by a wide spectrum of investors, both individual and institutional, in a wide variety of investment strategies. This is because ETFs have the following advantages:

- Diversification can be obtained easily with a single ETF transaction. With equity-oriented ETFs, investors can gain instant exposure to different market capitalizations, style (value or growth), sector or industries, or countries or geographic regions. With fixed income ETFs, they can gain exposure to different maturity segments and bond market sectors. Thus, ETFs provide a convenient way to diversify.
- Although ETFs represent interests in a portfolio of securities, they trade similarly to a stock on an organized exchange. For example, ETFs can be sold short and also bought on margin.
- ETFs trade throughout the whole trading day at market prices that are updated continuously, rather than only trading once a day at closing market prices, as do the traditional open-end mutual funds.
- For many ETFs, there exist futures and options contracts on the same index, which is convenient for risk management.

---

[5] ETFs usually publish an indicative intraday NAV every 15 seconds that is available from major data providers.

▶ Portfolio holdings of ETFs are transparent. The ETF sponsor publishes the constituents of the fund on a daily basis. This should closely resemble the constituents of the underlying index. This is in contrast to other funds, for which the manager publishes only the list of assets in the fund from time to time.

▶ ETFs are cost effective. There are no load fees. Moreover, because the ETFs are passively managed, the expense ratio (which includes management fee for open-end funds, trustee fee for UITs, and custody fee for HOLDRs) can be kept low relative to actively managed funds. The expense ratio is comparable to that of an index mutual fund. For example, management fee can be as low as 8 basis points for the most successful U.S. ETFs, and up to 90 basis points for sector and international products (Mussavian and Hirsch, 2002). ETFs have a cost advantage over traditional mutual funds because there is no shareholder accounting at the fund level.

▶ ETFs have an advantage over closed-end index funds because their structure can prevent a significant premium/discount. Although supply and demand determine the market price of an ETF just like any other security, arbitrage helps keep the traded price of an ETF much more in line with its underlying value. By simultaneously buying (or selling) the ETF basket of securities and selling (or buying) the ETF shares in the secondary market, and creating (or redeeming) ETF shares to be delivered against the sale, market makers can capture the price discrepancy and make an arbitrage profit. Thus, UIT and open-end ETFs have the capability to avoid trading at large premiums and discounts to the NAVs. This is in contrast to closed-end index funds, which offer a fixed supply of shares, and as demand changes, they frequently trade at appreciable discounts from—and sometimes premiums to—their NAVs.

▶ The exposure to capital gains distribution taxes is lower than for traditional funds, so the consequences of other shareholders' redemptions are limited. As mentioned, capital gains resulting from in-kind transfer for redemptions do not create a tax burden for the remaining ETF shareholders. For this reason, capital gains tax liability is expected to be lower for ETF shareholders than for mutual fund shareholders.

▶ Dividends are reinvested immediately for open-end ETFs (but not for UIT ETFs), whereas for index mutual funds, timing of dividend reinvestment varies.

However, ETFs are not necessarily the most efficient alternative for investing in a market segment.

▶ In many countries, actively traded ETFs track a narrow-based market index, including only stocks with large market capitalization. So, no ETF is available for mid or low market-cap stocks. This is not the case in the United States, where a variety of ETF products trade actively.

▶ Many investors do not require the intraday trading opportunity provided by ETFs, because they have a long investment horizon.

▶ Some ETFs do not have large trading volumes and the bid–ask spread can be quite large. For example, some U.S. ETFs based on some sector indexes or on some foreign indexes (e.g., emerging markets) do not trade actively, and directly investing in a managed fund can be a less costly alternative, especially for large investors. Sector and international ETFs have an expense ratio that can be substantial (close to 1 percent) compared with that of a managed portfolio.

▶ For large institutional investors, the alternative to international ETFs is to invest directly in an indexed, or actively managed, international portfolio; the costs could be less, and the tax situation equivalent or better.

Types of ETFs

ETFs can be grouped by investment category, based on their investment target (broad domestic market index, style, sector/industry, country or region). For a given investment target, ETFs can be created based on different indexes of the same market, as well as by different sponsors. The number of ETFs keeps growing, and the diversity of investment targets increases, although not all ETFs launched are successful. We cite only some notable examples under each of the following categories:

▶ *Broad domestic market index*: In many countries, the most active ETFs are those launched on the major local stock index. Hong Kong Tracker Fund was the first ETF listed in Asia and the largest ever IPO in Asia excluding Japan. In Japan, Nikkei 225 and TOPIX ETFs have amassed significant assets under management, and there are several competing sponsors offering ETFs on the same indexes. In Europe, ETFs based on the French CAC 40 index and the German DAX 30 index are by far the most actively traded. In the United States, there are many market indexes followed by investors, so there are many competing ETFs; the most notable examples in this category include S&P 500 Depositary Receipts, iShares S&P 500, NASDAQ-100 QQQ and DIA (Diamonds Trust Series tracking the Dow Jones index). There are also ETFs based on very broad U.S. market indexes, such as the Russell 1000, Russell 3000, or Wilshire 5000 indexes. It is fair to say that ETFs based on local market indexes now exist in most countries, including in many emerging countries.

▶ *Style*: Some ETFs track a specific investment style, namely, value and growth. These ETFs are based on value and growth indexes developed by several index providers. This type of ETF is primarily found in the United States because investors from other countries are less accustomed to style investing, but there are some pan-European and Japanese style ETFs. There also exist ETFs specialized by market capitalization (large, mid, and small cap).

▶ *Sector or industry*: Some ETFs track a sector index or invest in baskets of stocks from specific industry sectors, including consumer, cyclicals, energy, financial, health care, industrials, insurance, materials, media, staples, technology, telecommunications, transportation, and utilities. Some ETFs specialize on a narrow sector or industry. For example, some ETFs track indexes of traded U.S. real estate investment trusts (REITs). Sector and industry ETFs can be found in the United States, Europe, and Japan. Many European funds track pan-European or global-sector indexes. In the United States, industry HOLDRs offer a series of investment portfolios that are based not on an index but on a basket of 20 to 50 companies in the same industry.

▶ *Foreign country or region (multiple countries)*: A fast-growing segment of the ETF market is funds tracking foreign-country indexes and regional indexes. In the United States, for example, iShares are indexed to several developed and emerging equity markets as well as to international indexes such as MSCI Europe and EAFE. International ETFs now represent a significant segment of ETFs offered in the United States. Country and regional ETFs have also been launched in Europe and Asia. Again, several sponsors are sometimes competing for products on the same international indexes.

▶ *Fixed income*: This category is a recent addition to the universe of ETFs, and mostly in the United States. These have had less success than equity ETFs so far.

▶ *Commodity*: ETFs have been introduced on some commodities, such as precious metals, and on some broad-based commodity index such as the GSCI.

▶ *Actively managed funds*: Some providers have introduced "active" ETFs in Europe. As of 2007 U.S. listing of active ETFs was also considered by several providers. While relying on the traditional design of ETF products, active ETFs do not intend to passively replicate the performance of an index but rely on active management of the portfolio to manage the risk/return profile. A challenge to actively manage an ETF using some proprietary model is the required daily transparence of ETFs. Active managers do not want to divulge their holdings for fear of being "front-run" by the market. The cost and tax advantage of an ETF structure would also be reduced.

International ETFs have distinguishing features. An ETF indexed on some less-liquid emerging market is bound to have high bid–ask spreads. Managing an ETF on a broad international index means holding stocks from numerous countries with different custodial arrangement and time zones. Again, the bid–ask spreads are bound to be larger than for *plain-vanilla* ETFs. But the size (assets under management) of the ETF is an important factor influencing costs. The effect of non-overlapping time zones should be taken into account when comparing the ETF price and its NAV. Take the example of an ETF on a Japanese stock index, traded in New York. During Wall Street opening hours, the Tokyo stock market is closed. The NAV available in the morning in the United States is based on the closing prices in Tokyo several hours before New York opened. Except for currency fluctuations, the NAV will remain unchanged because Tokyo is closed throughout the New York trading session. However, the ETF price will be affected by expectations about future stock prices in Tokyo, so it could differ significantly from the official NAV. This is not an inefficiency and there are no arbitrage opportunities because the NAV is stale and does not correspond to current market pricing.

Risks in ETFs

Listed next are the major risks faced by ETFs. They, however, do not affect all ETFs to the same extent. For example, market risk, trading risk, and tracking error risk affect all ETFs, while sector risk, currency risk, and country risk may affect sector and country ETFs. Likewise, derivatives risk affects only those funds that employ derivatives in their investment strategies. In addition, different ETFs may face risks that are unique to the fund (not discussed in this reading).

▶ *Market risk*: ETF shareholders are subject to risks similar to those of holders of other diversified portfolios. The NAV of the ETF will change with changes in the market index tracked by the fund.

▶ *Asset class/sector risk*: Some ETFs invest in some market segment. The returns from the type of securities in which an ETF invests may underperform returns from the general securities markets or different asset classes. For example, the performance of a sector ETF may be susceptible to any single economic, market, political, or regulatory occurrence. Thus, a sector ETF also may be adversely affected by the performance of that specific sector or group of industries on which it is based. This risk is directly implied by the investment strategy offered by the fund.

▶ *Trading risk*: Although an ETF is designed to make it likely that it will trade close to its NAV, impediments to the securities markets may result in trading prices that differ, sometimes significantly, from NAV. Moreover, there is no assurance that an active trading market will always exist for the ETF on the exchange, so the bid–ask spread can be large for some ETFs. The overall depth and liquidity of the secondary market also may fluctuate.

▶ *Tracking error risk*: Although ETFs are designed to provide investment results that generally correspond to the price and yield performance of their respective underlying indexes, the funds/trusts may not be able to exactly replicate the performance of the indexes because of fund/trust expenses and other factors. Tracking risk comes from trading risk (the ETF market price deviates from its NAV), but also from the fact that the ETF NAV differs from the index value.

▶ *Derivatives risk*: ETFs that invest in index futures contracts and other derivatives to track an index are subject to additional risks that accrue to derivatives, for example, counterparty credit risk and higher leverage.

▶ *Currency risk and country risk*: ETFs that are based on international indexes may involve risk of capital loss from unfavorable fluctuations in currency values or from economic and political instability in other nations. ETFs invested in emerging markets bear greater risk of market shutdown and of the imposition of capital controls than those typically found in a developed market. Country risk also includes the risk of expropriation. It could be that foreign investors are discriminated against, so that the return of an ETF will significantly underperform the local market index return achieved by a local investor.

Applications of ETFs

ETFs can be used in a wide variety of investment strategies. Following are some suggested popular applications:

▶ *Implementing asset allocation*: ETFs can be used to effect asset allocation among baskets of stocks and bonds at either the strategic or the tactical level.

▶ *Diversifying sector/industry exposure*: ETFs on broad market indexes can be used to diversify away the sector- or industry-specific event risks borne in an otherwise undiversified portfolio. Such ETF exposure is a natural complement to an investment strategy of holding only a few attractive stocks.

▶ *Gaining exposure to international markets*: Money managers can quickly and easily purchase ETFs for instant and extensive international exposure to a single country or multiple countries within a geographic region, compared with the expense and difficulty of assembling a portfolio of foreign securities.

▶ *Equitizing cash*: By investing in ETFs, money managers can put idle cash to work temporarily while determining where to invest for the longer term. For example, a fund manager using the Nikkei 225 as its benchmark could invest cash inflows into one of the ETFs tied to this benchmark before he decides which stocks to buy. This can minimize cash drag or benchmark risk. It is a convenient alternative to buying futures contract on the market index.

▶ *Managing cash flows*: Investment managers can take advantage of ETFs' liquidity during periods of cash inflows and outflows. A portfolio manager can establish a position in an ETF that corresponds to the portfolio's benchmark or investment strategy, investing inflows into the ETF and liquidating the position as needed to meet redemptions or invest in specific stocks or bonds.

▶ *Completing overall investment strategy*: Fund or money managers can use ETFs to quickly establish or increase exposure to an industry or sector to "fill holes" in an overall investment strategy.

▶ *Bridging transitions in fund management*: Pension plan assets can often lie dormant during times of investment manager appointments, replacements, or shifts. Institutions can use ETFs as a cost-effective method to keep assets invested in the interim.

▶ *Managing portfolio risk*: Because ETFs can be sold short in a declining equity market (or rising interest rate market for fixed-income ETFs), portfolio managers can use ETFs to hedge overall portfolio risk or sector/industry exposure.

▶ *Applying relative value, long/short strategies*: Institutions can take advantage of ETF features to apply long/short strategies aimed at increasing returns. For example, an institution can establish a long position in a broad market, country, sector, style, or bond index expected to outperform while shorting an index expected to underperform. Doubling the size of the long position versus the short position can leverage the total position. Market makers can use ETFs to exploit price discrepancies between ETFs, the underlying index, the futures, and/or options.

2   REAL ESTATE

Real estate is usually considered to be buildings and buildable land, including offices, industrial warehouses, multifamily buildings, and retail space. Real estate is a form of tangible asset, one that can be touched and seen, as opposed to financial claims that are recorded as pieces of paper. Other forms of tangible assets are available for investment purposes. These include natural resources, timber, containers, artwork, and many others. We will focus on real estate, which is by far the most common form of investment in tangible assets.

Real estate as an investment has several unique characteristics as well as several characteristics common to other types of investments. Even the definition of real estate isolates it as a unique investment. Real estate is an immovable asset—land (earth surface) and the permanently attached improvements to it. Graaskamp defines real estate as artificially delineated space with a fourth dimension of time referenced to a fixed point on the face of the earth.[6] This astrophysical definition stresses the idea that ownership rights to earth areas can be divided up not only in the three dimensions of space, but also in a time dimension, as well as divided up among investors. One plot of land with its build-

---

[6] Jarchow (1991), p. 42.

ing can be divided into above ground (e.g., buildings) and below ground (e.g., minerals), into areas within the building (e.g., rooms), and into periods of time (timesharing). Different investors can own the different divisions. Many classifications can be adopted for real estate. Real estate can be classified by usage (office space, multifamily housing, retail space) and location. It can also be classified into four quadrants by form of ownership, public or private, and by form of financing, debt or equity.[7] Clearly, it is not possible to adopt a simple classification of real estate because this asset class covers so many different investment products.

Real estate is an important investment category. In many countries, domestic real estate is a common investment vehicle for pension funds and life insurance companies. It is not uncommon to have private European investors owning and renting directly a few real estate units, such as houses, condominium apartments, or parking spaces. But there are some obstacles for institutions and individuals wishing to invest in foreign real estate. First, it is difficult to monitor properties located abroad. Second, taxes, paperwork, and unforeseen risks may make foreign real estate investment impractical on a large scale, although investments can be made through specialized managers in the countries of interest. To be sure, private deals can be arranged for special projects, but these are well beyond the scope of this book. There is, however, a definite trend toward the development of negotiable forms for real property interest. In many countries, pooled funds have been created with the specific purpose of real estate investment. Mortgage-backed Eurobonds are rapidly growing in popularity. Many institutional investors, especially in Europe, have started to invest in international real estate. The time may not be too far off when real estate will be a normal component of international investment strategies.

Forms of Real Estate Investment

There are several forms of real estate investment: free and clear equity, leveraged equity, mortgages, and aggregation vehicles.

Free and Clear Equity

Free and clear equity, sometimes called *fee simple*, refers to full ownership rights for an indefinite period of time, giving the owner the right, for example, to lease the property to tenants and resell the property at will. This is straightforward purchase of some real estate property.

Leveraged Equity

Leveraged equity refers to the same ownership rights but subject to debt (a promissory note) and a pledge (mortgage) to hand over real estate ownership rights if the loan terms are not met. A mortgage is a pledge of real estate ownership rights to another party as security for debt owed to that party. Thus, leveraged equity involves equity ownership plus a debt and a requirement to transfer ownership of the equity in case of default on the debt. The debt and the mortgage are usually packaged together into a mortgage loan.

---

[7] See, for example, Hudson-Wilson (2001).

Mortgages

Mortgages (or more precisely, *mortgage loans*) themselves are another real estate investment vehicle, representing a type of debt investment. Investing in a mortgage provides the investor with a stream of bondlike payments. These payments include net interest, net of mortgage servicing fees, and a scheduled repayment of principal. This is a form of real estate investment because the creditor may end up owning the property being mortgaged. Mortgage loans often include a clause of early repayment (at a cost) at the option of the debtor. So, the debtholder may also receive excess principal repayments, called mortgage prepayments. These prepayments produce uncertainty in the amount and timing of mortgage cash flows.

To diversify risks, a typical investor does not invest in one mortgage, but in securities issued against a pool of mortgages. An intermediary buys a pool of mortgages and then issues securities backed by the mortgages, but with the securities passing through the net mortgage payments to the investors.

Aggregation Vehicles

Aggregation vehicles aggregate investors and serve the purpose of giving investors collective access to real estate investments. *Real estate limited partnerships* (*RELPs*) allow investors (the limited partners) to participate in real estate projects while preserving limited liability (the initial investment) and leaving management to the general partners who are real estate experts. *Commingled funds* are pools of capital created largely by like-minded institutional investors organized together by an intermediary to invest chiefly in real estate investment projects. The investors share in the investment rewards according to the amount of capital they invest. Commingled funds can be either open or closed end. Closed-end funds have a set termination date, typically allow no new investors after initiation of the fund, and typically buy and hold a real estate portfolio for the life of the fund, with no reinvestment as sales occur. By contrast, open-end funds have indefinite lives, accept new investors, and revise their real estate portfolios over time. Finally, *real estate investment trusts* (*REITs*) are a type of closed-end investment company. They issue shares that are traded on a stock market, and they invest in various types of real estate. Thus, they aggregate individual investors and provide them easy access to real estate and diversification within real estate. Of course, the risk and return characteristics of REITs depend on the type of investment they make. Mortgage REITs, which invest primarily in mortgages, are more akin to a bond investment, while equity REITs, which invest primarily in commercial or residential properties using leverage, are more akin to an investment in leveraged equity real estate. The shares of REITs trade freely on the stock market, so they are liquid investments, but their share price can trade at a discount (or premium) to the NAV of the properties in their portfolio.

Valuation Approaches

Real estate assets are quite different from securities traded on a financial market: "Because the real estate market is not an auction market offering divisible shares in every property, and information flows in the market are complex, these features place a premium on investment judgment. Managers who want to own some of IBM simply buy some shares. Managers who want to participate in the returns on, say, a $300 million office building must take a significant position in the property."[8] Following are some characteristics of real estate as an investable asset class:

▶ Properties are immovable, basically indivisible, and unique assets, as contrasted to fungible (perfectly interchangeable) and divisible assets such as currencies. Though unique, even art is movable and thus not as unique as real estate.

▶ Properties are only approximately comparable to other properties.

▶ Properties are generally illiquid, due to their immobility and indivisibility.

▶ There is no national, or international, auction market for properties. Hence, the "market" value of a given property is difficult to assess.

▶ Transaction costs and management fees for real estate investments are high.

▶ Real estate markets suffer inefficiencies because of the nature of real estate itself and because information is not freely available.

Valuation of real estate focuses on intrinsic value just as does the valuation of any asset. In real estate, the term *appraisal* is used for the process of estimating the market and the investment value of the property. The market value estimate is independent of the particular investor, but the investment value depends on the particular use that the investor plans for the property.

To estimate a property's value, a real estate appraiser generally uses one of three approaches or a combination of the approaches. The approaches are the cost approach, the sales comparison approach, and the income approach. An investor can further take into account her specific tax situation to value the property using a discounted after-tax cash flow approach. These four approaches are used worldwide.

The Cost Approach

The cost approach is analogous to the use of replacement cost of total assets in the calculation of Tobin's Q for equity valuation. What would it cost to replace the building in its present form? Of course, an estimate of the land value must be added to the building replacement cost estimate. The replacement cost approach is relatively easy to implement because it is based on current construction costs, but it suffers from severe limitations. First, an appraisal of the land value is required and that is not always an easy task. Second, the market value of an existing property could differ markedly from its construction cost. An office building could be very valuable because it has some prestigious and stable tenants that pay high rents, not because of the value of the construction. Conversely, an office building in poor condition, with a large vacancy rate and in a bad neighborhood, could be worth much less than its replacement cost.

The Sales Comparison Approach

The sales comparison approach is similar to the "price multiple comparables" approach in equity valuation. Market value is estimated relative to a benchmark value. The benchmark value may be the market price of a similar property, or the average or median value of the market prices of similar properties, in transactions

---

[8] Firstenberg, Ross, and Zisler (1988).

made near the time of the appraisal. The benchmark-based estimate needs to be adjusted for changing market conditions, the possibility that the benchmark itself is mispriced, and the unique features of the property relative to the benchmark. Properties with comparable characteristics might not have traded recently.

One formal variation of the sales comparison approach is the method of *hedonic price estimation*. In this method, the major characteristics of a property that can affect its value are identified. The characteristics of a residential property that are relevant to its value can be the age of the building, its size, its location, its vacancy rate, its amenities, and so on. Individual properties are given a quantitative rating for each of the characteristics. For example, location could be ranked from 1 (very bad) to 10 (very good). The sales price for all recent transactions of the properties in the benchmark are then regressed on their characteristics ratings. This is a regression in which there is one observation for each transaction. The dependent (left-hand side) variable is the transaction price, and the independent (right-hand side) variables are the ratings for each of the characteristics. The estimated slope coefficients are the valuation of each characteristic in the transaction price. The result is a benchmark monetary value associated with each characteristic's rating. It is then possible to estimate the selling price of a specific property by taking into account its rating on each feature (see Example 2). Although this has become a standard technique in residential property appraisal, it has also been applied to income producing property.[9]

EXAMPLE 2

Sales Comparison Approach: Hedonic Price Model

A real estate company has prepared a simple hedonic model to value houses in a specific area. Here is a summary list of the house's characteristics that can affect pricing:

▶ The number of main rooms
▶ The surface area of the garden
▶ The presence of a swimming pool
▶ The distance to a shopping center

A statistical analysis of a large number of recent transactions in the area allowed the company to estimate the following slope coefficients:

Characteristics	Units	Slope Coefficient in Pounds per Unit
Number of rooms	Number	20,000
Surface area of the garden	Square feet	5
Swimming pool	0 or 1	20,000
Distance to shopping center	In miles	−10,000

---

[9] See Söderberg (2002), pp. 157–180.

A typical house in the area has five main rooms, a garden of 10,000 square feet, a swimming pool, and a distance of one mile to the nearest shopping center. The transaction price for a typical house was £160,000.

You wish to value a house that has seven rooms, a garden of 10,000 square feet, a swimming pool, and a distance of two miles to the nearest shopping center. What is the appraisal value based on this sales comparison approach of hedonic price estimation?

Solution: The appraised value is given by the equation

$$
\begin{aligned}
\text{Value} &= 20{,}000 \times (\text{\# Rooms}) + 5 \times (\text{Garden surface}) + 20{,}000 \\
&\quad \times (\text{Pool}) - 10{,}000 \times (\text{Distance to shopping center}) \\
&= 20{,}000 \times 7 + 5 \times 10{,}000 + 20{,}000 \times 1 - 10{,}000 \times 2 \\
&= £190{,}000
\end{aligned}
$$

This specific house has an appraised value of £190,000. Compared to the typical house in the area, it has two more rooms but is one mile farther from the nearest shopping center.

The Income Approach

The income approach to real estate valuation values property using a perpetuity discount type of model. The perpetuity is the annual net operating income (NOI). This perpetual stream is discounted at a market required rate of return (the market capitalization or cap rate). NOI is gross potential income minus expenses, which include estimated vacancy and collection losses, insurance, taxes, utilities, and repairs and maintenance. Technically, the market cap rate is the rate used by the market in recent transactions to capitalize future income into a present market value. For a constant and perpetual stream of annual NOI, we have

$$
\text{Appraisal price} = \frac{\text{NOI}}{\text{Market cap rate}}
$$

And the market cap rate is calculated on the benchmark transactions as

$$
\text{Market cap rate} = \frac{\text{Benchmark NOI}}{\text{Benchmark transaction price}}
$$

Benchmark may refer to a single comparable property or the median or mean of several comparable properties, with any appropriate adjustments. A numerical illustration is presented in Example 3.

It must be stressed that the income approach makes the simplifying assumption of a constant and perpetual amount of annual income. The income approach can also be adjusted for the special cases of a constant growth rate in rentals or a constant growth rate in rentals coupled with long-term leases. Valuation with a constant growth rate in rentals parallels the constant growth dividend discount model. Inflation could make NOI grow at the inflation rate over time. As long as inflation can be passed through, it will not affect valuation, because the market cap rate also incorporates the inflation rate. In the long-term lease case, the growth in rentals is not fully reflected in the NOI growth

EXAMPLE 3

The Income Approach

An investor wants to evaluate an apartment complex using the income approach. Recent sales in the area consist of an office building and an apartment complex. He gathers the following data on the apartment complex, as well as on recent sales in the area. All income items are on an annual basis. According to the income approach, what is the value of the apartment complex?

	Apartment Investment under Consideration	Office Building Recently Sold	Apartment Complex Recently Sold
Gross potential rental income	$120,000		
Estimated vacancy and collection losses	6%		
Insurance and taxes	$10,000		
Utilities	$7,000		
Repairs and maintenance	$12,000		
Depreciation	$14,000		
Interest on proposed financing	$11,000		
Net operating income		$300,000	$60,000
Sales price		$2,000,000	$500,000

Solution: The NOI for the apartment complex is gross potential rental income minus estimated vacancy and collection costs minus insurance and taxes minus utilities minus repairs and maintenance.

$$NOI = 120,000 - 0.06 \times 120,000 - 10,000 - 7,000 - 12,000 = 83,800$$

The other apartment complex is the comparable property, and that has a capitalization rate of

$$NOI/(\text{Transaction price}) = 60,000/500,000 = 0.12$$

Applying this cap rate to the apartment complex under consideration gives an appraisal price of

$$NOI/(\text{Cap rate}) = 83,800/0.12 = \$698,333$$

Note that we do not use the financing costs to determine the NOI, because we wish to appraise the value of the property independently of its financing. Neither do we subtract depreciation. The implicit assumption is that repairs and maintenance will allow the investor to keep the building in good condition forever.

rate. The rent remains fixed over the term of the lease, while costs grow at the inflation rate. This is analogous to the inflation pass-through question raised in equity valuation. If expected inflation will cause operating expenses to rise, how much of the inflation can the owner pass through to the tenants? Longer lease terms delay the pass-through. Another limitation of this approach is that all calculations are performed before tax.

The Discounted After-Tax Cash Flow Approach

Supplementing the cost, sales comparison, and income approach used for market value appraisals, the discounted after-tax cash flow approach is a check on investment valuation. If the investor can deduct depreciation and any interest payments from NOI, then the investor's after-tax cash flows depend on the investor's marginal tax rate. Hence, the value of a property for a specific investor depends on the investor's marginal tax rate. Once these cash flows and after-tax proceeds from future property disposition are estimated, the net present value of the property to an equity investor is obtained as the present value of the cash flows, discounted at the investor's required rate of return on equity, minus the amount of equity required to make the investment.

For an equity investment to be worthwhile, its expected net present value must be positive. Alternatively, the investment's yield (internal rate of return) should exceed the investor's required rate of return. A numerical illustration is presented in Example 4.

EXAMPLE 4

The Discounted Cash Flow Approach

An analyst is assigned the task of evaluating a real estate investment project. The purchase price is $700,000, which is financed 20 percent by equity and 80 percent by a mortgage loan at a 10 percent pretax interest rate. According to the applicable country's tax rules, the interest on real estate financing for this project is tax-deductible. The mortgage loan has a long maturity and level annual payments of $59,404. This includes interest payments on the remaining principal at a 10 percent interest rate and a variable principal repayment that steps up with time. The analyst calculated NOI in the first year to be $83,800. NOI is expected to grow at a rate of 5 percent every year.

The analyst faces the following valuation tasks: determining the first year's after-tax cash flow, determining interim after-tax cash flows, determining the final year's after-tax cash flow, and calculating two measures of the project's profitability, the investment's net present value (NPV) and the investment's yield (internal rate of return).

i. Determine the first year's after-tax cash flow using the following data:

Net operating income (NOI) for first year	$83,800
Straight-line depreciation	$18,700
Mortgage payment	$59,404
Purchase price	$700,000
80% financing at a 10% interest rate	
NOI growth rate	5%
Marginal income tax rate	31%

ii. Determine the second year's after-tax cash flow, using the preceding table and with a growth rate of 5% in NOI.

iii. The property is sold at the end of the fifth year. Determine the after-tax cash flow for that property sale year, using the following data (the after-tax cash flow without property sale has been calculated as previously).

After-tax cash flow without property sale	$33,546
Straight-line depreciation	$18,700
Mortgage payment	$59,404
Cumulative mortgage principal repayments by end of fifth year	$20,783
Purchase price	$700,000
80% financing at 10% interest rate	
NOI growth factor	5%
Marginal income tax rate	31%
Capital gains tax rate	20%
Forecasted sales price	$875,000
Property sales expense as a percentage of sales price	6%

Use the information below to answer Parts iv and v.

The following data summarize the after-tax cash flows for all five years of the project's life (the table includes the results we have calculated previously for years 1, 2, and 5, as well as results for years 3 and 4):

Year	1	2	3	4	5
Cash flow	21,575	24,361	27,280	30,339	273,629

The analyst now turns to evaluating whether the project should be undertaken. She estimates the required rate of return for an equity investment in projects of similar risk as 16 percent. The purchase price for the property is $700,000. The financing plan calls for 80 percent debt financing, so the equity investment is only $140,000. The investor's cost of equity for projects with this level of risk is 16 percent, but a sensitivity analysis on cost of equity helps provide some perspective for the analyst. She decides to conduct a sensitivity analysis, calculating the present value of the year 1 to year 5 after-tax cash flows using a range of discount rates other than 16 percent; the results appear in the following table:

Discount Rate	Present Value
0.10	$250,867
0.14	$216,161
0.18	$187,637
0.22	$164,012
0.26	$144,303
0.30	$127,747
0.34	$113,750

iv. Determine the real estate project's NPV, using the analyst's required rate of return, and make a purchase recommendation based only on this analysis.

v. Determine an approximate yield for the real estate project, and make a purchase recommendation based only on this analysis.

Solution to i: Because interest is tax-deductible here, calculate the first year's interest, and then calculate after-tax net income. The amount borrowed is $560,000 = 700,000 × 0.8. The first year's interest at 10 percent is then $56,000 = 0.1 × $560,000. After-tax net income is then ($83,800 − $18,700 − $56,000) × (1 − 0.31) = $6,279.

To get after-tax cash flow from after-tax net income, depreciation must be added and the principal repayment component of the $59,404 mortgage payment must be subtracted. The principal repayment is the mortgage payment minus the interest payment, or $3,404 = $59,404 − $56,000. Thus, the after-tax cash flow is $21,575 = $6,279 + $18,700 − $3,404.

Solution to ii: First we calculate the new NOI, equal to $87,990 = $83,800 × (1.05).

Second, we calculate after-tax net income. We need to calculate the second year's interest payment on the mortgage balance after the first year's payment. This mortgage balance is the original principal balance minus the first year's principal repayment, or $556,596. The interest on this balance is then $55,660. After-tax net income is then ($87,990 − $18,700 − $55,660) × (1 − 0.31) = $9,405.

Third, the second year's principal repayment is the mortgage payment minus the interest payment, or $3,744 = $59,404 − $55,660.

Finally, then calculate the second year's after-tax cash flow, which equals the second year's after-tax net income plus depreciation minus the principal repayment, or $24,361 = $9,405 + $18,700 − $3,744.

Solution to iii: The after-tax cash flow for the property sale year is equal to the sum of the after-tax cash flow without the property sale plus the after-tax cash flow from the property sale. When a property is sold, the outstanding mortgage principal balance (the outstanding mortgage, for short) must be paid to the lender. In the following calculations, we incorporate that effect into the after-tax cash flow from the property sale.

To begin, we calculate the capital gains on the sale of the property. To do that, first determine the ending book value as the original purchase price minus five years' worth of depreciation, or $606,500 = $700,000 − 5 × $18,700. The net sale price is equal to the forecasted sale price, $875,000, minus sales expenses of 6 percent, or $52,500. Capital gains taxes are paid on the difference between the net sales price and the book value, or a difference of $216,000 = ($875,000 − $52,500) − $606,500. The capital gains taxes are then $43,200 = 0.2 × $216,000. The after-tax cash flow from the property sale is then the net sales price minus the outstanding mortgage minus the capital gains taxes. The outstanding mortgage is the original mortgage minus five years' worth of principal repayments, or $539,217 = $560,000 − $20,783. Thus the after-tax cash flow from the property sale is $240,083 = ($875,000 − $52,500) − $539,217 − $43,200. The after-tax cash flow for the property sale year is then $273,629 = $33,546 + $240,083.

Solution to iv: At a cost of equity of 16 percent, the present value of the cash flow is $201,215 = $21,575/1.16 + $24,361/1.16^2 + $27,280/1.16^3 + $30,339/1.16^4 + $273,629/1.16^5. The investment requires equity of $140,000 = 0.2 × $700,000. Thus, the NPV is $61,215 = $201,215 − $140,000. The analyst recommends this investment because it has a positive NPV.

Solution to v: We can address the question using the results of the analyst's sensitivity analysis. The yield or internal rate of return is the discount rate that makes the project's NPV equal to zero. The yield must be between 26 percent and 30 percent because discounting at 26 percent gives a present value ($144,303) that is larger than the initial investment (of $140,000), or a positive NPV, while discounting at 30 percent gives a present value ($127,747) that is smaller than the initial investment, or a negative NPV. Consequently, the project's yield must lie between 26 percent and 30 percent. Actually, the internal rate of return of this project is slightly below 27 percent. The analyst recommends the investment because the investment's yield exceeds the investor's required rate of return (16 percent).

Real Estate in a Portfolio Context

Some real estate indexes have been developed to attempt to measure the average return on real estate investment. Good-quality indexes with a long-term historical record exist in the United States and United Kingdom, but they are more recent in other countries. There are also global real estate indexes.

Real estate returns consist of income and capital gain or loss. The income on a property can usually be measured in a straightforward fashion. The value appreciation is more difficult to assess. The most common method is to use changes in *appraised* value. Appraisal of each property is conducted by specialists fairly infrequently (typically once a year). Appraisals are generally based on the approaches discussed previously. In practice, appraisal prices exhibit remarkable inertia. The value of a real estate portfolio is further smoothed because properties are appraised infrequently, so their prices remain constant between appraisals.

The major U.S. real estate index based on appraisal values is the National Council of Real Estate Investment Fiduciaries (NCREIF) property index, or NPI. This is a quarterly index, starting in 1978 and broken down by regions and property types.

Another method of measuring price appreciation is to use a reference to REITs. The total return on a REIT is made up of the income paid to shareholders as well as the stock market appreciation of the REIT share price. Various REIT indexes are used to proxy the average total return on real estate investments. REIT indexes are easy to construct because they are simply some weighted average of market-traded shares. The major REIT indexes are as follows:

▶ The National Association of Real Estate Investment Trusts (NAREIT), a monthly index of over 100 REITs, starting in 1972

▶ REIT indexes published by various institutions, for example, Dow Jones Wilshire or MSCI

For all the REIT indexes mentioned above, one can access a global index, broken down by regions or individual countries.

Appraisal-based indexes and REIT stock market indexes provide very different performance and risk characteristics for real estate. Appraisal-based indexes are much less volatile than REIT indexes. For example, Goetzmann and Ibbotson (1990) found that a REIT index had an annual standard deviation of 15.4 percent, comparable to that of the S&P 500 index but six times larger than that of an appraisal-based index of 2.6 percent. Furthermore, appraisal-based indexes and REIT indexes have very little correlation. Appraisal-based indexes exhibit persistent returns (returns are correlated over time), showing the inertia in appraisals. REIT indexes are strongly correlated with the rest of the stock market.

In summary, real estate returns can be calculated using either appraisal indexes or REIT indexes. Appraisals do not provide continuous price data, and they do not provide market prices but only market price estimates. REIT indexes provide continuous market prices of REITs but not of the underlying real estate. Thus, they reflect the amount of leverage used in the REITs. Therefore neither approach to calculating returns is entirely satisfactory. In any case, the issue in investment is one of forecasting returns, standard deviations, and correlations. For example, in analyzing a particular real estate project, an investor would supplement cash flow forecasts and discounted cash flow analysis with considerations of how the project's cash flows will covary with his existing portfolio. An individual investor will not receive diversification benefits from a real estate project whose returns are highly correlated with his own business employment income.

A few studies have looked at real estate from a global viewpoint. These studies examine the proposed portfolio benefits of real estate, risk reduction (through diversification), and inflation protection. These studies involve either appraisal-based real estate indexes or returns on publicly traded real companies such as REITs. Eichholtz (1996) looked at the diversification benefits of real estate shares quoted in many countries. He found that international diversification strongly reduces the risk of a real estate portfolio. The argument seems even stronger than for international equity diversification because the international correlation of real estate appears lower than that of equity. Hoesli, Lekander, and Witkiewicz (2004) confirm that international diversification is useful within a real estate portfolio. They also show that real estate provides a useful element of diversification within a portfolio of stocks and bonds. Their study uses appraisal-based indexes, with their well-known smoothing characteristic, although they attempt to correct for it. However, Mull and Soenen (1997) showed that REITs are strongly correlated with other U.S. stocks, so that foreign investors who buy U.S. REITs do not gain a large diversification benefit beyond the U.S. stock market exposure. Quan and Titman (1997) studied commercial real estate values in 17 countries where property values and rents are calculated using an appraisal-based approach. Commercial real estate prices and stock prices are both affected by the general level of economic activity, so they should be correlated. Pooling their international data, Quan and Titman did find that the relation between stock returns and changes in real estate values is strong. Two other statistical properties of real estate prices are worth mentioning. Liu, Hartzell, and Hoesli (1997) looked at real estate securities traded on seven national stock markets and concluded that their correlation with inflation is low, so they do not provide a good hedge against inflation. Furthermore, there is a general finding that real estate prices tend to react negatively to interest rate levels and changes.

Although research studies have not provided overwhelming evidence to support the risk reduction and inflation protection benefits of real estate, such studies are always limited by the use of either appraisal indexes or REIT indexes. Judgment is needed in assessing the impact of real estate on a portfolio. First, what are the projected cash flows and what are the predicted covariances of the cash flows with the current portfolio? Second, what are the inflation pass-through characteristics of the real estate investment?

3   PRIVATE EQUITY

Private equity investing has grown rapidly in the 2000s. *Private equity* is a broad term that commonly refers to an equity investment in a potentially successful company or asset not publicly traded on capital market. *Private equity investments* are equity investments that are not traded on exchanges. Institutional and individual investors usually invest in private equity through limited partnerships, which allow investors (the limited partners) to participate in a portfolio of private equity projects while preserving limited liability (the initial investment) and leaving management to the general partners, who are private equity experts. General partners often get involved in the management of the companies they invest in. Typically, the general partners are associated with a firm that specializes in private equity or with the private equity department of a financial institution. The limited partnership is often called the fund, and the general partners are sometimes designated as the management company (although at times that is a separate company affiliated with the general partner). Funds of funds are also offered that pool investments in several private equity funds. There are several overlapping categories of private equity investing. The three main categories are described below.

Venture capital is one of the main categories of private equity investing and the most traditional one. Venture capital investments are private equity investments in business ventures from idea stage through expansion of a company already producing and selling a product and through preparation for exit from the investment via buyout or initial public offering. Venture capital investing may be done at several stages along the way, but eventual exit is a primary consideration. By its very nature, such investing requires a horizon of several years and the willingness to accept several failures for every success in the venture capital portfolio: The possibly enormous return on the winning venture must compensate for many likely failed ventures. Venture capital is detailed below.

Leveraged buyout investing has become the largest category of private equity. Buyout investors typically take a majority control in acquired companies, as opposed to venture capitalists who only take a minority interest. These companies are established, ongoing concerns and are often publicly traded on some exchange. In buyouts, investors put up an equity stake, typically between 20 and 40 percent of the total purchase price, and borrow the rest; hence the term *leveraged*. After acquisition, the purchased company is taken private. The private equity firm gets involved in the management of the acquired company and takes steps to increase its value. The objective is to resell the acquired company, or part of it, within a few years at a higher price. The sale is done privately or through an *initial public offering (IPO)*. A *management buyout* (*MBO*) is a special form of leveraged buyout in which the managers of the acquired company become large investors in the company after its privatization. Large buyouts of public companies can exceed $10 billion and make news headlines. But there are also numerous deals involving "middle market" companies that enter the portfolio of companies held by a private equity fund. The leveraged buyout market has become global; private equity firms from many nationalities invest all over the world, including in emerging countries. While the concept of leveraged buyout investing is simple, success primarily depends on the ability of the managers to restructure the portfolio companies to extract value when they are taken private.

Distressed investing, also called *special situations* or *vulture investing*, refers to investing in the equity and debt of companies in financial distress. Because the private equity firm typically buys out the distressed company, there is some overlap with the previous category. But debtholders have a priority claim over equity holders, so any improvement in the company's situation will first accrue to debtholders. The concept is to invest in operationally sound, financially distressed companies and to reorganize them. A further discussion of distressed investing is provided later in the reading.

It must be stressed that hedge funds (described on page 218) have also ventured into private equity, especially in buyouts of small companies and distressed-debt investing. While most hedge funds shy away from taking control of companies and restructuring them, instead focusing on somewhat liquid financial investments, many experts predict that the move into private equity is a natural progression for hedge funds, so the line between private equity funds and hedge funds will get blurred.

The rest of this section is devoted to venture capital, which is the original form of private equity investment. The success of buyouts and distress investing relies on the restructuring of the acquired companies, a topic beyond the scope of this reading.

Stages of Venture Capital Investing

Schilit (1996) provides a good review of the various stages of venture capital investing. Several rounds of financing take place, and these can be characterized by where they occur in the development of the venture itself. Here, Schilit's classification review is adapted and blended with other common industry terminology.[10] Each stage of financing is matched by investments, so that aggregate investment activity is often reported by the amount in different stage funds.

1. *Seed-stage* financing is capital provided for a business idea. The capital generally supports product development and market research.

2. *Early stage* financing is capital provided for companies moving into operation and before commercial manufacturing and sales have occurred.

   ▶ *Start-up* is capital provided for companies just moving into operation but without any commercial product or service sales. The capital generally supports product development and initial marketing.

   ▶ *First-stage* financing is capital provided to initiate commercial manufacturing and sales.

3. *Formative-stage* financing includes seed stage and early stage.

4. *Later-stage* financing is capital provided after commercial manufacturing and sales have begun but before any initial public offering.

   ▶ *Second-stage* financing refers to capital used for initial expansion of a company already producing and selling a product but perhaps not yet profitably.

   ▶ *Third-stage* financing is capital provided for major expansion, such as physical plant expansion, product improvement, or a major marketing campaign.

   ▶ *Mezzanine* (bridge) financing is capital provided to prepare for the step of going public and represents the bridge between the expanding company and the initial public offering (IPO).

Expansion-stage financing includes second and third stage. *Balanced-stage* financing is a term used to refer to all the stages, seed through mezzanine.

Investment Characteristics

Venture capital investing has several characteristics, some of which are common to alternative investing in general, but many of which are unique:

   ▶ *Illiquidity*: Venture capital investments do not provide an easy or short-term path for cashing out. Liquidation or divestment of each venture within a portfolio is dependent on the success of the fund manager in creating a buyout or IPO opportunity. One particular risk is that inexperienced venture fund managers will "grandstand" and bring ventures to the market too early, especially when the IPO market is good. Conversely, a poor IPO

---

[10] See, for example, Thomson Venture Economics, the National Venture Capital Association (in the United States), the European Venture Capital Association, and the British Venture Capital Association.

market may mean that otherwise successful ventures may afford no immediate path to liquidity.

▶ *Long-term commitment required*: Venture capital requires a long-term commitment because of the time lag to liquidity. If the average investor is averse to illiquidity, there will be a liquidity risk premium on venture capital. Thus, an investor with a longer than average time horizon can expect to profit from this liquidity risk premium. It is not surprising that university endowments (with their long horizons) have sought venture capital vehicles.

▶ *Difficulty in determining current market values*: Because there is no continuous trading of the investments within a venture fund portfolio, there is no objective way of determining the current market value of the portfolio. This poses a problem for reporting the market value exposure of the current venture capital portion of an investor's portfolio.

▶ *Limited historical risk and return data*: Because there is no continuous market in venture capital, historical risk and return data have limitations.

▶ *Limited information*: Because entrepreneurs operate in previously uncharted territory, there is little information on which to base estimates of cash flows or the probability of success of their ventures.

▶ *Entrepreneurial/management mismatches*: Although surely profit motivated, some entrepreneurs may be more wedded to the success of their favorite idea than to the financial success of the venture. During the early life of a firm, there are also two major problems that may arise. First, the entrepreneur may not be a good manager, so the existence or creation of a good management team is critical. Second, rapid growth produces a change in the type of managerial expertise required, so that entrepreneurs/managers who can succeed with small ventures need the ability to adapt to the different demands of larger companies, or the investors must be in a position to replace them.

▶ *Fund manager incentive mismatches*: Fund managers may be rewarded by size of their fund rather than by performance of their fund. Investors interested in performance must look for fund managers whose incentives are aligned with theirs.

▶ *Lack of knowledge of how many competitors exist*: Because entrepreneurs operate in uncharted territory, there is often little way for them or for analysts to know how many other entrepreneurs are developing substitute ideas or products at the same time. Thus, competitive analysis for venture capital investments is even more difficult than for investments in established companies in established industries.

▶ *Vintage cycles*: Some years are better than others. Both entry and exit are factors here. If too many entrepreneurial firms enter at the prompt of increased venture capital availability, the economics of perfect competition will prevail and returns will be weak. On the exit side, poor financial market conditions can cause venture capital to dry up, and perhaps some firms that could be successful will not find the financing needed for their success. Thus, some years provide better firm planting and growing conditions than others.

▶ *Extensive operations analysis and advice may be required*: More than financial engineering skill is required of fund managers. Venture capital investments require extensive investment analysis, but they also require extensive operating management experience. Thus, a venture capital manager who can add value will be the one who has both financial and operating experience, and knowledge of the emerging industry in which the entrepreneur is operating. The venture capital manager must be able to act as both a financial and an operations management consultant to the venture. Reflecting David Swensen's philosophy[11] at the Yale Endowment, the investor is well advised to choose a fund manager who knows the business and can add value.

Types of Liquidation/Divestment[12]

Exit strategies are critical for venture capital investing. The main types of liquidation/divestment are trade sales, IPOs followed by the sale of quoted equity, and write-offs. Trade sales are sales or mergers of the private company for cash or stock of the acquirer. An IPO is the initial issuance of shares registered for public trading. Shares are distributed to the private equity investors who can sell them in the marketplace only after the expiration of a lock-up period. (In rare cases, a sale or merger of the private company follows the IPO.) Write-offs are voluntary liquidations that may or may not produce any proceeds. In addition to the main types of liquidation, there are cases of bankruptcy as well as the situation in which the founder/entrepreneur buys out the outside venture capital investors and takes the company back to a privately held company without institutional shareholders.

Participating in a venture capital fund, investors get distributions of public stock or cash from realized venture capital investments. The fund may require additional investments (drawdowns) from limited partners and may make cash or share distributions at random times during the life of the fund. Investors might also be able to sell their interests if they can find a buyer. Also, at the end of the fund's life, there are often illiquid, barely alive companies ("living dead") that are transferred to a liquidating vehicle with minimal fees. A very few funds have an evergreen type of structure, which rolls old fund investments into a new fund that has new cash commitments.

Valuation and Performance Measurement

In the venture capital area, valuation and performance measurement is a difficult exercise. This is true at the level of a single venture project, but also at the level of an investment in a venture capital fund.

Valuation and Project Risk

Valuing a prospective venture capital project is a challenging task. Although some valuation methods can be applied, quantifying future cash flows is difficult. Investing in a particular venture capital project is motivated by an anticipated large payoff at time of exit. But many projects will fail along the way. In addition to the normal risk of equity investments, the particular risk of venture capital stems from the increased uncertainty created by possibly inexperienced entrepreneurs with innovative products or product ideas and uncertain time to success, even if successful. Some of the unique risks of venture capital projects come from their investment characteristics, as described. Of course, the risk of a portfolio of venture capital investments is less than the risk of any individual venture project, because of risk diversification.

---

[11] See pages 17 and 18 in Lerner (2000).

[12] This section has benefited from correspondence with Dean Takahashi.

So, there are three main parameters that enter into valuing a venture capital project:

▶ An assessment of the expected payoff at time of exit, if the venture is successful

▶ An assessment of the time it will take to exit the venture successfully

▶ An assessment of the probability of failure

This is illustrated in Example 5.

The payoff structure of actual projects is generally more complex than that of Example 5. Practitioners may use a multiple-scenario approach to valuation. In this approach, payoffs are simulated under each scenario (from optimistic to pessimistic) and weighted by the probability of occurrence of the scenario.

EXAMPLE 5

Venture Capital Valuation and Risk

An investor estimates that investing $1 million in a particular venture capital project will pay $16 million at the end of seven years if it succeeds; however, she realizes that the project may fail at any time between now and the end of seven years. The investor is considering an equity investment in the project and her cost of equity for a project with this level of risk is 18 percent. In the following table are the investor's estimates of some probabilities of failure for the project. First, 0.25 is the probability of failure in year 1. For year 2, 0.22 is the probability that the project fails in the second year, given that it has survived through year 1. For year 3, 0.20 is the probability that the project fails, given that it has survived through year 2, and so forth.

Year	1	2	3	4	5	6	7
Failure probability	0.25	0.22	0.20	0.20	0.20	0.20	0.20

i. Determine the probability that the project survives to the end of the seventh year.

ii. Determine the expected NPV of the project.

iii. Make a recommendation.

Solution to i: The probability that the project survives to the end of the first year is $(1 - 0.25) = 1$ minus the probability of failure in the first year; the probability that it survives to the end of the second year is the product of the probability it survives the first year times the probability it survives the second year, or $(1 - 0.25)(1 - 0.22)$. Using this pattern, the probability that the firm survives to the end of the seventh year is $(1 - 0.25)(1 - 0.22)(1 - 0.20)^5 = (0.75)(0.78)(0.80)^5 = 0.192$ or 19.2%.

Solution to ii: The NPV of the project, given that it survives to the end of the seventh year and thus earns $16 million, equals $4.02 million $= -\$1$ million $+ \$16$ million$/1.18^7$. The NPV of project given that it fails is $-\$1$

million. Thus, the project's expected NPV is a probability-weighted average of these two amounts, or (0.192) ($4.02 million) + (0.808) (−$1 million) = −$36,160.

Solution to iii: Based on its negative NPV, the recommendation is to decline the investment.

Performance Measurement

Investors in a venture capital fund need to evaluate the performance of their investment not only at time of liquidation but also during the life of their investment. This is usually done by calculating an internal rate of return based on cash flows since inception and the end-of-period valuation of the unliquidated remaining holdings (residual value or net asset value). The European Private Equity and Venture Capital Association (www.evca.com), the British Private Equity and Venture Capital Association (www.bvca.co.uk), and CFA Institute have valuation guidelines bearing on this.

There are several challenges to performance measurement in the venture capital area. Lerner (2000) points these out in a discussion of future directions for an endowment fund:

▶ The difficulty in determining precise valuations. Venture capital funds do not have market prices to value their holdings, so they use some arbitrary technique to value their portfolios of ongoing projects. For example, some managers apply an average internal rate of return to the historical investment costs of their ongoing projects. Of course, the actual exit value is used at the time of exit of a project, or a zero value is used if a project failed.

▶ The lack of meaningful benchmarks against which fund manager and investment success can be measured.

▶ The long-term nature of any reliable performance feedback in the venture capital asset class.

4   HEDGE FUNDS AND ABSOLUTE RETURN STRATEGIES

The early 1990s saw the explosive development of *hedge funds*. Even though the attraction of these funds was tempered by many huge losses suffered in 1994 and 1998, the hedge fund industry continued to prosper. The assets under management of hedge funds passed the $2 trillion mark in 2007, and the number of hedge funds was estimated to be over 13,000 in mid-2007.[13] The growth in the past few years has been explosive. On the global scene, the asset base of hedge funds managed in the United States tends to dominate, but many hedge fund managers are based in Europe (especially London) and Asia is starting to develop a hedge fund industry.

---

[13] See www.HedgeFund.net.

Although wealthy individual investors have been the traditional client bases of hedge funds, institutional investors, especially endowments and foundations, have started to invest en masse. We start this section by describing the different types of hedge funds available, including funds of funds. A discussion of the leverage and unique risk characteristics of hedge funds will complete this description. Hedge funds follow strategies that promise a large absolute return and deserve a close investigation of the actual performance and risk of those strategies. We therefore present the case for investing in hedge funds in some detail, but we also provide the caveats.

Definition of Hedge Funds

Objective

It is difficult to provide a general definition of hedge funds. The original concept of a hedge fund was to offer plays *against* the markets, using short selling, futures, and other derivative products. Today, funds using the hedge fund appellation follow all kinds of strategies and cannot be considered a homogeneous asset class. Some funds are highly leveraged; others are not. Some engage in hedging activities; others do not. Some focus on making macroeconomic bets on commodities, currencies, interest rates, and so on. Some are mostly "technical" funds trying to take advantage of the mispricing of some securities within their market. Futures funds belong to the world of hedge funds. In fact, the common denominator of hedge funds is not their investment strategy but the *search for absolute returns*.

Money management has progressively moved toward a focus on performance *relative to preassigned benchmarks*. An institutional money manager's performance is generally evaluated relative to some market index that is assigned as a mandate. In turn, these benchmarks guide (some would say unduly constrain) the money manager's investment policy. The risk of deviating from the performance of the benchmark has become huge, given all of the publicity surrounding relative performance in a very competitive money management industry. The development of hedge funds can be seen as a reaction against this trend, with the search for absolute return in all directions. In practice, this means that hedge funds might have more appropriately been termed *isolation funds*. They generally try to isolate specific bets for the purpose of generating alpha. One can infer the particular bet from each hedge fund position. Hedge fund managers seek freedom to achieve high absolute returns and wish to be rewarded for their performance. These objectives are apparent in the legal organization and the fee structure of hedge funds. These two aspects are probably the only uniform characteristics of hedge funds.

Legal Structure

Hedge funds are typically set up as a *limited partnership, limited liability corporation* (in the United States), or *offshore corporation*. These legal structures allow the fund manager to take short and long positions in any asset, to use all kinds of derivatives, and to leverage the fund without restrictions.

Hedge funds based in the United States most often take the form of a limited partnership organized under section 3(c)(1) or section 3(c)(7) of the Investment Company Act of 1940, thereby gaining exemption from registration with the U.S. Securities and Exchange Commission (SEC) and therefore from most SEC regulations.[14] Investment in a hedge fund, whatever its legal structure, is a security for purposes of the Securities Act of 1933. In order to avoid the registration requirements of the Securities Act with respect to the sale of their securities, hedge funds generally rely on the private offering exemption in section 4(2) of that act and on the safe harbor contained in Regulation D promulgated thereunder. Section 4(2) exempts from registration securities sold without any "public offering." As a practical matter, this means that there can be no communication (electronic or otherwise) that could be viewed as a general solicitation or advertisement. Under section 3(c)(1) of the Investment Company Act, the fund is limited to no more than 100 partners. In practice, those investors must be "accredited investors,"[15] although up to 35 partners could be unaccredited. Under section 3(c)(7) of the Investment Company Act, the fund is limited to no more than 499 investors, who must be "qualified purchasers".[16] As of early 2006, the SEC imposed much stricter rules that prompted many hedge funds to register with the SEC as investment advisers. But this new rule was struck down by a federal appeals court in June 2006. Rather than imposing stricter registration requirements, the SEC then decided to propose a new anti-fraud rule under the Investment Advisers Act, which applies to all investment advisers regardless of their registration status. Advisers to funds (or other pooled investment vehicles) are prohibited from making false, misleading, or deceptive statements or acts. The effect of the proposed anti-fraud rule would be to permit the SEC to bring enforcement actions against advisers that violate the rule. While hedge funds remain under light regulation throughout the world, some countries are pushing for tighter regulation; Germany has been the most vocal proponent of tighter regulations.

Given the small number of partners, a minimum investment is typically several hundred thousand dollars. Institutional investors can become partners. U.S. hedge funds are typically incorporated in a "fund-friendly" state such as Delaware.

Offshore funds have also proved to be an attractive legal structure. These are incorporated in locations such as the British Virgin Islands, the Cayman Islands, Bermuda, or other locations attractive from a fiscal and legal point of view. A hedge fund might consider using "feeders" (vehicles that have an ownership interest in the hedge fund) that enable it to solicit funds from investors in every imaginable tax and legal domain—one feeder for ordinary U.S. investors, another for tax-free pensions, another for Japanese who want their profits hedged in yen, and still another for European institutions, which invest only in shares that are listed on an exchange (e.g., a dummy listing on the Irish Stock Exchange). These feeders don't keep the money; they are used as paper conduits that channel the money to a central fund, typically a Cayman Islands partnership.

Fee Structure

The manager is compensated through a *base management fee* based on the value of assets under management (at one time as much as 2 to 3 percent, now more typically 1 percent of the asset base) plus an *incentive fee* proportional to the

---

[14] Congress enacted the Investment Advisers Act of 1940 ("Advisers Act") in conjunction with the Investment Company Act of 1940.

[15] An accredited investor under the Securities Act of 1933 is an individual with a net worth in excess of $1 million or an annual income in excess of $200,000, or an entity with total assets of $5 million or more. This standard was enacted in 1982 and is being upgraded. The SEC proposed in 2007 to add the requirement that investors own at least $2.5 million in investments (excluding the personal residence and some other personal assets). This addition applies only to new investors.

[16] A qualified purchaser (or qualified investor) is an individual with at least $5 million in investments or an entity with at least $25 million in investments.

realized profits (ranging from 15 percent to 30 percent, typically 20 percent of total profits).[17] The base fee is paid whatever the performance of the fund. The incentive fee cannot be negative, so a negative return on the funds implies a zero incentive fee. The incentive fee is sometimes applied to profits measured above a risk-free rate applied to the assets. In other words, the hedge fund return has to be greater than the risk-free rate before the incentive fee is activated. The fee structure sometimes includes a "high-water mark" stating that following a year in which the fund declined in value, the hedge fund would first have to recover those losses before any incentive fee would be paid. Example 6 shows the effect of a hedge fund's fee structure on its net return.

EXAMPLE 6

Hedge Fund Fee

A hedge fund has an annual 1 percent base management fee plus a 20 percent incentive fee applied to profits above the risk-free rate, taken to be the Treasury bill rate. Hence, the incentive fee is applied to annual profits after deduction of the Treasury bill rate applied to the amount of assets under management at the start of the year. The gross return during the year is 40 percent. What is the net return (the return after fees) for an investor if the risk-free rate is 5 percent?

Solution:

$$\text{Fee} = 1\% + 20\% \times (40\% - 5\%) = 8\%$$
$$\text{Net return} = 40\% - 8\% = 32\%$$

Classification

Hedge funds have become quite global, as evidenced by the wide array of global investments used by these hedge funds and the international diversity of their client base. Some classifications of hedge funds by investment strategy is provided in the media and by hedge funds databases. These classifications are somewhat arbitrary, exhibit a large degree of overlap, and differ extensively across sources. Following is one possible classification system:

▶ *Long/short funds* are the traditional types of hedge funds, taking short and long bets in common stocks. They vary their short and long exposures according to forecasts, use leverage, and now operate on numerous markets throughout the world. These funds often maintain net positive or negative market exposures, so they are not necessarily market neutral. In fact, a subgroup within this category is funds that have a systematic short bias, known as dedicated short funds or short-seller funds. Long/short funds represent a large amount of hedge fund assets. An illustration is presented in Example 7.

▶ *Market-neutral funds* are a form of long/short funds that attempt to be hedged against a general market movement. They take bets on valuation differences of individual securities within some market segment. This could involve simultaneous long and short positions in closely related securities with a zero net exposure to the market itself. A market-neutral long-short portfolio is

---

[17] Besides the management and incentive fees that all hedge funds charge their clients, some hedge funds may charge other fees, such as surrender fees, ticket charges, and financing fees.

EXAMPLE 7

Long/Short Market-Neutral Strategy

A hedge fund has a capital of $10 million and invests in a market-neutral long/short strategy on the British equity market. Shares can be borrowed from a primary broker with a cash margin deposit equal to 18 percent of the value of the shares. No additional costs are charged to borrow the shares. The hedge fund has drawn up a list of shares regarded as undervalued (list A) and a list of shares regarded as overvalued (list B). The hedge fund expects that shares in list A will outperform the British index by 5 percent over the year, while shares in list B will underperform the British index by 5 percent over the year. The hedge fund wishes to retain a cash cushion of $1 million for unforeseen events. What specific investment actions would you suggest?

Solution: The hedge fund would sell short shares from list B and use the proceeds to buy shares from list A for an equal amount such that the overall beta of the portfolio with respect to the market equals zero. Some capital needs to be invested in the margin deposit. The hedge funds could take long/short positions for $50 million:

▶ Keep $1 million in cash.

▶ Deposit $9 million in margin.

▶ Borrow $25 million of shares from list B from a broker, and sell those shares short.

▶ Use the sale proceeds to buy $25 million worth of shares from list A.

The positions in shares from lists A and B are established so that the portfolio's beta is zero. Also, note that the invested assets of $50 million equals $9 million divided by 0.18. The ratio of invested assets to equity capital is roughly 5:1.

If expectations materialize, the return for investors in the hedge fund will be high. The long/short portfolio of shares should have a gain over the year of 10 percent on $50 million, whatever the movement in the general market index. This $5 million gain will translate into an annual return before fees of 50 percent on the invested capital of $10 million. This calculation does not take into account the return on invested cash ($1 million) and assumes that the dividends on long positions will offset dividends on short positions.

constructed so that the total value of the positions held long equals the total value of the positions sold short (dollar neutrality) and so that the total sensitivity of the long positions equals and offsets the total sensitivity of the short positions (beta neutrality). The long position would be in stocks considered undervalued, and the short position would be in stocks considered overvalued. Leverage is generally used, so that the investment in the long position (or the short position) is a multiple of the hedge fund equity. Another alternative is to use derivatives to hedge market risk. For example, a manager could buy some bond deemed to be underpriced with a simultaneous short position in bond futures or other fixed-income derivatives. This type of fund is sometimes called a fixed-income arbitrage fund. Other types of arbitrage make use of complex securities with option-like clauses, such as convertibles, warrants, or collateralized mortgage obligations (CMOs). Among the various techniques used by market-neutral funds are the following:

► Equity long/short

► Fixed-income arbitrage

► Pairs trading

► Warrant arbitrage

► Mortgage arbitrage

► Convertible bond arbitrage

► Closed-end fund arbitrage

► Statistical arbitrage

It must be stressed that despite their labels ("arbitrage," "neutral"), these funds are not riskless because hedges can never be perfect. Loss can be incurred if the model used is imperfect, and it can be high because hedge funds tend to be highly leveraged.

► *Global macro funds* take bets on the direction of a market, a currency, an interest rate, a commodity, or any macroeconomic variable. These funds tend to be highly leveraged and make extensive use of derivatives. There are many subgroups in this category, including the following:

  ► *Futures funds* (or *managed futures funds*) are commodity pools that include commodity trading advisor funds (CTAs). They take bets on directional moves in the positions they hold (long and short) in a single asset class, such as currency, fixed income, or commodities, and tend to use many actively traded futures contracts.

  ► *Emerging-market funds* primarily take bets on all types of securities in emerging markets. The securities markets in these economies are typically less efficient and less liquid than those in developed markets. There typically is not an organized lending market for securities, so it is difficult to sell short most issues. Emerging market investments tend to be fairly volatile and greatly influenced by economic and political factors.

► *Event-driven funds* take bets on some event specific to a company or a security. Typically the events are special situations or opportunities to capitalize on price fluctuations. These include the following, among others:

  ► *Distressed securities funds*: The manager invests in the debt and/or equity of companies having financial difficulty. Such companies are generally in bankruptcy reorganization or are emerging from reorganization or appear likely to declare bankruptcy in the near future. Because of their distressed situations, the manager can buy such companies' securities at deeply discounted prices. The manager stands to make money should the company successfully reorganize and return to profitability. The manager may take short positions in companies whose situations he believes will worsen, rather than improve, in the short term.

  ► *Risk arbitrage in mergers and acquisitions*: Before the effective date of a merger, the stock of the acquired company will typically sell at a discount to its acquisition value as officially announced. A hedge fund manager simultaneously buys stock in a company being acquired and sells stock in its acquirers. Even though a merger has been accepted by the board of directors of the two companies, there is always a chance that the merger will not go through, possibly because of objections by regulatory authorities. This is a reason for the existence of the discount. If the takeover falls through, fund managers can be left with large losses. An illustration is presented in Example 8.

EXAMPLE 8

Merger Risk Arbitrage and Long/Short Market-Neutral Strategy

A merger has been announced between a French company A and a German company B. A will acquire B by offering one share of A for two shares of B. Shares of B were trading in a €15 to €20 range prior to the merger announcement. Shares of B currently trade at €24, while shares of A trade at €50. The merger has been approved by both boards of directors but is awaiting ratification by all shareholders (which is extremely likely) and approval by the EU commission (there is a slight risk of non-approval because the combined company has a large European market share in some products). How could a hedge fund take advantage of the situation? What are the risks?

Solution: The hedge fund should construct a hedged position whereby it buys two shares of B for every share of A that it sells short. Because the proceeds of the short sale of one share of A (€50) can be used to buy two shares of B (€48), the position can be highly leveraged. Of course, the cost of securities lending and margin deposit should also be taken into account. When the merger is completed, the hedge fund will make a profit of approximately two euros for each share of A.

The risk is that the merger will fall through. If it does, the stock price of B will drop sharply, because it was to be acquired at a price well above its premerger market value. If the stock price of A also falls, it should be by less than for B, resulting in an overall loss. The stock price of A might also rise, adding to the loss related to the position in B. That would mean a sizable loss for the hedge fund.

Funds of Funds

Funds of funds (*FOF*) have been created to allow easier access to small investors, but also to institutional investors. An FOF is open to investors and, in turn, invests in a selection of hedge funds. If an FOF has a large client base, it can invest large sums of money in each hedge fund. With their attractive benefits, FOFs have grown rapidly and now hold more than a third of all hedge fund assets. An FOF provides investors with several benefits:

▶ *Retailing*: Typically, a single hedge fund requires an investment of one to several hundred thousand dollars or euros. For the same amount, an investor can get exposure to a large number of hedge funds.

▶ *Access*: FOF managers may be able to offer investments in successful hedge funds that are closed to individual investors because the maximum number of investors has been reached. As long-time investors, they may have "old" money invested with funds that have been closed to new investment. They are also privileged clients that will have priority in buying shares of individual investors who cash out from the hedge fund for personal reasons.

▶ *Diversification*: An FOF allows investors to diversify the risk of a single hedge fund. The good performance of a single hedge fund could be due to specific market conditions prevailing in the past. An FOF can diversify across several types of hedge funds that may have good performance in different market conditions.

▶ *Expertise*: The manager of the FOF is supposed to have expertise in finding reliable and good-quality hedge funds in a world where information on the investment strategies of hedge funds is difficult to obtain. Selecting the right hedge fund and strategy requires a large database and intimate knowledge of strategies, and their advantages and potential pitfalls.

▶ *Due diligence process*: The due diligence (both at the outset and ongoing) that has to be performed by an institutional investor when selecting a hedge fund is highly specialized and time consuming, given the secretive nature of hedge funds and their complex investment strategies. An FOF may be better equipped to perform this due diligence than is a typical institutional investor.

However, there are drawbacks with an FOF:

▶ *Fee*: The fee charged by its manager is in addition to that charged by each hedge fund. The total fee can be quite hefty.

▶ *Performance*: Individual hedge funds are mostly selected by the FOF on the basis of past performance, which in practice often gives little indication of future performance. Biases of the existing databases on hedge funds used by FOFs in their selection process are described subsequently. There is little evidence of persistence in the performance delivered by FOFs.

▶ *Diversification is a double-edged sword*: Blending a high expected return hedge fund with many others for risk reduction purposes means that the overall FOF expected return will be lowered by this diversification. But the fees paid are still very high.

Leverage and Unique Risks of Hedge Funds

Prior to discussing the performance of hedge funds, we review the use of leverage by hedge funds and the unique risks for hedge funds. Some people regard the use of leverage as one of the main sources of risk for hedge funds, while others maintain that proper use of leverage with appropriate risk management benefits hedge fund investors. In addition, risks that are unique to hedge funds may make hedge funds look unduly risky. Thus, we can usefully discuss hedge funds' risks prior to presenting their historical track record.

Use of Leverage

One of the common characteristics of hedge funds is their use of leverage as part of their trading strategy, although some hedge funds do not use leverage at all. For certain strategies (such as arbitrage strategies), leverage is essential because the arbitrage return is so small that leverage is needed for amplifying the profit. However, leverage is a double-edged sword that also magnifies losses on the downside. In this traditional sense, leveraged investments are more aggressive than those without leverage, and to some people, this may mean high risk.

Leverage in hedge funds often runs from 2:1 to 10:1 (depending on the type of assets held and strategies used) and can run higher than 100:1 [e.g., at one point in time, a well-known hedge fund, Long Term Capital Management or LTCM, had leverage that stood over 500:1 (Lhabitant, 2002)]. Thus, some hedge funds may specifically limit the leverage they will employ in the limited partnership agreement so that hedge fund managers are legally bound by that limit. Within the limit, however, hedge fund managers have considerable flexibility.

In general, hedge fund managers can create leverage in trading by

▶ borrowing external funds to invest more or sell short more than the equity capital they put in,

▶ borrowing through a brokerage margin account, and

▶ using financial instruments and derivatives that require posting margins (typically a fraction of the full value of the position) in lieu of trading in the cash securities that require full payment.

Unique Risks of Hedge Funds

In addition to market and trading risks in different markets, hedge funds face the following unique risks:

▶ *Liquidity risk*: The liquidity risk is common to all investors who trade in illiquid or thin markets. However, the lack of liquidity under extreme market conditions can cause irreversible damage to hedge funds whose strategies rely on the presence of liquidity in specific markets. For example, the demise of LTCM was attributed to the unexpected absence of normal liquidity.

▶ *Pricing risk*: Hedge funds often invest in complex securities traded over-the-counter. Pricing securities that trade infrequently is a difficult task, especially in periods of high volatility. Broker-dealers tend to adopt an extremely conservative pricing policy to protect themselves in periods of high volatility. The marking-to-market (margin calls) of positions based on these prices can create severe cash needs for hedge funds, even if the funds do not try to liquidate their positions. For example, it is widely believed that the cash drain of marking-to-market positions based on brokers' conservative pricing of derivatives compounded the problems of LTCM.

▶ *Counterparty credit risk*: Because hedge funds deal with broker-dealers in most transactions—from buying securities on margin to mortgage trading—counterparty credit risk can arise from many sources. Thus, hedge funds face significant counterparty risk.

▶ *Settlement risk*: Settlement risk refers to the failure to deliver the specified security or money by one of the parties to the transaction on the settlement day.

▶ *Short squeeze risk*: A short squeeze arises when short sellers must buy in their positions at rising prices, for example because owners of the borrowed stock demand their shares back. Because some hedge fund strategies require short selling (e.g., long/short strategies), this risk can affect fund performance significantly.

▶ *Financing squeeze*: If a hedge fund has reached or is near its borrowing capacity, its ability to borrow cash is constrained. Margin calls and marking position to market might result in a cash need for the fund. This risk puts the hedge fund in a vulnerable position when it is forced to reduce the levered positions, say, in an illiquid market at substantial losses, in order to stop the leverage from rising. If the hedge fund were able to borrow more cash, these substantial losses could be avoided.

Hedge Funds Universe and Indexes

Hedge funds are not publicly offered or listed. Hence, information must be obtained directly from each hedge fund or through data providers who specialize in collecting data on some universe of hedge funds and funds of funds. Data providers also publish hedge fund indexes. The performance of these indexes is widely disseminated and is used to build the case for investing in hedge funds. Indexes also allow a comparison of the performance of specific hedge funds to competitors.

Indexes

A number of indexes track the hedge fund industry. Specialized hedge fund firms (such as Hedge Fund Research, Van Hedge, Hennessee, Greenwich), banks (such as Credit Suisse/Tremont,[18] ABN AMRO EurekaHedge), index providers (such as MSCI, S&P, FTSE), and even educational institutions (CISDM, EDHEC) offer dedicated hedge fund indexes.[19] These indexes are also broken down in subindexes for various classifications of hedge funds according to investment strategy, but the classifications vary across providers.

Some indexes are equal-weighted, while others are weighted by the assets under management for each fund. One reason for using equal weights is that hedge funds are reluctant to provide information on their size. But asset-weighted indexes are more representative of the performance of money invested in hedge funds. Some are audited and have a transparent composition, but others are not. The criteria for inclusion vary; in many cases, all that is required is that the hedge fund volunteers to be included in the database used for the index construction. Any database only includes a number of the existing hedge funds; furthermore, most providers build their hedge fund indexes from a selection of the funds in their database. For any month, the performance reported by the various index providers can vary widely.

Investable indexes are created from funds that can be actually bought and sold by investors, the so-called open funds. Investability is an attractive property for an index because it makes the index more relevant to the choices truly available to investors. Several providers publish investable indexes that use various eligibility criteria to include specific hedge funds in the index. Typically, the hedge fund should be accepting new investments and redemption should have no lock-up period; however, such indexes do not represent the total universe of hedge funds and may underrepresent the more successful managers, who may not find the requirements for inclusion in the index attractive. Funds of funds have been created to track these investable indexes.

---

[18] As of 2007, the Credit Suisse/Tremont indexes are based on the TASS database that is managed by Tremont but owned and distributed by Lipper.

[19] The launching dates of these indexes differ. Some were launched in the 1990s, others in the 2000s. In some cases, the historical value of the index was back-calculated to an earlier date, with the risk of including only surviving hedge funds and biasing the performance upward.

Biases

Investors should exercise caution when using the historical track record of hedge funds in reaching asset allocation decisions. The hedge fund industry does not adhere to rigorous performance presentation standards. Biases in historical performance data can make it difficult to interpret hedge fund performance; past winners may also not repeat. The performance data from hedge fund databases and indexes suffer from serious biases:

▶ *Self-selection bias*: Hedge fund managers themselves decide whether they want to be included in a database. Managers who have funds with an unimpressive track record will not wish to have that information exposed.

▶ *Backfilling bias*: When a hedge fund enters a database, it brings with it its track record. Only hedge funds with good track records enter the database, creating a positive bias in past performance in the database. Ibbotson and Chen (2006) studied the TASS database from 1995 to 2006 and estimate that excluding backfilled data reduces the average annual return by some 350 basis points. Reliable index providers have recently taken steps to minimize backfill bias.

▶ *Survivorship bias*: In the investment industry, unsuccessful funds and managers tend to disappear over time. Only successful ones search for new clients and present their track records. This trend creates a survivor bias. The problem is acute because hedge funds often do not have to comply with performance presentation standards. It is not uncommon to see hedge fund managers present the track records of only their successful funds, omitting those that have been closed. If a fund begins to perform poorly, perhaps even starting to go out of business, it may stop reporting its performance entirely, thus inflating the reported average performance. Hedge fund indexes and databases may include only funds that have survived; funds with bad performance disappear and are removed from the database that is used by investors to select among existing funds. Most academic studies suggest that survivorship bias overstates return by 200 to 400 basis points per year. Malkiel and Saha (2005) studied the TASS database from 1996 to 2003 and estimated the average annual bias in performance to be 442 basis points. A similar survivorship bias exists for equity mutual funds, but it is smaller because the attrition rate of mutual funds is much smaller than the hedge fund attrition rate (on the order of 8 to 15 percent per year, on average). Reliable hedge fund indexes are now much less susceptible to survivorship bias as defunct hedge funds are kept in the database; however, funds that simply stop reporting still pose a problem.

Hedge funds risk measures are also affected by biases:

▶ *Smoothed pricing of infrequently traded assets*: Some assets trade infrequently. This is the case for many alternative assets that are not exchange-traded, such as real estate or private equity. This is also the case for illiquid exchange-traded securities or OTC instruments often used by hedge funds. Because prices used are often not up-to-date market prices but estimates of fair value, their volatility is reduced (*smoothing effect*). The infrequent nature of price updates for alternative investments induces serial correlation of returns and a downward bias to the measured risk of the assets. In addition, correlations of alternative investment returns with conventional equity and fixed income returns, and correlations among the alternative investments, are often artificially low simply because of the smoothing effect and the absence of market-observable returns. The bias can be large, so the true risk is much larger than the reported estimates. As suggested by Asness, Krail, and Liew (2001), Lo (2002), and Getmansky, Lo, and Mei (2004), the correction requires taking serial correlation of return into account. This will lead to an increase in the estimated standard deviation and a decrease in the Sharpe ratio commonly used to measure risk-adjusted performance. After adjusting for serial correlation, Lo (2002) finds estimates that differ from the naive Sharpe ratio estimator by as much as 70 percent. Some hedge funds purport to be market neutral (i.e., funds with relatively small market betas), but Asness, Krail, and Liew (2001) show that including both contemporaneous and lagged market returns as regressors and summing the coefficients yields significantly higher market exposure.

▶ *Option-like investment strategies*: Traditional risk measures used in performance appraisal assume that portfolio returns are drawn from normal, or at least symmetric, distributions. Standard deviation (and hence the Sharpe ratio) is a good estimate of risk if the return distributions are close to normal. As shown in Malkiel and Saha (2005), distributions of hedge funds return tend to deviate strongly from normality (with high kurtosis, or "fat" tails, and negative skewness). Many investment strategies followed by hedge funds have some option-like features that violate the normal distributional assumptions. For example, hedge funds following so-called arbitrage strategies will generally make a small profit when asset prices converge to their estimated fair value, but they run the risk of a huge loss if their arbitrage model fails. Standard deviation or traditional value-at-risk (VaR) measures understate the true risk of losses, and the Sharpe ratio can be an inappropriate performance measure, even after correcting for smoothed pricing.

▶ *Fee structure and gaming*: It is also important to remember the high fees charged by hedge funds, typically a fixed fee of 1 percent plus an incentive fee of 20 percent of the total return, if positive. This compensation structure is option-like. Clearly, fund managers are paid to take risks. One can argue that they have strong incentives to take a huge amount of risk if their recent performance has been bad. However, one can also argue that because of the high-water mark provision, hedge fund managers may not want to ruin their chance to stage a comeback by taking more risk as their performance diminishes. In either case, past risk measures may be misleading for forecasting future performance and risk for a fund that has performed badly in the recent past.

To summarize, investors need to exercise caution in interpreting the reported performance of hedge funds (see Example 9). Furthermore, the risks in hedge fund investments are easily underestimated.

EXAMPLE 9

Biases in Reported Performance

A manager without any expertise has decided to launch five long/short hedge funds with some seed money. The investment strategies of the five funds are quite different. Actually, the investment strategy of fund A is just the opposite of that of fund E. After a couple of years, some funds have performed well and some badly, as could be expected by pure chance. The annualized standard deviation is 10 percent, and the annual risk-free rate is 3 percent. The manager decides to close funds A, B, and C and to enter funds D and E in a well-known hedge fund database. The marketing pitch of the manager is that the funds have superior performance (Sharpe ratio of 1.7 and 2.7). What do you think?

Fund Name	Mean Annual Return	Standard Deviation	Sharpe Ratio
Fund A	−30%	10%	−3.3
Fund B	−20%	10%	−2.3
Fund C	0%	10%	−0.3
Fund D	+20%	10%	1.7
Fund E	+30%	10%	2.7

Solution: The performance on the funds is purely random; however, only the good-performing funds are included in the hedge fund database. The performance reported for a selection of funds is misleading. There is obvious survivorship and self-selection bias. Similarly, the performance of the hedge fund index is biased upward and misleading.

The Case for Investing in Hedge Funds

Hedge funds are attractive because of their risk and performance characteristics. Proponents stress that the unique value of hedge funds is their ability to produce attractive risk-adjusted returns, independent of broad market trends. Most types of hedge funds seek positive returns regardless of market conditions. This approach differs from traditional funds that take only long positions in the markets and therefore have returns that are strongly correlated with the market in which they invest. For example, most equity hedge fund strategies (long/short, market neutral, merger arbitrage, etc.) are designed to have limited correlation with the equity market; thus, they may not fully capture the upside potential during equity bull markets, but they aim to generate positive returns and preserve capital during equity bear markets. Hedge funds aim at providing "good" returns in all stock market phases. Furthermore, hedge funds cover a wide diversity of investment strategies in a variety of instruments and markets; such investment strategies are not available within traditional asset classes. Hence, as a group, reflected in a broad hedge fund index, hedge funds offer attractive risk diversification benefits to traditional investments, so hedge funds are often marketed as an attractive asset class.[20]

---

[20] Some are hesitant to call hedge funds an asset class because of their heterogeneity, but we will keep the appellation for lack of a better term.

EXHIBIT 2	Performance and Risk Characteristics of Various Market Indexes January 1994–December 2006, in U.S. Dollars					
	Credit Suisse/Tremont Hedge Fund Index	MSCI World Index	S&P 500	DJ EURO STOXX	TOPIX	Lehman Global Aggregate
Average annualized return	10.9%	7.2%	10.9%	12.2%	1.2%	6.1%
Annualized volatility (standard deviation)	7.7%	13.4%	14.3%	17.7%	16.8%	5.1%
Correlation with MSCI World index	0.5	1.0	0.9	0.9	0.5	0.1
Beta with MSCI World index	0.3	1.0	1.0	1.1	0.7	—
Sharpe ratio	0.9	0.2	0.5	0.5	(0.2)	0.4

Source: Credit Suisse/Tremont Hedge Fund Index, www.hedgeindex.com, February 2007.

Asset Class

Many suggest that investors should allocate part of their assets to hedge funds, even in a passive way. The usual argument in favor of hedge funds as an asset class is illustrated in Exhibit 2, which gives risk and performance estimates for a variety of indexes over the period January 1994 to December 2006. All calculations are conducted in U.S. dollars. The first is the Credit Suisse/Tremont hedge fund index, a broad index of all hedge funds. Next is the MSCI World equity index, followed by the U.S., European, and Japanese equity indexes. The last column is the Lehman Global Aggregate bond index. The first observation is that the volatility of the broad hedged fund index, measured by the standard deviation of returns, is considerably smaller than that of the global equity market (7.7% instead of 13.4%). Another interesting parameter is the correlation with the global equity index. The correlation of the global hedge fund index with the equity market is 0.5. It is clearly positive but far from one, suggesting excellent diversification benefits. Part of the explanation for a low correlation comes from the fact that hedge funds do not experience big negative return or drawdown in periods when the equity market drops, as was the case from 2001 to 2003. Estimating correlation over shorter periods, the correlation between hedge fund returns and equity returns tends to decrease in periods of bear markets and increase in periods of bull markets (see Lo, 2002). For example, the correlation increased drastically in the bull market period of 2003 to 2006. Again, hedge fund marketers would argue that the diversification benefits of hedge funds are less needed in periods of booming equity markets but badly needed in periods of falling markets. The last row gives the Sharpe ratio, namely, the average return in excess of the U.S. 90-day Treasury bill rate divided by the standard deviation. The Sharpe ratio for the broad hedge fund index (0.9) is superior to that of all the other asset classes. While the empirical case for allocating investments to the hedge funds asset class is impressive, one should not forget the statistical caveats mentioned above: the performance and risk estimates of hedge funds indexes suffer from some bias.

Individual Funds

Within the universe of hedge funds, individual funds can follow vastly different investment strategies using different instruments and markets. Some strategies and managers can deliver outstanding performance. Investors often wish to go beyond a passive allocation to the hedge fund class and find top-performing hedge funds. The fee structure and flexibility of hedge funds attract talented fund managers. Someone having an outstanding investment idea can apply it in a hedge fund with few constraints. The investment idea can be leveraged to generate high returns for investors and for the manager. So, the search for an attractive hedge fund is based in part on the perceived talent of the manager to generate superior performance. The hedge fund class is different from traditional asset classes in many respects, including the fact that there is an enormous dispersion in returns of individual hedge funds. Malkiel and Saha (2005) stress, "The cross-sectional variation and the range of individual hedge fund returns are far greater than they are for traditional asset classes. Investors in hedge funds take on a substantial risk of selecting a dismally performing fund or, worse, a failing one" (p. 87). Of course, investors take this risk in the hope of finding top-performing hedge funds.

Performance of individual hedge funds can come from many sources, but two primary sources of return on a specific fund are the selection of market exposures (often called beta) and the skill in constructing strategies or selecting securities (often called alpha). When a fund takes some market exposure (beta), its performance is partly attributable to its exposure to market movements. If a fund were totally market neutral, it would have no beta. Part of the performance (alpha) also comes from the good (bad) skill of the manager in implementing the strategy with a given market exposure. Take the example of a U.S. equity long/short fund with a market exposure (beta) of 0.3, or 30 percent, relative to the U.S. equity market. If the equity market goes up (down), the market exposure will have a positive (negative) contribution to the fund return. However, the manager could have skills in selecting individual securities, say an alpha of 5 percent per year, that induce a positive return in any market environment, on top of the market exposure contribution. Investors must try to disentangle the two effects (beta and alpha) in attributing performance of a hedge fund. Investors sometimes use multifactor market models to estimate the fund's exposures (betas) to various market factors. Performing such a calculation for individual hedge funds is a difficult task because of data availability and because hedge funds tend to follow nonlinear strategies implying that the betas vary considerably over time.

Some argue that it is not worth paying the large fees of hedge funds for simply taking some market exposures that can be replicated at a very low cost. Hence, some replication funds ("clones") have been created with risk market exposures similar to various hedge fund indexes. They offer risk diversification benefits that are somewhat similar to those of hedge funds, without their high management fee. But they cannot deliver any of the alpha that is promised by individual hedge funds.

5   CLOSELY HELD COMPANIES AND INACTIVELY TRADED SECURITIES

Investments in closely held companies and inactively traded securities require analysis of legal, financial, and ownership considerations with account taken of the effects of illiquidity. *Closely held companies* are those that are not publicly traded. *Inactively traded securities* are securities of companies that are infrequently traded; they generally do not trade on major exchanges. Illiquidity, limited information availability, and minority ownership issues are common to such companies.

Legal Environment

Closely held companies may be organized in various legal forms, such as special tax-advantaged corporations (subchapter S corporations in the United States), regular corporations, general partnerships, limited partnerships, and sole proprietorships. These forms have tax implications, as well as ownership differences, for the investor. Ownership is a bundle of rights, and these rights differ, depending on the business form. Because valuations can be required to provide evidence in litigation—for example, minority shareholder claims—much case law defines terms such as *intrinsic value, fundamental value,* and *fair value.* These definitions may vary in different jurisdictions. Even what is judged as evidence for a valuation can vary. There has long been a tension between the theory of value as based on projected cash flows and the acceptance of the *hard* evidence of recent cash flows. In a real sense, then, valuation of closely held and inactively traded securities requires extensive knowledge of the law and the purposes of the valuation.[21]

Valuation Alternatives

The basic types of valuation are the cost approach, the comparables approach, and the income approach.

The Cost Approach

This approach attempts to determine what it would cost to replace the company's assets in their present form.

The Comparables Approach

In the company comparison approach, market value is estimated relative to a benchmark value. The benchmark value may be the market price of a similar but actively traded company, or the average or median value of the market prices of similar companies, in transactions made near the time of the appraisal. The benchmark-based estimate needs to be adjusted for changing market conditions, the possibility that the benchmark itself is mispriced, and the unique features of the company relative to the benchmark. Companies with comparable characteristics might not have traded recently.

The Income Approach

For business valuation, Pratt, Reilly, and Schweihs (2000) essentially define the income approach as one of appropriately discounting any anticipated future economic income stream.

---

[21] See Pratt, Reilly, and Schweihs (2000) for an extensive treatment of the analysis and appraisal of closely held companies.

Bases for Discounts/Premiums

Because closely held companies and inactively traded securities are illiquid, some discount must be made for that illiquidity. For infrequently traded stocks, share prices should reflect a liquidity discount compensating investors for illiquidity in the market for the shares. Shares of closely held companies lack a public market (lack marketability) and so their valuation should reflect a marketability discount to account for the extra return investors should require on those shares. In addition to a discount for lack of marketability for a closely held company, the analyst may also need to apply a discount for minority interest, or a premium for control. The minority interest discount is applied if the interest will not be able to influence corporate strategy and other business decisions. To estimate a marketability discount, minority discount, or control premium, the analyst must carefully define the amount or base to which the discount or premium should be applied.

To estimate a marketability discount for a closely held company, the analyst identifies a publicly traded comparable company with a liquid market. The comparable's market value of equity is the base to which the marketability discount is applied.

To estimate a minority interest discount for a company, the base is an estimate of that company's value of equity inclusive of the value arising from ownership of all rights of control. To estimate a control premium, the base is an estimate of that company's value of equity not reflecting control (the value of equity from a minority shareholder perspective).

6   DISTRESSED SECURITIES/BANKRUPTCIES

Distressed securities are securities of companies that have filed or are close to filing for bankruptcy court protection, or that are seeking out-of-court debt restructuring to avoid bankruptcy. The legal framework of bankruptcy proceedings differs across countries. In the United States, two types of bankruptcy protection are available: protection for liquidation (called Chapter 7) and protection for reorganization (called Chapter 11). Valuation of such securities requires legal, operational, and financial analysis.

To understand distressed securities, one must appreciate the inherent divergence of interests between the stockholders and bondholders of a company. Stockholders own the successful company, but bondholders have a prior claim to the assets of the bankrupt company. In reorganizations, bondholders' prior claim can allow them to negotiate for ownership in the postbankruptcy company, thus diluting the original shareholders' claims. Investing in distressed securities, then, usually means investing in distressed company bonds with a view toward equity ownership in the eventually reconstituted company. In this regard, such investments have characteristics somewhat similar to those of venture capital investing. For example, they are illiquid and require a long horizon, as well as intense investor participation in guiding the venture to a successful outcome. Another similarity, though, is the possibility of mispricing. Hooke (1998) reports on the disappointment of some traditional distressed-securities investors that these investments are attracting attention and efficient prices; but he suggests that business volatility and high leverage will guarantee many problem companies with inevitable value discrepancies (mispricing).

Distressed-security investing may be viewed as the ultimate in value investing. A distressed company with low enterprise value (EV) to earnings before interest, taxes, depreciation, and amortization (EBITDA) will attract the attention of an investor looking for positive, postrestructuring cash flows. The primary question for any distressed security is the question of the distress source. Is the company operationally sound but financially hampered by too much gearing (leverage), or is the company weak operationally? If the company is weak operationally, is it a candidate to be turned around by cost cutting and improvement in the business cycle or else by new management and/or a new competitive strategy? Distressed-security investing requires intense industry analysis, as well as analysis of business strategies and of the management team that will conduct the restructuring.

COMMODITY MARKETS AND COMMODITY DERIVATIVES

7

Commodities present an unusual investment alternative. Investing in commodities complements the investment opportunities offered by shares of corporations that extensively use those commodities in their production process. Investing directly in agricultural products and other commodities gives the investor a share in the commodity components of the country's production and consumption. Money managers and average investors, however, usually prefer commodity derivatives (financial instruments that derive their value from the value of the underlying commodity) rather than commodities themselves. The average investor does not want to store grains, cattle, crude oil, or metals. There are several indirect ways to invest in commodities:

▶ *Futures contracts*: A commodity futures contract is a standardized, exchange-traded agreement between two parties in which the buyer agrees to buy a commodity from the seller at a future date at a price agreed upon today.

▶ Bonds indexed on some commodity price.

▶ Stocks of companies producing the commodity.

Investing in commodity futures is the most common strategy. Commodity trading advisers (CTAs) offer *managed futures funds* that take positions in exchange-traded derivatives on commodities and financials.[22]

Commodity Futures

Futures contracts are the easiest and cheapest way to invest in commodities. Commodities can be grouped into three major categories:

▶ *Agricultural products*, including fibers (wool, cotton), grains (wheat, corn, soybeans), food (coffee, cocoa, orange juice), and livestock (cattle, hogs, pork bellies). These are often called soft commodities by professionals.

▶ *Energy*, including crude oil, heating oil, and natural gas

▶ *Metals*, such as copper, aluminum, gold, silver, and platinum

Numerous commodity indexes have been developed. Some traditional indexes are broadly based, with a global economic perspective; they aim to track

---

[22] See Jaeger (2002), p. 18.

the evolution of input prices. Other indexes have been developed as *investable* indexes. They are based on the most liquid commodity futures contracts, so they can easily be replicated by taking positions in individual commodities. For example, the Goldman Sachs Commodity Index (GSCI) is a world-production weighted index of 24 commodities with liquid futures contracts. The composition and weights of the GSCI are periodically revised. Futures contracts on the GSCI trade in Chicago. The composition and weights of the various commodity indexes differ widely, and so do their performances.

Motivation and Investment Vehicles

Commodities are sometimes treated as an asset class because they represent a direct participation in the real economy. The motivation for investing in commodities ranges from the diversification benefits achievable by a passive investor to the speculative profits sought by an *active* investor. The design of the investment vehicle used reflects these different motivations.

Passive Investment

A passive investor would buy commodities for their risk-diversification benefits. A passive investor would typically invest through a collateralized position in a futures contract (see Example 10). Many banks and money managers offer collateralized futures funds based on one of the investable commodity indexes. A collateralized position in futures is a portfolio in which an investor takes a long position in futures for a given amount of underlying value and simultaneously invests the same amount in government securities, such as Treasury bills. The various investable indexes and collateralized futures indexes are published both in excess-return and total-return form. The indexes reported assume that the *total return* on the index is continuously reinvested. The *excess return* is the return above the risk-free rate. The total return is the risk-free rate plus the excess return.

EXAMPLE 10

Collateralized Futures

Assume that the futures price is currently $100. If $100 million is added to the fund, the manager will take a long position in the futures contract for $100 million of underlying value and simultaneously buy $100 million worth of Treasury bills (part of this will be deposited as margin). If the futures price drops to $95 the next day, the futures position will be marked to market, and the manager will have to sell $5 million of the Treasury bills to cover the loss. Conversely, if the futures price rises to $105, the manager will receive a marked-to-market profit of $5 million, which will be invested in additional Treasury bills. Discuss the sources of total return from such an investment.

Solution: The total return on the collateralized futures position comes from the change in futures price and the interest income on the Treasury bills.

Generally, the volatility of commodity futures is higher than that of domestic or international equity, but commodities tend to have a low to negative correlation with stock and bond returns and a desirable positive correlation with inflation. Looking at the period from 1959 to 2004, Gorton and Rouwenhorst (2006) find that commodities have an average return comparable to stocks and a low to negative correlation with stocks and bonds. While stocks and bonds are negatively correlated with unexpected inflation, commodity prices tend to be positively correlated with unexpected inflation—an attractive feature. However, Erb and Harvey (2006) point out that over the period 1969–2004 there is a wide dispersion of results across individual commodities, so all conclusions on performance and risk of commodities strongly depend on the composition and weighting scheme of the commodity index used. For example, energy-related commodities offer the best hedge against inflation, but precious metals have not provided an inflation hedge over the period under study. Furthermore, the excellent long-term performance of some commodity indexes requires a word of caution. The commodities and weights selected to enter indexes reflect a selection bias when they include data from time periods prior to the initiation of the index, which biases any back-calculated performance. Index providers are now careful to avoid this bias.

Active Investment

Besides making inflation bets, another motivation for investing in commodities is their link to economic growth. In periods of rapid economic growth, commodities are in strong demand to satisfy production needs, and their prices tend to go up. Because of productivity gains, the prices of finished goods are unlikely to rise as fast as those of raw materials. This suggests an active management strategy in which specific commodities are bought and sold at various times. Managed futures are proposed by a large number of institutions.

As with any investments, the risk-and-return characteristics of managed futures must be analyzed carefully. Schneeweis (2002) discusses the proposed attraction of managed futures: the possibility of positive returns in months when the market does well and in the months when it does poorly. Jaeger (2002) proposes several principles for the risk management of managed futures portfolios:

- ▶ Diversification
- ▶ Liquidity monitoring, because diversification into a larger universe of contracts can include illiquid contracts
- ▶ Volatility dependent allocation where the weight of the different contracts in the portfolio is determined by their historical or implied volatility
- ▶ Quantitative risk management techniques such as value at risk (VaR) and stress tests
- ▶ Risk budgeting on various aggregation levels to detect undesired risk concentrations
- ▶ Limits on leverage
- ▶ Use of derivatives to hedge any unwanted currency risk
- ▶ Care in model selection with respect to data mining, in and out of sample performance, and adequate performance adjustments for risk

The Example of Gold

Gold has always played a special role in investments. It is a commodity traded worldwide, but more important, it has been regarded by many Europeans and Asians as the ultimate store of value. It is considered an international monetary asset that offers protection in case of a major disruption. Central banks and many investors regard gold as a monetary asset because it has been the core of domestic and international monetary systems for many centuries. This section focuses on gold investment because of the historical importance of gold in investment strategies, and as an example of a real asset investment. Of course, precious stones, stamps, or paintings could also be profitable long-term investments, but they usually require high transaction costs; moreover, each stone or painting is in a sense unique, which reduces its marketability. Gold is offered in a wide variety of investment vehicles that can be used in passive or active strategies. Gold-linked investments include gold bullion, coins, bonds, mining equity, futures, and options on gold and on mining equity or bonds.

The Motivation for Investing in Gold

The traditional role of gold as the ultimate hedge and store of value is well known. For centuries, Europeans and Asians alike have regarded gold as the best possible protection against inflation and social, political, or economic crises because it can easily be traded worldwide at any time, and its real value increases during crises. Europeans and others who have suffered revolutions, invasions, and periods of hyperinflation need no correlation coefficients to be convinced of this attractive portfolio hedge characteristic. For example, gold kept its real value during the U.S. stock market crash from 1929 to 1932 and the London Stock Exchange collapse in equity and bonds from 1973 to 1975. Furthermore, the central role gold has played in domestic and international monetary systems for thousands of years makes it, in part, a monetary asset with exceptional liquidity. Other real assets, such as diamonds or stamps, do not have this characteristic.

In general, gold often allows investors to diversify against the kinds of risks that affect all stock markets simultaneously. For example, in 1973 and 1974, the price of bullion tripled when stock markets worldwide dropped dramatically during the oil crisis; the NYSE dropped approximately 50 percent.

A theoretical comment is in order here. In modern portfolio theory, a small or negative beta implies that the expected return on gold should be small. For example, a negative beta caused by a negative correlation between gold and the market portfolio implies that in the capital asset pricing model (CAPM) framework, the expected return on gold should be less than the risk-free interest rate. Indeed, it can be claimed that we should expect a modest long-term performance in gold and a greater return on the other assets in the portfolio; however, gold assets will reduce the risk of the portfolio in the event of adverse economic conditions. The question for a prudent portfolio manager, then, is whether these hedge benefits are worth the implicit cost she must pay in the form of a smaller expected long-term return for a small part of the portfolio.

Gold Price Determinants

The following material is intended to indicate the kind of information and methods that analysts and investment managers use to analyze real asset investments. Commodities other than gold could also serve as examples.

Gold is a tangible international asset in limited supply. Gold can be extracted at a cost but cannot be produced artificially. Although gold is immune to the effects of weather, water, and oxygen, it suffers from human habits. The tradition of hiding gold treasures in the ground is consistent with the observation that gold is the ultimate physical store of value during major disruptions such as civil unrest, coup d'état, and war. During World War II, most Europeans dug a hole in their gardens or cellars to hide their gold holdings. Part of this hidden gold is never recovered if the owner dies. Most of the gold used in dentistry also disappears with the owner. Despite these losses, the stock of gold keeps slowly increasing with the amount extracted.

In a sense, the price of gold should be easy to forecast: The product is well defined. The supply sources are well identified, and reserves can be reasonably estimated. The major demands are clearly identified: carat jewelry, industrial needs, coins, and investment.

Supply and demand clearly determine the price of gold. It is therefore necessary to study the various components of supply and demand to forecast the price of gold. A different model may be required for each component. For example, Western mine production is affected by technological considerations, South African extraction policy, and political situations in sensitive countries. Russia's gold sales depend on that country's need for hard currencies. Official sales may also be induced by monetary and balance of payments problems. Industrial demand depends on technological innovation and the discovery of cheaper substitutes. Jewelry demand is sensitive to short-term gold price movements, as well as fashion; the investment motivation is often present in jewelry purchases. Investment demand for bullion and coins is a component of the total demand affecting gold price but is also determined by expectations of future price movements.

So, although gold is a single, well-identified, extensively researched product, its analysis and valuation is not a simple exercise. This difficulty may add another dimension to gold's mystical attraction.

Commodity-Linked Securities

Holding commodities provides no income, so the sole return to the owner is through price increase. Investors can select securities that are linked to some commodity prices and also provide some income. This can be an attractive alternative for investors who wish to, or must, hold financial investments rather than real assets. The two major types of commodity-linked securities are bonds and equity. The indexation clause is explicit for commodity-linked bonds but implicit for equity. Again, we focus on the example of gold.

Commodity-Linked Bonds

There are many examples of commodity-linked bonds in the world capital markets. In periods of high inflation, governments have often been forced to offer loans with coupons or principal indexed to either the price of a specific good or a global inflation index. Inflation-indexed gilts became popular in the United Kingdom during the 1980s. The capital and coupons of these bonds are indexed to British retail prices.

In 1997, the U.S. Treasury started to offer Inflation-Indexed Securities, also known as Treasury Inflation Protected Securities (TIPS). The first such security was a 10-year bond, issued with a real yield of 3.45 percent. The principal value is adjusted for changes in the consumer price index (CPI) on each semiannual coupon payment date. So, the nominal coupon, equal to the real yield times the

CPI-adjusted principal, increases with inflation. At maturity, the CPI-adjusted principal is reimbursed. In the United States, some government agencies, municipalities, and corporations have also issued inflation-indexed bonds. Often, the inflation adjustment to the principal is paid out immediately rather than at final maturity. This structure has been adopted because seeing their nominal credit exposure on nongovernment issues accumulate automatically over time worried investors.

Several countries have issued inflation-indexed bonds (United Kingdom, France, Sweden, Canada, etc.), and corporations and governments have issued bonds indexed to a variety of specific prices, such as oil prices. Gold bonds, and bonds with warrants on gold, have been an attractive alternative to holding gold ingots.

Commodity-Linked Equity

The value of some companies is directly affected by commodity prices. This is clearly the case with the so-called energy companies. For example, companies in the oil and gas industries are affected by the evolution of oil prices. The link between commodity prices and stock prices is more evident for small, undiversified companies that specialize in one type of activity, for example, oil and gas exploration and production. However, large oil companies tend to be quite diversified across activities and the link between commodity prices and stock prices is weaker. An integrated exploration, production, and refining company will be less affected by oil price increases than a company operating in only one of the industry segments.

Gold mining companies are another example of commodity-linked equity. Gold mining shares differ from commodity-linked bonds in that the indexation clause is not fixed by contract but depends on mining economics. In fact, the mining industry is probably the simplest activity to describe in a valuation model. The economics of mining can be described by a simple discounted cash flow model. The principal relationship in the model is the cost structure of the mine as measured by the ratio of costs to revenues. The cost to remove an ounce or a gram of gold from so-called storage and refine it depends on several factors: technology, wage rates, power rates, and the grade and depth of the mine. Revenues depend on the world price of gold. Any movement in the market price of gold will directly affect the cash flows of a mine and therefore its market value; the higher the ratio of costs to revenues, the more sensitive will be the cash flows to gold price movements. However, note that the correlation between gold mine share prices and the price of gold is far from perfect. Gold mine values are influenced by factors other than gold prices; for example, social and political factors have strongly affected South African share prices over time.

SUMMARY

▶ Alternative investments usually involve illiquidity, difficulty in the determination of current market values, limited historical risk and return data, the requirement for extensive investment analysis, a liquidity risk premium, and a segmentation risk premium. Alternative assets are assets not traded on exchanges. Alternative strategies are strategies that mostly use traded assets for the purpose of isolating betas and generating alpha.

▶ An open-end fund stands ready to redeem investor shares at market value, but a closed-end fund does not. A load fund has sales commission charges, and a no-load fund does not. Sales fees may also appear in annual distribution fees.

▶ The net asset value of a fund is calculated as the per-share value of the investment company's assets minus liabilities.

▶ Mutual funds may charge several different fees: Loads and redemption fees provide sales incentives; distribution and operating fees are annual fees; the part of the operating fee that is allocated to the fund manager can be considered an investment performance incentive.

▶ An exchange traded fund (ETF) is a special type of fund that tracks some market index but that is traded on a stock market like any common share.

▶ A mutual fund's purchases and sales of stocks held in the fund lead to taxable gains at the level of the fund, but this is not the case for an ETF because of its in-kind creation and redemption process.

▶ The advantages of ETFs are diversification, trading similarly to a stock, management of their risk augmented by futures and options contracts on them, transparency, cost-effectiveness, avoidance of significant premiums or discounts to NAV, tax savings from payment of in-kind redemption, and immediate dividend reinvestment for open-end ETFs. The disadvantages are these: only a narrow-based market index is tracked in some countries; intraday trading opportunity is not important for long-horizon investors; large bid–ask spreads on some ETFs; and possibly better cost structures and tax advantages to direct index investing for large institutions.

▶ Some characteristics of real estate as an investable asset class are that each property is immovable, basically indivisible, and unique; real estate is not directly comparable to other properties; it is illiquid; and it is bought and sold intermittently in a generally local marketplace, with high transaction costs and market inefficiencies.

▶ The main approaches to real estate valuation are the cost approach, the sales comparison approach, the income approach, and the discounted after-tax cash flow approach.

▶ The net operating income from a real estate investment is gross potential income minus expenses, which include estimated vacancy and collection costs, insurance, taxes, utilities, and repairs and maintenance.

▶ The value of a property can be calculated as the cost to replace the building in its present form in the cost approach; an adjusted value from a benchmark of comparable sales in the sales comparison approach; a hedonic price estimate from a regression model in the sales comparison approach; and capitalized net operating income in the income approach.

▶ The net present value of a property to an equity investor is obtained as the present value of the after-tax cash flows, discounted at the investor's required rate of return on equity, minus the amount of equity required to make the investment.

▶ The three main categories of private equity are venture capital, leveraged buy-outs, and distressed investing.

▶ Venture capital investing is done in many stages from seed through mezzanine.

▶ Venture capital investment characteristics include illiquidity, long-term commitment, difficulty in determining current market values, limited historical risk and return data, limited information, entrepreneurial/management mismatches, fund manager incentive mismatches, lack of knowledge of how many competitors exist, vintage cycles, and the requirement for extensive operations analysis and advice. The challenges to venture capital performance measurement are the difficulty in determining precise valuations, the lack of meaningful benchmarks, and the long-term nature of any performance feedback.

▶ The expected net present value of a venture capital project with a single terminal payoff and a single initial investment can be calculated, given its possible payoff and its conditional failure probabilities, as the present value of the expected payoff minus the required initial investment.

▶ The term *hedge fund* is not fully descriptive because the hedged position is generally designed to isolate a bet rather than to reduce risk. Hedge funds can be defined as funds that seek absolute returns; have a legal structure avoiding some government regulations; and have option-like fees, including a base management fee and an incentive fee proportional to realized profits.

▶ The net performance of a hedge fund can be calculated by subtracting its fees from its gross performance.

▶ Hedge funds can be categorized in a variety of ways: long/short, market neutral, global macro, event driven, convertible arbitrage, fixed-income arbitrage.

▶ The advantages of fund of funds (FOF) investing are availability to the small investor, the fact that access to funds is closed to new investors, diversification, managerial expertise, and a due diligence process. The disadvantages of FOF investing are high fees, little evidence of persistent performance, and the absolute return loss through diversification.

▶ High leverage is often present in hedge funds as part of the trading strategy and is an essential part of some strategies in which the arbitrage return is so small that leverage is needed to amplify the profit. The unique risks of hedge funds are liquidity risk, pricing risk, counterparty credit risk, settlement risk, short squeeze risk, and financing squeeze risk.

▶ In terms of performance, hedge funds are generally viewed as delivering a good return in both up and down markets. The net return on hedge fund indexes tends to be attractive, with a lower standard deviation of return than equity investments, a Sharpe ratio that is higher than that of equity investments, and a low correlation with conventional investments. The biases present in hedge fund performance and risk reporting include self-selection bias, backfilling bias, survivorship bias, smoothed pricing on infrequently traded assets, option-like investment strategies, and fee structure–induced gaming.

▶ For closely held companies and inactively traded securities, a discount is used for lack of liquidity, for lack of marketability, and for a minority interest, but a control premium is added for controlling ownership. The base for the marketability discount is the market value of equity for a comparable publicly traded company.

▶ Distressed-securities investing usually means investing in distressed company bonds with a view to equity ownership in the eventually reconstituted company. Such investments are similar to venture capital investments because they are illiquid, they require a long investment horizon, they require intense investor participation/consulting, and they offer the possibility of alpha because of mispricing.

▶ As a vehicle for investing in production and consumption, commodities complement the investment opportunities offered by shares of corporations that extensively use these as raw materials in their production processes. Investing directly in agricultural products and other commodities gives the investor exposure to the commodity components of the country's production and consumption.

▶ Commodity trading advisors (CTAs) offer managed futures funds that take positions in exchange traded derivatives on commodities and financials.

▶ The return on a collateralized futures position comes from the change in the futures price plus the interest income on risk-free government securities.

▶ The motivation for investing in commodities, commodity derivatives, and commodity-linked securities is that they may have negative correlation with stock and bond returns and a desirable positive correlation with inflation. In the case of commodity-linked securities, the investor can receive some income rather than depending solely on commodity price changes.

▶ The risk of managed futures can be managed through diversification, liquidity monitoring, volatility dependent allocation, quantitative techniques such as VaR, risk budgeting on various aggregation levels, limits on leverage, use of derivatives, and care in model selection.

PRACTICE PROBLEMS FOR READING 73

Use the following information for Problems 1 and 2

Global Leveraged Equity Fund (GLEF) has three classes of shares, each holding the same portfolio of securities but having a different expense structure. The following table summarizes the expenses of these classes of shares.

Expense Comparison for Four Classes of GLEF

	Class A	Class B*	Class C
Sales charge (load) on purchases	5%	None	None
Deferred sales charge (load) on redemptions	None	4% in the first year, declining by 1% each year thereafter	1% for the initial 2 years only
Annual expenses:			
Distribution fee	0.25%	0.50%	0.50%
Management fee	0.50%	0.50%	0.50%
Other expenses	0.50%	0.50%	0.50%
	1.25%	1.50%	1.50%

* Class B shares automatically convert to Class A shares 72 months (6 years) after purchase.

Assume that expense percentages given will be constant at the given values. Assume that the deferred sales charges are computed on the basis of NAV.

An investor is considering the purchase of GLEF shares. The investor expects equity investments with risk characteristics similar to GLEF to earn 9 percent per year. He decides to make his selection of fund share class based on an assumed 9 percent return each year, gross of any of the expenses given in the preceding table.

1. Decide which class of shares of GLEF is best for the investor if he plans to liquidate his investment toward the end of

   A. year 1.

   B. year 3.

   C. year 5.

   D. year 15.

2. You have analyzed the relative performance of different classes of GLEF shares for liquidation in several years. Specifically, you have looked at liquidation in years 1, 3, 5, and 15. Your results are as follows. (The > symbol implies that the class preceding the sign performs better than the class following and the = symbol implies equal performance of the two classes.)

▶ Liquidation in year 1: Class C > Class B > Class A

▶ Liquidation in year 3: Class C > Class B > Class A

▶ Liquidation in year 5: Class B = Class C > Class A

▶ Liquidation in year 15: Class B > Class C > Class A

Provide an intuitive explanation for the pattern of relative performance that you observe.

3. Using the price data for several houses recently sold in a particular area, a real estate firm has identified the main characteristics that affect the prices of houses in that area. The characteristics identified include the living area, the number of bathrooms, whether the house has a fireplace, and how old the house is. The estimated slope coefficient for each of these characteristics and the constant term are as follows:

Characteristic	Units	Coefficient in Euros per Unit
Intercept	—	140,000
Living area	Square meters	210
Number of bathrooms	Number	10,000
Fireplace	0 or 1	15,000
Age of the house	Years	−6,000

Use these above estimates to value a five-year-old house with a living area of 500 square meters, three bathrooms, and a fireplace.

4. A real estate firm is evaluating an office building using the income approach. The real estate firm has compiled the following information for the office building. All information is on an annual basis.

Gross potential rental income	$350,000
Estimated vacancy and collection losses*	4%
Insurance and taxes	$26,000
Utilities	$18,000
Repairs and maintenance	$23,000
Depreciation	$40,000
Interest on proposed financing	$18,000

* As a percentage of gross potential rental income

There have been two recent sales of office buildings in the area. The first building had a net operating income of $500,000 and was sold at $4 million. The second building had a net operating income of $225,000 and was sold at $1.6 million.

A. Compute the net operating income for the office building to be valued.

B. Use the income approach to compute the appraisal price of the office building.

5. An analyst is evaluating a real estate investment project using the discounted cash flow approach. The purchase price is $3 million, which is financed 15 percent by equity and 85 percent by a mortgage loan. It is expected that the property will be sold in five years. The analyst has estimated the following after-tax cash flows during the first four years of the real estate investment project.

Year	1	2	3	4
Cash flow	$60,000	$75,000	$91,000	$108,000

For the fifth year, that is, the year when the property would be sold by the investor, the after-tax cash flow without the property sale is estimated to be $126,000 and the after-tax cash flow from the property sale is estimated to be $710,000.

Compute the NPV of this project. State whether the investor should undertake the project. The investor's cost of equity for projects with level of risk comparable to this real estate investment project is 18 percent.

6. An investment firm is evaluating a real estate investment project using the discounted cash flow approach. The purchase price is $1.5 million, which is financed 20 percent by equity and 80 percent by a mortgage loan at a 9 percent pre-tax interest rate. The mortgage loan has a long maturity and constant annual payments of $120,000. This includes interest payments on the remaining principal at a 9 percent interest rate and a variable principal repayment that steps up with time. The net operating income (NOI) in the first year is estimated to be $170,000. NOI is expected to grow at a rate of 4 percent every year. The interest on real estate financing for the project is tax-deductible. The marginal income tax rate for the investment firm is 30 percent. Using straight-line depreciation, the annual depreciation of the property is $37,500.

  A. Compute the after-tax cash flows in years 1, 2, and 3 of the project.

  B. It is expected that the property will be sold at the end of three years. The projected sale price is $1.72 million. The property's sales expenses are 6.5 percent of the sale price. The capital gains tax rate is 20 percent. Compute the after-tax cash flow from the property sale in year 3.

  C. The investor's cost of equity for projects with level of risk comparable to this real estate investment project is 19 percent. Recommend whether to invest in the project or not, based on the NPV of the project.

7. Would you suggest using real estate appraisal-based indexes in a global portfolio optimization?

8. Suppose the estimated correlation matrix of the Wilshire 5000 U.S. stock index and two real estate indexes, the Federal Russell Company index (FRC) and the National Association of Real Estate Investment Trusts (NAREIT) is as follows:

	Wilshire 5000	NAREIT	FRC
Wilshire 5000	1.00	0.79	0.18
NAREIT	0.79	1.00	0.02
FRC	0.18	0.02	1.00

Based on this matrix, compare the expected price behavior of the two real estate indexes.

9. An investor is evaluating a venture capital project that will require an investment of $1.4 million. The investor estimates that she will be able to exit the venture successfully in eight years. She also estimates that there is an 80 percent chance that the venture will not survive until the end of the eighth year. If the venture does survive until then, it is equally likely that the payoff at the time of exit will be either $25 million or $35 million. The investor is considering an equity investment in the project, and her cost of equity for a project with similar risk is 20 percent.

  A. Compute the NPV of the venture capital project.

  B. Recommend whether to accept or reject the project.

10. VenCap, Inc. is a venture capital financier. It estimates that investing £4.5 million in a particular venture capital project can return £60 million at the end of six years if it succeeds; however, it realizes that the project may fail at any time between now and the end of six years. The following table has VenCap's estimates of probabilities of failure for the project. First, 0.28 is the probability of failure in year 1. The probability that the project fails in the second year, given that it has survived through year 1, is 0.25. The probability that the project fails in the third year, given that it has survived through year 2, is 0.22, and so forth. VenCap is considering an equity investment in the project, and its cost of equity for a project with this level of risk is 22 percent.

Year	1	2	3	4	5	6
Failure probability	0.28	0.25	0.22	0.18	0.18	0.10

Compute the expected net present value of the venture capital project and recommend whether VenCap should accept or reject the project.

11. Consider a hedge fund that has an annual fee structure of 1.5 percent base management fee plus a 15 percent incentive fee applied to profits above the risk-free rate. If the risk-free rate is 5.5 percent, compute the net percentage return for an investor if the gross return during the year is

A. 35%.

B. 5%.

C. −6%.

12. A hedge fund currently has assets of $2 billion. The annual fee structure of this fund consists of a fixed fee of 1 percent of portfolio assets plus a 20 percent incentive fee. The fund applies the incentive fee to the gross return each year in excess of the portfolio's previous high-water mark, which is the maximum portfolio value since the inception of the fund. The maximum value the fund has achieved so far since its inception was a little more than a year ago when its value was $2.1 billion. Compute the fee that the manager would earn in dollars if the return on the fund this year turns out to be

A. 29%.

B. 4.5%.

C. −1.8%.

13. Consider a hedge fund whose annual fee structure has a fixed fee and an incentive fee with a high-water mark provision. The fund manager earns an incentive fee only if the fund is above the high-water mark of the maximum portfolio value since the inception of the fund. Discuss the positive and negative implications of the high-water mark provision for the investors of the hedge fund.

14. A hedge fund has compiled a list of French firms that it believes will outperform the overall French stock market by 7 percent over the year. It also has compiled a list of French firms that it believes will underperform the overall French stock market by 7 percent. The hedge fund wants to invest in a market-neutral long/short strategy on the French stock market. It has a capital of €25 million for this purpose. However, it would like to retain a cash cushion of €1 million for unforeseen events. The hedge fund can borrow shares from a primary broker with a cash margin deposit equal to 20 percent of the value of the shares. No additional costs are charged to borrow the shares.

   A. Outline the strategy for the hedge fund.

   B. Compute the return on the hedge fund's capital of €25 million if the returns on both lists of stocks are as expected. Ignore the return on invested cash of €1 million, and assume that dividends on the long stocks will offset dividends on the short stocks.

15. The shares of an Italian firm have been trading earlier around €6. Recently, a Spanish firm entered into talks with the Italian firm to acquire it. The Spanish firm offered two of its shares for every three shares of the Italian firm. The boards of directors of both firms have approved the merger, and ratification by shareholders is expected soon. The shares of the Spanish firm are currently trading at €12.50, and the shares of the Italian firm are trading at €8.

   A. Should the shares of the Italian firm trade at a discount? Explain.

   B. What position do you think a hedge fund that specializes in risk arbitrage in mergers and acquisitions will take in the two firms? Assume that the hedge fund's position will involve 250,000 shares of the Italian firm.

   C. It turns out that the European Union commission does not approve the merger because it fears that the merged firm will have a monopolistic position in its industry. After this announcement, the shares of the Italian firm fell to €6.10 each. The shares of the Spanish firm are still trading at €12.50 each. Discuss the consequences for the hedge fund. Ignore the cost of securities lending and margins deposit.

16. Global group manages hedge funds and has three hedge funds invested in the stock market of a particular emerging country. These three hedge funds have very different investment strategies. As expected, the 2007 returns on the three funds were quite different. Over the year 2007, an index based on the overall stock market of the emerging country went up by 20 percent. Here are the performances of the three funds before management fees set at 15 percent of gross profits:

Fund	Gross Return
A	50%
B	20%
C	−10%

At year end, most clients had left fund C, and Global group closed this fund. At the start of 2008, Global group launched an aggressive publicity campaign among portfolio managers, stressing the remarkable return on fund A. If potential clients asked whether the firm had other hedge funds invested in the particular emerging market, it mentioned the only other fund, fund B, and claimed that the group's average gross performance during 2008 was 35 percent.

A. Compare the average gross return and the average net return on the three hedge funds with the percentage increase in the stock market index.

B. Comment on the publicity campaign launched by Global group.

17. An analyst is examining the performance of hedge funds. He looks at the 90 hedge funds that are in existence today and notes that the average annual return on these funds during the last 10 years is 25.17 percent. The standard deviation of these returns is 17.43 percent and the Sharpe ratio is 1.15. The analyst also observes that the average of the annual returns on a stock market index during the last 10 years is 14.83 percent. The standard deviation of these returns is 11.87 percent and the Sharpe ratio is 0.81. The analyst concludes that the hedge funds have substantially outperformed the stock market index. Discuss why the comparison by the analyst could be misleading.

18. Consider the four major commodities traded on a commodity futures exchange today (year 10). The following table lists the average annualized price movements from year 1 to year 10, as well as the production volumes, expressed in the local currency unit, today (year 10) and ten years ago (year 1).

Commodity	Average Return	Annual Production	
		Year 1	Year 10
A	20%	10	50
B	20%	5	20
C	−10%	50	10
D	0%	35	20

The futures exchange has now decided to create a commodity index based on the four commodities, with weights equal to their current relative importance in economic production. These indexes are back-calculated till year 1 using today's weights.

A. Would such an index give unbiased indications over the past 10 years?

B. What suggestions do you have regarding weights that can be used to back-calculate the indexes?

19. The beta of gold relative to the market portfolio is −0.3. The risk-free rate is 7 percent, and the market risk premium is 4 percent.

A. What is the expected return on gold based on the capital asset pricing model (CAPM)?

B. Give an intuitive explanation for the magnitude of the expected return on gold.

20. An analyst compared the performance of a hedge fund index with the performance of a major stock index over the past eight years. She noted that the hedge fund index (created from a database) had a higher average return, lower standard deviation, and higher Sharpe ratio than the stock index. All the successful funds that have been in the hedge fund database continued to accept new money over the eight-year period. Are the average return and the Sharpe ratio, respectively, for the hedge fund index *most likely* overstated or understated?

	Average return for the hedge fund index	Sharpe ratio for the hedge fund index
A.	Overstated	Overstated
B.	Overstated	Understated
C.	Understated	Overstated

21. In-kind redemption is a process available to investors participating in:

A. traditional mutual funds but not exchange traded funds.

B. exchange traded funds but not traditional mutual funds.

C. both traditional mutual funds and exchange traded funds.

22. Does trading take place only once a day at closing market prices in the case of:

	exchange traded funds?	traditional mutual funds?
A.	No	No
B.	No	Yes
C.	Yes	No

23. Do funds that are likely to trade at substantial discounts from their net asset values include:

	exchange traded funds?	closed-end funds?
A.	No	No
B.	No	Yes
C.	Yes	No

24. Forms of real estate investment that typically involve issuing shares that are traded on the stock market include:

A. real estate investment trusts but not commingled funds.

B. commingled funds but not real estate investment trusts.

C. both real estate investment trusts and commingled funds.

25. An investor gathered the following information about a real estate investment:

Cost of the property	$800,000
Amount financed by mortgage loan	80%
Interest rate on mortgage loan	13%
Present value of after-tax cash flows from the investment	$226,000
Investor's required rate of return for an equity investment	16%

The investment's net present value (NPV) and yield to an equity investor, respectively, are *best* described as being:

	Investment's NPV	Investment's yield to an equity investor
A.	Positive	Greater than 16%
B.	Positive	Between 13% and 16%
C.	Negative	Less than 13%

26. An investor is considering the purchase of an apartment building. The investor expects that net operating income will remain constant over the life of the investment. The investor plans to depreciate the property using straight-line depreciation and expects that his 35 percent tax rate will not change over the life of the investment. The investor will finance 80 percent of the purchase price with a long-term mortgage loan that will require a level annual payment of $62,600 and he intends to hold the property for at least ten years. During the years prior to the sale of the property, the investor's annual after-tax cash flow from the investment will *most likely*:

   A. be lower in the third year than in the second year.

   B. be higher in the third year than in the second year.

   C. remain constant, because net operating income is expected to remain constant.

27. An investor gathered the following information about a real estate investment:

Amount financed by mortgage loan	$640,000
Interest rate on mortgage loan	10%
Term of mortgage loan	30 years
Year 1 gross potential rental income	$160,000
Year 1 estimated vacancy and collection losses	5%
Year 1 estimated insurance, taxes, and electricity	$35,000
Year 1 estimated repairs and maintenance	$20,000
Annual straight-line depreciation	$25,000
Investor's tax rate	30%

   The mortgage loan requires level end-of-year annual payments of $67,891 and interest on the loan is tax-deductible. The investment's expected after-tax cash flow in Year 1 is *closest* to:

   A. $5,600.

   B. $26,709.

   C. $30,600.

28. A long time horizon is typically required for investments in:

   A. distressed securities but not for investments in venture capital.

   B. venture capital but not for investments in distressed securities.

   C. both distressed securities and investments in venture capital.

29. An investor gathered the following information about a venture capital project:

Initial investment in project	$400,000
Estimated payoff if project is successful	$12 million
Time to payoff for project	8 years
Probability of project's survival until end of year 8	15%
Investor's required rate of return	17%

The net present value of the venture capital project is *closest* to:

A. $112,608.

B. $172,608.

C. $452,608.

SOLUTIONS FOR READING 73

1. Let us compute the terminal value of $1 invested. The share class with the highest terminal value net of all expenses would be the most appropriate, because all classes are based on the same portfolio and thus have the same portfolio risk characteristics.

A. Class A. $1 × (1 − 0.05) = $0.95 is the amount available for investment at $t = 0$, after paying the front-end sales charge. Because this amount grows at 9% per year, reduced by annual expenses of 0.0125, the terminal value per $1 invested after one year is $0.95 × 1.09 × (1 − 0.0125) = $1.0226.

Class B. Ignoring any deferred sales charge, after one year, $1 invested grows to $1 × 1.09 × (1 − 0.015) = $1.0737. According to the table, the deferred sales charge would be 4%; therefore, the terminal value is $1.0737 × 0.96 = $1.0308.

Class C. Ignoring any deferred sales charge, after one year, $1 invested grows to $1 × 1.09 × (1 − 0.015) = $1.0737. According to the table, the deferred sales charge would be 1%; therefore, the terminal value is $1.0737 × 0.99 = $1.063.

Class C is the best.

B. Class A. The terminal value per $1 invested after three years is $0.95 × 1.09^3 × $(1 − 0.0125)^3$ = $1.1847.

Class B. Ignoring any deferred sales charge, after three years, $1 invested grows to $1 × 1.09^3 × $(1 − 0.015)^3$ = $1.2376. The deferred sales charge would be 2%; therefore, the terminal value is $1.2376 × 0.98 = $1.2128.

Class C. There would be no deferred sales charge. Thus, after three years, $1 invested grows to $1 × 1.09^3 × $(1 − 0.015)^3$ = $1.2376.

Class C is the best.

C. Class A. The terminal value per $1 invested after five years is $0.95 × 1.09^5 × $(1 − 0.0125)^5$ = $1.3726.

Class B. There would be no deferred sales charge. So, the terminal value per $1 invested after five years is $1 × 1.09^5 × $(1 − 0.015)^5$ = $1.4266.

Class C. There would be no deferred sales charge. So, the terminal value per $1 invested after five years is $1 × 1.09^5 × $(1 − 0.015)^5$ = $1.4266.

Classes B and C are the best.

D. Class A. The terminal value per $1 invested after 15 years is $0.95 × 1.09^{15} × $(1 − 0.0125)^{15}$ = $2.8653.

Class B. There would be no deferred sales charge. So, the terminal value per $1 invested after 15 years is $1 × 1.09^{15} × $(1 − 0.015)^6$ × $(1 − 0.0125)^9$ = $2.9706.

Class C. There would be no deferred sales charge. So, the terminal value per \$1 invested after 15 years is $\$1 \times 1.09^{15} \times (1 - 0.015)^{15} = \$2.9036$.

Class B is the best.

2. Class A performs quite poorly unless the investment horizon is very long. The reason is the high sales charge of 5 percent on purchases. Even though the annual expenses for Class A are low, that is not enough to offset the high sales charge on purchases until a very long investment horizon. One could verify that Class A outperforms Class C for an investment horizon of 21 years or more.

Class B performs worse than Class C at very short-term horizons because of its higher deferred sales charges. However, after its deferred sales charges disappear, the relative performance of Class B starts improving. After six years, Class B shares convert to Class A with its lower annual expenses. At longer horizons, Class B starts to outperform Class C due to its annual expenses, which are lower than those of Class C.

Class C performs well at shorter investment horizons because it has no initial sales charge and it has a low deferred sales charge.

3. The estimated model is

House value in euros = 140,000 + (210 × Living area) + (10,000 × Number of bathrooms) + (15,000 × Fireplace) − (6,000 × Age)

so, the value of the specific house is

$$140,000 + (210 \times 500) + (10,000 \times 3) + (15,000 \times 1) - (6,000 \times 5) = €260,000$$

4. **A.** The net operating income for the office building is gross potential rental income minus estimated vacancy and collection costs, minus insurance and taxes, minus utilities, minus repairs and maintenance.

$$\begin{aligned} \text{NOI} &= 350,000 - 0.04 \times 350,000 - 26,000 - 18,000 - 23,000 \\ &= \$269,000 \end{aligned}$$

B. The capitalization rate of the first office building recently sold in the area is

$$\text{NOI/(Transaction price)} = 500,000/4,000,000 = 0.125$$

The capitalization rate of the second office building recently sold in the area is

$$\text{NOI/(Transaction price)} = 225,000/1,600,000 = 0.141$$

The average of the two capitalization rates is 0.133.

Applying this capitalization rate to the office building under consideration, which has an NOI of \$269,000, gives an appraisal value of:

$$\text{NOI/(Capitalization rate)} = 269,000/0.133 = \$2,022,556$$

5. The after-tax cash flow for the property sale year is $126,000 + $710,000 = $836,000. At a cost of equity of 18%, the present value of the after-tax cash flows in years 1 through 5 is as follows:

$60,000/1.18 + $75,000/1.18^2 + $91,000/1.18^3 + $108,000/1.18^4 + 836,000/1.18^5 = $581,225

The investment requires equity of 0.15 × $3,000,000 = $450,000. Thus, the NPV = $581,225 − $450,000 = $131,225. The recommendation based on NPV would be to accept the project, because the NPV is positive.

6. A. The amount borrowed is 80% of $1.5 million, which is $1.2 million. The first year's interest = 9% of $1.2 million = $108,000. So,

After-tax net income in year 1 = (NOI − Depreciation − Interest) × (1 − Marginal tax rate) = ($170,000 − $37,500 − $108,000) × (1 − 0.30) = $17,150

After-tax cash flow = After-tax net income + Depreciation − Principal repayment

and,

Principal repayment = Mortgage payment − Interest = $120,000 − $108,000 = $12,000

so,

After-tax cash flow in year 1 = $17,150 + $37,500 − $12,000 = $42,650.

New NOI in year 2 = 1.04 × $170,000 = $176,800. We need to calculate the second year's interest payment on the mortgage balance after the first year's payment. This mortgage balance is the original principal balance minus the first year's principal repayment, or $1,200,000 – $12,000 = $1,188,000. The interest on this balance is $106,920.

So,

After-tax net income = ($176,800 − $37,500 − $106,920) × (1 − 0.30) = $22,666

Principal repayment = $120,000 − $106,920 = $13,080

so,

After-tax cash flow in year 2 = $22,666 + $37,500 − $13,080 = $47,086

New NOI in year 3 = 1.04 × $176,800 = $183,872. We need to calculate the third year's interest payment on the mortgage balance after the second year's payment. This mortgage balance is the original principal balance minus the first two years' principal repayments, or $1,200,000 − $12,000 − $13,080 = $1,174,920. The interest on this balance is $105,743.

So,

After-tax net income = ($183,872 − $37,500 − $105,743) × (1 − 0.30) = $28,440

Principal repayment = $120,000 − $105,743 = $14,257

so,

After-tax cash flow in year 3 = $28,440 + $37,500 − $14,257 = $51,683

B. Ending book value = Original purchase price − Total depreciation during three years = $1,500,000 − 3 × $37,500 = $1,387,500.

The net sale price = $1,720,000 × (1 − 0.065) = $1,608,200

Capital gains tax = 0.20 × ($1,608,200 − $1,387,500) = $44,140

After-tax cash flow from property sale = Net sales price − Outstanding mortgage − Capital gains tax

and,

Outstanding mortgage = Original mortgage − Three years' worth of principal repayments,

or

$$\$1,200,000 - (\$12,000 + \$13,080 + \$14,257) = \$1,160,663$$

so,

After-tax cash flow from the property sale = $1,608,200 − $1,160,663 − $44,140 = $403,397

C. The total after-tax cash flow for the property sale year is $51,683 + $403,397 = $455,080. At a cost of equity of 19%, the present value of the after-tax cash flows in years 1 through 3 is as follows:

$$\$42,650/1.19 + \$47,086/1.19^2 + \$455,080/1.19^3 = \$339,142$$

The investment requires equity of 0.20 × $1,500,000 = $300,000. Thus, the NPV = $339,142 − $300,000 = $39,142. The recommendation based on NPV would be to accept the project, because the NPV is positive.

7. No, one would not suggest using real estate appraisal-based indexes in a global portfolio optimization. Real estate appraisal values are a smoothed series. One of the reasons for this smoothness is that the appraisals are done quite infrequently. Another reason is that the appraised values typically show relatively few changes. Due to these two reasons, an appraisal-based index understates volatility. This spuriously low volatility would inflate the attractiveness of real estate.

8. Clearly, the two real estate indexes have very different price behaviors. Their correlation is almost null. As expected, the NAREIT *index* exhibits a strong correlation with U.S. stocks because the REIT share prices are strongly influenced by the stock market. In contrast, the FRC index, which is much less volatile, is not highly correlated with the stock market.

9. A. There are three possibilities.

Project does not survive until the end of the eighth year.

Project survives and the investor exits with a payoff of $25 million.

Project survives and the investor exits with a payoff of $35 million.

There is an 80 percent chance that the project will not survive until the end of the eighth year. That is, there is a 20 percent chance that the project will survive, and the investor will exit the project then. If the project survives, it is equally likely that the payoff at the time of exit will be either $25 million or $35 million.

The project's NPV is the present value of the expected payoffs minus the required initial investment of $1.4 million.

NPV = $0.8 \times \$0 + 0.2 \times [(0.5 \times \$25 \text{ million} + 0.5 \times \$35 \text{ million})/1.2^8] - \$1.4 \text{ million} = -\$0.004592 \text{ million or} -\$4,592$

B. Because the expected NPV of the project is negative, the project should be rejected.

10. The probability that the venture capital project survives to the end of the first year is $(1 - 0.28)$, 1 minus the probability of failure in the first year; the probability that it survives to the end of second year is the product of the probability it survives the first year times the probability it survives the second year, or $(1 - 0.28)(1 - 0.25)$. So, the probability that the project survives to end of the sixth year is $(1 - 0.28)(1 - 0.25)(1 - 0.22)(1 - 0.18)(1 - 0.18)(1 - 0.10) = (0.72)(0.75)(0.78)(0.82)(0.82)(0.90) = 0.255$, or 25.5%. The probability that the project fails is $1 - 0.255 = 0.745$, or 74.5%.

The net present value of the project, if it survives to the end of the sixth year and thus earns €60 million, is $-€4.5 \text{ million} + €60 \text{ million}/1.22^6 = €13.70 \text{ million}$. The net present value of the project if it fails is $-€4.5$ million. Thus, the project's expected NPV is a probability-weighted average of these two amounts, or $(0.255)(€13.70 \text{ million}) + (0.745)(-€4.5 \text{ million}) = €141,000$.

Based on the project's positive net present value, VenCap should accept the investment.

11. A. Fee = $1.5\% + 15\% \times (35\% - 5.5\%) = 1.5\% + 4.425\% = 5.925\%$

Net return = $35\% - 5.925\% = 29.1\%$

B. Because the gross return is less than the risk-free rate, the incentive fee is zero. The only fee incurred is the base management fee of 1.5%.

Net return = $5\% - 1.5\% = 3.5\%$.

C. Again, the incentive fee is zero.

Net return = $-6\% - 1.5\% = -7.5\%$.

12. A. Fixed fee = 1% of $2 billion = $20 million.

If the return is 29%, new value of the fund would be $2 billion $\times$ 1.29 = $2.58 billion. This new value would be $2.58 billion − $2.1 billion = $0.48 billion above the high watermark. So, the incentive fee = 20% $\times$ $0.48 billion = $0.096 billion, or $96 million.

Total fee = $20 million + $96 million = $116 million

B. Fixed fee = 1% of $2 billion = $20 million.

If the return is 4.5%, new value of the fund would be $2 billion $\times$ 1.045 = $2.09 billion. Because this new value is below the high watermark of $2.1 billion, no incentive fee would be earned.

Total fee = $20 million

C. Fixed fee = 1% of $2 billion = $20 million.

If the return is −1.8%, no incentive fee would be earned.

Total fee = $20 million

13. Clearly, the high watermark provision has the positive implication for the investors that they would have to pay the manager an incentive fee only when they make a profit. Further, the hedge fund manager would need to make up any earlier losses before becoming eligible for the incentive fee payment. However, a negative implication is that the option-like characteristic of the high watermark provision (the incentive fee being zero everywhere below the benchmark and increasing above the benchmark) may induce risk-taking behavior when the fund is below the high watermark. The manager may take more risky positions when the fund is below the high watermark in order to get to above the high watermark and earn an incentive fee. The worst case for the manager is a zero incentive fee, regardless of how far below the benchmark the fund turns out to be. Another negative implication is that the incentive fees, if the fund exceeds the high watermark, are set quite high (typically at 20%), which reduces long-run asset growth.

14. A. The hedge fund would sell short the overvalued shares and use the proceeds to buy the undervalued shares. The fund has €25 million − €1 million = €24 million to be used toward cash margin deposit. Because the cash margin deposit requirement is 20%, the fund could take long and short positions totalling €24 million/0.20 = €120 million. So, the fund would do the following:

Keep €1 million in cash

Deposit €24 million in a margin account

Borrow €120 million of overvalued stocks from a broker

Sell the overvalued stocks for €120 million

Use the sale proceeds to purchase undervalued stocks for €120 million

B. If the performances of both lists of stocks are as expected, there would be a gain of 7% on the long position of €120 million and a gain of 7% on the short position of €120 million. So, the total gain would be 7% × €120 million × 2 = €16.8 million. Ignoring the return on invested cash of €1 million, and assuming that dividends on the long stocks will offset dividends on the short stocks, this translates to an annual return of (€16.8 million/€25 million) × 100 = 67.2%. The return is so high when the expectations are realized, because the position is highly levered.

15. A. The Spanish firm will give two of its shares, which are worth €25, for three of the Italian firm's shares, which are worth €24. Thus, the shares of the Italian firm are trading at a discount. The reason for the discount is that there is a possibility that the merger may not go through. If the merger does not go through, the shares of the Italian firm are likely to fall back to the premerger announcement level. An investor currently buying shares of the Italian firm is taking the risk that the merger will not occur.

B. The hedge fund will take a hedged position by selling two shares of the Spanish firm short for every three shares of the Italian firm that it buys. So, the hedge fund will buy 250,000 shares of the Italian firm by selling (2/3) × 250,000 = 166,666.67, that is, 166,667 shares of the Spanish firm. The proceeds from the short sale are 166,667 × €12.50 = €2,083,338, which is €83,338 more than the cost of buying the shares of the Italian firm, which is 250,000 × €8 = €2,000,000.

C.   Because the merger did not go through and the stock price of the Italian firm fell, the hedge fund incurs a substantial loss. The loss is $250,000 \times (€8 - €6.10) = €475,000$.

16. **A.**   Net return on Fund A = $50\% \times (1 - 0.15) = 42.5\%$

Net return on Fund B = $20\% \times (1 - 0.15) = 17\%$

Net return on Fund C = -10%

So, average net return = $(42.5\% + 17\% - 10\%)/3 = 16.5\%$

Average gross return = $(50\% + 20\% - 10\%)/3 = 20\%$

Thus, the average gross return on the three hedge funds is the same as the percentage increase in the stock market index, and the average net return is lower.

B.   The publicity campaign launched by Global group illustrates the problem of survivorship bias in performance measure of hedge funds. Although the average gross return on the three hedge funds is the same as the percentage increase in the stock market index, the performance reported by Global group seems much better because it is based on only the funds that survive. That is, the average performance reported by Global group is inflated.

17. The measurement of the performance of the hedge funds suffers from survivorship bias. The 90 hedge funds that the analyst has examined include only those funds that have survived during the last 10 years. Thus, any poorly performing funds that have been discontinued due to low return or high volatility, or both, have been excluded. Accordingly, the average return on hedge funds has been overstated, while the volatility has been understated. Consequently, the Sharpe ratio for the hedge funds has been overstated. Furthermore, the Sharpe ratio may be a misleading measure of risk-adjusted performance for hedge funds because of the optionality in their investment strategies.

18. **A.**   The construction of the index is okay in year 10 but not in the earlier years. By using today's weights in construction of the index in earlier years, the exchange is over-weighing those commodities that have become important over the period, and have simultaneously gone up in price.

B.   For each year, use the relative economic importance of the commodities in that year as the weights for that year. That is, use year one weights for the index calculated in year one, and so on.

19. **A.**   The expected return on gold, as theoretically derived by the CAPM, is

$$E(R_{gold}) = 7\% + \beta_{gold} \times 4\%$$
$$= 7\% - 0.3\,(4\%) = 5.8\%$$

B.   Given its negative beta, gold is likely to perform well when the overall market performs poorly. Thus, our investment in gold is likely to offset some of the loss on the rest of the portfolio. Investors should be willing to accept an overall lower expected return on gold because, in periods of financial distress, gold tends to do well.

20. A is correct. Survivorship bias affects both the returns and the risk (standard deviation) reported for the hedge funds. Hedge funds with low or negative returns will be excluded from the index as will funds with high volatility; those funds will not survive for eight years. If only the successful

funds remain in the index, the returns are overstated and risk is understated. Overstated returns and understated risk will both tend to overstate the Sharpe ratio.

21. B is correct. A major distinguishing feature of exchange traded funds is the in-kind redemption process. The process allows the remaining investors in exchange traded funds to avoid capital gains taxes because the portfolio does not realize capital gains with in-kind redemptions. Traditional mutual funds use in-cash redemptions that may result in a capital gains tax liability for all participants in the fund.

22. B is correct. One of the advantages of ETFs is that trading takes place continuously throughout the trading day. Traditional mutual funds trade once a day at closing market values.

23. B is correct. Supply and demand determine the market prices of both types of funds. However, the easy arbitrage available between ETF shares and the assets held by the ETF keeps the traded price of an ETF more in line with its underlying value. Closed-end funds offer a fixed supply of shares, and, as demand changes, can trade at large discounts or premiums to underlying value.

24. A is correct. Real estate investment trusts are closed-end investment companies and trade on the stock market. Comingled funds are pools of capital created by institutions to invest in real estate projects. They do not trade actively.

25. A is correct. The equity investment in the property is $800,000(100% − 80%) = $160,000. The present value of the after-tax cash flows is greater than the cost of the investment, so the NPV is positive. If the NPV is positive the IRR (yield) must be greater than the investor's required rate of return.

26. A is correct. Even though NOI, the annual mortgage payment, the tax rate, and the tax benefit from depreciation remain the same, the tax benefit from the interest deduction will decline over time. The allocation of the mortgage payment between interest and principal will change as the amount of the principal outstanding is reduced over time; the portion of the payment allocated to interest will decline. The reduction in interest expense will lower the tax benefits associated with the mortgage payment and thus reduce the after-tax cash flow over time.

27. B is correct. The after-tax net income from the investment would be:

Net rental income (0.95 × 160,000)	152,000
Insurance, taxes and electric	−35,000
Repairs and maintenance	−20,000
Depreciation	−25,000
Interest (0.10 × 640,000)	−64,000
Before tax income	8,000
Taxes (0.30 × 8000)	−2,400
After tax income	5,600
Add back depreciation	+25,000
Subtract principal payment (67,891 − 64,000)	−3,891
After-tax cash flow	26,709

28. C is correct. The similarities between distressed securities investing and venture capital investing include illiquidity, a long time horizon, intense investor participation, and the possibility of mispricing.

29. A is correct. First, multiply the payoff ($12 million) by the probability of survival (15%). The expected payoff is $1,800,000. The present value of $1,800,000 eight years into the future using the required return of 17% is $512,608. Finally, subtracting the cost of the project ($400,000) results in a present value of $112,608.

INVESTING IN COMMODITIES
by Ronald G. Layard-Liesching

LEARNING OUTCOMES

The candidate should be able to:	Mastery
a. explain the relationship between spot prices and expected future prices in terms of contango and backwardation;	☐
b. describe the sources of return and risk for a commodity investment and the effect on a portfolio of adding an allocation to commodities;	☐
c. explain why a commodity index strategy is generally considered an active investment.	☐

Investing in commodities remains controversial. But a long-only allocation to commodities brings risk reduction and inflation protection to a traditional portfolio asset mix. As more public and private pension funds are searching for higher-returning and liability-matching assets, interest in commodity investment is rising rapidly. Currently, the majority of institutional investment in commodities is index based, and trading to maintain index exposure makes this an active strategy. And although institutional commodity investment is in its infancy, newer strategies, such as index plus and active long-only, are increasing in popularity.

Commodities are now capturing the interest of institutional investors because, to put it simply, the math works. The average U.S. public pension fund has a return target of 8 percent, but the prospect over the next few years for the basic 60 percent/40 percent equity/fixed-income mix is dim. With the estimated return for bonds around 5 percent, a gross equity return of nearly 11 percent a year is needed to make up the difference. Few investors believe this type of return is achievable. Thus, plan sponsors are seeking new uncorrelated sources of return, such as commodities, to introduce into the traditional portfolio mix.

Note:
Commodity index strategies, unlike U.S. equity index strategies, are active strategies because of the high turnover.

Ronald G. Layard-Liesching is chief investment officer at Pareto Partners, New York City.

This presentation comes from the 2006 Financial Analysts Seminar held in Evanston, Illinois, on 16–21 July 2006.

265

Funds are also increasingly concerned with managing liability-relative risks and are turning to liability-driven investment strategies. The United States has a huge problem with underfunded retirement benefits, but in many other countries, the situation is even worse. Hence, around the globe, pension fund chief investment officers are trying to find the asset class with an expected risk–return profile that improves upon that of more traditional investments and more closely matches their funds' growing liabilities. This quest is driving managers to alternative investments, in general, and to commodities, in particular.

This reading will begin with a basic introduction to commodities before proceeding to a discussion of the controversies surrounding the commodity markets. Then, I will explain how commodities fit into a portfolio and will suggest a lens other than mean–variance analysis with which to view their contribution. Through that lens, commodity investment appears rather attractive. The existence of a commodity return premium is currently actively debated mainly because the asset class does not produce cash flow. So, I will outline the sources of commodity returns. Finally, I will explain the alternatives for institutions seeking to implement commodity investment programs.

1   COMMODITY BASICS

Commodity strategies require investing cash collateral to support derivatives exposure. The principal derivatives are forwards and futures contracts. Note that a relationship exists between the spot (current) price of the commodity and the expected spot price of the commodity at the maturity date of the derivative contract. If the future price is above the spot price, this is referred to as "contango." If the future price is below the spot price, this is referred to as "backwardation."

Contango

When a commodity market is in contango, as illustrated in Figure 1, futures prices are higher than the spot price because market participants believe the spot price will be higher in the future. Contango often occurs when a commodity's price is high and volatile, as is the case currently with oil. For example, the oil consumer, such as an airline, drives the price of the futures higher than the spot price as it attempts to hedge against the risk of higher spot prices, which could ultimately cause it to go out of business.

The amount by which the relative price of the futures can rise is limited, however, by a classic arbitrage trade. If the futures price goes too high, an investor can buy the commodity at the spot price, store it, insure it, and sell it forward. This "carry trade" is a pure financing activity and theoretically limits the futures price to a level called "full carry." A commodity like gold can be easily borrowed in large size, and the borrowing cost of gold is usually below dollar cash interest rates. Hence, this arbitrage means that gold will often be at full carry in the forward market. But different commodities have unique features that affect this relationship.

FIGURE 1 Contango Illustration

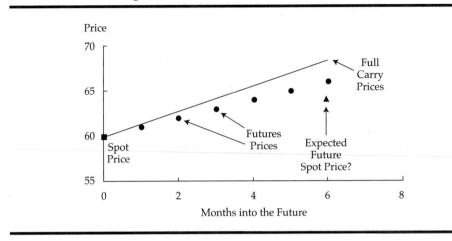

For example, there may be limitations on storing commodities for future delivery. Hogs, for instance, cannot be stored indefinitely because they have finite lives. There also may be physical limits on available storage for delivery. In these cases, the classic carry trade does not apply. So, forward prices can rise far above the spot price, reflecting a future supply shortage.

For most commodities, the investor buys a futures contract with a set maturity date. When the futures contract is purchased, the investor deposits cash as collateral for the contract with the exchange. This cash generates an additional return called the "collateral yield." But the investor wishes to maintain long-only commodity exposure. So, when the contract matures, it is closed out and another one is bought with a longer maturity. This trade is called "rolling the contract." This contract rolling creates a small profit or loss that is unrelated to the spot price movement. In this way, the investor maintains long exposure to the commodity. For most commodities, exceptions being precious metals, such as silver and gold, it would not be practical to actually hold the physical commodity.

Backwardation

The opposite of contango is when the forward price or futures price of a commodity is below its spot price. This situation is referred to as "backwardation" and is illustrated in Figure 2. Backwardation used to be common in the oil market. When the price of oil was low, producers wanted to hedge their risk of further price declines. Lower prices threatened their ability to stay in business. Backwardation actually used to be the norm in most commodities because a potential price fall had a proportionally bigger impact on the few large producers than on the many small consumers. This feature was analyzed by John Maynard Keynes, who referred to it as "natural backwardation." Commodity producers were willing to sell their commodity below the price they expected it to be in the future to protect against business risk. There was substantial disutility to this large group of producers if the price fell. So, long-only speculators gained by taking over this price risk from the producers. This natural backwardation may be changing, however, because derivatives trading and institutional investing make for greater symmetry. When prices are low and volatile, producers hedge and the market enters backwardation. When prices are high and volatile, consumers

FIGURE 2   Backwardation Illustration

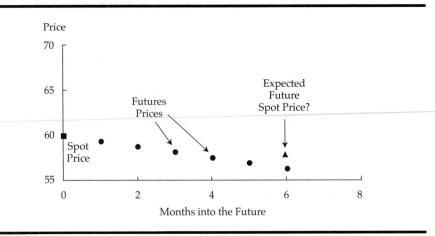

FIGURE 3   Yield Components of Commodities, January 1986–December 2004

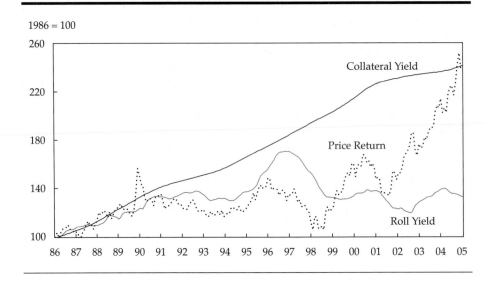

Source: Based on monthly data from the Gresham TAP Index.

hedge. At the same time, investors are attempting to hedge inflation risk. The combination of these two actions creates contango.

Sources of Return

Long-only investment in commodities is usually obtained via collateralized long positions in commodity futures, forwards, or swaps. The institutional investor receives three distinct sources of return: collateral yield, roll or convenience yield, and the spot price return. Figure 3 plots the three yield components of a commodity index investment. The collateral yield is the return on cash used as margin to take long derivatives exposure. Generally, this is a T-bill return. Active collateral management can enhance this return.

The roll yield (also known as "convenience yield") is the return from rolling forward the maturity of the derivatives position. During the period shown in Figure 3, the roll yield was both positive and negative. The return to the long investor is positive when the market is in backwardation; the long investor can buy the commodity below the current spot level from a hedger. On maturity, the hedger pays the long investor the convergence in price between the forward and spot rates. Currently, the roll yield on commodity indices is negative because, on average, commodity markets are in contango. This negative roll yield is particularly the case for oil, which has a large weight in the major commodity indices. Because of future expected oil supply shortages, speculators have driven the futures price of oil above the spot price. For the majority of commodities, long investors are buying futures at a price higher than the spot price. Hence, if the spot price moves sideways, the long position will be closed out at a loss. That difference in price is lost, and as a result, the roll yield is negative.

The price return can obviously be positive or negative based on fluctuations in its spot price caused by supply and demand. Over the past 25 years, price returns, although volatile, have been strong.

COMMODITY CONTROVERSIES ■ **2** ▸

Much controversy exists about whether commodities are an asset class. Fueling the debate over the classification of commodities as an asset class are the arguments that commodity prices decline in the very long run, roll yield may disappear, rolling costs may reduce returns, and the return premium may result from rebalancing. Of course, the argument that commodities cannot be an asset class because they do not generate cash flow is frequently heard, but I will address that later in the reading.

Commodity Prices

Some argue that commodity prices decline in the long run (and hence are not an asset class). Over the last century, spot commodity prices have fallen by some 1.5 percent a year. The time horizons of most portfolios, however, are much shorter than 100 years. Figure 3 shows that from 1989 to 2000, the spot price basically moved sideways, generating minimal price return, but took off like a rocket in early 2001. Investors who bought the argument against holding commodities missed out on this spectacular run-up in price.

Commodity prices decline because of the introduction of new supplies and new production technology (such as the Alaska oil sands and coal gasification), substitution of one commodity for another when prices rise (such as aluminum for copper in power lines), and reduction in the use of certain commodities in technological processes (such as optical fibers for copper).

Offsetting these effects are the facts that global supplies are finite for many commodities, demand for storable commodities is rising, and the engagement in the global economy of the postemergent economies of China and India fundamentally alters global demand and supply.

Most of the fluctuation in commodity prices comes from the demand side of the equation. The supply-side shifts are usually smaller and slower to respond than are demand fluctuations (note that this is not true of electricity, for example, where supply disruptions can cause dramatic price moves). So, as demand rises for a finite supply of a commodity, the price of the commodity is bound to rise.

The demand for storable commodities, which can be held as hard assets, is also increasing. The lack of cash flow from these commodities is irrelevant: Investors hold U.S. dollar balances because of their usefulness as a store of value. The same dynamic is affecting the demand for commodities. Commodities are perceived as a good store of value in an increasingly risky and unstable world.

The prices of commodities will also rise because they are denominated in units of paper currency. As the value of a currency falls, prices of commodities denominated in that currency rise. In other words, the price of commodities operates as an exchange rate. It is the exchange rate between the commodity and the value of a paper currency—the U.S. dollar. So, if the dollar depreciates or loses its purchasing power, the value of commodities will appreciate. The existence of truly massive unfunded U.S. dollar deficits explains one component of the long-term return premium to long commodity investing.

Roll Yield

The roll yield is the yield that has historically existed in situations when the forward price is below the spot price. Producers sell commodities at prices lower than the expected future price to hedge their business risk, which benefits long investors and speculators. But the rapid growth in institutional long-only investors and growing worldwide demand for commodities may have created permanent structural change in the marketplace. It is raising fears that the roll yield may disappear. At the moment, it is indeed negative, but this has been seen before.

When Keynes formulated his theory of natural backwardation, developed futures markets did not exist and the preponderance of market participants were hedgers. The bottom line was that long investors won and hedgers lost. Today's market is no longer dominated by participants with a single motive, so the market can move both ways. Opportunities to add value have thus increased because of the disassociation between the price of the futures and the expected future price.

Rolling Costs

Investing in indices requires that the investor roll his or her exposure. In other words, at the maturity date of the futures contract, the investor can either take physical delivery of the commodity or roll the futures contract, which means buying another contract with a new maturity date. The rolling cost is the cost to sell the maturing contract and buy a new one.

The indices, such as the Goldman Sachs Commodity Index (GSCI) and the Dow Jones-AIG Commodity Index (DJ-AIG), roll on specified dates over five business days. During this period, a very high volume of contracts trades because of the tremendous size of the indices' long holdings. The market makers know which contracts are involved, so the roll, not surprisingly, becomes more expensive. Thus, the dynamics of the roll inflict a hidden, but significant, cost on long-only investors that definitely reduces returns. Roll costs, however, can be reduced or avoided through active roll maturity and timing management.

Return Premium

An academic debate is stirring about the commodity return premium. The debate basically revolves around the fact that over the same time period, the long-term geometric return of the average commodity was close to zero but the geometric return of the commodity index was strong. How can the commodity basket have a higher geometric return than the components? The answer is that index volatility is lower than the average volatility of its constituents (29 percent). Rebalancing occurs when the weights of holdings in different commodities need to be adjusted back to the index weights after large price moves. So, if the oil price rises sharply, oil must be sold and the other commodities purchased. Rebalancing can thus add value. Therefore, the geometric return of a rebalanced portfolio is higher than the average return of its constituents. The approximate relationship, according to Booth and Fama (1992), is

$$G = M - \frac{\sigma^2}{2},$$

where G is the geometric return, M is the arithmetic return, and σ is the volatility. Erb and Harvey (2006) argued that this rebalancing return provides essentially all the return to commodity investing. Gorton and Rouwenhorst (2006) countered this argument, showing that rebalancing interacts with return seriality. The crucial point is that the primary driver of return in commodities is not simply the rebalancing process.

COMMODITIES IN A PORTFOLIO   3

Long-term commodity investment offers several positives to a portfolio. The risk–return profile of commodities over the past 25 years is similar to that of U.S. equities. Commodities also provide a reduction in portfolio risk, which is the primary argument for adding commodities to traditional portfolios. Return-timing diversification as well as inflation shock and liability matching are other reasons for adding commodities to a portfolio.

Long-Term Return

Figure 4 shows long-term bond, stock, and commodity futures returns. All three returns were positive over the period. From January 1991 to April 2006, the volatilities of the two major commodity indices—the DJ-AIG (12.1 percent) and the GSCI (18.6 percent)—and the volatility of equities as measured by the S&P 500 Index (14.2 percent) were quite similar, as shown in Table 1. As one would assume, the volatility of bonds as measured by the Lehman Brothers U.S. Aggregate Index (3.8 percent) was much lower than that for either equities or commodities. Note that the volatility of the DJ-AIG was lower than that of the GSCI because it is a much more evenly weighted basket of commodities; the GSCI is currently 73 percent energy weighted versus 33 percent for the DJ-AIG. A mean–variance optimizer loves commodities because of their negative correlation with other markets and their interesting risk–return characteristics. As a result, it will allocate a higher percentage of the portfolio to commodities than prudence dictates is wise. There is a better way to analyze the commodity allocation.

FIGURE 4   Inflation-Adjusted Performance of Stocks, Bonds, and Commodity Futures, July 1959–December 2004

July 1959 = 100

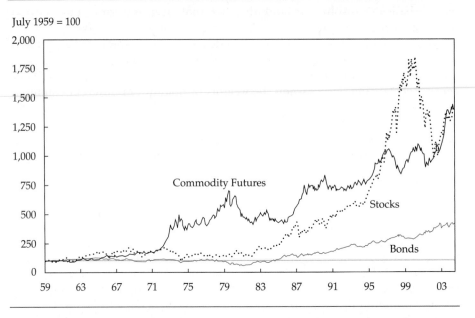

Source: Gorton and Rouwenhorst (2006).

TABLE 1   Return and Volatility, January 1991–April 2006

Index	Return	Volatility
S&P 500	11.2%	14.2%
DJ-AIG	4.2	12.1
GSCI	7.8	18.6
Lehman Brothers U.S. Aggregate	7.0	3.8

Note: Data are monthly.

Sources: Based on data from Standard & Poor's, Lehman Brothers, and Goldman, Sachs & Co.

Portfolio Risk

A. D. Roy, who published a paper in 1952 at about the same time Harry M. Markowitz was writing his Nobel Prize–winning paper on modern portfolio theory, said that investors do not want to know the long-run average expected rate of return on their portfolios. They want to know what will happen next year. Roy's point was that to be a long-term investor, you have to be able to survive the short run. As an alternative to mean–variance portfolio selection, Roy developed "safety-first" investing—choosing the highest-returning portfolio subject to the worst-case short-run outcome being acceptable.

Table 2 illustrates the portfolio impact of commodities during the period from January 1991 to April 2006. The first row shows the return, volatility, and worst-case return for a portfolio of 60 percent U.S. equities and 40 percent U.S. bonds. Hedge funds, alternatives, and international investing could also be

TABLE 2	Portfolio Impact of Commodities, January 1991–April 2006						
Portfolio	Equities	Bonds	GSCI	DJ-AIG	Return	Volatility	Worst 12 Months
1	60%	40%	—	—	11.3%	8.6%	−12.3%
2	55	40	5%	—	11.3	8.0	−11.7
3	50	40	10	—	11.2	7.5	−11.2
4	55	40	—	5%	11.0	8.0	−11.2
5	50	40	—	10	10.6	7.4	−10.1

Note: Data are monthly.

Sources: Based on data from Standard & Poor's, Lehman Brothers, AIG, and Goldman, Sachs & Co.

included without changing the results. The annualized return was 11.3 percent, which easily exceeds the current 8.0–8.5 percent target return of most U.S. funds. Annualized volatility for this 60/40 portfolio was 8.6 percent. The return for the 60/40 portfolio over the worst 12 months of the period was −12.3 percent.

Note one caveat to this analysis: It assesses only the asset side of the fund, not the fund surplus over liabilities. A typical U.S. corporate pension plan has a liability duration of 14 years, which is equivalent to being short a 14-year-duration bond. Analyzing the surplus for this period would mean the worst-case 12-month return would be −24 percent because liabilities rose at the same time asset prices fell in the perfect storm of 2000 through 2002. The proper analysis should thus always consider assets in relationship to liabilities. If the analysis outlined in Table 2 included the liability side of the equation, then the outcome—that adding commodities to a portfolio improves the worst-case return scenario—would be even more strikingly positive.

When 5 percent of the equity allocation is moved to the GSCI, the worst-case return is reduced by 60 bps, and with a 10 percent allocation to the GSCI, the reduction is more than 1 percentage point. The improvement is a result of the fact that when paper assets fall in value, the value of commodities tends to rise.

In the case of a 10.0 percent allocation to the DJ-AIG, the worst-case return is reduced to −10.1 percent, an improvement of more than 100 bps versus the 10.0 percent allocation to the GSCI. The GSCI does not produce as large an improvement as the DJ-AIG because of the dominant presence of oil in the GSCI. The price of oil is highly volatile and pushes the total index value up and down as the price of oil fluctuates; the DJ-AIG, in contrast, is influenced by the broader trend in commodities and demonstrates greater persistence. The bottom line is that in terms of risk reduction, the more diversified DJ-AIG historically has provided a more potent impact than the GSCI.

Return-Timing Diversification

Long-term returns of any asset class are concentrated in brief periods of time. If the past 20 years of equity returns were sorted from the highest-returning months to the lowest-returning months and then 7 percent of the highest-returning months were removed, the result would be a return equal to bonds. If 10 percent of the highest-returning months were removed, equities would have zero return. If daily returns are used, the return pattern is even more concentrated. Additionally, these periods of high excess return performance vary for different asset classes. So, not only are asset returns concentrated over time, but the periods of outperformance also vary for different asset classes.

Financial assets tend to perform weakly in the late stages of economic recovery, when there are inflation shocks and also when monetary policy becomes restrictive. These are the times when commodities tend to have strong returns because investors perceive that global capacity utilization is high, a shortage of raw commodities is at hand, and inflation is lurking around the corner. Ultimately, rising commodity prices will trigger further monetary tightening, which is not good news for bonds or equities. Clearly, the commodity markets are a natural complement to traditional markets and provide the element of time diversification of returns that is so beneficial in controlling portfolio risk.

The prices of commodities react much more to current supply–demand conditions than do the prices of equities and bonds, which respond more closely to the longer-term outlook. This deviation between time horizons of the two markets provides another interesting aspect of time diversification. Commodity investment also provides diversification across economic environments, which is an excellent corollary to time diversification. Some argue that energy cost is a core source of inflation and thus favor concentrated investment in, for example, the GSCI, which has a high energy weight. As good a solution as that might appear to be as a counterbalance to inflationary pressures, an equally important consideration is the diversification of risk, which argues for investment in a more equally weighted basket of commodities.

Inflation-Liability Matching

Long-term liabilities, whether they are pension payments from pension funds or grants from foundations and endowments, are exposed to erosion from inflation. In order to match the long-term inflation exposure in liabilities, long-only commodity investing provides a natural hedge. Of course, commodities do not match the U.S. Consumer Price Index definition of inflation, but they do match components of the index. Thus, not only does adding commodities to a portfolio reduce risk in the short run, but it also reduces the risk of longer-term inflation exposure.

4   IMPLEMENTATION OF COMMODITY STRATEGIES

Commodity index strategies, unlike U.S. equity index strategies, are active strategies because of the high turnover. For example, the constituent weights change, which is driven by changes in the weighting formula of the respective benchmark index. Second, a rolling methodology is implied by the index and largely determines the roll frequency of the portfolio. And last, the cash collateral position is continually reinvested as short-term cash equivalents mature and are replaced. Thus, my view is that all commodity investment is active.

Unlike in conventional investment indices, the return correlations between the commodity index constituents in different subcategories are close to zero. Obviously, heating oil correlates with West Texas Intermediate—a type of crude oil used as a benchmark—which correlates with unleaded gasoline. But the average correlation between pork belly futures and gasoline is zero. Within some of the clusters, such as the energy complex and base metals, correlations are high, but between the blocks, correlations are, in essence, zero, which maximizes the rebalance yield.

Commodity indices differ dramatically in their investability, their exposures, and their risk and return characteristics. Although new indices are created all the time, I will focus on just two of them: the GSCI and DJ-AIG. Started in December 1992, the GSCI includes 24 commodities, is production weighted, and gives oil a direct weight of 73.5 percent. The DJ-AIG began in July 1998, includes 19 commodities, and is weighted one-third to production and two-thirds to trading. Individual commodities are limited to 15 percent of the index, and concentration constraints limit energy to a 33 percent weight.

The current estimate of institutional investment in long-only commodity strategies is $120 billion. Of this amount, about $50 billion is invested in the GSCI. Another $30 billion is invested in the DJ-AIG and is expected to increase with the introduction of a new exchange-traded fund (ETF).

Note that a separate, but also growing, activity is institutional investment in active commodity trading. This trading includes the activities of managers of global macro strategies as well as those of long–short commodity trading advisers (CTAs). These long–short strategies, however, are an entirely different beast from long only and have absolute return targets.

The commodity trading industry has a notoriously poor information ratio. Furiously trading long and short commodity positions will not hedge the risk in a pension portfolio. Diversification provided by CTA strategies is beneficial, but allocations are too small for this to be relevant: A 0.5 percent CTA allocation having a correlation with the S&P 500 of −0.1 has minimal impact on portfolio return if the market drops 20 percent. For a CTA strategy to affirmatively impact portfolio-level risk, an allocation of at least 5 percent is required. That allocation would be very hard to sell to investment committees. So, although a CTA strategy is definitely an interesting component in a portfolio and earns its place in the alternative investments pool, that is where it belongs.

Core Commodity Investment Approaches

Commodity investment approaches range from pure index exposure to a CTA long–short strategy. To play a core role in a portfolio, commodity investment can be made by using one of three structures: an index fund, an index-plus strategy, or an active long-only strategy.

Index Fund

An index fund strategy can be implemented simply by purchasing an ETF as well as an index swap or note directly from a dealer.

Index Plus

The goal of an index-plus strategy is to provide an incremental return over the index. About a dozen firms currently offer this type of strategy. Four common ways to enhance the return of the index are through high-collateral return, roll management, rebalancing, and maturity management. In a high-collateral-return strategy, the cash held as margin collateral is worked as hard as possible to pick up any available return and often means moving into short-dated notes and weaker credits. Roll management involves a tactical approach to the timing of the roll on commodity futures contracts. The $80 billion invested in the GSCI and DJ-AIG indices roll on the prespecified five days in each contract settlement month. Deviating from this pattern and rolling earlier than the rest of the market or managing the maturities on forward contracts can result in a positive incremental return over the index. Rebalancing to the index can also be done more or less frequently to add value.

Active Long-Only

Active long-only strategies are a new and developing market. At present, they stand roughly equivalent in development to the currency strategies of the early 1990s. These strategies are usually built around several unique characteristics of commodities markets. These characteristics include the short-run seriality of commodity returns and the long-run reversion of commodity prices driven by market fundamentals. Another active strategy is broader diversification, which, as with any portfolio, improves risk-adjusted performance. For example, the quest for new reserves or alternative energy sources is being diligently pursued by many, and sooner or later, the price of energy will drop because someone will be successful. Portfolio diversification among commodities will protect against this eventuality.

The structural dynamics of commodities argue for active investing. The following quote is from a recent article by Kat and Oomen (2006):

> We have shown that commodity futures returns and volatility may vary considerably over different phases of the business cycle, under different monetary conditions as well as with the shape of the futures curve. This suggests that a purely passive investment in commodities may not be optimal and, given the differences in behavior of different commodities, that some commodities will be better at diversifying equity and bond portfolios than others. (p. 18)

Basically, Kat and Oomen argue that there are real reasons to believe the commodity markets are less than entirely efficient.

Impact of Institutional Investment

The commodity markets are being profoundly changed by the influx of institutional money. Backwardation, when the forward price is below the spot price, has become less stable. Because larger numbers of investors are putting on the same trades, rolls are becoming more expensive and dynamic, which is similar to what has happened to the cost of swapping between small-cap and large-cap U.S. equities.

Because of the influx of institutional money into the market, value is diverging from fundamentals. Copper is an excellent example; its price has risen 300 percent in two years. The situation is similar to what occurred in the currency market as institutional investors became involved. Thirty years ago, currency was primarily used to finance international exports and imports. There was minimal international portfolio investment by institutions in the 1970s, and so, there were minimal currency transactions by institutional investors. Today, institutional investor flows totally dominate currency markets; only some 1.6 percent of daily currency market activity is related to exports and imports. As institutional investor participation builds in commodities, prices will detach from fundamentals. But a commodity's price cannot detach indefinitely from fundamentals because supply will adjust to meet demand. A massive supply response in both the energy and copper markets is in progress and will reverse the dramatic price appreciation of the past few years for these commodities.

More extreme price moves will occur in commodity markets as demand and supply become more frequently misaligned, thus creating forced sales or purchases. In most commodities, a spectacular squeeze occurs as a result of a large market participant's exploitation of structural supply–demand imbalances in a certain commodity. More position squeezes are on the horizon as this market changes.

CONCLUSION 5

Commodity investment improves portfolios. The improvement comes not just from return but from reducing the risk of losing money when stressful market environments occur. An equally important point is that all commodity investment is active; even a so-called passive program involves very high turnover and management of cash. But the real source of added value from active management is utility arbitrage, which is based on the premise that different investors have different objectives and thus accept a cost for transferring risk. Note, however, that institutional investing is altering, and will continue to alter at an escalating pace, the dynamics of the commodity markets. Institutional commodity investment is truly in its infancy.

REFERENCES 6

Booth, David G., and Eugene F. Fama. 1992. "Diversification Returns and Asset Contributions." *Financial Analysts Journal*, vol. 48, no. 3 (May/June):26–32.

Erb, Claude B., and Campbell R. Harvey. 2006. "The Strategic and Tactical Value of Commodity Futures." *Financial Analysts Journal*, vol. 62, no. 2 (March/April):69–97.

Gorton, Gary, and K. Geert Rouwenhorst. 2006. "Facts and Fantasies about Commodity Futures." *Financial Analysts Journal*, vol. 62, no. 2 (March/April):47–68.

Kat, Harry, and Roel Oomen. 2006. "What Every Investor Should Know about Commodities, Part 1: Univariate Return Analysis." Alternative Investment Research Centre Working Paper No. 29 (January).

Roy, A. D. 1952. "Safety First and Holding of Assets." *Econometrica*, vol. 20, no. 3 (July):431–449.

APPENDIX 74A

MORE FROM RONALD G. LAYARD-LIESCHING

This section presents the speaker's lively question and answer session with the conference audience.

Question: How would you characterize the commodity markets today?

Layard-Liesching: Some commodities are experiencing a price bubble—copper, for example. When a commodity trades at a multiple of its marginal extraction cost, it is without a doubt in the midst of a bubble. In my view, this does not preclude a strategic portfolio exposure to commodities.

The driver of the rise in commodity prices is the growth of the global middle class, not growth in China and India per se. Take sugar, for example. Poor people cannot afford it, but when formerly poor people migrate into the middle class and can afford it, they want it. The Chinese government estimates that the size of its middle class is now equal to the population of the United Kingdom, Germany, and France combined. And India, which is expected to overtake China in population, is experiencing a similar dynamic in its rapidly expanding middle class. This is why as an investor you want to be long commodities from a purely strategic point of view.

Individual commodities have always experienced price bubbles, and now, these bubbles will be even bigger as demographic change creates demand spikes.

Question: Can commodities offer protection against inflationary pressures in the cost of services, such as medical care?

Layard-Liesching: No. Obviously, service inflation is a big risk at the moment, but I don't think any investment can really hedge such steeply rising costs.

Question: Could you expand on your comment that commodity prices react more to current supply and demand conditions whereas financial asset prices respond to a longer-term outlook?

Layard-Liesching: The classic formula for the P/E multiple, which is commonly used in equity valuation, incorporates discounted future earnings. In today's stock market, if you eliminated the next three years' estimated earnings, 90 percent of the share-price valuation would still remain. So clearly, the price of shares is determined by long-term expectations of earnings. Commodities, however, have price dynamics that are related to a short-run storage component that in situations of excess causes the price to plummet, and vice versa.

A good example is the electricity market in the United States. When the market has excess electricity, the price plummets because electricity cannot be stored, and when electricity is in short supply, the price goes through the roof because stored capacity does not exist to relieve the demand. In contrast, an equity investment in a utility operates with a much longer time horizon so that the shares of the commodity producer and the commodity itself represent two extremes in time horizon with corresponding implications for the pricing of each.

Question: Can investors get exposure to commodities through commodity producers and extractors?

Layard-Liesching: When you invest in a commodity-producing or extracting company, you are also buying exposure to labor costs and political risk. Because of this, the bottom line is that commodities do better than commodity companies, and in the long run, commodities are also a better inflation hedge than the commodity companies.

Some very interesting opportunities present themselves, however, when commodity companies are severely underpriced in the market. In these instances, the companies will outperform commodities, and when the companies become overpriced, the opposite will be true. So in a portfolio, the two strategies would complement each other nicely.

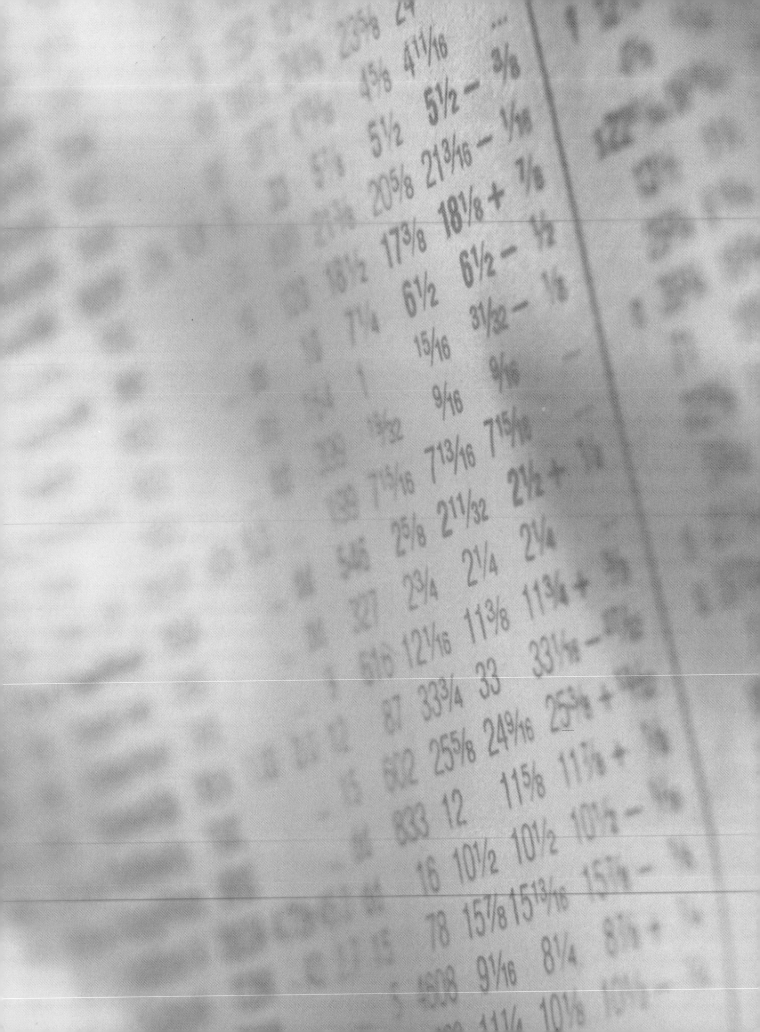

A priori probability A probability based on logical analysis rather than on observation or personal judgment.

Abandonment option The ability to terminate a project at some future time if the financial results are disappointing.

Abnormal rate of return The amount by which a security's actual return differs from its expected rate of return which is based on the market's rate of return and the security's relationship with the market.

Above full-employment equilibrium A macroeconomic equilibrium in which real GDP exceeds potential GDP.

Absolute dispersion The amount of variability present without comparison to any reference point or benchmark.

Absolute frequency The number of observations in a given interval (for grouped data).

Accelerated methods of depreciation Depreciation methods that allocate a relatively large proportion of the cost of an asset to the early years of the asset's useful life.

Account With the accounting systems, a formal record of increases and decreases in a specific asset, liability, component of owners' equity, revenue, or expense.

Account format A method of presentation of accounting transactions in which effects on assets appear at the left and effects on liabilities and equity appear at the right of a central dividing line; also known as T-account format.

Accounting profit (income before taxes or pretax income) Income as reported on the income statement, in accordance with prevailing accounting standards, before the provisions for income tax expense.

Accounting risk The risk associated with accounting standards that vary from country to country or with any uncertainty about how certain transactions should be recorded.

Accounts payable Amounts that a business owes to its vendors for goods and services that were purchased from them but which have not yet been paid.

Accounts receivable turnover Ratio of sales on credit to the average balance in accounts receivable.

Accrual basis Method of accounting in which the effect of transactions on financial condition and income are recorded when they occur, not when they are settled in cash.

Accrued expenses (accrued liabilities) Liabilities related to expenses that have been incurred but not yet paid as of the end of an accounting period—an example of an accrued expense is rent that has been incurred but not yet paid, resulting in a liability "rent payable."

Accrued interest Interest earned but not yet paid.

Accumulated benefit obligation Under U.S. GAAP, a measure used in estimating a defined-benefit pension plan's liabilities, defined as "the actuarial present value of benefits (whether vested or nonvested) attributed by the pension benefit formula to employee service rendered before a specified date and based on employee service and compensation (if applicable) prior to that date."

Accumulated depreciation An offset to property, plant, and equipment (PPE) reflecting the amount of the cost of PPE that has been allocated to current and previous accounting periods.

Accumulation phase Phase in the investment life cycle during which individuals in the early-to-middle years of their working career attempt to accumulate assets to satisfy short-term needs and longer-term goals.

Acquiring company, or acquirer The company in a merger or acquisition that is acquiring the target.

Acquisition The purchase of some portion of one company by another; the purchase may be for assets, a definable segment of another entity, or the purchase of an entire company.

Acquisition method A method of accounting for a business combination where the acquirer is required to measure each identifiable asset and liability at fair value. This method was the result of a joint project of the IASB and FASB aiming at convergence in standards for the accounting of business combinations.

Active factor risk The contribution to active risk squared resulting from the portfolio's different-than-benchmark exposures relative to factors specified in the risk model.

Active return The return on a portfolio minus the return on the portfolio's benchmark.

Active risk The standard deviation of active returns.

Active risk squared The variance of active returns; active risk raised to the second power.

Active specific risk or asset selection risk The contribution to active risk squared resulting from the portfolio's active weights on individual assets as those weights interact with assets' residual risk.

G-1

Active strategy In reference to short-term cash management, an investment strategy characterized by monitoring and attempting to capitalize on market conditions to optimize the risk and return relationship of short-term investments.

Activity ratios (asset utilization or operating efficiency ratios) Ratios that measure how efficiently a company performs day-to-day tasks, such as the collection of receivables and management of inventory.

Addition rule for probabilities A principle stating that the probability that A or B occurs (both occur) equals the probability that A occurs, plus the probability that B occurs, minus the probability that both A and B occur.

Add-on interest A procedure for determining the interest on a bond or loan in which the interest is added onto the face value of a contract.

Adjusted beta Historical beta adjusted to reflect the tendency of beta to be mean reverting.

Adjusted R^2 A measure of goodness-of-fit of a regression that is adjusted for degrees of freedom and hence does not automatically increase when another independent variable is added to a regression.

Agency costs Costs associated with the conflict of interest present when a company is managed by non-owners. Agency costs result from the inherent conflicts of interest between managers and equity owners.

Agency costs of equity The smaller the stake that managers have in the company, the less is their share in bearing the cost of excessive perquisite consumption or not giving their best efforts in running the company.

Agency problem, or principal-agent problem A conflict of interest that arises when the agent in an agency relationship has goals and incentives that differ from the principal to whom the agent owes a fiduciary duty.

Agency relationships An arrangement whereby someone, an agent, acts on behalf of another person, the principal.

Aggregate demand The relationship between the quantity of real GDP demanded and the price level.

Aggregate hours The total number of hours worked by all the people employed, both full time and part time, during a year.

Aging schedule A breakdown of accounts into categories of days outstanding.

Allowance for bad debts An offset to accounts receivable for the amount of accounts receivable that are estimated to be uncollectible.

Alternative hypothesis The hypothesis accepted when the null hypothesis is rejected.

American option An option contract that can be exercised at any time until its expiration date.

Amortization The process of allocating the cost of intangible long-term assets having a finite useful life to accounting periods; the allocation of the amount of a bond premium or discount to the periods remaining until bond maturity.

Amortizing and accreting swaps A swap in which the notional principal changes according to a formula related to changes in the underlying.

Analysis of variance (ANOVA) The analysis of the total variability of a dataset (such as observations on the dependent variable in a regression) into components representing different sources of variation; with reference to regression, ANOVA provides the inputs for an F-test of the significance of the regression as a whole.

Annual percentage rate The cost of borrowing expressed as a yearly rate.

Annuity A finite set of level sequential cash flows.

Annuity due An annuity having a first cash flow that is paid immediately.

Anomalies Security price relationships that appear to contradict a well-regarded hypothesis; in this case, the efficient market hypothesis.

Anticipation stock Excess inventory that is held in anticipation of increased demand, often because of seasonal patterns of demand.

Antidilutive With reference to a transaction or a security, one that would increase earnings per share (EPS) or result in EPS higher than the company's basic EPS—antidilutive securities are not included in the calculation of diluted EPS.

Arbitrage 1) The simultaneous purchase of an undervalued asset or portfolio and sale of an overvalued but equivalent asset or portfolio, in order to obtain a riskless profit on the price differential. Taking advantage of a market inefficiency in a risk-free manner. 2) A trading strategy designed to generate a guaranteed profit from a transaction that requires no capital commitment or risk bearing on the part of the trader. A simple example of an arbitrage trade would be the simultaneous purchase and sale of the same security in different markets at different prices. 3) The condition in a financial market in which equivalent assets or combinations of assets sell for two different prices, creating an opportunity to profit at no risk with no commitment of money. In a well-functioning financial market, few arbitrage opportunities are possible. 4) A risk-free operation that earns an expected positive net profit but requires no net investment of money.

Arbitrage opportunity An opportunity to conduct an arbitrage; an opportunity to earn an expected positive net profit without risk and with no net investment of money.

Arbitrage portfolio The portfolio that exploits an arbitrage opportunity.

Arithmetic mean The sum of the observations divided by the number of observations.

Arrears swap A type of interest rate swap in which the floating payment is set at the end of the period and the interest is paid at that same time.

Asian call option A European-style option with a value at maturity equal to the difference between the stock price at maturity and the average stock price during the life of the option, or $0, whichever is greater.

Asset allocation The process of deciding how to distribute an investor's wealth among different asset classes for investment purposes.

Asset beta The unlevered beta; reflects the business risk of the assets; the asset's systematic risk.

Asset class Securities that have similar characteristics, attributes, and risk/return relationships.

Asset purchase An acquisition in which the acquirer purchases the target company's assets and payment is made directly to the target company.

Asset retirement obligations (AROs) The fair value of the estimated costs to be incurred at the end of a tangible asset's service life. The fair value of the liability is determined on the basis of discounted cash flows.

Asset-based loan A loan that is secured with company assets.

Assets Resources controlled by an enterprise as a result of past events and from which future economic benefits to the enterprise are expected to flow.

Assignment of accounts receivable The use of accounts receivable as collateral for a loan.

Asymmetric information The differential of information between corporate insiders and outsiders regarding the company's performance and prospects. Managers typically have more information about the company's performance and prospects than owners and creditors.

At the money An option in which the underlying value equals the exercise price.

Autocorrelation The correlation of a time series with its own past values.

Autocorrelation test A test of the efficient market hypothesis that compares security price changes over time to check for predictable correlation patterns.

Automated Clearing House An electronic payment network available to businesses, individuals, and financial institutions in the United States, U.S. Territories, and Canada.

Automatic fiscal policy A fiscal policy action that is triggered by the state of the economy.

Automatic stabilizers Mechanisms that stabilize real GDP without explicit action by the government.

Autonomous tax multiplier The magnification effect of a change in taxes on aggregate demand.

Autoregressive (AR) model A time series regressed on its own past values, in which the independent variable is a lagged value of the dependent variable.

Available-for-sale investments Debt and equity securities not classified as either held-to-maturity or held-for-trading securities. The investor is willing to sell but not actively planning to sell. In general, available-for-sale securities are reported at fair value on the balance sheet.

Average cost pricing rule A rule that sets price to cover cost including normal profit, which means setting the price equal to average total cost.

Average fixed cost Total fixed cost per unit of output.

Average product The average product of a factor of production. It equals total product divided by the quantity of the factor employed.

Average tax rate A person's total tax payment divided by his or her total income.

Average total cost Total cost per unit of output.

Average variable cost Total variable cost per unit of output.

Backtesting With reference to portfolio strategies, the application of a strategy's portfolio selection rules to historical data to assess what would have been the strategy's historical performance.

Backward integration A merger involving the purchase of a target ahead of the acquirer in the value or production chain; for example, to acquire a supplier.

Backwardation A condition in the futures markets in which the benefits of holding an asset exceed the costs, leaving the futures price less than the spot price.

Balance sheet (statement of financial position or statement of financial condition) The financial statement that presents an entity's current financial position by disclosing resources the entity controls (its assets) and the claims on those resources (its liabilities and equity claims), as of a particular point in time (the date of the balance sheet).

Balance sheet ratios   Financial ratios involving balance sheet items only.

Balanced budget   A government budget in which tax revenues and outlays are equal.

Balanced budget multiplier   The magnification effect on aggregate demand of a simultaneous change in government expenditure and taxes that leaves the budget balanced.

Balance-sheet-based accruals ratio   The difference between net operating assets at the end and the beginning of the period compared to the average net operating assets over the period.

Balance-sheet-based aggregate accruals   The difference between net operating assets at the end and the beginning of the period.

Bank discount basis   A quoting convention that annualizes, on a 360-day year, the discount as a percentage of face value.

Bargain purchase   When a company is acquired and the purchase price is less than the fair value of the net assets. The current treatment of the excess of fair value over the purchase price is different under IFRS and U.S. GAAP. The excess is never accounted for as negative goodwill.

Barriers to entry   Legal or natural constraints that protect a firm from potential competitors.

Barter   The direct exchange of one good or service for other goods and services.

Basic EPS   Net earnings available to common shareholders (i.e., net income minus preferred dividends) divided by the weighted average number of common shares outstanding.

Basis   The difference between the spot price of the underlying asset and the futures contract price at any point in time (e.g., the *initial* basis at the time of contract origination, the *cover* basis at the time of contract termination).

Basis point value (BPV)   Also called *present value of a basis point* or *price value of a basis point* (PVBP), the change in the bond price for a 1 basis point change in yield.

Basis swap   1) An interest rate swap involving two floating rates. 2) A swap in which both parties pay a floating rate.

Bayes' formula   A method for updating probabilities based on new information.

Bear hug   A tactic used by acquirers to circumvent target management's objections to a proposed merger by submitting the proposal directly to the target company's board of directors.

Bear spread   An option strategy that involves selling a put with a lower exercise price and buying a put with a higher exercise price. It can also be executed with calls.

Behavioral finance   Involves the analysis of various psychological traits of individuals and how these traits affect how they act as investors, analysts, and portfolio managers.

Below full-employment equilibrium   A macroeconomic equilibrium in which potential GDP exceeds real GDP.

Benchmark   A comparison portfolio; a point of reference or comparison.

Benchmark error   Situation where an inappropriate or incorrect benchmark is used to compare and assess portfolio returns and management.

Benchmark portfolio   A comparison standard of risk and assets included in the policy statement and similar to the investor's risk preference and investment needs, which can be used to evaluate the investment performance of the portfolio manager.

Bernoulli random variable   A random variable having the outcomes 0 and 1.

Bernoulli trial   An experiment that can produce one of two outcomes.

Beta   A standardized measure of systematic risk based upon an asset's covariance with the market portfolio.

Big tradeoff   The conflict between equality and efficiency.

Bilateral monopoly   A situation in which a single seller (a monopoly) faces a single buyer (a monopsony).

Binomial model   A model for pricing options in which the underlying price can move to only one of two possible new prices.

Binomial random variable   The number of successes in n Bernoulli trials for which the probability of success is constant for all trials and the trials are independent.

Binomial tree   The graphical representation of a model of asset price dynamics in which, at each period, the asset moves up with probability p or down with probability $(1 - p)$.

Black market   An illegal market in which the price exceeds the legally imposed price ceiling.

Block   Orders to buy or sell that are too large for the liquidity ordinarily available in dealer networks or stock exchanges.

Bond equivalent yield   A calculation of yield that is annualized using the ratio of 365 to the number of days to maturity. Bond equivalent yield allows for the restatement and comparison of securities with different compounding periods.

Bond option   An option in which the underlying is a bond; primarily traded in over-the-counter markets.

Bond yield plus risk premium approach An estimate of the cost of common equity that is produced by summing the before-tax cost of debt and a risk premium that captures the additional yield on a company's stock relative to its bonds. The additional yield is often estimated using historical spreads between bond yields and stock yields.

Bond-equivalent basis A basis for stating an annual yield that annualizes a semiannual yield by doubling it.

Bond-equivalent yield The yield to maturity on a basis that ignores compounding.

Bonding costs Costs borne by management to assure owners that they are working in the owners' best interest (e.g., implicit cost of non-compete agreements).

Book value equity per share The amount of book value (also called carrying value) of common equity per share of common stock, calculated by dividing the book value of shareholders' equity by the number of shares of common stock outstanding.

Bootstrapping earnings An increase in a company's earnings that results as a consequence of the idiosyncrasies of a merger transaction itself rather than because of resulting economic benefits of the combination.

Bottom-up analysis With reference to investment selection processes, an approach that involves selection from all securities within a specified investment universe, i.e., without prior narrowing of the universe on the basis of macroeconomic or overall market considerations.

Box spread An option strategy that combines a bull spread and a bear spread having two different exercise prices, which produces a risk-free payoff of the difference in the exercise prices.

Break point In the context of the weighted average cost of capital (WACC), a break point is the amount of capital at which the cost of one or more of the sources of capital changes, leading to a change in the WACC.

Breakeven point The number of units produced and sold at which the company's net income is zero (revenues = total costs).

Breakup value The value that can be achieved if a company's assets are divided and sold separately.

Breusch–Pagan test A test for conditional heteroskedasticity in the error term of a regression.

Broker 1) An agent who executes orders to buy or sell securities on behalf of a client in exchange for a commission. 2) *See* Futures commission merchants.

Budget deficit A government's budget balance that is negative—outlays exceed tax revenues.

Budget surplus A government's budget balance that is positive—tax revenues exceed outlays.

Bull spread An option strategy that involves buying a call with a lower exercise price and selling a call with a higher exercise price. It can also be executed with puts.

Business risk The risk associated with operating earnings. Operating earnings are uncertain because total revenues and many of the expenditures contributed to produce those revenues are uncertain.

Butterfly spread An option strategy that combines two bull or bear spreads and has three exercise prices.

Call An option that gives the holder the right to buy an underlying asset from another party at a fixed price over a specific period of time.

Call market A market in which trading for individual stocks only takes place at specified times. All the bids and asks available at the time are combined and the market administrators specify a single price that will possibly clear the market at that time.

Cannibalization Cannibalization occurs when an investment takes customers and sales away from another part of the company.

Cap 1) A contract on an interest rate, whereby at periodic payment dates, the writer of the cap pays the difference between the market interest rate and a specified cap rate if, and only if, this difference is positive. This is equivalent to a stream of call options on the interest rate. 2) A combination of interest rate call options designed to hedge a borrower against rate increases on a floating-rate loan.

Capital allocation line (CAL) A graph line that describes the combinations of expected return and standard deviation of return available to an investor from combining the optimal portfolio of risky assets with the risk-free asset.

Capital appreciation A return objective in which the investor seeks to increase the portfolio value, primarily through capital gains, over time to meet a future need rather than dividend yield.

Capital asset pricing model (CAPM) An equation describing the expected return on any asset (or portfolio) as a linear function of its beta relative to the market portfolio.

Capital budgeting The allocation of funds to relatively long-range projects or investments.

Capital market line (CML) The line with an intercept point equal to the risk-free rate that is tangent to the efficient frontier of risky assets; represents the efficient frontier when a risk-free asset is available for investment.

Capital preservation   A return objective in which the investor seeks to minimize the risk of loss; generally a goal of the risk-averse investor.

Capital rationing   A capital rationing environment assumes that the company has a fixed amount of funds to invest.

Capital structure   The mix of debt and equity that a company uses to finance its business; a company's specific mixture of long-term financing.

Capitalized inventory costs   Costs of inventories including costs of purchase, costs of conversion, other costs to bring the inventories to their present location and condition, and the allocated portion of fixed production overhead costs.

Caplet   Each component call option in a cap.

Capped swap   A swap in which the floating payments have an upper limit.

Captive finance subsidiary   A wholly-owned subsidiary of a company that is established to provide financing of the sales of the parent company.

Carrying amount (book value)   The amount at which an asset or liability is valued according to accounting principles.

Cartel   A group of firms that has entered into a collusive agreement to restrict output and increase prices and profits.

Cash   In accounting contexts, cash on hand (e.g., petty cash and cash not yet deposited to the bank) and demand deposits held in banks and similar accounts that can be used in payment of obligations.

Cash basis   Accounting method in which the only relevant transactions for the financial statements are those that involve cash.

Cash conversion cycle (net operating cycle)   A financial metric that measures the length of time required for a company to convert cash invested in its operations to cash received as a result of its operations; equal to days of inventory on hand + days of sales outstanding – number of days of payables.

Cash equivalents   Very liquid short-term investments, usually maturing in 90 days or less.

Cash flow additivity principle   The principle that dollar amounts indexed at the same point in time are additive.

Cash flow at risk (CFAR)   A variation of VAR that reflects the risk of a company's cash flow instead of its market value.

Cash flow from operations (cash flow from operating activities or operating cash flow)   The net amount of cash provided from operating activities.

Cash flow statement (statement of cash flows)   A financial statement that reconciles beginning-of-period and end-of-period balance sheet values of cash; consists of three parts: cash flows from operating activities, cash flows from investing activities, and cash flows from financing activities.

Cash offering   A merger or acquisition that is to be paid for with cash; the cash for the merger might come from the acquiring company's existing assets or from a debt issue.

Cash price or spot price   The price for immediate purchase of the underlying asset.

Cash ratio   A liquidity ratio calculated as (cash + short-term marketable investments) divided by current liabilities; measures a company's ability to meet its current obligations with just the cash and cash equivalents on hand.

Cash settlement   A procedure used in certain derivative transactions that specifies that the long and short parties engage in the equivalent cash value of a delivery transaction.

Cash-flow-statement-based accruals ratio   The difference between reported net income on an accrual basis and the cash flows from operating and investing activities compared to the average net operating assets over the period.

Cash-flow-statement-based aggregate accruals   The difference between reported net income on an accrual basis and the cash flows from operating and investing activities.

Central bank   A bank's bank and a public authority that regulates the nation's depository institutions and controls the quantity of money.

Central limit theorem   A result in statistics that states that the sample mean computed from large samples of size n from a population with finite variance will follow an approximate normal distribution with a mean equal to the population mean and a variance equal to the population variance divided by n.

Centralized risk management or companywide risk management   When a company has a single risk management group that monitors and controls all of the risk-taking activities of the organization. Centralization permits economies of scale and allows a company to use some of its risks to offset other risks. See also *enterprise risk management*.

Chain rule of forecasting   A forecasting process in which the next period's value as predicted by the forecasting equation is substituted into the right-hand side of the equation to give a predicted value two periods ahead.

Characteristic line Regression line that indicates the systematic risk (beta) of a risky asset.

Chart of accounts A list of accounts used in an entity's accounting system.

Cheapest to deliver A bond in which the amount received for delivering the bond is largest compared with the amount paid in the market for the bond.

Cherry-picking When a bankrupt company is allowed to enforce contracts that are favorable to it while walking away from contracts that are unfavorable to it.

Classical A macroeconomist who believes that the economy is self-regulating and that it is always at full employment.

Classified balance sheet A balance sheet organized so as to group together the various assets and liabilities into subcategories (e.g., current and noncurrent).

Clean-surplus accounting The bottom-line income reflects all changes in shareholders' equity arising from other than owner transactions. In the absence of owner transactions, the change in shareholders' equity should equal net income. No adjustments such as translation adjustments bypass the income statement and go directly to shareholders equity.

Clearinghouse An entity associated with a futures market that acts as middleman between the contracting parties and guarantees to each party the performance of the other.

Clientele effect The preference some investors have for shares that exhibit certain characteristics.

Closeout netting Netting the market values of *all* derivative contracts between two parties to determine one overall value owed by one party to another in the event of bankruptcy.

Coefficient of variation (CV) The ratio of a set of observations' standard deviation to the observations' mean value.

Cointegrated Describes two time series that have a long-term financial or economic relationship such that they do not diverge from each other without bound in the long run.

Collar An option strategy involving the purchase of a put and sale of a call in which the holder of an asset gains protection below a certain level, the exercise price of the put, and pays for it by giving up gains above a certain level, the exercise price of the call. Collars also can be used to provide protection against rising interest rates on a floating-rate loan by giving up gains from lower interest rates.

Collusive agreement An agreement between two (or more) producers to restrict output, raise the price, and increase profits.

Combination A listing in which the order of the listed items does not matter.

Command system A method of allocating resources by the order (command) of someone in authority. In a firm a managerial hierarchy organizes production.

Commercial paper Unsecured short-term corporate debt that is characterized by a single payment at maturity.

Commission brokers Employees of a member firm who buy or sell securities for the customers of the firm.

Committed lines of credit A bank commitment to extend credit up to a pre-specified amount; the commitment is considered a short-term liability and is usually in effect for 364 days (one day short of a full year).

Commodity forward A contract in which the underlying asset is oil, a precious metal, or some other commodity.

Commodity futures Futures contracts in which the underlying is a traditional agricultural, metal, or petroleum product.

Commodity option An option in which the asset underlying the futures is a commodity, such as oil, gold, wheat, or soybeans.

Commodity swap A swap in which the underlying is a commodity such as oil, gold, or an agricultural product.

Common size statements Financial statements in which all elements (accounts) are stated as a percentage of a key figure such as revenue for an income statement or total assets for a balance sheet.

Common-size analysis The restatement of financial statement items using a common denominator or reference item that allows one to identify trends and major differences; an example is an income statement in which all items are expressed as a percent of revenue.

Company fundamental factors Factors related to the company's internal performance, such as factors relating to earnings growth, earnings variability, earnings momentum, and financial leverage.

Company share-related factors Valuation measures and other factors related to share price or the trading characteristics of the shares, such as earnings yield, dividend yield, and book-to-market value.

Comparable company   A company that has similar business risk; usually in the same industry and preferably with a single line of business.

Competitive bid   An underwriting alternative wherein an issuing entity (governmental body or a corporation) specifies the type of security to be offered (bonds or stocks) and the general characteristics of the issue, and the issuer solicits bids from competing investment banking firms with the understanding that the issuer will accept the highest bid from the bankers.

Complement   In probability, with reference to an event S, the event that S does not occur; in economics, a good that is used in conjunction with another good.

Completed contract   A method of revenue recognition in which the company does not recognize any revenue until the contract is completed; used particularly in long-term construction contracts.

Completely diversified portfolio   A portfolio in which all unsystematic risk has been eliminated by diversification.

Component cost of capital   The rate of return required by suppliers of capital for an individual source of a company's funding, such as debt or equity.

Compounding   The process of accumulating interest on interest.

Comprehensive income   The change in equity of a business enterprise during a period from nonowner sources; includes all changes in equity during a period except those resulting from investments by owners and distributions to owners; comprehensive income equals net income plus other comprehensive income.

Conditional expected value   The expected value of a stated event given that another event has occurred.

Conditional heteroskedasticity   Heteroskedasticity in the error variance that is correlated with the values of the independent variable(s) in the regression.

Conditional probability   The probability of an event given (conditioned on) another event.

Conditional variances   The variance of one variable, given the outcome of another.

Confidence interval   A range that has a given probability that it will contain the population parameter it is intended to estimate.

Conglomerate merger   A merger involving companies that are in unrelated businesses.

Consistency   A desirable property of estimators; a consistent estimator is one for which the probability of estimates close to the value of the population parameter increases as sample size increases.

Consistent   With reference to estimators, describes an estimator for which the probability of estimates close to the value of the population parameter increases as sample size increases.

Consolidation   The combining of the results of operations of subsidiaries with the parent company to present financial statements as if they were a single economic unit. The asset, liabilities, revenues and expenses of the subsidiaries are combined with those of the parent company, eliminating intercompany transactions.

Consolidation phase   Phase in the investment life cycle during which individuals who are typically past the midpoint of their career have earnings that exceed expenses and invest them for future retirement or estate planning needs.

Constant maturity swap or CMT swap   A swap in which the floating rate is the rate on a security known as a constant maturity treasury or CMT security.

Constant maturity treasury or CMT   A hypothetical U.S. Treasury note with a constant maturity. A CMT exists for various years in the range of 2 to 10.

Constant returns to scale   Features of a firm's technology that lead to constant long-run average cost as output increases. When constant returns to scale are present, the *LRAC* curve is horizontal.

Construct the portfolio   Given the strategy and economic outlook, what specific stocks and/or bonds will be put into the portfolio at the present time that are consistent with the client's policy statement.

Consumer Price Index (CPI)   An index that measures the average of the prices paid by urban consumers for a fixed "basket" of the consumer goods and services.

Consumer surplus   The value (or marginal benefit) of a good minus the price paid for it, summed over the quantity bought.

Contango   A situation in a futures market where the current futures price is greater than the current spot price for the underlying asset.

Contestable market   A market in which firms can enter and leave so easily that firms in the market face competition from potential entrants.

Contingent claims   Derivatives in which the payoffs occur if a specific event occurs; generally referred to as options.

Continual monitoring   The constant evaluation of the economic environment, the policy statement, and the portfolio to ensure that it is consistent with the policy statement. Also involves evaluating performance to determine if changes are required in the portfolio, the strategy, or the policy statement.

Continuous market A market where stocks are priced and traded continuously by an auction process or by dealers when the market is open.

Continuous random variable A random variable for which the range of possible outcomes is the real line (all real numbers between $-\infty$ and $+\infty$ or some subset of the real line.

Continuous time Time thought of as advancing in extremely small increments.

Continuously compounded return The natural logarithm of 1 plus the holding period return, or equivalently, the natural logarithm of the ending price over the beginning price.

Contra account An account that offsets another account.

Contribution margin The amount available for fixed costs and profit after paying variable costs; revenue minus variable costs.

Controlling interest An investment where the investor exerts control over the investee, typically by having a greater than 50 percent ownership in the investee.

Convenience yield The nonmonetary return offered by an asset when the asset is in short supply, often associated with assets with seasonal production processes.

Conventional cash flow A conventional cash flow pattern is one with an initial outflow followed by a series of inflows.

Conversion factor An adjustment used to facilitate delivery on bond futures contracts in which any of a number of bonds with different characteristics are eligible for delivery.

Convertible debt Debt with the added feature that the bondholder has the option to exchange the debt for equity at prespecified terms.

Cooperative equilibrium The outcome of a game in which the players make and share the monopoly profit.

Core inflation rate A measure of inflation based on the core CPI—the CPI excluding food and fuel.

Corporate governance The system of principles, policies, procedures, and clearly defined responsibilities and accountabilities used by stakeholders to overcome the conflicts of interest inherent in the corporate form.

Corporate raider A person or organization seeking to profit by acquiring a company and reselling it, or seeking to profit from the takeover attempt itself (e.g. greenmail).

Corporation A legal entity with rights similar to those of a person. The chief officers, executives, or top managers act as agents for the firm and are legally entitled to authorize corporate activities and to enter into contracts on behalf of the business.

Correlation A number between -1 and $+1$ that measures the co-movement (linear association) between two random variables.

Correlation analysis The analysis of the strength of the linear relationship between two data series.

Correlation coefficient A standardized measure of the relationship between two variables that ranges from -1.00 to $+1.00$.

Cost averaging The periodic investment of a fixed amount of money.

Cost of capital The rate of return that suppliers of capital require as compensation for their contribution of capital.

Cost of carry The cost associated with holding some asset, including financing, storage, and insurance costs. Any yield received on the asset is treated as a negative carrying cost.

Cost of carry model A model for pricing futures contracts in which the futures price is determined by adding the cost of carry to the spot price.

Cost of debt The cost of debt financing to a company, such as when it issues a bond or takes out a bank loan.

Cost of goods sold For a given period, equal to beginning inventory minus ending inventory plus the cost of goods acquired or produced during the period.

Cost of preferred stock The cost to a company of issuing preferred stock; the dividend yield that a company must commit to pay preferred stockholders.

Cost recovery method A method of revenue recognition in which the seller does not report any profit until the cash amounts paid by the buyer—including principal and interest on any financing from the seller—are greater than all the seller's costs for the merchandise sold.

Cost structure The mix of a company's variable costs and fixed costs.

Cost-push inflation An inflation that results from an initial increase in costs.

Council of Economic Advisers The President's council whose main work is to monitor the economy and keep the President and the public well informed about the current state of the economy and the best available forecasts of where it is heading.

Covariance   A measure of the co-movement (linear association) between two random variables.

Covariance matrix   A matrix or square array whose entries are covariances; also known as a variance–covariance matrix.

Covariance stationary   Describes a time series when its expected value and variance are constant and finite in all periods and when its covariance with itself for a fixed number of periods in the past or future is constant and finite in all periods.

Covered call   An option strategy involving the holding of an asset and sale of a call on the asset.

Covered interest arbitrage   A transaction executed in the foreign exchange market in which a currency is purchased (sold) and a forward contract is sold (purchased) to lock in the exchange rate for future delivery of the currency. This transaction should earn the risk-free rate of the investor's home country.

Credit   With respect to double-entry accounting, a credit records increases in liability, owners' equity, and revenue accounts or decreases in asset accounts; with respect to borrowing, the willingness and ability of the borrower to make promised payments on the borrowing.

Credit analysis   The evaluation of credit risk; the evaluation of the creditworthiness of a borrower or counterparty.

Credit derivatives   A contract in which one party has the right to claim a payment from another party in the event that a specific credit event occurs over the life of the contract.

Credit risk or default risk   The risk of loss caused by a counterparty's or debtor's failure to make a promised payment.

Credit scoring model   A statistical model used to classify borrowers according to creditworthiness.

Credit spread option   An option on the yield spread on a bond.

Credit swap   A type of swap transaction used as a credit derivative in which one party makes periodic payments to the other and receives the promise of a payoff if a third party defaults.

Credit VAR, Default VAR, or Credit at Risk   A variation of VAR that reflects credit risk.

Credit-linked notes   Fixed-income securities in which the holder of the security has the right to withhold payment of the full amount due at maturity if a credit event occurs.

Creditworthiness   The perceived ability of the borrower to pay what is owed on the borrowing in a timely manner; it represents the ability of a company to withstand adverse impacts on its cash flows.

Cross elasticity of demand   The responsiveness of the demand for a good to a change in the price of a substitute or complement, other things remaining the same. It is calculated as the percentage change in the quantity demanded of the good divided by the percentage change in the price of the substitute or complement.

Cross-product netting   Netting the market values of all contracts, not just derivatives, between parties.

Cross-sectional analysis   Analysis that involves comparisons across individuals in a group over a given time period or at a given point in time.

Cross-sectional data   Observations over individual units at a point in time, as opposed to time-series data.

Crowding-out effect   The tendency for a government budget deficit to decrease investment.

Cumulative distribution function   A function giving the probability that a random variable is less than or equal to a specified value.

Cumulative relative frequency   For data grouped into intervals, the fraction of total observations that are less than the value of the upper limit of a stated interval.

Currency   The notes and coins held by individuals and businesses.

Currency drain ratio   The ratio of currency to deposits.

Currency forward   A forward contract in which the underlying is a foreign currency.

Currency option   An option that allows the holder to buy (if a call) or sell (if a put) an underlying currency at a fixed exercise rate, expressed as an exchange rate.

Currency swap   A swap in which each party makes interest payments to the other in different currencies.

Current assets, or liquid assets   Assets that are expected to be consumed or converted into cash in the near future, typically one year or less.

Current cost   With reference to assets, the amount of cash or cash equivalents that would have to be paid to buy the same or an equivalent asset today; with reference to liabilities, the undiscounted amount of cash or cash equivalents that would be required to settle the obligation today.

Current credit risk   The risk associated with the possibility that a payment currently due will not be made.

Current exchange rate   For accounting purposes, the spot exchange rate on the balance sheet date.

Current income   A return objective in which the investor seeks to generate income rather than capital gains; generally a goal of an investor who wants to supplement earnings with income to meet living expenses.

Current liabilities Short-term obligations, such as accounts payable, wages payable, or accrued liabilities, that are expected to be settled in the near future, typically one year or less.

Current rate method Approach to translating foreign currency financial statements for consolidation in which all assets and liabilities are translated at the current exchange rate. The current rate method is the prevalent method of translation.

Current ratio A liquidity ratio calculated as current assets divided by current liabilities.

Current taxes payable Tax expenses that have been recognized and recorded on a company's income statement but which have not yet been paid.

Cyclical change An economic trend arising from the ups and downs of the business cycle.

Cyclical company A firm whose earnings rise and fall with general economic activity.

Cyclical stock A stock with a high beta; its gains typically exceed those of a rising market and its losses typically exceed those of a falling market.

Cyclical surplus or deficit The actual surplus or deficit minus the structural surplus or deficit.

Cyclical unemployment The fluctuating unemployment over the business cycle.

Daily settlement See *marking to market*.

Data mining The practice of determining a model by extensive searching through a dataset for statistically significant patterns.

Day trader A trader holding a position open somewhat longer than a scalper but closing all positions at the end of the day.

Days of inventory on hand (DOH) An activity ratio equal to the number of days in the period divided by inventory turnover over the period.

Days of sales outstanding (DSO) An activity ratio equal to the number of days in the period divided by receivables turnover.

Dead-hand provision A poison pill provision that allows for the redemption or cancellation of a poison pill provision only by a vote of continuing directors (generally directors who were on the target company's board prior to the takeover attempt).

Deadweight loss A measure of inefficiency. It is equal to the decrease in total surplus that results from an inefficient level of production.

Dealing securities Securities held by banks or other financial intermediaries for trading purposes.

Debit With respect to double-entry accounting, a debit records increases of asset and expense accounts or decreases in liability and owners' equity accounts.

Debt covenants Agreements between the company as borrower and its creditors.

Debt incurrence test A financial covenant made in conjunction with existing debt that restricts a company's ability to incur additional debt at the same seniority based on one or more financial tests or conditions.

Debt rating approach A method for estimating a company's before-tax cost of debt based upon the yield on comparably rated bonds for maturities that closely match that of the company's existing debt.

Debt ratings An objective measure of the quality and safety of a company's debt based upon an analysis of the company's ability to pay the promised cash flows, as well as an analysis of any indentures.

Debt with warrants Debt issued with warrants that give the bondholder the right to purchase equity at prespecified terms.

Debt-to-assets ratio A solvency ratio calculated as total debt divided by total assets.

Debt-to-capital ratio A solvency ratio calculated as total debt divided by total debt plus total shareholders' equity.

Debt-to-equity ratio A solvency ratio calculated as total debt divided by total shareholders' equity.

Decentralized risk management A system that allows individual units within an organization to manage risk. Decentralization results in duplication of effort but has the advantage of having people closer to the risk be more directly involved in its management.

Deciles Quantiles that divide a distribution into 10 equal parts.

Decision rule With respect to hypothesis testing, the rule according to which the null hypothesis will be rejected or not rejected; involves the comparison of the test statistic to rejection point(s).

Declaration date The day that the corporation issues a statement declaring a specific dividend.

Declining trend channel The range defined by security prices as they move progressively lower.

Deductible temporary differences Temporary differences that result in a reduction of or deduction from taxable income in a future period when the balance sheet item is recovered or settled.

Deep in the money Options that are far in-the-money.

Deep out of the money Options that are far out-of-the-money.

Default risk premium An extra return that compensates investors for the possibility that the borrower will fail to make a promised payment at the contracted time and in the contracted amount.

Defensive company   Firms whose future earnings are likely to withstand an economic downturn.

Defensive interval ratio   A liquidity ratio that estimates the number of days that an entity could meet cash needs from liquid assets; calculated as (cash + short-term marketable investments + receivables) divided by daily cash expenditures.

Defensive stock   A stock whose return is not expected to decline as much as that of the overall market during a bear market (a beta less than one).

Deferred tax assets   A balance sheet asset that arises when an excess amount is paid for income taxes relative to accounting profit. The taxable income is higher than accounting profit and income tax payable exceeds tax expense. The company expects to recover the difference during the course of future operations when tax expense exceeds income tax payable.

Deferred tax liabilities   A balance sheet liability that arises when a deficit amount is paid for income taxes relative to accounting profit. The taxable income is less than the accounting profit and income tax payable is less than tax expense. The company expects to eliminate the liability over the course of future operations when income tax payable exceeds tax expense.

Defined-benefit pension plans   Plan in which the company promises to pay a certain annual amount (defined benefit) to the employee after retirement. The company bears the investment risk of the plan assets.

Defined-contribution pension plans   Individual accounts to which an employee and typically the employer makes contributions, generally on a tax-advantaged basis. The amounts of contributions are defined at the outset, but the future value of the benefit is unknown. The employee bears the investment risk of the plan assets.

Definitive merger agreement   A contract signed by both parties to a merger that clarifies the details of the transaction, including the terms, warranties, conditions, termination details, and the rights of all parties.

Degree of confidence   The probability that a confidence interval includes the unknown population parameter.

Degree of financial leverage (DFL)   The ratio of the percentage change in net income to the percentage change in operating income; the sensitivity of the cash flows available to owners when operating income changes.

Degree of operating leverage (DOL)   The ratio of the percentage change in operating income to the percentage change in units sold; the sensitivity of operating income to changes in units sold.

Degree of total leverage   The ratio of the percentage change in net income to the percentage change in units sold; the sensitivity of the cash flows to owners to changes in the number of units produced and sold.

Degrees of freedom (df)   The number of independent observations used.

Delivery   A process used in a deliverable forward contract in which the long pays the agreed-upon price to the short, which in turn delivers the underlying asset to the long.

Delivery option   The feature of a futures contract giving the short the right to make decisions about what, when, and where to deliver.

Delta   The relationship between the option price and the underlying price, which reflects the sensitivity of the price of the option to changes in the price of the underlying.

Delta hedge   An option strategy in which a position in an asset is converted to a risk-free position with a position in a specific number of options. The number of options per unit of the underlying changes through time, and the position must be revised to maintain the hedge.

Delta-normal method   A measure of VAR equivalent to the analytical method but that refers to the use of delta to estimate the option's price sensitivity.

Demand for money   The relationship between the quantity of money demanded and the interest rate when all other influences on the amount of money that people wish to hold remain the same.

Demand-pull inflation   An inflation that results from an initial increase in aggregate demand.

Dependent   With reference to events, the property that the probability of one event occurring depends on (is related to) the occurrence of another event.

Dependent variable   The variable whose variation about its mean is to be explained by the regression; the left-hand-side variable in a regression equation.

Depository institution   A firm that takes deposits from households and firms and makes loans to other households and firms.

Depreciation   The process of systematically allocating the cost of long-lived (tangible) assets to the periods during which the assets are expected to provide economic benefits.

Derivative   A financial instrument whose value depends on the value of some underlying asset or

factor (e.g., a stock price, an interest rate, or exchange rate).

Derivatives dealers Commercial and investment banks that make markets in derivatives.

Derived demand Demand for a factor of production, which is derived from the demand for the goods and services produced by that factor.

Descriptive statistics The study of how data can be summarized effectively.

Designated fair value instruments Financial instruments that an entity chooses to measure at fair value per IAS 39 or SFAS 159. Generally, the election to use the fair value option is irrevocable.

Desired reserve ratio The ratio of reserves to deposits that banks want to hold.

Diff swaps A swap in which the payments are based on the difference between interest rates in two countries but payments are made in only a single currency.

Diffuse prior The assumption of equal prior probabilities.

Diluted EPS The EPS that would result if all dilutive securities were converted into common shares.

Diluted shares The number of shares that would be outstanding if all potentially dilutive claims on common shares (e.g., convertible debt, convertible preferred stock, and employee stock options) were exercised.

Diminishing balance method An accelerated depreciation method, i.e., one that allocates a relatively large proportion of the cost of an asset to the early years of the asset's useful life.

Diminishing marginal returns The tendency for the marginal product of an additional unit of a factor of production to be less than the marginal product of the previous unit of the factor.

Direct debit program An arrangement whereby a customer authorizes a debit to a demand account; typically used by companies to collect routine payments for services.

Direct financing lease A type of finance lease, from a lessor perspective, where the present value of the lease payments (lease receivable) equals the carrying value of the leased asset. The revenues earned by the lessor are financing in nature.

Direct format (direct method) With reference to the cash flow statement, a format for the presentation of the statement in which cash flow from operating activities is shown as operating cash receipts less operating cash disbursements.

Direct write-off method An approach to recognizing credit losses on customer receivables in which the company waits until such time as a customer has defaulted and only then recognizes the loss.

Dirty-surplus accounting Accounting in which some income items are reported as part of stockholders' equity rather than as gains and losses on the income statement; certain items of comprehensive income bypass the income statement and appear as direct adjustments to shareholders' equity.

Dirty-surplus items Direct adjustments to shareholders' equity that bypass the income statement.

Disbursement float The amount of time between check issuance and a check's clearing back against the company's account.

Discount To reduce the value of a future payment in allowance for how far away it is in time; to calculate the present value of some future amount. Also, the amount by which an instrument is priced below its face value.

Discount interest A procedure for determining the interest on a loan or bond in which the interest is deducted from the face value in advance.

Discount rate The interest rate at which the Fed stands ready to lend reserves to depository institutions.

Discounted cash flow analysis In the context of merger analysis, it is an estimate of a target company's value found by discounting the company's expected future free cash flows to the present.

Discouraged workers People who are available and willing to work but have not made specific effort to find a job in the previous four weeks.

Discrete random variable A random variable that can take on at most a countable number of possible values.

Discrete time Time thought of as advancing in distinct finite increments.

Discretionary fiscal policy A fiscal action that is initiated by an act of Congress.

Discriminant analysis A multivariate classification technique used to discriminate between groups, such as companies that either will or will not become bankrupt during some time frame.

Diseconomies of scale Features of a firm's technology that lead to rising long-run average cost as output increases.

Dispersion The variability around the central tendency.

Disposable income Aggregate income minus taxes plus transfer payments.

Divestiture The sale, liquidation, or spin-off of a division or subsidiary.

Dividend discount model (DDM) A technique for estimating the value of a stock issue as the present value of all future dividends.

Dividend discount model based approach An approach for estimating a country's equity risk premium. The market rate of return is estimated as the sum of the dividend yield and the growth rate in dividends for a market index. Subtracting the risk-free rate of return from the estimated market return produces an estimate for the equity risk premium.

Dividend payout policy The strategy a company follows with regard to the amount and timing of dividend payments.

Dividend payout ratio The ratio of cash dividends paid to earnings for a period.

Dividends per share The dollar amount of cash dividends paid during a period per share of common stock.

Dominant strategy equilibrium A Nash equilibrium in which the best strategy for each player is to cheat (deny) regardless of the strategy of the other player.

Double declining balance depreciation An accelerated depreciation method that involves depreciating the asset at double the straight-line rate. This rate is multiplied by the book value of the asset at the beginning of the period (a declining balance) to calculate depreciation expense.

Double taxation Corporate earnings are taxed twice when paid out as dividends. First, corporate earnings are taxed regardless of whether they will be distributed as dividends or retained at the corporate level, and second, dividends are taxed again at the individual shareholder level.

Double-entry accounting The accounting system of recording transactions in which every recorded transaction affects at least two accounts so as to keep the basic accounting equation (assets = liabilities + owners' equity) in balance.

Down transition probability The probability that an asset's value moves down in a model of asset price dynamics.

Downstream A transaction between two affiliates, an investor company and an associate company such that the investor company records a profit on its income statement. An example is a sale of inventory by the investor company to the associate.

Drag on liquidity When receipts lag, creating pressure from the decreased available funds.

Dummy variable A type of qualitative variable that takes on a value of 1 if a particular condition is true and 0 if that condition is false.

Duopoly A market structure in which two producers of a good or service compete.

DuPont analysis An approach to decomposing return on investment, e.g., return on equity, as the product of other financial ratios.

Duration A measure of an option-free bond's average maturity. Specifically, the weighted average maturity of all future cash flows paid by a security, in which the weights are the present value of these cash flows as a fraction of the bond's price. A measure of a bond's price sensitivity to interest rate movements.

Dutch Book theorem A result in probability theory stating that inconsistent probabilities create profit opportunities.

Dynamic hedging A strategy in which a position is hedged by making frequent adjustments to the quantity of the instrument used for hedging in relation to the instrument being hedged.

Earnings at risk (EAR) A variation of VAR that reflects the risk of a company's earnings instead of its market value.

Earnings expectation management Attempts by management to influence analysts' earnings forecasts.

Earnings game Management's focus on reporting earnings that meet consensus estimates.

Earnings management activity Deliberate activity aimed at influencing reporting earnings numbers, often with the goal of placing management in a favorable light; the opportunistic use of accruals to manage earnings.

Earnings multiplier model A technique for estimating the value of a stock issue as a multiple of its future earnings per share.

Earnings per share The amount of income earned during a period per share of common stock.

Earnings surprise A company announcement of earnings that differ from analysts' prevailing expectations.

Economic depreciation The change in the market value of capital over a given period.

Economic efficiency A situation that occurs when the firm produces a given output at the least cost.

Economic exposure The risk associated with changes in the relative attractiveness of products and services offered for sale, arising out of the competitive effects of changes in exchange rates.

Economic order quantity–reorder point An approach to managing inventory based on expected demand and the predictability of demand; the ordering point for new inventory is determined based on the costs of ordering and carrying inventory, such that the total cost associated with inventory is minimized.

Economic profit A firm's total revenue minus its total cost.

Economic rent Any surplus—consumer surplus, producer surplus or economic profit. The income received by the owner of a factor of production over and above the amount required to induce that owner to offer the factor for use.

Economies of scale Features of a firm's technology that lead to a falling long-run average cost as output increases. In reference to mergers, it is the savings achieved through the consolidation of operations and elimination of duplicate resources.

Economies of scope Decreases in average total cost that occur when a firm uses specialized resources to produce a range of goods and services.

Effective annual rate The amount by which a unit of currency will grow in a year with interest on interest included.

Effective annual yield (EAY) An annualized return that accounts for the effect of interest on interest; EAY is computed by compounding 1 plus the holding period yield forward to one year, then subtracting 1.

Efficiency In statistics, a desirable property of estimators; an efficient estimator is the unbiased estimator with the smallest variance among unbiased estimators of the same parameter.

Efficiency wage A real wage rate that is set above the equilibrium wage rate and that balances the costs and benefits of this higher wage rate to maximize the firm's profit.

Efficient capital market A market in which security prices rapidly reflect all information about securities.

Efficient frontier The portion of the minimum-variance frontier beginning with the global minimum-variance portfolio and continuing above it; the graph of the set of portfolios offering the maximum expected return for their level of variance of return.

Efficient portfolio A portfolio offering the highest expected return for a given level of risk as measured by variance or standard deviation of return.

Elastic demand Demand with a price elasticity greater than 1; other things remaining the same, the percentage change in the quantity demanded exceeds the percentage change in price.

Elasticity A measure of sensitivity; the incremental change in one variable with respect to an incremental change in another variable.

Elasticity of supply The responsiveness of the quantity supplied of a good to a change in its price, other things remaining the same.

Electronic funds transfer The use of computer networks to conduct financial transactions electronically.

Empirical probability The probability of an event estimated as a relative frequency of occurrence.

Employment Act of 1946 A landmark Congressional act that recognizes a role for government actions to keep unemployment low, the economy expanding, and inflation in check.

Employment-to-population ratio The percentage of people of working age who have jobs.

Enhanced derivatives products companies (EDPC) A type of subsidiary engaged in derivatives transactions that is separated from the parent company in order to have a higher credit rating than the parent company.

Enterprise risk management A form of *centralized risk management* that typically encompasses the management of a broad variety of risks, including insurance risk.

Equitizing cash A strategy used to replicate an index. It is also used to take a given amount of cash and turn it into an equity position while maintaining the liquidity provided by the cash.

Equity Assets less liabilities; the residual interest in the assets after subtracting the liabilities.

Equity carve-out A form of restructuring that involves the creation of a new legal entity and the sale of equity in it to outsiders.

Equity forward A contract calling for the purchase of an individual stock, a stock portfolio, or a stock index at a later date at an agreed-upon price.

Equity method A basis for reporting investment income in which the investing entity recognizes a share of income as earned rather than as dividends when received. These transactions are typically reflected in Investments in Associates or Equity Method Investments.

Equity options Options on individual stocks; also known as stock options.

Equity risk premium The expected return on equities minus the risk-free rate; the premium that investors demand for investing in equities.

Equity swap A swap transaction in which at least one cash flow is tied to the return to an equity portfolio position, often an equity index.

Error autocorrelation The autocorrelation of the error term.

Error term The portion of the dependent variable that is not explained by the independent variable(s) in the regression.

Estimate The particular value calculated from sample observations using an estimator.

Estimated (or fitted) parameters With reference to regression analysis, the estimated values of the population intercept and population slope coefficient(s) in a regression.

Estimated rate of return The rate of return an investor anticipates earning from a specific investment over a particular future holding period.

Estimation With reference to statistical inference, the subdivision dealing with estimating the value of a population parameter.

Estimator An estimation formula; the formula used to compute the sample mean and other sample statistics are examples of estimators.

Eurodollar A dollar deposited outside the United States.

European-style option or European option An option contract that can only be exercised on its expiration date.

Event Any outcome or specified set of outcomes of a random variable.

Event study Research that examines the reaction of a security's price to a specific company, world event, or news announcement.

Excess kurtosis Degree of peakedness (fatness of tails) in excess of the peakedness of the normal distribution.

Excess reserves A bank's actual reserves minus its desired reserves.

Exchange for physicals (EFP) A permissible delivery procedure used by futures market participants, in which the long and short arrange a delivery procedure other than the normal procedures stipulated by the futures exchange.

Exchange ratio The number of shares that target stockholders are to receive in exchange for each of their shares in the target company.

Ex-dividend Trading ex-dividend refers to shares that no longer carry the right to the next dividend payment.

Ex-dividend date The first date that a share trades without (i.e. "ex") the dividend.

Exercise or exercising the option The process of using an option to buy or sell the underlying.

Exercise date The day that employees actually exercise the options and convert them to stock.

Exercise price (strike price, striking price, or strike) The fixed price at which an option holder can buy or sell the underlying.

Exercise rate or strike rate The fixed rate at which the holder of an interest rate option can buy or sell the underlying.

Exhaustive Covering or containing all possible outcomes.

Expected rate of return The return that analysts' calculations suggest a security should provide, based on the market's rate of return during the period and the security's relationship to the market.

Expected value The probability-weighted average of the possible outcomes of a random variable.

Expensed Taken as a deduction in arriving at net income.

Expenses Outflows of economic resources or increases in liabilities that result in decreases in equity (other than decreases because of distributions to owners); reductions in net assets associated with the creation of revenues.

Expiration date The date on which a derivative contract expires.

Exposure to foreign exchange risk The risk of a change in value of an asset or liability denominated in a foreign currency due to a change in exchange rates.

External diseconomies Factors outside the control of a firm that raise the firm's costs as the industry produces a larger output.

External economies Factors beyond the control of a firm that lower the firm's costs as the industry produces a larger output.

External efficiency A market in which prices adjust quickly to new information regarding supply or demand. Also referred to as *informational efficiency*.

External growth Company growth in output or sales that is achieved by buying the necessary resources externally (i.e., achieved through mergers and acquisitions).

Externality The effect of an investment on other things besides the investment itself.

Face value (also principal, par value, stated value, or maturity value) The amount of cash payable by a company to the bondholders when the bonds mature; the promised payment at maturity separate from any coupon payment.

Factor A common or underlying element with which several variables are correlated.

Factor risk premium (or factor price) The expected return in excess of the risk-free rate for a portfolio with a sensitivity of 1 to one factor and a sensitivity of 0 to all other factors.

Factor sensitivity (also factor betas or factor loadings) A measure of the response of return to each unit of increase in a factor, holding all other factors constant.

Fair market value The market price of an asset or liability that trades regularly.

Fair value The amount at which an asset could be exchanged, or a liability settled, between knowledgeable, willing parties in an arm's-length transaction; the price that would be received to sell an asset or paid to transfer a liability in an orderly transaction between market participants.

Federal budget The annual statement of the outlays and tax revenues of the government of the United States, together with the laws and regulations that approve and support those outlays and taxes.

Federal funds rate The interest rate that the banks charge each other on overnight loans.

Federal Open Market Committee The main policy-making organ of the Federal Reserve System.

Federal Reserve System (the Fed) The central bank of the United States.

Fiduciary call A combination of a European call and a risk-free bond that matures on the option expiration day and has a face value equal to the exercise price of the call.

FIFO method The first in, first out, method of accounting for inventory, which matches sales against the costs of items of inventory in the order in which they were placed in inventory.

Filter rule A trading rule that recommends security transactions when price changes exceed a previously determined percentage.

Finance lease (capital lease) Essentially, the purchase of some asset by the buyer (lessee) that is directly financed by the seller (lessor).

Financial analysis The process of selecting, evaluating, and interpreting financial data in order to formulate an assessment of a company's present and future financial condition and performance.

Financial distress Heightened uncertainty regarding a company's ability to meet its various obligations because of lower or negative earnings.

Financial flexibility The ability to react and adapt to financial adversities and opportunities.

Financial futures Futures contracts in which the underlying is a stock, bond, or currency.

Financial leverage The extent to which a company can effect, through the use of debt, a proportional change in the return on common equity that is greater than a given proportional change in operating income; also, short for the financial leverage ratio.

Financial leverage ratio A measure of financial leverage calculated as average total assets divided by average total equity.

Financial reporting quality The accuracy with which a company's reported financials reflect its operating performance and their usefulness for forecasting future cash flows.

Financial risk The risk that environmental, social, or governance risk factors will result in significant

costs or other losses to a company and its shareholders; the risk arising from a company's obligation to meet required payments under its financing agreements.

Financing activities Activities related to obtaining or repaying capital to be used in the business (e.g., equity and long-term debt).

Firm An economic unit that hires factors of production and organizes those factors to produce and sell goods and services.

First-differencing A transformation that subtracts the value of the time series in period $t-1$ from its value in period t.

First-order serial correlation Correlation between adjacent observations in a time series.

Fiscal imbalance The present value of the government's commitments to pay benefits minus the present value of its tax revenues.

Fiscal policy The government's attempt to achieve macroeconomic objectives such as full employment, sustained long-term economic growth, and price level stability by setting and changing tax rates, making transfer payments, and purchasing goods and services.

Fixed asset turnover An activity ratio calculated as total revenue divided by average net fixed assets.

Fixed charge coverage A solvency ratio measuring the number of times interest and lease payments are covered by operating income, calculated as (EBIT + lease payments) divided by (interest payments + lease payments).

Fixed costs Costs that remain at the same level regardless of a company's level of production and sales.

Fixed rate perpetual preferred stock Nonconvertible, noncallable preferred stock that has a fixed dividend rate and no maturity date.

Fixed-income forward A forward contract in which the underlying is a bond.

Flat trend channel The range defined by security prices as they maintain a relatively steady level.

Flip-in pill A poison pill takeover defense that dilutes an acquirer's ownership in a target by giving other existing target company shareholders the right to buy additional target company shares at a discount.

Flip-over pill A poison pill takeover defense that gives target company shareholders the right to purchase shares of the acquirer at a significant discount to the market price, which has the effect of causing dilution to all existing acquiring company shareholders.

Float In the context of customer receipts, the amount of money that is in transit between payments made by customers and the funds that are usable by the company.

Float factor   An estimate of the average number of days it takes deposited checks to clear; average daily float divided by average daily deposit.

Floating-rate loan   A loan in which the interest rate is reset at least once after the starting date.

Floor   A combination of interest rate put options designed to hedge a lender against lower rates on a floating-rate loan.

Floor brokers   Independent members of an exchange who act as brokers for other members.

Floor traders or locals   Market makers that buy and sell by quoting a bid and an ask price. They are the primary providers of liquidity to the market.

Floored swap   A swap in which the floating payments have a lower limit.

Floorlet   Each component put option in a floor.

Flotation cost   Fees charged to companies by investment bankers and other costs associated with raising new capital.

Foreign currency transactions   Transactions that are denominated in a currency other than a company's functional currency.

Forward contract   An agreement between two parties in which one party, the buyer, agrees to buy from the other party, the seller, an underlying asset at a later date for a price established at the start of the contract.

Forward integration   A merger involving the purchase of a target that is farther along the value or production chain; for example, to acquire a distributor.

Forward price or forward rate   The fixed price or rate at which the transaction scheduled to occur at the expiration of a forward contract will take place. This price is agreed on at the initiation date of the contract.

Forward rate agreement (FRA)   A forward contract calling for one party to make a fixed interest payment and the other to make an interest payment at a rate to be determined at the contract expiration.

Forward swap   A forward contract to enter into a swap.

Four-firm concentration ratio   A measure of market power that is calculated as the percentage of the value of sales accounted for by the four largest firms in an industry.

Free cash flow   The actual cash that would be available to the company's investors after making all investments necessary to maintain the company as an ongoing enterprise (also referred to as free cash flow to the firm); the internally generated funds that can be distributed to the company's investors (e.g., shareholders and bondholders) without impairing the value of the company.

Free cash flow hypothesis   The hypothesis that higher debt levels discipline managers by forcing them to make fixed debt service payments and by reducing the company's free cash flow.

Free cash flow to equity   The cash flow available to a company's common shareholders after all operating expenses, interest, and principal payments have been made, and necessary investments in working and fixed capital have been made.

Free cash flow to the firm   The cash flow available to the company's suppliers of capital after all operating expenses have been paid and necessary investments in working capital and fixed capital have been made.

Frequency distribution   A tabular display of data summarized into a relatively small number of intervals.

Frequency polygon   A graph of a frequency distribution obtained by drawing straight lines joining successive points representing the class frequencies.

Frictional unemployment   The unemployment that arises from normal labor turnover—from people entering and leaving the labor force and from the ongoing creation and destruction of jobs.

Friendly transaction   A potential business combination that is endorsed by the managers of both companies.

Full employment   A situation in which the quantity of labor demanded equals the quantity supplied. At full employment, there is no cyclical unemployment—all unemployment is frictional and structural.

Full-employment equilibrium   A macroeconomic equilibrium in which real GDP equals potential GDP.

Full price   The price of a security with accrued interest.

Functional currency   The currency of the primary economic environment in which an entity operates.

Fundamental beta   A beta that is based at least in part on fundamental data for a company.

Fundamental factor models   A multifactor model in which the factors are attributes of stocks or companies that are important in explaining cross-sectional differences in stock prices.

Future value (FV)   The amount to which a payment or series of payments will grow by a stated future date.

Futures commission merchants (FCMs) Individuals or companies that execute futures transactions for other parties off the exchange.

Futures contract A variation of a forward contract that has essentially the same basic definition but with some additional features, such as a clearinghouse guarantee against credit losses, a daily settlement of gains and losses, and an organized electronic or floor trading facility.

Futures exchange A legal corporate entity whose shareholders are its members. The members of the exchange have the privilege of executing transactions directly on the exchange.

Gains Asset inflows not directly related to the ordinary activities of the business.

Game theory A tool that economists use to analyze strategic behavior—behavior that takes into account the expected behavior of others and the recognition of mutual interdependence.

Gamma A numerical measure of how sensitive an option's delta is to a change in the underlying.

Generalized least squares A regression estimation technique that addresses heteroskedasticity of the error term.

Generational accounting An accounting system that measures the lifetime tax burden and benefits of each generation.

Generational imbalance The division of the fiscal imbalance between the current and future generations, assuming that the current generation will enjoy the existing levels of taxes and benefits.

Geometric mean A measure of central tendency computed by taking the nth root of the product of n non-negative values.

Gifting phase Phase in the investment life cycle during which individuals use excess assets to financially assist relatives or friends, establish charitable trusts, or construct trusts to minimize estate taxes.

Giro system An electronic payment system used widely in Europe and Japan.

Goodwill An intangible asset that represents the excess of the purchase price of an acquired company over the value of the net assets acquired.

Government debt The total amount that the government has borrowed. It equals the sum of past budget deficits minus the sum of past budget surpluses.

Government expenditure multiplier The magnification effect of a change in government expenditure on goods and services on equilibrium expenditure and real GDP.

Grant date The day that options are granted to employees; usually the date that compensation expense is measured if both the number of shares and option price are known.

Greenmail The purchase of the accumulated shares of a hostile investor by a company that is targeted for takeover by that investor, usually at a substantial premium over market price.

Gross profit (gross margin) Sales minus the cost of sales (i.e., the cost of goods sold for a manufacturing company).

Gross profit margin The ratio of gross profit to revenues.

Grouping by function With reference to the presentation of expenses in an income statement, the grouping together of expenses serving the same function, e.g. all items that are costs of goods sold.

Grouping by nature With reference to the presentation of expenses in an income statement, the grouping together of expenses by similar nature, e.g., all depreciation expenses.

Growth company A company that consistently has the opportunities and ability to invest in projects that provide rates of return that exceed the firm's cost of capital. Because of these investment opportunities, it retains a high proportion of earnings, and its earnings grow faster than those of average firms.

Growth investors With reference to equity investors, investors who seek to invest in high-earnings-growth companies.

Growth option or expansion option The ability to make additional investments in a project at some future time if the financial results are strong.

Growth stock A stock issue that generates a higher rate of return than other stocks in the market with similar risk characteristics.

Harmonic mean A type of weighted mean computed by averaging the reciprocals of the observations, then taking the reciprocal of that average.

Hedge ratio The relationship of the quantity of an asset being hedged to the quantity of the derivative used for hedging.

Hedging A general strategy usually thought of as reducing, if not eliminating, risk.

Held-for-trading securities (trading securities) Debt or equity financial assets bought with the intention to sell them in the near term, usually less than three months; securities that a company intends to trade.

Held-to-maturity investments Debt (fixed-income) securities that a company intends to hold to maturity; these are presented at their original cost, updated for any amortization of discounts or premiums.

Herfindahl–Hirschman Index   A measure of market concentration that is calculated by summing the squared market shares for competing companies in an industry; high HHI readings or mergers that would result in large HHI increases are more likely to result in regulatory challenges.

Heteroskedastic   With reference to the error term of a regression, having a variance that differs across observations.

Heteroskedasticity   The property of having a non-constant variance; refers to an error term with the property that its variance differs across observations.

Heteroskedasticity-consistent standard errors   Standard errors of the estimated parameters of a regression that correct for the presence of heteroskedasticity in the regression's error term.

Histogram   A bar chart of data that have been grouped into a frequency distribution.

Historical cost   In reference to assets, the amount paid to purchase an asset, including any costs of acquisition and/or preparation; with reference to liabilities, the amount of proceeds received in exchange in issuing the liability.

Historical equity risk premium approach   An estimate of a country's equity risk premium that is based upon the historical averages of the risk-free rate and the rate of return on the market portfolio.

Historical exchange rates   For accounting purposes, the exchange rates that existed when the assets and liabilities were initially recorded.

Historical method   A method of estimating VAR that uses data from the returns of the portfolio over a recent past period and compiles this data in the form of a histogram.

Historical simulation (or back simulation)   Another term for the historical method of estimating VAR. This term is somewhat misleading in that the method involves not a *simulation* of the past but rather what *actually happened* in the past, sometimes adjusted to reflect the fact that a different portfolio may have existed in the past than is planned for the future.

Holder-of-record date   The date that a shareholder listed on the corporation's books will be deemed to have ownership of the shares for purposes of receiving an upcoming dividend; two business days after the ex-dividend date.

Holding period return   The return that an investor earns during a specified holding period; a synonym for total return.

Holding period yield (HPY)   The return that an investor earns during a specified holding period; holding period return with reference to a fixed-income instrument.

Homogenization   Creating a contract with standard and generally accepted terms, which makes it more acceptable to a broader group of participants.

Homoskedasticity   The property of having a constant variance; refers to an error term that is constant across observations.

Horizontal analysis   Common-size analysis that involves comparing a specific financial statement with that statement in prior or future time periods; also, cross-sectional analysis of one company with another.

Horizontal common-size analysis   A form of common-size analysis in which the accounts in a given period are used as the benchmark or base period, and every account is restated in subsequent periods as a percentage of the base period's same account.

Horizontal merger   A merger involving companies in the same line of business, usually as competitors.

Hostile transaction   An attempt to acquire a company against the wishes of the target's managers.

Hurdle rate   The rate of return that must be met for a project to be accepted.

Hypothesis   With reference to statistical inference, a statement about one or more populations.

Hypothesis testing   With reference to statistical inference, the subdivision dealing with the testing of hypotheses about one or more populations.

Identifiable intangible   An intangible that can be acquired singly and is typically linked to specific rights or privileges having finite benefit periods (e.g., a patent or trademark).

If-converted method   A method for accounting for the effect of convertible securities on earnings per share (EPS) that specifies what EPS would have been if the convertible securities had been converted at the beginning of the period, taking account of the effects of conversion on net income and the weighted average number of shares outstanding.

Impairment   Diminishment in value as a result of carrying (book) value exceeding fair value and/or recoverable value.

Impairment of capital rule   A legal restriction that dividends cannot exceed retained earnings.

Implicit rental rate   The firm's opportunity cost of using its own capital.

Implied repo rate   The rate of return from a cash-and-carry transaction implied by the futures price relative to the spot price.

Implied volatility   The volatility that option traders use to price an option, implied by the price of the option and a particular option-pricing model.

Implied yield   A measure of the yield on the underlying bond of a futures contract implied by pricing it as though the underlying will be delivered at the futures expiration.

Imputation   In reference to corporate taxes, a system that imputes, or attributes, taxes at only one level of taxation. For countries using an imputation tax system, taxes on dividends are effectively levied only at the shareholder rate. Taxes are paid at the corporate level but they are *attributed* to the shareholder. Shareholders deduct from their tax bill their portion of taxes paid by the company.

Incentive system   A method of organizing production that uses a market-like mechanism inside the firm.

Income   Increases in economic benefits in the form of inflows or enhancements of assets, or decreases of liabilities that result in an increase in equity (other than increases resulting from contributions by owners).

Income elasticity of demand   The responsiveness of demand to a change in income, other things remaining the same. It is calculated as the percentage change in the quantity demanded divided by the percentage change in income.

Income statement (statement of operations or profit and loss statement)   A financial statement that provides information about a company's profitability over a stated period of time.

Income tax paid   The actual amount paid for income taxes in the period; not a provision, but the actual cash outflow.

Income tax payable   The income tax owed by the company on the basis of taxable income.

Income tax recoverable   The income tax expected to be recovered, from the taxing authority, on the basis of taxable income. It is a recovery of previously remitted taxes or future taxes owed by the company.

Incremental cash flow   The cash flow that is realized because of a decision; the changes or increments to cash flows resulting from a decision or action.

Independent   With reference to events, the property that the occurrence of one event does not affect the probability of another event occurring.

Independent and identically distributed (IID)   With respect to random variables, the property of random variables that are independent of each other but follow the identical probability distribution.

Independent projects   Independent projects are projects whose cash flows are independent of each other.

Independent variable   A variable used to explain the dependent variable in a regression; a right-hand-side variable in a regression equation.

Index amortizing swap   An interest rate swap in which the notional principal is indexed to the level of interest rates and declines with the level of interest rates according to a predefined schedule. This type of swap is frequently used to hedge securities that are prepaid as interest rates decline, such as mortgage-backed securities.

Index option   An option in which the underlying is a stock index.

Indexing   An investment strategy in which an investor constructs a portfolio to mirror the performance of a specified index.

Indirect format (indirect method)   With reference to cash flow statements, a format for the presentation of the statement which, in the operating cash flow section, begins with net income then shows additions and subtractions to arrive at operating cash flow.

Induced taxes   Taxes that vary with real GDP.

Inelastic demand   A demand with a price elasticity between 0 and 1; the percentage change in the quantity demanded is less than the percentage change in price.

Inflation premium   An extra return that compensates investors for expected inflation.

Inflation rate   The annual percentage change in the price level.

Inflation rate targeting   A monetary policy strategy in which the central bank makes a public commitment to achieve an explicit inflation rate and to explain how its policy actions will achieve that target.

Inflationary gap   The amount by which real GDP exceeds potential GDP.

Information   An attribute of a good market that includes providing buyers and sellers with timely, accurate information on the volume and prices of past transactions and on all currently outstanding bids and offers.

Information ratio (IR)   Mean active return divided by active risk.

Informationally efficient market   A more technical term for an efficient capital market that emphasizes the role of information in setting the market price.

Initial margin requirement   The margin requirement on the first day of a transaction as well as on any day in which additional margin funds must be deposited.

Initial public offering (IPO) A new issue by a firm that has no existing public market.

In-sample forecast errors The residuals from a fitted time-series model within the sample period used to fit the model.

Instability in the minimum-variance frontier The characteristic of minimum-variance frontiers that they are sensitive to small changes in inputs.

Installment Said of a sale in which proceeds are to be paid in installments over an extended period of time.

Installment method (installment-sales method) With respect to revenue recognition, a method that specifies that the portion of the total profit of the sale that is recognized in each period is determined by the percentage of the total sales price for which the seller has received cash.

Instrument rule A decision rule for monetary policy that sets the policy instrument at a level that is based on the current state of the economy.

Intangible assets Assets lacking physical substance, such as patents and trademarks.

Interest coverage A solvency ratio calculated as EBIT divided by interest payments.

Interest rate A rate of return that reflects the relationship between differently dated cash flows; a discount rate.

Interest rate call An option in which the holder has the right to make a known interest payment and receive an unknown interest payment.

Interest rate cap or cap A series of call options on an interest rate, with each option expiring at the date on which the floating loan rate will be reset, and with each option having the same exercise rate. A cap in general can have an underlying other than an interest rate.

Interest rate collar A combination of a long cap and a short floor, or a short cap and a long floor. A collar in general can have an underlying other than an interest rate.

Interest rate floor or floor A series of put options on an interest rate, with each option expiring at the date on which the floating loan rate will be reset, and with each option having the same exercise rate. A floor in general can have an underlying other than the interest rate.

Interest rate forward (See *forward rate agreement*)

Interest rate option An option in which the underlying is an interest rate.

Interest rate parity A formula that expresses the equivalence or parity of spot and forward rates, after adjusting for differences in the interest rates.

Interest rate put An option in which the holder has the right to make an unknown interest payment and receive a known interest payment.

Interest rate swap A swap in which the underlying is an interest rate. Can be viewed as a currency swap in which both currencies are the same and can be created as a combination of currency swaps.

Intergenerational data mining A form of data mining that applies information developed by previous researchers using a dataset to guide current research using the same or a related dataset.

Internal rate of return (IRR) The discount rate that makes net present value equal 0; the discount rate that makes the present value of an investment's costs (outflows) equal to the present value of the investment's benefits (inflows).

Interquartile range The difference between the third and first quartiles of a dataset.

Interval With reference to grouped data, a set of values within which an observation falls.

Interval scale A measurement scale that not only ranks data but also gives assurance that the differences between scale values are equal.

In-the-money Options that, if exercised, would result in the value received being worth more than the payment required to exercise.

Intrinsic value or exercise value The value obtained if an option is exercised based on current conditions.

Inventory The unsold units of product on hand.

Inventory blanket lien The use of inventory as collateral for a loan. Though the lender has claim to some or all of the company's inventory, the company may still sell or use the inventory in the ordinary course of business.

Inventory turnover An activity ratio calculated as cost of goods sold divided by average inventory.

Inverse floater A floating-rate note or bond in which the coupon is adjusted to move opposite to a benchmark interest rate.

Investing activities Activities which are associated with the acquisition and disposal of property, plant, and equipment; intangible assets; other long-term assets; and both long-term and short-term investments in the equity and debt (bonds and loans) issued by other companies.

Investment decision process Estimation of intrinsic value for comparison with market price to determine whether or not to invest.

Investment opportunity schedule A graphical depiction of a company's investment opportunities ordered from highest to lowest expected return. A company's optimal capital budget is found where the investment opportunity schedule intersects with the company's marginal cost of capital.

Investment strategy A decision by a portfolio manager regarding how he or she will manage the portfolio to meet the goals and objectives of the client. This will include either active or passive management and, if active, what style in terms of top-down or bottom-up or fundamental versus technical.

IRR rule An investment decision rule that accepts projects or investments for which the IRR is greater than the opportunity cost of capital.

Joint probability The probability of the joint occurrence of stated events.

Joint probability function A function giving the probability of joint occurrences of values of stated random variables.

Joint venture An entity (partnership, corporation, or other legal form) where control is shared by two or more entities called venturers.

Just-in-time method Method of managing inventory that minimizes in-process inventory stocks.

Keynesian A macroeconomist who believes that left alone, the economy would rarely operate at full employment and that to achieve full employment, active help from fiscal policy and monetary policy is required.

Keynesian cycle theory A theory that fluctuations in investment driven by fluctuations in business confidence—summarized in the phrase "animal spirits"—are the main source of fluctuations in aggregate demand.

k-percent rule A rule that makes the quantity of money grow at a rate of k percent a year, where k equals the growth rate of potential GDP.

kth Order autocorrelation The correlation between observations in a time series separated by k periods.

Kurtosis The statistical measure that indicates the peakedness of a distribution.

Labor force The sum of the people who are employed and who are unemployed.

Labor force participation rate The percentage of the working-age population who are members of the labor force.

Labor union An organized group of workers whose purpose is to increase wages and to influence other job conditions.

Laddering strategy A form of active strategy which entails scheduling maturities on a systematic basis within the investment portfolio such that investments are spread out equally over the term of the ladder.

Laffer curve The relationship between the tax rate and the amount of tax revenue collected.

Law of diminishing returns As a firm uses more of a variable input, with a given quantity of other inputs (fixed inputs), the marginal product of the variable input eventually diminishes.

Law of one price The condition in a financial market in which two equivalent financial instruments or combinations of financial instruments can sell for only one price. Equivalent to the principle that no arbitrage opportunities are possible.

Legal monopoly A market structure in which there is one firm and entry is restricted by the granting of a public franchise, government license, patent, or copyright.

Legal risk The risk that failures by company managers to effectively manage a company's environmental, social, and governance risk exposures will lead to lawsuits and other judicial remedies, resulting in potentially catastrophic losses for the company; the risk that the legal system will not enforce a contract in case of dispute or fraud.

Legislative and regulatory risk The risk that governmental laws and regulations directly or indirectly affecting a company's operations will change with potentially severe adverse effects on the company's continued profitability and even its long-term sustainability.

Leptokurtic Describes a distribution that is more peaked than a normal distribution.

Lessee The party obtaining the use of an asset through a lease.

Lessor The owner of an asset that grants the right to use the asset to another party.

Level of significance The probability of a Type I error in testing a hypothesis.

Leverage In the context of corporate finance, leverage refers to the use of fixed costs within a company's cost structure. Fixed costs that are operating costs (such as depreciation or rent) create operating leverage. Fixed costs that are financial costs (such as interest expense) create financial leverage.

Leveraged buyout (LBO) A transaction whereby the target company management team converts the target to a privately held company by using heavy borrowing to finance the purchase of the target company's outstanding shares.

Leveraged floating-rate note or leveraged floater A floating-rate note or bond in which the coupon is adjusted at a multiple of a benchmark interest rate.

Leveraged recapitalization A post-offer takeover defense mechanism that involves the assumption of a large amount of debt that is then used to finance share repurchases; the effect is to dramatically change the company's capital structure while attempting to deliver a value to target shareholders in excess of a hostile bid.

Liabilities　Present obligations of an enterprise arising from past events, the settlement of which is expected to result in an outflow of resources embodying economic benefits; creditors' claims on the resources of a company.

LIFO layer liquidation (LIFO liquidation)　With respect to the application of the LIFO inventory method, the liquidation of old, relatively low-priced inventory; happens when the volume of sales rises above the volume of recent purchases so that some sales are made from relatively old, low-priced inventory.

LIFO method　The last in, first out, method of accounting for inventory, which matches sales against the costs of items of inventory in the reverse order the items were placed in inventory (i.e., inventory produced or acquired last are assumed to be sold first).

LIFO reserve　The difference between inventory reported at FIFO and inventory reported at LIFO (FIFO inventory value less LIFO inventory value).

Likelihood　The probability of an observation, given a particular set of conditions.

Limit down　A limit move in the futures market in which the price at which a transaction would be made is at or below the lower limit.

Limit move　A condition in the futures markets in which the price at which a transaction would be made is at or beyond the price limits.

Limit order　An order that lasts for a specified time to buy or sell a security when and if it trades at a specified price.

Limit pricing　The practice of setting the price at the highest level that inflicts a loss on an entrant.

Limit up　A limit move in the futures market in which the price at which a transaction would be made is at or above the upper limit.

Linear association　A straight-line relationship, as opposed to a relationship that cannot be graphed as a straight line.

Linear interpolation　The estimation of an unknown value on the basis of two known values that bracket it, using a straight line between the two known values.

Linear regression　Regression that models the straight-line relationship between the dependent and independent variable(s).

Linear trend　A trend in which the dependent variable changes at a constant rate with time.

Liquid　Term used to describe an asset that can be quickly converted to cash at a price close to fair market value.

Liquidation　To sell the assets of a company, division, or subsidiary piecemeal, typically because of bankruptcy; the form of bankruptcy that allows for the orderly satisfaction of creditors' claims after which the company ceases to exist.

Liquidity　The ability to buy or sell an asset quickly and at a reasonable price based on information. A company's ability to satisfy its short-term obligations using assets that are most readily converted into cash; the ability to trade a futures contract, either selling a previously purchased contract or purchasing a previously sold contract.

Liquidity premium　An extra return that compensates investors for the risk of loss relative to an investment's fair value if the investment needs to be converted to cash quickly.

Liquidity ratios　Financial ratios measuring the company's ability to meet its short-term obligations.

Liquidity risk　The risk that a financial instrument cannot be purchased or sold without a significant concession in price due to the size of the market.

Living wage　An hourly wage rate that enables a person who works a 40-hour work week to rent adequate housing for not more than 30 percent of the amount earned.

Local currency　The currency of the country where a company is located.

Lockbox system　A payment system in which customer payments are mailed to a post office box and the banking institution retrieves and deposits these payments several times a day, enabling the company to have use of the fund sooner than in a centralized system in which customer payments are sent to the company.

Locked limit　A condition in the futures markets in which a transaction cannot take place because the price would be beyond the limits.

Logit model　A qualitative-dependent-variable multiple regression model based on the logistic probability distribution.

Log-linear model　With reference to time-series models, a model in which the growth rate of the time series as a function of time is constant.

Log-log regression model　A regression that expresses the dependent and independent variables as natural logarithms.

London Interbank Offer Rate (LIBOR)　The Eurodollar rate at which London banks lend dollars to other London banks; considered to be the best representative rate on a dollar borrowed by a private, high-quality borrower.

Long The buyer of a derivative contract. Also refers to the position of owning a derivative.

Long run A period of time in which the quantities of all resources can be varied.

Longitudinal data Observations on characteristic(s) of the same observational unit through time.

Long-lived assets (or long-term assets) Assets that are expected to provide economic benefits over a future period of time, typically greater than one year.

Long-run aggregate supply The relationship between the quantity of real GDP supplied and the price level in the long run when real GDP equals potential GDP.

Long-run average cost curve The relationship between the lowest attainable average total cost and output when both plant size and labor are varied.

Long-run industry supply curve A curve that shows how the quantity supplied by an industry varies as the market price varies after all the possible adjustments have been made, including changes in plant size and the number of firms in the industry.

Long-run macroeconomic equilibrium A situation that occurs when real GDP equals potential GDP—the economy is on its long-run aggregate supply curve.

Long-run Phillips curve A curve that shows the relationship between inflation and unemployment when the actual inflation rate equals the expected inflation rate.

Long-term contract A contract that spans a number of accounting periods.

Long-term debt-to-assets ratio The proportion of a company's assets that is financed with long-term debt.

Long-term equity anticipatory securities (LEAPS) Options originally created with expirations of several years.

Long-term liability An obligation that is expected to be settled, with the outflow of resources embodying economic benefits, over a future period generally greater than one year.

Long-term, high-priority goal A long-term financial investment goal of personal importance that typically includes achieving financial independence, such as being able to retire at a certain age.

Look-ahead bias A bias caused by using information that was unavailable on the test date.

Losses Asset outflows not directly related to the ordinary activities of the business.

Lower bound The lowest possible value of an option.

Lower-priority goal A financial investment goal of lesser personal importance, such as taking a luxurious vacation or buying a car every few years.

M1 A measure of money that consists of currency and traveler's checks plus checking deposits owned by individuals and businesses.

M2 A measure of money that consists of M1 plus time deposits, savings deposits, and money market mutual funds, and other deposits.

Macaulay duration The duration without dividing by 1 plus the bond's yield to maturity. The term, named for one of the economists who first derived it, is used to distinguish the calculation from modified duration. See also *modified duration.*

Macroeconomic factor A factor related to the economy, such as the inflation rate, industrial production, or economic sector membership.

Macroeconomic factor model A multifactor model in which the factors are surprises in macroeconomic variables that significantly explain equity returns.

Macroeconomic long run A time frame that is sufficiently long for the real wage rate to have adjusted to achieve full employment: real GDP equal to potential GDP, unemployment equal to the natural unemployment rate, the price level is proportional to the quantity of money, and the inflation rate equal to the money growth rate minus the real GDP growth rate.

Macroeconomic short run A period during which some money prices are sticky and real GDP might be below, above, or at potential GDP and unemployment might be above, below, or at the natural rate of unemployment.

Maintenance margin The required proportion that the investor's equity value must be to the total market value of the stock. If the proportion drops below this percent, the investor will receive a margin call.

Maintenance margin requirement The margin requirement on any day other than the first day of a transaction.

Managerialism theories Theories that posit that corporate executives are motivated to engage in mergers to maximize the size of their company rather than shareholder value.

Manufacturing resource planning (MRP) The incorporation of production planning into inventory management. A MRP analysis provides both a materials acquisition schedule and a production schedule.

Margin The percent of cost a buyer pays in cash for a security, borrowing the balance from the broker. This introduces leverage, which increases the risk of the transaction. Also the amount of money that a trader deposits in a margin account. In futures markets, there is no borrowing so the margin is more of a down payment or performance bond.

Margin call A request by an investor's broker for additional capital for a security bought on margin if the investor's equity value declines below the required maintenance margin.

Marginal cost The opportunity cost of producing one more unit of a good or service. It is the best alternative forgone. It is calculated as the increase in total cost divided by the increase in output.

Marginal cost pricing rule A rule that sets the price of a good or service equal to the marginal cost of producing it.

Marginal product The increase in total product that results from a one-unit increase in the variable input, with all other inputs remaining the same. It is calculated as the increase in total product divided by the increase in the variable input employed, when the quantities of all other inputs are constant.

Marginal revenue The change in total revenue that results from a one-unit increase in the quantity sold. It is calculated as the change in total revenue divided by the change in quantity sold.

Marginal revenue product The change in total revenue that results from employing one more unit of a factor of production (labor) while the quantity of all other factors remains the same. It is calculated as the increase in total revenue divided by the increase in the quantity of the factor (labor).

Marginal tax rate The part of each additional dollar in income that is paid as tax.

Market The means through which buyers and sellers are brought together to aid in the transfer of goods and/or services.

Market order An order to buy or sell a security immediately at the best price available.

Market portfolio The portfolio that includes all risky assets with relative weights equal to their proportional market values.

Market power The ability to influence the market, and in particular the market price, by influencing the total quantity offered for sale.

Market price of risk The slope of the capital market line, indicating the market risk premium for each unit of market risk.

Market rate The rate demanded by purchasers of bonds, given the risks associated with future cash payment obligations of the particular bond issue.

Market risk The risk associated with interest rates, exchange rates, and equity prices.

Market risk premium The expected excess return on the market over the risk-free rate.

Market-oriented investors With reference to equity investors, investors whose investment disciplines cannot be clearly categorized as value or growth.

Marking to market A procedure used primarily in futures markets in which the parties to a contract settle the amount owed daily. Also known as the *daily settlement.*

Markowitz decision rule A decision rule for choosing between two investments based on their means and variances.

Mark-to-market The revaluation of a financial asset or liability to its current market value or fair value.

Matching principle The accounting principle that expenses should be recognized when the associated revenue is recognized.

Matching strategy An active investment strategy that includes intentional matching of the timing of cash outflows with investment maturities.

Materiality The condition of being of sufficient importance so that omission or misstatement of the item in a financial report could make a difference to users' decisions.

Matrix pricing In the fixed income markets, to price a security on the basis of valuation-relevant characteristics (e.g. debt-rating approach).

Maturity premium An extra return that compensates investors for the increased sensitivity of the market value of debt to a change in market interest rates as maturity is extended.

McCallum rule A rule that makes the growth rate of the monetary base respond to the long-term average growth rate of real GDP and medium-term changes in the velocity of circulation of the monetary base.

Mean The sum of all values in a distribution or dataset, divided by the number of values summed; a synonym of arithmetic mean.

Mean absolute deviation With reference to a sample, the mean of the absolute values of deviations from the sample mean.

Mean excess return The average rate of return in excess of the risk-free rate.

Mean rates of return The average of an investment's returns over an extended period of time.

Mean reversion The tendency of a time series to fall when its level is above its mean and rise when its level is below its mean; a mean-reverting time series tends to return to its long-term mean.

Mean–variance analysis An approach to portfolio analysis using expected means, variances, and covariances of asset returns.

Means of payment A method of settling a debt.

Measure of central tendency A quantitative measure that specifies where data are centered.

Measure of location A quantitative measure that describes the location or distribution of data; includes not only measures of central tendency but also other measures such as percentiles.

Measurement scales A scheme of measuring differences. The four types of measurement scales are nominal, ordinal, interval, and ratio.

Median The value of the middle item of a set of items that has been sorted into ascending or descending order; the 50th percentile.

Merger The absorption of one company by another; that is, two companies become one entity and one or both of the pre-merger companies ceases to exist as a separate entity.

Mesokurtic Describes a distribution with kurtosis identical to that of the normal distribution.

Minimum efficient scale The smallest quantity of output at which the long-run average cost curve reaches its lowest level.

Minimum wage A regulation that makes the hiring of labor below a specified wage rate illegal. The lowest wage at which a firm may legally hire labor.

Minimum-variance frontier The graph of the set of portfolios that have minimum variance for their level of expected return.

Minimum-variance portfolio The portfolio with the minimum variance for each given level of expected return.

Minority active investments Investments in which investors exert significant influence, but not control, over the investee. Typically, the investor has 20 to 50% ownership in the investee.

Minority interest (noncontrolling interest) The proportion of the ownership of a subsidiary not held by the parent (controlling) company.

Minority passive investments (passive investments) Investments in which the investor has no significant influence or control over the operations of the investee.

Mismatching strategy An active investment strategy whereby the timing of cash outflows is not matched with investment maturities.

Mixed factor models Factor models that combine features of more than one type of factor model.

Mixed offering A merger or acquisition that is to be paid for with cash, securities, or some combination of the two.

Modal interval With reference to grouped data, the most frequently occurring interval.

Mode The most frequently occurring value in a set of observations.

Model risk The use of an inaccurate pricing model for a particular investment, or the improper use of the right model.

Model specification With reference to regression, the set of variables included in the regression and the regression equation's functional form.

Modified duration A measure of a bond's price sensitivity to interest rate movements. Equal to the Macaulay duration of a bond divided by one plus its yield to maturity.

Monetarist A macroeconomist who believes that the economy is self-regulating and that it will normally operate at full employment, provided that monetary policy is not erratic and that the pace of money growth is kept steady.

Monetarist cycle theory A theory that fluctuations in both investment and consumption expenditure, driven by fluctuations in the growth rate of the quantity of money, are the main source of fluctuations in aggregate demand.

Monetary assets and liabilities Assets and liabilities with value equal to the amount of currency contracted for, a fixed amount of currency. Examples are cash, accounts receivable, mortgages receivable, accounts payable, bonds payable, and mortgages payable. Inventory is not a monetary asset. Most liabilities are monetary.

Monetary base The sum of Federal Reserve notes, coins and banks' deposits at the Fed.

Monetary policy The Fed conducts the nation's monetary policy by changing interest rates and adjusting the quantity of money.

Monetary policy instrument A variable that the Fed can control directly or closely target.

Monetary/nonmonetary method Approach to translating foreign currency financial statements for consolidation in which monetary assets and liabilities are translated at the current exchange rate. Nonmonetary assets and liabilities are translated at historical exchange rates (the exchange rates that existed when the assets and liabilities were acquired).

Money Any commodity or token that is generally acceptable as the means of payment.

Money market The market for short-term debt instruments (one-year maturity or less).

Money market yield (or CD equivalent yield) A yield on a basis comparable to the quoted yield on an interest-bearing money market instrument that pays interest on a 360-day basis; the annualized holding period yield, assuming a 360-day year.

Money multiplier The ratio of the change in the quantity of money to the change in the monetary base.

Moneyness   The relationship between the price of the underlying and an option's exercise price.

Money-weighted rate of return   The internal rate of return on a portfolio, taking account of all cash flows.

Monitoring costs   Costs borne by owners to monitor the management of the company (e.g., board of director expenses).

Monopolistic competition   A market structure in which a large number of firms compete by making similar but slightly different products.

Monopoly   A market structure in which there is one firm, which produces a good or service that has no close substitutes and in which the firm is protected from competition by a barrier preventing the entry of new firms.

Monopsony   A market in which there is a single buyer.

Monte Carlo simulation method   An approach to estimating a probability distribution of outcomes to examine what might happen if particular risks are faced. This method is widely used in the sciences as well as in business to study a variety of problems.

Moving average   The continually recalculating average of security prices for a period, often 200 days, to serve as an indication of the general trend of prices and also as a benchmark price.

Multicollinearity   A regression assumption violation that occurs when two or more independent variables (or combinations of independent variables) are highly but not perfectly correlated with each other.

Multiple linear regression model   A linear regression model with two or more independent variables.

Multiple R   The correlation between the actual and forecasted values of the dependent variable in a regression.

Multiplication rule for probabilities   The rule that the joint probability of events A and B equals the probability of A given B times the probability of B.

Multi-step format   With respect to the format of the income statement, a format that presents a subtotal for gross profit (revenue minus cost of goods sold).

Multivariate distribution   A probability distribution that specifies the probabilities for a group of related random variables.

Multivariate normal distribution   A probability distribution for a group of random variables that is completely defined by the means and variances of the variables plus all the correlations between pairs of the variables.

Mutually exclusive events   Events such that only one can occur at a time.

Mutually exclusive projects   Mutually exclusive projects compete directly with each other. For example, if Projects A and B are mutually exclusive, you can choose A or B, but you cannot choose both.

n Factorial   For a positive integer n, the product of the first n positive integers; 0 factorial equals 1 by definition. n factorial is written as $n!$.

Nash equilibrium   The outcome of a game that occurs when player A takes the best possible action given the action of player B and player B takes the best possible action given the action of player A.

Natural monopoly   A monopoly that occurs when one firm can supply the entire market at a lower price than two or more firms can.

Natural unemployment rate   The unemployment rate when the economy is at full employment. There is no cyclical unemployment; all unemployment is frictional, structural, and seasonal.

Near-term, high-priority goal   A short-term financial investment goal of personal importance, such as accumulating funds for making a house down payment or buying a car.

Needs-tested spending   Government spending on programs that pay benefits to suitably qualified people and businesses.

Negative serial correlation   Serial correlation in which a positive error for one observation increases the chance of a negative error for another observation, and vice versa.

Negotiated sales   An underwriting arrangement wherein the sale of a security issue by an issuing entity (governmental body or a corporation) is done using an investment banking firm that maintains an ongoing relationship with the issuer. The characteristics of the security issue are determined by the issuer in consultation with the investment banker.

Net asset balance sheet exposure   When assets translated at the current exchange rate are greater in amount than liabilities translated at the current exchange rate. Assets exposed to translation gains or losses exceed the exposed liabilities.

Net book value   The remaining (undepreciated) balance of an asset's purchase cost. For liabilities, the face value of a bond minus any unamortized discount, or plus any unamortized premium.

Net income (loss)   The difference between revenue and expenses; what remains after subtracting all expenses (including depreciation, interest, and taxes) from revenue.

Net liability balance sheet exposure When liabilities translated at the current exchange rate are greater than assets translated at the current exchange rate. Liabilities exposed to translation gains or losses exceed the exposed assets.

Net operating assets The difference between operating assets (total assets less cash) and operating liabilities (total liabilities less total debt).

Net operating cycle An estimate of the average time that elapses between paying suppliers for materials and collecting cash from the subsequent sale of goods produced.

Net operating profit less adjusted taxes, or NOPLAT A company's operating profit with adjustments to normalize the effects of capital structure.

Net present value (NPV) The present value of an investment's cash inflows (benefits) minus the present value of its cash outflows (costs).

Net profit margin (profit margin or return on sales) An indicator of profitability, calculated as net income divided by revenue; indicates how much of each dollar of revenues is left after all costs and expenses.

Net realizable value Estimated selling price in the ordinary course of business less the estimated costs necessary to make the sale.

Net revenue Revenue after adjustments (e.g., for estimated returns or for amounts unlikely to be collected).

Netting When parties agree to exchange only the net amount owed from one party to the other.

New classical A macroeconomist who holds the view that business cycle fluctuations are the efficient responses of a well-functioning market economy bombarded by shocks that arise from the uneven pace of technological change.

New classical cycle theory A rational expectations theory of the business cycle that regards unexpected fluctuations in aggregate demand as the main source of fluctuations of real GDP around potential GDP.

New issue Common stocks or bonds offered by companies for public sale.

New Keynesian A macroeconomist who holds the view that not only is the money wage rate sticky but also that the prices of goods and services are sticky.

New Keynesian cycle theory A rational expectations theory of the business cycle that regards unexpected and currently expected fluctuations in aggregate demand as the main source of fluctuations of real GDP around potential GDP.

Node Each value on a binomial tree from which successive moves or outcomes branch.

Nominal rate A rate of interest based on the security's face value.

Nominal risk-free interest rate The sum of the real risk-free interest rate and the inflation premium.

Nominal scale A measurement scale that categorizes data but does not rank them.

Nonconventional cash flow In a nonconventional cash flow pattern, the initial outflow is not followed by inflows only, but the cash flows can flip from positive (inflows) to negative (outflows) again (or even change signs several times).

Noncurrent Not due to be consumed, converted into cash, or settled within one year after the balance sheet date.

Noncurrent assets Assets that are expected to benefit the company over an extended period of time (usually more than one year).

Nondeliverable forwards (NDFs) Cash-settled forward contracts, used predominately with respect to foreign exchange forwards.

Nonlinear relation An association or relationship between variables that cannot be graphed as a straight line.

Nonmonetary assets and liabilities Assets and liabilities that are not monetary assets and liabilities. Nonmonetary assets include inventory, fixed assets, and intangibles, and nonmonetary liabilities include deferred revenue.

Nonparametric test A test that is not concerned with a parameter, or that makes minimal assumptions about the population from which a sample comes.

Nonrenewable natural resources Natural resources that can be used only once and that cannot be replaced once they have been used.

Nonstationarity With reference to a random variable, the property of having characteristics such as mean and variance that are not constant through time.

Normal backwardation The condition in futures markets in which futures prices are lower than expected spot prices.

Normal contango The condition in futures markets in which futures prices are higher than expected spot prices.

Normal distribution A continuous, symmetric probability distribution that is completely described by its mean and its variance.

Normal profit The return that an entrepreneur can expect to receive on the average.

Notes payable Amounts owed by a business to creditors as a result of borrowings that are evidenced by (short-term) loan agreements.

***n*-Period moving average** The average of the current and immediately prior *n* − 1 values of a time series.

NPV rule An investment decision rule that states that an investment should be undertaken if its NPV is positive but not undertaken if its NPV is negative.

Null hypothesis The hypothesis to be tested.

Number of days of inventory An activity ratio equal to the number of days in a period divided by the inventory ratio for the period; an indication of the number of days a company ties up funds in inventory.

Number of days of payables An activity ratio equal to the number of days in a period divided by the payables turnover ratio for the period; an estimate of the average number of days it takes a company to pay its suppliers.

Number of days of receivables Estimate of the average number of days it takes to collect on credit accounts.

Objective probabilities Probabilities that generally do not vary from person to person; includes a priori and objective probabilities.

Objectives The investor's goals expressed in terms of risk and return and included in the policy statement.

Off-balance sheet financing Arrangements that do not result in additional liabilities on the balance sheet but nonetheless create economic obligations.

Off-market FRA A contract in which the initial value is intentionally set at a value other than zero and therefore requires a cash payment at the start from one party to the other.

Offsetting A transaction in exchange-listed derivative markets in which a party re-enters the market to close out a position.

Oligopoly A market structure in which a small number of firms compete.

One-sided hypothesis test (or one-tailed hypothesis test) A test in which the null hypothesis is rejected only if the evidence indicates that the population parameter is greater than (smaller than) θ_0. The alternative hypothesis also has one side.

Open market operation The purchase or sale of government securities—U.S. Treasury bills and bonds—by the Federal Reserve in the open market.

Operating activities Activities that are part of the day-to-day business functioning of an entity, such as selling inventory and providing services.

Operating breakeven The number of units produced and sold at which the company's operating profit is zero (revenues = operating costs).

Operating cycle A measure of the time needed to convert raw materials into cash from a sale; it consists of the number of days of inventory and the number of days of receivables.

Operating lease An agreement allowing the lessee to use some asset for a period of time; essentially a rental.

Operating leverage The use of fixed costs in operations.

Operating profit (operating income) A company's profits on its usual business activities before deducting taxes.

Operating profit margin (operating margin) A profitability ratio calculated as operating income (i.e., income before interest and taxes) divided by revenue.

Operating return on assets (operating ROA) A profitability ratio calculated as operating income divided by average total assets.

Operating risk The risk attributed to the operating cost structure, in particular the use of fixed costs in operations; the risk arising from the mix of fixed and variable costs; the risk that a company's operations may be severely affected by environmental, social, and governance risk factors.

Operations risk or operational risk The risk of loss from failures in a company's systems and procedures (for example, due to computer failures or human failures) or events completely outside of the control of organizations (which would include "acts of God" and terrorist actions).

Opportunity cost The value that investors forgo by choosing a particular course of action; the value of something in its best alternative use.

Opportunity set The set of assets available for investment.

Optimal capital structure The capital structure at which the value of the company is maximized.

Optimal portfolio The portfolio on the efficient frontier that has the highest utility for a given investor. It lies at the point of tangency between the efficient frontier and the curve with the investor's highest possible utility.

Optimizer A specialized computer program or a spreadsheet that solves for the portfolio weights that will result in the lowest risk for a specified level of expected return.

Option A financial instrument that gives one party the right, but not the obligation, to buy or sell an underlying asset from or to another party at a fixed price over a specific period of time. Also referred to as contingent claims.

Option price, option premium, or premium The amount of money a buyer pays and seller receives to engage in an option transaction.

Ordinal scale A measurement scale that sorts data into categories that are ordered (ranked) with respect to some characteristic.

Ordinary annuity An annuity with a first cash flow that is paid one period from the present.

Ordinary least squares (OLS) An estimation method based on the criterion of minimizing the sum of the squared residuals of a regression.

Ordinary shares (**common stock or common shares**) Equity shares that are subordinate to all other types of equity (e.g., preferred equity).

Organic growth Company growth in output or sales that is achieved by making investments internally (i.e., excludes growth achieved through mergers and acquisitions).

Orthogonal Uncorrelated; at a right angle.

Other comprehensive income Items of comprehensive income that are not reported on the income statement; comprehensive income minus net income.

Other post-retirement benefits Promises by the company to pay benefits in the future, other than pension benefits, such as life insurance premiums and all or part of health care insurance for its retirees.

Other receivables Amounts owed to the company from parties other than customers.

Outcome A possible value of a random variable.

Outliers Small numbers of observations at either extreme (small or large) of a sample.

Out-of-sample forecast errors The differences between actual and predicted value of time series outside the sample period used to fit the model.

Out-of-sample test A test of a strategy or model using a sample outside the time period on which the strategy or model was developed.

Out-of-the-money Options that, if exercised, would require the payment of more money than the value received and therefore would not be currently exercised.

Output gap Real GDP minus potential GDP.

Overnight index swap (OIS) A swap in which the floating rate is the cumulative value of a single unit of currency invested at an overnight rate during the settlement period.

Overweighted A condition in which a portfolio, for whatever reason, includes more of a class of securities than the relative market value alone would justify.

Owners' equity The excess of assets over liabilities; the residual interest of shareholders in the assets of an entity after deducting the entity's liabilities.

Paired comparisons test A statistical test for differences based on paired observations drawn from samples that are dependent on each other.

Paired observations Observations that are dependent on each other.

Pairs arbitrage trade A trade in two closely related stocks involving the short sale of one and the purchase of the other.

Panel data Observations through time on a single characteristic of multiple observational units.

Parameter A descriptive measure computed from or used to describe a population of data, conventionally represented by Greek letters.

Parameter instability The problem or issue of population regression parameters that have changed over time.

Parametric test Any test (or procedure) concerned with parameters or whose validity depends on assumptions concerning the population generating the sample.

Partial regression coefficients or partial slope coefficients The slope coefficients in a multiple regression.

Partnership A business owned and operated by more than one individual.

Passive strategy In reference to short-term cash management, it is an investment strategy characterized by simple decision rules for making daily investments.

Payables turnover An activity ratio calculated as purchases divided by average trade payables.

Payer swaption A swaption that allows the holder to enter into a swap as the fixed-rate payer and floating-rate receiver.

Payment date The day that the company actually mails out (or electronically transfers) a dividend payment.

Payment netting A means of settling payments in which the amount owed by the first party to the second is netted with the amount owed by the second party to the first; only the net difference is paid.

Payoff The value of an option at expiration.

Payoff matrix A table that shows the payoffs for every possible action by each player for every possible action by each other player.

Payout ratio The percentage of total earnings paid out in dividends in any given year (in per-share terms, DPS/EPS).

Peak The culmination of a bull market when prices stop rising and begin declining.

Pecking order theory   The theory that managers take into account how their actions might be interpreted by outsiders and thus order their preferences for various forms of corporate financing. Forms of financing that are least visible to outsiders (e.g., internally generated funds) are most preferable to managers and those that are most visible (e.g., equity) are least preferable.

Per unit contribution margin   The amount that each unit sold contributes to covering fixed costs—that is, the difference between the price per unit and the variable cost per unit.

Percentage-of-completion   A method of revenue recognition in which, in each accounting period, the company estimates what percentage of the contract is complete and then reports that percentage of the total contract revenue in its income statement.

Percentiles   Quantiles that divide a distribution into 100 equal parts.

Perfect collinearity   The existence of an exact linear relation between two or more independent variables or combinations of independent variables.

Perfect competition   A market in which there are many firms each selling an identical product; there are many buyers; there are no restrictions on entry into the industry; firms in the industry have no advantage over potential new entrants; and firms and buyers are well informed about the price of each firm's product.

Perfect price discrimination   Price discrimination that extracts the entire consumer surplus.

Perfectly elastic demand   Demand with an infinite price elasticity; the quantity demanded changes by an infinitely large percentage in response to a tiny price change.

Perfectly inelastic demand   Demand with a price elasticity of zero; the quantity demanded remains constant when the price changes.

Performance appraisal   The evaluation of risk-adjusted performance; the evaluation of investment skill.

Performance guarantee   A guarantee from the clearinghouse that if one party makes money on a transaction, the clearinghouse ensures it will be paid.

Performance measurement   The calculation of returns in a logical and consistent manner.

Period costs   Costs (e.g., executives' salaries) that cannot be directly matched with the timing of revenues and which are thus expensed immediately.

Periodic rate   The quoted interest rate per period; the stated annual interest rate divided by the number of compounding periods per year.

Permanent differences   Differences between tax and financial reporting of revenue (expenses) that will not be reversed at some future date. These result in a difference between the company's effective tax rate and statutory tax rate and do not result in a deferred tax item.

Permutation   An ordered listing.

Perpetuity   A perpetual annuity, or a set of never-ending level sequential cash flows, with the first cash flow occurring one period from now.

Pet projects   Projects in which influential managers want the corporation to invest. Often, unfortunately, pet projects are selected without undergoing normal capital budgeting analysis.

Phillips curve   A curve that shows a relationship between inflation and unemployment.

Plain vanilla swap   An interest rate swap in which one party pays a fixed rate and the other pays a floating rate, with both sets of payments in the same currency.

Platykurtic   Describes a distribution that is less peaked than the normal distribution.

Point estimate   A single numerical estimate of an unknown quantity, such as a population parameter.

Point of sale   Systems that capture transaction data at the physical location in which the sale is made.

Poison pill   A pre-offer takeover defense mechanism that makes it prohibitively costly for an acquirer to take control of a target without the prior approval of the target's board of directors.

Poison puts   A pre-offer takeover defense mechanism that gives target company bondholders the right to sell their bonds back to the target at a pre-specified redemption price, typically at or above par value; this defense increases the need for cash and raises the cost of the acquisition.

Policy statement   A statement in which the investor specifies investment goals, constraints, and risk preferences.

Pooled estimate   An estimate of a parameter that involves combining (pooling) observations from two or more samples.

Pooling of interests accounting method   A method of accounting in which combined companies were portrayed as if they had always operated as a single economic entity. Called pooling of interests under U.S. GAAP and uniting of interests under IFRS. (No longer allowed under U.S. GAAP or IFRS.)

Population   All members of a specified group.

Population mean   The arithmetic mean value of a population; the arithmetic mean of all the observations or values in the population.

Population standard deviation A measure of dispersion relating to a population in the same unit of measurement as the observations, calculated as the positive square root of the population variance.

Population variance A measure of dispersion relating to a population, calculated as the mean of the squared deviations around the population mean.

Portfolio performance attribution The analysis of portfolio performance in terms of the contributions from various sources of risk.

Portfolio possibilities curve A graphical representation of the expected return and risk of all portfolios that can be formed using two assets.

Position trader A trader who typically holds positions open overnight.

Positive serial correlation Serial correlation in which a positive error for one observation increases the chance of a positive error for another observation, and a negative error for one observation increases the chance of a negative error for another observation.

Posterior probability An updated probability that reflects or comes after new information.

Potential credit risk The risk associated with the possibility that a payment due at a later date will not be made.

Potential GDP The value of production when all the economy's labor, capital, land, and entrepreneurial ability are fully employed; the quantity of real GDP at full employment.

Power of a test The probability of correctly rejecting the null—that is, rejecting the null hypothesis when it is false.

Precautionary stocks A level of inventory beyond anticipated needs that provides a cushion in the event that it takes longer to replenish inventory than expected or in the case of greater than expected demand.

Pre-investing The strategy of using futures contracts to enter the market without an immediate outlay of cash.

Prepaid expense A normal operating expense that has been paid in advance of when it is due.

Present (price) value of a basis point (PVBP) The change in the bond price for a 1 basis point change in yield. Also called *basis point value* (BPV).

Present value (PV) The present discounted value of future cash flows: For assets, the present discounted value of the future net cash inflows that the asset is expected to generate; for liabilities, the present discounted value of the future net cash outflows that are expected to be required to settle the liabilities.

Presentation currency The currency in which financial statement amounts are presented.

Pretax margin A profitability ratio calculated as earnings before taxes divided by revenue.

Price ceiling A regulation that makes it illegal to charge a price higher than a specified level.

Price continuity A feature of a liquid market in which there are small price changes from one transaction to the next due to the depth of the market.

Price discovery A feature of futures markets in which futures prices provide valuable information about the price of the underlying asset.

Price discrimination The practice of selling different units of a good or service for different prices or of charging one customer different prices for different quantities bought.

Price elasticity of demand A units-free measure of the responsiveness of the quantity demanded of a good to a change in its price, when all other influences on buyers' plans remain the same.

Price floor A regulation that makes it illegal to trade at a price lower than a specified level.

Price limits Limits imposed by a futures exchange on the price change that can occur from one day to the next.

Price relative A ratio of an ending price over a beginning price; it is equal to 1 plus the holding period return on the asset.

Price taker A firm that cannot influence the price of the good or service it produces.

Price to book value A valuation ratio calculated as price per share divided by book value per share.

Price to cash flow A valuation ratio calculated as price per share divided by cash flow per share.

Price to sales A valuation ratio calculated as price per share divided by sales per share.

Price/earnings (P/E) ratio The number by which expected earnings per share is multiplied to estimate a stock's value; also called the *earnings multiplier*.

Priced risk Risk for which investors demand compensation for bearing (e.g. equity risk, company-specific factors, macroeconomic factors).

Price-setting option The operational flexibility to adjust prices when demand varies from forecast. For example, when demand exceeds capacity, the company could benefit from the excess demand by increasing prices.

Price-weighted index An index calculated as an arithmetic mean of the current prices of the sampled securities.

Primary market   The market in which newly issued securities are sold by their issuers, who receive the proceeds.

Principal   The amount of funds originally invested in a project or instrument; the face value to be paid at maturity.

Principal–agent problem   The problem of devising compensation rules that induce an *agent* to act in the best interest of a *principal.*

Prior probabilities   Probabilities reflecting beliefs prior to the arrival of new information.

Private placement   A new issue sold directly to a small group of investors, usually institutions.

Probability   A number between 0 and 1 describing the chance that a stated event will occur.

Probability density function   A function with non-negative values such that probability can be described by areas under the curve graphing the function.

Probability distribution   A distribution that specifies the probabilities of a random variable's possible outcomes.

Probability function   A function that specifies the probability that the random variable takes on a specific value.

Probit model   A qualitative-dependent-variable multiple regression model based on the normal distribution.

Producer surplus   The price of a good minus its minimum supply-price, summed over the quantity sold.

Product differentiation   Making a product slightly different from the product of a competing firm.

Production quota   An upper limit to the quantity of a good that may be produced in a specified period.

Production-flexibility   The operational flexibility to alter production when demand varies from forecast. For example, if demand is strong, a company may profit from employees working overtime or from adding additional shifts.

Profitability ratios   Ratios that measure a company's ability to generate profitable sales from its resources (assets).

Project sequencing   To defer the decision to invest in a future project until the outcome of some or all of a current project is known. Projects are sequenced through time, so that investing in a project creates the option to invest in future projects.

Projected benefit obligation   Under U.S. GAAP, a measure used in estimating a defined-benefit pension plan's liabilities, defined as "the actuarial present value as of a date of all benefits attributed by the pension benefit formula to employee ser-

vice rendered prior to that date. The projected benefit obligation is measured using assumptions as to future compensation if the pension benefit formula is based on those future compensation levels."

Proportionate consolidation   A method of accounting for joint ventures where the venturer's share of the assets, liabilities, income and expenses of the joint venture are combined on a line-by-line basis with similar items on the venturer's financial statements.

Protective put   An option strategy in which a long position in an asset is combined with a long position in a put.

Provision   In accounting, a liability of uncertain timing or amount.

Proxy fight   An attempt to take control of a company through a shareholder vote.

Proxy statement   A public document that provides the material facts concerning matters on which shareholders will vote.

Pseudo-random numbers   Numbers produced by random number generators.

Pull on liquidity   When disbursements are paid too quickly or trade credit availability is limited, requiring companies to expend funds before they receive funds from sales that could cover the liability.

Purchase method   A method of accounting for a business combination where the acquiring company allocates the purchase price to each asset acquired and liability assumed at fair value. If the purchase price exceeds the allocation, the excess is recorded as goodwill.

Purchased in-process research and development costs   The costs of research and development in progress at an acquired company.

Purchasing power gain   A gain in value caused by changes in price levels. Monetary liabilities experience purchasing power gains during periods of inflation.

Purchasing power loss   A loss in value caused by changes in price levels. Monetary assets experience purchasing power losses during periods of inflation.

Pure discount instruments   Instruments that pay interest as the difference between the amount borrowed and the amount paid back.

Pure factor portfolio   A portfolio with sensitivity of 1 to the factor in question and a sensitivity of 0 to all other factors.

Pure-play method   A method for estimating the beta for a company or project; it requires using a comparable company's beta and adjusting it for financial leverage differences.

Put   An option that gives the holder the right to sell an underlying asset to another party at a fixed price over a specific period of time.

Put–call parity   An equation expressing the equivalence (parity) of a portfolio of a call and a bond with a portfolio of a put and the underlying, which leads to the relationship between put and call prices

Put–call–forward parity   The relationship among puts, calls, and forward contracts.

p-Value   The smallest level of significance at which the null hypothesis can be rejected; also called the marginal significance level.

Qualifying special purpose entities   Under U.S. GAAP, a special purpose entity structured to avoid consolidation that must meet qualification criteria.

Qualitative dependent variables   Dummy variables used as dependent variables rather than as independent variables.

Quantile (or fractile)   A value at or below which a stated fraction of the data lies.

Quantity theory of money   The proposition that in the long run, an increase in the quantity of money brings an equal percentage increase in the price level.

Quartiles   Quantiles that divide a distribution into four equal parts.

Quick assets   Assets that can be most readily converted to cash (e.g., cash, short-term marketable investments, receivables).

Quick ratio, or acid test ratio   A stringent measure of liquidity that indicates a company's ability to satisfy current liabilities with its most liquid assets, calculated as (cash + short-term marketable investments + receivables) divided by current liabilities.

Quintiles   Quantiles that divide a distribution into five equal parts.

Random number   An observation drawn from a uniform distribution.

Random number generator   An algorithm that produces uniformly distributed random numbers between 0 and 1.

Random variable   A quantity whose future outcomes are uncertain.

Random walk   A time series in which the value of the series in one period is the value of the series in the previous period plus an unpredictable random error.

Range   The difference between the maximum and minimum values in a dataset.

Ratio scales   A measurement scale that has all the characteristics of interval measurement scales as well as a true zero point as the origin.

Ratio spread   An option strategy in which a long position in a certain number of options is offset by a short position in a certain number of other options on the same underlying, resulting in a risk-free position.

Rational expectation   The most accurate forecast possible, a forecast that uses all the available information, including knowledge of the relevant economic forces that influence the variable being forecasted.

Real business cycle theory   A theory of the business cycle that regards random fluctuations in productivity as the main source of economic fluctuations.

Real exchange rate   The relative price of foreign-made goods and services to U.S.-made goods and services.

Real risk-free interest rate   The single-period interest rate for a completely risk-free security if no inflation were expected.

Real wage rate   The quantity of goods and services that an hour's work can buy. It is equal to the money wage rate divided by the price level and multiplied by 100.

Realizable value (settlement value)   With reference to assets, the amount of cash or cash equivalents that could currently be obtained by selling the asset in an orderly disposal; with reference to liabilities, the undiscounted amount of cash or cash equivalents expected to be paid to satisfy the liabilities in the normal course of business.

Realized capital gains   Capital gains that result when an appreciated asset is sold; realized capital gains are taxable.

Receivables turnover   An activity ratio equal to revenue divided by average receivables.

Receiver swaption   A swaption that allows the holder to enter into a swap as the fixed-rate receiver and floating-rate payer.

Recessionary gap   The amount by which potential GDP exceeds real GDP.

Reference base period   The period in which the CPI is defined to be 100.

Regime   With reference to a time series, the underlying model generating the times series.

Registered competitive market makers (RCMMs)   Members of an exchange who are allowed to use their memberships to buy or sell for their own account within the specific trading obligations set down by the exchange.

Registered traders   Members of the stock exchange who are allowed to use their memberships to buy and sell for their own account, which means they save commissions on their trading but they provide liquidity to the market, and they abide by exchange regulations on how they can trade.

Regression coefficients The intercept and slope coefficient(s) of a regression.

Regulatory risk The risk associated with the uncertainty of how derivative transactions will be regulated or with changes in regulations.

Rejection point (or critical value) A value against which a computed test statistic is compared to decide whether to reject or not reject the null hypothesis.

Relative dispersion The amount of dispersion relative to a reference value or benchmark.

Relative frequency With reference to an interval of grouped data, the number of observations in the interval divided by the total number of observations in the sample.

Relative-strength (RS) ratio The ratio of a stock price or an industry index value to a market indicator series, indicating the stock's or the industry's performance relative to the overall market.

Renewable natural resources Natural resources that can be used repeatedly without depleting what is available for future use.

Rent ceiling A regulation that makes it illegal to charge a rent higher than a specified level.

Rent seeking The pursuit of wealth by capturing economic rent—consumer surplus, producer surplus, or economic profit.

Reorganization Agreements made by a company in bankruptcy under which a company's capital structure is altered and/or alternative arrangements are made for debt repayment; U.S. Chapter 11 bankruptcy. The company emerges from bankruptcy as a going concern.

Replacement value The market value of a swap.

Report format With respect to the format of a balance sheet, a format in which assets, liabilities, and equity are listed in a single column.

Reputational risk The risk that a company will suffer an extended diminution in market value relative to other companies in the same industry due to a demonstrated lack of concern for environmental, social, and governance risk factors.

Required reserve ratio The minimum percentage of deposits that banks are required to hold as reserves.

Reserve ratio The fraction of a bank's total deposits that are held in reserves.

Reserves A bank's reserves consist of notes and coins in its vaults plus its deposit at the Federal Reserve.

Residual autocorrelations The sample autocorrelations of the residuals.

Residual claim The owners' remaining claim on the company's assets after the liabilities are deducted.

Residual dividend approach A dividend payout policy under which earnings in excess of the funds necessary to finance the equity portion of company's capital budget are paid out in dividends.

Residual loss Agency costs that are incurred despite adequate monitoring and bonding of management.

Resistance level A price at which a technician would expect a substantial increase in the supply of a stock to reverse a rising trend.

Retail method An inventory accounting method in which the sales value of an item is reduced by the gross margin to calculate the item's cost.

Return on assets (ROA) A profitability ratio calculated as net income divided by average total assets; indicates a company's net profit generated per dollar invested in total assets.

Return on common equity (ROCE) A profitability ratio calculated as (net income – preferred dividends) divided by average common equity; equal to the return on equity ratio when no preferred equity is outstanding.

Return on equity (ROE) A profitability ratio calculated as net income divided by average shareholders' equity.

Return on total capital A profitability ratio calculated as EBIT divided by the sum of short- and long-term debt and equity.

Return prediction studies Studies wherein investigations attempt to predict the time series of future rates of return using public information. An example would be predicting above-average returns for the stock market based on the aggregate dividend yield—e.g., high dividend yield indicates above average future market returns.

Revaluation The process of valuing long-lived assets at fair value, rather than at cost less accumulated depreciation. Any resulting profit or loss is either reported on the income statement and/or through equity under revaluation surplus.

Revenue The amount charged for the delivery of goods or services in the ordinary activities of a business over a stated period; the inflows of economic resources to a company over a stated period.

Reverse stock split A reduction in the number of shares outstanding with a corresponding increase in share price, but no change to the company's underlying fundamentals.

Revolving credit agreements   The strongest form of short-term bank borrowing facilities; they are in effect for multiple years (e.g., 3–5 years) and may have optional medium-term loan features.

Rho   The sensitivity of the option price to the risk-free rate.

Ricardo-Barro equivalence   The proposition that taxes and government borrowing are equivalent—a budget deficit has no effect on the real interest rate or investment.

Rising trend channel   The range defined by security prices as they move progressively higher.

Risk averse   The assumption about investors that they will choose the least risky alternative, all else being equal.

Risk budgeting   The establishment of objectives for individuals, groups, or divisions of an organization that takes into account the allocation of an acceptable level of risk.

Risk governance   The setting of overall policies and standards in risk management

Risk management   The process of identifying the level of risk an entity wants, measuring the level of risk the entity currently has, taking actions that bring the actual level of risk to the desired level of risk, and monitoring the new actual level of risk so that it continues to be aligned with the desired level of risk.

Risk premium   The expected return on an investment minus the risk-free rate.

Risk-free asset   An asset with returns that exhibit zero variance.

Risk-neutral probabilities   Weights that are used to compute a binomial option price. They are the probabilities that would apply if a risk-neutral investor valued an option.

Risk-neutral valuation   The process by which options and other derivatives are priced by treating investors as though they were risk neutral.

Risky asset   An asset with uncertain future returns.

Robust   The quality of being relatively unaffected by a violation of assumptions.

Robust standard errors   Standard errors of the estimated parameters of a regression that correct for the presence of heteroskedasticity in the regression's error term.

Root mean squared error (RMSE)   The square root of the average squared forecast error; used to compare the out-of-sample forecasting performance of forecasting models.

Roy's safety first criterion   A criterion asserting that the optimal portfolio is the one that minimizes the probability that portfolio return falls below a threshold level.

Rule of 72   The principle that the approximate number of years necessary for an investment to double is 72 divided by the stated interest rate.

Runs test   A test of the weak-form efficient market hypothesis that checks for trends that persist longer in terms of positive or negative price changes than one would expect for a random series.

Safety stock   A level of inventory beyond anticipated needs that provides a cushion in the event that it takes longer to replenish inventory than expected or in the case of greater than expected demand.

Safety-first rules   Rules for portfolio selection that focus on the risk that portfolio value will fall below some minimum acceptable level over some time horizon.

Sales   Generally, a synonym for revenue; "sales" is generally understood to refer to the sale of goods, whereas "revenue" is understood to include the sale of goods or services.

Sales returns and allowances   An offset to revenue reflecting any cash refunds, credits on account, and discounts from sales prices given to customers who purchased defective or unsatisfactory items.

Sales risk   Uncertainty with respect to the quantity of goods and services that a company is able to sell and the price it is able to achieve; the risk related to the uncertainty of revenues.

Sales-type lease   A type of finance lease, from a lessor perspective, where the present value of the lease payments (lease receivable) exceeds the carrying value of the leased asset. The revenues earned by the lessor are operating (the profit on the sale) and financing (interest) in nature.

Salvage value   The amount the company estimates that it can sell the asset for at the end of its useful life.

Sample   A subset of a population.

Sample excess kurtosis   A sample measure of the degree of a distribution's peakedness in excess of the normal distribution's peakedness.

Sample kurtosis   A sample measure of the degree of a distribution's peakedness.

Sample mean   The sum of the sample observations, divided by the sample size.

Sample selection bias   Bias introduced by systematically excluding some members of the population according to a particular attribute—for example, the bias introduced when data availability leads to certain observations being excluded from the analysis.

Sample skewness   A sample measure of degree of asymmetry of a distribution.

Sample standard deviation The positive square root of the sample variance.

Sample statistic or statistic A quantity computed from or used to describe a sample.

Sample variance A sample measure of the degree of dispersion of a distribution, calculated by dividing the sum of the squared deviations from the sample mean by the sample size (n) minus 1.

Sampling The process of obtaining a sample.

Sampling distribution The distribution of all distinct possible values that a statistic can assume when computed from samples of the same size randomly drawn from the same population.

Sampling error The difference between the observed value of a statistic and the quantity it is intended to estimate.

Sampling plan The set of rules used to select a sample.

Sandwich spread An option strategy that is equivalent to a short butterfly spread.

Sarbanes–Oxley Act An act passed by the U.S. Congress in 2002 that created the Public Company Accounting Oversight Board (PCAOB) to oversee auditors.

Scalper A trader who offers to buy or sell futures contracts, holding the position for only a brief period of time. Scalpers attempt to profit by buying at the bid price and selling at the higher ask price.

Scatter plot A two-dimensional plot of pairs of observations on two data series.

Scenario analysis Analysis that shows the changes in key financial quantities that result from given (economic) events, such as the loss of customers, the loss of a supply source, or a catastrophic event; a risk management technique involving examination of the performance of a portfolio under specified situations. Closely related to stress testing.

Screening The application of a set of criteria to reduce a set of potential investments to a smaller set having certain desired characteristics.

Search activity The time spent looking for someone with whom to do business.

Seasoned equity issues New equity shares offered by firms that already have stock outstanding.

Seats Memberships in a derivatives exchange.

Secondary market The market in which outstanding securities are bought and sold by owners other than the issuers. Purpose is to provide liquidity for investors.

Sector neutralizing Measure of financial reporting quality by subtracting the mean or median ratio for a given sector group from a given company's ratio.

Securities Act of 1933 An act passed by the U.S. Congress in 1933 that specifies the financial and other significant information that investors must receive when securities are sold, prohibits misrepresentations, and requires initial registration of all public issuances of securities.

Securities Exchange Act of 1934 An act passed by the U.S. Congress in 1934 that created the Securities and Exchange Commission (SEC), gave the SEC authority over all aspects of the securities industry, and empowered the SEC to require periodic reporting by companies with publicly traded securities.

Securities offering A merger or acquisition in which target shareholders are to receive shares of the acquirer's common stock as compensation.

Security market index An index created as a statistical measure of the performance of an entire market or segment of a market based on a sample of securities from the market or segment of a market.

Security market line (SML) The graph of the capital asset pricing model.

Segment debt ratio Segment liabilities divided by segment assets.

Segment margin Segment profit (loss) divided by segment revenue.

Segment ROA Segment profit (loss) divided by segment assets.

Segment turnover Segment revenue divided by segment assets.

Semideviation The positive square root of semivariance (sometimes called semistandard deviation).

Semilogarithmic Describes a scale constructed so that equal intervals on the vertical scale represent equal rates of change, and equal intervals on the horizontal scale represent equal amounts of change.

Semistrong-form efficient market hypothesis The belief that security prices fully reflect all publicly available information, including information from security transactions and company, economic, and political news.

Semivariance The average squared deviation below the mean.

Sensitivity analysis Analysis that shows the range of possible outcomes as specific assumptions are changed.

Separation theorem The proposition that the investment decision, which involves investing in the market portfolio on the capital market line, is separate from the financing decision, which targets a specific point on the CML based on the investor's risk preference.

Serially correlated   With reference to regression errors, errors that are correlated across observations.

Service period   The period benefited by the employee's service, usually the period between the grant date and the vesting date.

Settlement date or payment date   The date on which the parties to a swap make payments.

Settlement period   The time between settlement dates.

Settlement price   The official price, designated by the clearinghouse, from which daily gains and losses will be determined and marked to market.

Settlement risk   When settling a contract, the risk that one party could be in the process of paying the counterparty while the counterparty is declaring bankruptcy.

Share repurchase   A transaction in which a company buys back its own shares. Unlike stock dividends and stock splits, share repurchases use corporate cash.

Shark repellents   A pre-offer takeover defense mechanism involving the corporate charter (e.g., staggered boards of directors and supermajority provisions).

Sharpe ratio   The average return in excess of the risk-free rate divided by the standard deviation of return; a measure of the average excess return earned per unit of standard deviation of return.

Short   The seller of a derivative contract. Also refers to the position of being short a derivative.

Short run   The period of time in which the quantity of at least one factor of production is fixed and the quantities of the other factors can be varied. The fixed factor is usually capital—that is, the firm has a given plant size.

Shortfall risk   The risk that portfolio value will fall below some minimum acceptable level over some time horizon.

Short-run aggregate supply   The relationship between the quantity of real GDP supplied and the price level when the money wage rate, the prices of other resources, and potential GDP remain constant.

Short-run industry supply curve   A curve that shows the quantity supplied by the industry at each price when the plant size of each firm and the number of firms in the industry remain the same.

Short-run macroeconomic equilibrium   A situation that occurs when the quantity of real GDP demanded equals the quantity of real GDP supplied—at the point of intersection of the *AD* curve and the *SAS* curve.

Short-run Phillips curve   A curve that shows the tradeoff between inflation and unemployment, when the expected inflation rate and the natural unemployment rate remain the same.

Short sale   The sale of borrowed securities with the intention of repurchasing them later at a lower price and earning the difference.

Shutdown point   The output and price at which the firm just covers its total variable cost. In the short run, the firm is indifferent between producing the profit-maximizing output and shutting down temporarily.

Signal   An action taken by an informed person (or firm) to send a message to uninformed people or an action taken outside a market that conveys information that can be used by the market.

Simple interest   The interest earned each period on the original investment; interest calculated on the principal only.

Simple random sample   A subset of a larger population created in such a way that each element of the population has an equal probability of being selected to the subset.

Simple random sampling   The procedure of drawing a sample to satisfy the definition of a simple random sample.

Simulation   Computer-generated sensitivity or scenario analysis that is based on probability models for the factors that drive outcomes.

Simulation trial   A complete pass through the steps of a simulation.

Single-payment loan   A loan in which the borrower receives a sum of money at the start and pays back the entire amount with interest in a single payment at maturity.

Single-price monopoly   A monopoly that must sell each unit of its output for the same price to all its customers.

Single-step format   With respect to the format of the income statement, a format that does not subtotal for gross profit (revenue minus cost of goods sold).

Skewed   Not symmetrical.

Skewness   A quantitative measure of skew (lack of symmetry); a synonym of skew.

Sole proprietorship   A business owned and operated by a single person.

Solvency   With respect to financial statement analysis, the ability of a company to fulfill its long-term obligations.

Solvency ratios   Ratios that measure a company's ability to meet its long-term obligations.

Sovereign yield spread   An estimate of the country spread (country equity premium) for a developing nation that is based on a comparison of bonds yields in country being analyzed and a developed country. The sovereign yield spread is the difference between a government bond yield in the country being analyzed, denominated in the currency of the developed country, and the Treasury bond yield on a similar maturity bond in the developed country.

Spearman rank correlation coefficient A measure of correlation applied to ranked data.

Special purpose entity (special purpose vehicle or variable interest entity) A non-operating entity created to carry out a specified purpose, such as leasing assets or securitizing receivables; can be a corporation, partnership, trust, limited liability, or partnership formed to facilitate a specific type of business activity.

Specialist The major market maker on U.S. stock exchanges who acts as a broker or dealer to ensure the liquidity and smooth functions of the secondary stock market.

Specific identification method An inventory accounting method that identifies which specific inventory items were sold and which remained in inventory to be carried over to later periods.

Speculative company A firm with a great degree of business and/or financial risk, with commensurate high earnings potential.

Speculative stock A stock that appears to be highly overpriced compared to its intrinsic valuation.

Spending phase Phase in the investment life cycle during which individuals' earning years end as they retire. They pay for expenses with income from social security and returns from prior investments and invest to protect against inflation.

Spin-off A form of restructuring in which shareholders of the parent company receive a proportional number of shares in a new, separate entity; shareholders end up owning stock in two different companies where there used to be one.

Split-off A form of restructuring in which shareholders of the parent company are given shares in a newly created entity in exchange for their shares of the parent company.

Split-rate In reference to corporate taxes, a split-rate system taxes earnings to be distributed as dividends at a different rate than earnings to be retained. Corporate profits distributed as dividends are taxed at a lower rate than those retained in the business.

Spread An option strategy involving the purchase of one option and sale of another option that is identical to the first in all respects except either exercise price or expiration.

Spurious correlation A correlation that misleadingly points towards associations between variables.

Stagflation The combination of inflation and recession.

Standard cost With respect to inventory accounting, the planned or target unit cost of inventory items or services.

Standard deviation The positive square root of the variance; a measure of dispersion in the same units as the original data.

Standard normal distribution (or unit normal distribution) The normal density with mean (μ) equal to 0 and standard deviation (σ) equal to 1.

Standardized beta With reference to fundamental factor models, the value of the attribute for an asset minus the average value of the attribute across all stocks, divided by the standard deviation of the attribute across all stocks.

Standardizing A transformation that involves subtracting the mean and dividing the result by the standard deviation.

Stated annual interest rate or quoted interest rate A quoted interest rate that does not account for compounding within the year.

Stated rate (nominal rate or coupon rate) The rate at which periodic interest payments are calculated.

Statement of cash flows (cash flow statement) A financial statement that reconciles beginning-of-period and end-of-period balance sheet values of cash; provides information about an entity's cash inflows and cash outflows as they pertain to operating, investing, and financing activities.

Statement of changes in shareholders' equity (statement of owners' equity) A financial statement that reconciles the beginning-of-period and end-of-period balance sheet values of shareholders' equity; provides information about all factors affecting shareholders' equity.

Statement of retained earnings A financial statement that reconciles beginning-of-period and end-of-period balance sheet values of retained income; shows the linkage between the balance sheet and income statement.

Static trade-off theory of capital structure A theory pertaining to a company's optimal capital structure; the optimal level of debt is found at the point where additional debt would cause the costs of financial distress to increase by a greater amount than the benefit of the additional tax shield.

Statistic A quantity computed from or used to describe a sample of data.

Statistical factor models A multifactor model in which statistical methods are applied to a set of historical returns to determine portfolios that best explain either historical return covariances or variances.

Statistical inference   Making forecasts, estimates, or judgments about a larger group from a smaller group actually observed; using a sample statistic to infer the value of an unknown population parameter.

Statistically significant   A result indicating that the null hypothesis can be rejected; with reference to an estimated regression coefficient, frequently understood to mean a result indicating that the corresponding population regression coefficient is different from 0.

Statistics   The science of describing, analyzing, and drawing conclusions from data; also, a collection of numerical data.

Statutory merger   A merger in which one company ceases to exist as an identifiable entity and all its assets and liabilities become part of a purchasing company.

Stock grants   The granting of stock to employees as a form of compensation.

Stock options (stock option grants)   The granting of stock options to employees as a form of compensation.

Stock purchase   An acquisition in which the acquirer gives the target company's shareholders some combination of cash and securities in exchange for shares of the target company's stock.

Stock-out losses   Profits lost from not having sufficient inventory on hand to satisfy demand.

Storage costs or carrying costs   The costs of holding an asset, generally a function of the physical characteristics of the underlying asset.

Straddle   An option strategy involving the purchase of a put and a call with the same exercise price. A straddle is based on the expectation of high volatility of the underlying.

Straight-line method   A depreciation method that allocates evenly the cost of a long-lived asset less its estimated residual value over the estimated useful life of the asset.

Strangle   A variation of a straddle in which the put and call have different exercise prices.

Strap   An option strategy involving the purchase of two calls and one put.

Strategies   All the possible actions of each player in a game.

Stratified random sampling   A procedure by which a population is divided into subpopulations (strata) based on one or more classification criteria. Simple random samples are then drawn from each stratum in sizes proportional to the relative size of

each stratum in the population. These samples are then pooled.

Stress testing   A set of techniques for estimating losses in extremely unfavorable combinations of events or scenarios.

Strip   An option strategy involving the purchase of two puts and one call.

Strong-form efficient market hypothesis   The belief that security prices fully reflect all information from both public and private sources.

Structural change   Economic trend occurring when the economy is undergoing a major change in organization or in how it functions.

Structural surplus or deficit   The budget balance that would occur if the economy were at full employment and real GDP were equal to potential GDP.

Structural unemployment   The unemployment that arises when changes in technology or international competition change the skills needed to perform jobs or change the locations of jobs.

Structured note   A variation of a floating-rate note that has some type of unusual characteristic such as a leverage factor or in which the rate moves opposite to interest rates.

Subjective probability   A probability drawing on personal or subjective judgment.

Subsidiary merger   A merger in which the company being purchased becomes a subsidiary of the purchaser.

Subsidy   A payment made by the government to a producer.

Sunk cost   A cost that has already been incurred.

Supply-side effects   The effects of fiscal policy on employment, potential GDP, and aggregate supply.

Support level   A price at which a technician would expect a substantial increase in price and volume for a stock to reverse a declining trend that was due to profit taking.

Surprise   The actual value of a variable minus its predicted (or expected) value.

Survey approach   An estimate of the equity risk premium that is based upon estimates provided by a panel of finance experts.

Survivorship bias   The bias resulting from a test design that fails to account for companies that have gone bankrupt, merged, or are otherwise no longer reported in a database.

Sustainable growth rate   The rate of dividend (and earnings) growth that can be sustained over time for a given level of return on equity, keeping the capital structure constant and without issuing additional common stock.

Swap An agreement between two parties to exchange a series of future cash flows.

Swap spread The difference between the fixed rate on an interest rate swap and the rate on a Treasury note with equivalent maturity; it reflects the general level of credit risk in the market.

Swaption An option to enter into a swap.

Symmetry principle A requirement that people in similar situations be treated similarly.

Synthetic call The combination of puts, the underlying, and risk-free bonds that replicates a call option.

Synthetic forward contract The combination of the underlying, puts, calls, and risk-free bonds that replicates a forward contract.

Synthetic index fund An index fund position created by combining risk-free bonds and futures on the desired index.

Synthetic put The combination of calls, the underlying, and risk-free bonds that replicates a put option.

Systematic factors Factors that affect the average returns of a large number of different assets.

Systematic risk The variability of returns that is due to macroeconomic factors that affect all risky assets. Because it affects all risky assets, it cannot be eliminated by diversification.

Systematic sampling A procedure of selecting every kth member until reaching a sample of the desired size. The sample that results from this procedure should be approximately random.

Takeover A merger; the term may be applied to any transaction, but is often used in reference to hostile transactions.

Takeover premium The amount by which the takeover price for each share of stock must exceed the current stock price in order to entice shareholders to relinquish control of the company to an acquirer.

Tangible assets Long-term assets with physical substance that are used in company operations, such as land (property), plant, and equipment.

Target balance A minimum level of cash to be held available—estimated in advance and adjusted for known funds transfers, seasonality, or other factors.

Target capital structure A company's chosen proportions of debt and equity.

Target company, or target The company in a merger or acquisition that is being acquired.

Target payout ratio A strategic corporate goal representing the long-term proportion of earnings that the company intends to distribute to shareholders as dividends.

Target semideviation The positive square root of target semivariance.

Target semivariance The average squared deviation below a target value.

Targeting rule A decision rule for monetary policy that sets the policy instrument at a level that makes the forecast of the ultimate policy target equal to the target.

Tax base (tax basis) The amount at which an asset or liability is valued for tax purposes.

Tax expense An aggregate of an entity's income tax payable (or recoverable in the case of a tax benefit) and any changes in deferred tax assets and liabilities. It is essentially the income tax payable or recoverable if these had been determined based on accounting profit rather than taxable income.

Tax incidence The division of the burden of the tax between the buyer and the seller.

Tax loss carry forward A taxable loss in the current period that may be used to reduce future taxable income.

Tax risk The uncertainty associated with tax laws.

Tax wedge The gap between the before-tax and after-tax wage rates.

Taxable income The portion of an entity's income that is subject to income taxes under the tax laws of its jurisdiction.

Taxable temporary differences Temporary differences that result in a taxable amount in a future period when determining the taxable profit as the balance sheet item is recovered or settled.

Taylor rule A rule that sets the federal funds rate at the equilibrium real interest rate (which Taylor says is 2 percent a year) plus amounts based on the inflation rate and the output gap.

t-Distribution A symmetrical distribution defined by a single parameter, degrees of freedom, that is largely used to make inferences concerning the mean of a normal distribution whose variance is unknown.

Technical analysis Estimation of future security price movements based on past price and volume movements.

Technological efficiency A situation that occurs when the firm produces a given output by using the least amount of inputs.

Technology Any method of producing a good or service.

Temporal method A variation of the monetary/nonmonetary translation method that requires not only monetary assets and liabilities, but also nonmonetary assets and liabilities that are measured at their current value on the balance sheet date to be translated at the current exchange rate. Assets and liabilities are translated at rates consistent with the timing of their measurement value. This method is typically used when the functional currency is other than the local currency.

Tender offer   A public offer whereby the acquirer invites target shareholders to submit ("tender") their shares in return for the proposed payment.

Tenor   The original time to maturity on a swap.

Termination date   The date of the final payment on a swap; also, the swap's expiration date.

Test statistic   A quantity, calculated based on a sample, whose value is the basis for deciding whether or not to reject the null hypothesis.

Theta   The rate at which an option's time value decays.

Third market   Over-the-counter trading of securities listed on an exchange.

Time series   A set of observations on a variable's outcomes in different time periods.

Time to expiration   The time remaining in the life of a derivative, typically expressed in years.

Time value or speculative value   The difference between the market price of the option and its intrinsic value, determined by the uncertainty of the underlying over the remaining life of the option.

Time value decay   The loss in the value of an option resulting from movement of the option price toward its payoff value as the expiration day approaches.

Time value of money   The principles governing equivalence relationships between cash flows with different dates.

Time-period bias   The possibility that when we use a time-series sample, our statistical conclusion may be sensitive to the starting and ending dates of the sample.

Time-series analysis   An examination of a firm's performance data over a period of time.

Time-series data   Observations of a variable over time.

Time-weighted rate of return   The compound rate of growth of one unit of currency invested in a portfolio during a stated measurement period; a measure of investment performance that is not sensitive to the timing and amount of withdrawals or additions to the portfolio.

Top-down analysis   With reference to investment selection processes, an approach that starts with macro selection (i.e., identifying attractive geographic segments and/or industry segments) and then addresses selection of the most attractive investments within those segments.

Total asset turnover   An activity ratio calculated as revenue divided by average total assets.

Total cost   The cost of all the productive resources that a firm uses.

Total fixed cost   The cost of the firm's fixed inputs.

Total invested capital   The sum of market value of common equity, book value of preferred equity, and face value of debt.

Total probability rule   A rule explaining the unconditional probability of an event in terms of probabilities of the event conditional on mutually exclusive and exhaustive scenarios.

Total probability rule for expected value   A rule explaining the expected value of a random variable in terms of expected values of the random variable conditional on mutually exclusive and exhaustive scenarios.

Total product   The total output produced by a firm in a given period of time.

Total return   A return objective in which the investor wants to increase the portfolio value to meet a future need by both capital gains and current income reinvestment.

Total return swap   A swap in which one party agrees to pay the total return on a security. Often used as a credit derivative, in which the underlying is a bond.

Total revenue   The value of a firm's sales. It is calculated as the price of the good multiplied by the quantity sold.

Total revenue test   A method of estimating the price elasticity of demand by observing the change in total revenue that results from a change in the price, when all other influences on the quantity sold remain the same.

Total variable cost   The cost of all the firm's variable inputs.

Tracking error   The standard deviation of the difference in returns between an active investment portfolio and its benchmark portfolio; also called tracking error volatility, tracking risk, and active risk.

Tracking portfolio   A portfolio having factor sensitivities that are matched to those of a benchmark or other portfolio.

Tracking risk   The standard deviation of the differences between a portfolio's returns and its benchmark's returns; a synonym of active risk.

Trade credit   A spontaneous form of credit in which a purchaser of the goods or service is financing its purchase by delaying the date on which payment is made.

Trade receivables (commercial receivables or accounts receivable)   Amounts customers owe the company for products that have been sold as well as amounts that may be due from suppliers (such as for returns of merchandise).

Trading securities (held-for-trading securities) Securities held by a company with the intent to trade them.

Transaction cost The cost of executing a trade. Low costs characterize an operationally efficient market.

Transaction exposure The risk of a change in value between the transaction date and the settlement date of an asset or liability denominated in a foreign currency.

Transactions motive In the context of inventory management, the need for inventory as part of the routine production–sales cycle.

Translation exposure The risk associated with the conversion of foreign financial statements into domestic currency.

Treasury bill A negotiable U.S. government security with a maturity of less than one year that pays no periodic interest but yields the difference between its par value and its discounted purchase price.

Treasury bond A U.S. government security with a maturity of more than 10 years that pays interest periodically.

Treasury note A U.S. government security with maturities of 1 to 10 years that pays interest periodically.

Treasury shares Shares that were issued and subsequently repurchased by the company.

Treasury stock method A method for accounting for the effect of options (and warrants) on earnings per share (EPS) that specifies what EPS would have been if the options and warrants had been exercised and the company had used the proceeds to repurchase common stock.

Tree diagram A diagram with branches emanating from nodes representing either mutually exclusive chance events or mutually exclusive decisions.

Trend A long-term pattern of movement in a particular direction.

Trimmed mean A mean computed after excluding a stated small percentage of the lowest and highest observations.

Trough The culmination of a bear market at which prices stop declining and begin rising.

Trust receipt arrangement The use of inventory as collateral for a loan. The inventory is segregated and held in trust, and the proceeds of any sale must be remitted to the lender immediately.

_t_-Test A hypothesis test using a statistic (_t_-statistic) that follows a _t_-distribution.

Two-sided hypothesis test (or two-tailed hypothesis test) A test in which the null hypothesis is rejected in favor of the alternative hypothesis if the evidence indicates that the population parameter is either smaller or larger than a hypothesized value.

Type I error The error of rejecting a true null hypothesis.

Type II error The error of not rejecting a false null hypothesis.

Unbiasedness Lack of bias. A desirable property of estimators, an unbiased estimator is one whose expected value (the mean of its sampling distribution) equals the parameter it is intended to estimate.

Unbilled revenue (accrued revenue) Revenue that has been earned but not yet billed to customers as of the end of an accounting period.

Unclassified balance sheet A balance sheet that does not show subtotals for current assets and current liabilities.

Unconditional heteroskedasticity Heteroskedasticity of the error term that is not correlated with the values of the independent variable(s) in the regression.

Unconditional probability (or marginal probability) The probability of an event _not_ conditioned on another event.

Underlying An asset that trades in a market in which buyers and sellers meet, decide on a price, and the seller then delivers the asset to the buyer and receives payment. The underlying is the asset or other derivative on which a particular derivative is based. The market for the underlying is also referred to as the spot market.

Underweighted A condition in which a portfolio, for whatever reason, includes less of a class of securities than the relative market value alone would justify.

Unearned fees Unearned fees are recognized when a company receives cash payment for fees prior to earning them.

Unearned revenue (deferred revenue) A liability account for money that has been collected for goods or services that have not yet been delivered; payment received in advance of providing a good or service.

Unemployment rate The number of unemployed people expressed as a percentage of all the people who have jobs or are looking for one. It is the percentage of the labor force who are unemployed.

Unidentifiable intangible An intangible that cannot be acquired singly and that typically possesses an indefinite benefit period; an example is accounting goodwill.

Unit elastic demand   Demand with a price elasticity of 1; the percentage change in the quantity demanded equals the percentage change in price.

Unit root   A time series that is not covariance stationary is said to have a unit root.

Uniting of interests method   A method of accounting in which combined companies were portrayed as if they had always operated as a single economic entity. Called pooling of interests under U.S. GAAP and uniting of interests under IFRS. (No longer allowed under U.S. GAAP or IFRS.)

Units-of-production method   A depreciation method that allocates the cost of a long-lived asset based on actual usage during the period.

Univariate distribution   A distribution that specifies the probabilities for a single random variable.

Unlimited funds   An unlimited funds environment assumes that the company can raise the funds it wants for all profitable projects simply by paying the required rate of return.

Unrealized capital gains   Capital gains that reflect the price appreciation of currently held unsold assets.

Unsystematic risk   Risk that is unique to an asset, derived from its particular characteristics. It can be eliminated in a diversified portfolio.

Unweighted index   An indicator series affected equally by the performance of each security in the sample regardless of price or market value. Also referred to as an *equal-weighted series*.

Up transition probability   The probability that an asset's value moves up.

Upstream   A transaction between two affiliates, an investor company and an associate company such that the associate company records a profit on its income statement. An example is a sale of inventory by the associate to the investor company.

Utilitarianism   A principle that states that we should strive to achieve "the greatest happiness for the greatest number of people."

Valuation   The process of determining the value of an asset or service.

Valuation allowance   A reserve created against deferred tax assets, based on the likelihood of realizing the deferred tax assets in future accounting periods.

Valuation process   Part of the investment decision process in which you estimate the value of a security.

Valuation ratios   Ratios that measure the quantity of an asset or flow (e.g., earnings) in relation to the

price associated with a specified claim (e.g., a share or ownership of the enterprise).

Value   The amount for which one can sell something, or the amount one must pay to acquire something.

Value at risk (VAR)   A money measure of the minimum value of losses expected during a specified time period at a given level of probability.

Value investors   With reference to equity investors, investors who are focused on paying a relatively low share price in relation to earnings or assets per share.

Value stocks   Stocks that appear to be undervalued for reasons besides earnings growth potential. These stocks are usually identified based on high dividend yields, low *P/E* ratios, or low price-to-book ratios.

Value-weighted index   An index calculated as the total market value of the securities in the sample. Market value is equal to the number of shares or bonds outstanding times the market price of the security.

Variable costs   Costs that fluctuate with the level of production and sales.

Variance   The expected value (the probability-weighted average) of squared deviations from a random variable's expected value.

Variation margin   Additional margin that must be deposited in an amount sufficient to bring the balance up to the initial margin requirement.

Vega   The relationship between option price and volatility.

Velocity of circulation   The average number of times a dollar of money is used annually to buy the goods and services that make up GDP.

Venturers   The owners of a joint venture. Each is active in the management and shares control of the joint venture.

Vertical analysis   Common-size analysis using only one reporting period or one base financial statement; for example, an income statement in which all items are stated as percentages of sales.

Vertical common-size analysis   The most common type of common-size analysis, in which the accounts in a given period are compared to a benchmark item in that same year.

Vertical merger   A merger involving companies at different positions of the same production chain; for example, a supplier or a distributor.

Vested benefit obligation   Under U.S. GAAP, a measure used in estimating a defined-benefit pension plan's liabilities, defined as the "actuarial present value of vested benefits."

Vested benefits   Future benefits promised to the employee regardless of continuing service. Benefits typically vest after a specified period of service or a specified period of service combined with age.

Vesting date The date that employees can first exercise stock options; vesting can be immediate or over a future period.

Volatility As used in option pricing, the standard deviation of the continuously compounded returns on the underlying asset.

Warehouse receipt arrangement The use of inventory as collateral for a loan; similar to a trust receipt arrangement except there is a third party (i.e., a warehouse company) that supervises the inventory.

Weak-form efficient market hypothesis The belief that security prices fully reflect all security market information.

Weighted average cost method An inventory accounting method that averages the total cost of available inventory items over the total units available for sale.

Weighted mean An average in which each observation is weighted by an index of its relative importance.

Weighted-average cost of capital A weighted average of the after-tax required rates of return on a company's common stock, preferred stock, and long-term debt, where the weights are the fraction of each source of financing in the company's target capital structure.

White knight A third party that is sought out by the target company's board to purchase the target in lieu of a hostile bidder.

White squire A third party that is sought out by the target company's board to purchase a substantial minority stake in the target—enough to block a hostile takeover without selling the entire company.

White-corrected standard errors A synonym for robust standard errors.

Winner's curse The tendency for the winner in certain competitive bidding situations to overpay, whether because of overestimation of intrinsic value, emotion, or information asymmetries.

Winsorized mean A mean computed after assigning a stated percent of the lowest values equal to one specified low value, and a stated percent of the highest values equal to one specified high value.

Working capital The difference between current assets and current liabilities.

Working capital management The management of a company's short-term assets (such as inventory) and short-term liabilities (such as money owed to suppliers).

Working capital turnover A comparison of revenues with working capital to produce a measure that shows how efficiently working capital is employed.

Working-age population The total number of people aged 15 years and over.

Yield The actual return on a debt security if it is held to maturity.

Yield beta A measure of the sensitivity of a bond's yield to a general measure of bond yields in the market that is used to refine the hedge ratio.

Yield spread The difference between the yield on a bond and the yield on a default-free security, usually a government note, of the same maturity. The yield spread is primarily determined by the market's perception of the credit risk on the bond.

Yield to maturity The annual return that an investor earns on a bond if the investor purchases the bond today and holds it until maturity.

Zero-cost collar A transaction in which a position in the underlying is protected by buying a put and selling a call with the premium from the sale of the call offsetting the premium from the purchase of the put. It can also be used to protect a floating-rate borrower against interest rate increases with the premium on a long cap offsetting the premium on a short floor.

BLS. *See* U.S. Bureau of Labor
　Statistics (BLS)
Blue Bayou: cash flow statements,
　V3: 268
board, V4: 173
board committees
　audit committee, V4: 181–183
　nominations committee, V4:
　　185–186
　other committees, V4: 186
　remuneration/compensation
　　committee, V4: 183–185
board of directors
　authority to hire external
　　consultants, V4: 178
　board committees, V4: 181–186
　defined, V4: 172–173
　independence, V4: 172, 175–176
　limiting number of, V4: 176n10
　qualifications, V4: 174, 176–177
　related-party transactions, V4:
　　179–180
　summary considerations, V4: 170
　terms of election, V4: 178–179
　two-tier (dual) board, V4: 173
　unitary board, V4: 173–174
Board of Governors, Federal Reserve,
　V2: 370, 371, 462, 465, 486
Bobls (German government-issued
　notes), V5: 310
Bolsa de Mercadorias & Futuros of
　Brazil: forward contracts, V6: 15
bond covenants. *See* financial
　covenants
bond insurance: as credit
　enhancement, V5: 338
bond-equivalent basis, V1: 257
bond-equivalent yield
　cash flow yield role, V5: 460–461
　defined, V1: 257
　in forward rate calculation, V5:
　　480–483
　overview, V5: 450–451
bondholders
　conversion privilege, V5: 248
　as creditors for debenture bonds,
　　V5: 327
　distressed securities, V6: 234
　embedded options for, V5: 243,
　　248, 249
　redemption prices, V5: 247
　rights of (U.S.), V5: 324–325
bond-market indexes
　described, V5: 44, 54–57
　government issued, V5: 57–59
　international, V5: 61–62
bonds and bond markets. *See also*
　callable bonds; U.S. Treasury,
　Treasury securities

annual compounding of, V5: 134n3
bankruptcy and, V5: 324–325
bond forward contracts, V6: 39–40
bonds payable
　accounting for bonds, V3: 515–520
　amortizing a bond discount, V3:
　　521–522
　bond amortization accounting,
　　V3: 520–523
　bonds issued at a discount, V3:
　　518–519
　bonds issued at face value, V3:
　　516–517
　current market rates, V3: 527
　debt covenants, V3: 524–525
　debt extinguishment, V3:
　　523–524
　fair values, V3: 527
　interest expenses/payments
　　accounting, V3: 520–523
　long-term debt presentation/
　　disclosure, V3: 525–527
　as long-term liability, V3: 514–527
borrowing funds to purchase, V5:
　250–251
calculating yield on, V1: 257
characteristics of, V1: 421–422
cheapest-to-deliver, V6: 69–70
collateral trust, V5: 327
collateralized bond obligation
　(CBO), V5: 338
commodity-linked, V6: 239–240
convertible, V5: 248, 249, 400
convexity, V5: 403, 527–528, 530,
　531, 539, 545–548
corporate, V5: 9, 13, 326–329, 330;
　V6: 92
coupon rate, V5: 237–242
covenants, V5: 235, 326
credit rating factors, V5: 325–326
currency denomination, V5: 248
day count conventions, V5:
　414–415
debenture, V5: 327–328
debt financing with, V2: 443–444
default spread, V5: 75–76
deferred coupon, V5: 238–242
defined, V3: 514, 515
electronic trading in, V5: 341–342
embedded options for
　for bondholders, V5: 249
　impact on interest rate risk,
　　V5: 267
　importance of, V5: 249–250
　for issuers, V5: 249
　option-adjusted spread (OAS),
　　V5: 476–479
　overview, V5: 248–249
　valuation models, V5: 424–425

volatility risk and, V5: 284, 528–532
　yield spread and, V5: 373–374
ERPs vs. (1900–2002), V4: 53–54
estimating defaults in, V1: 433
exchangeable, V5: 248, 400
external, V5: 305
federal funds rate and, V2: 475, 483
futures, V6: 68–69
futures market, V5: 13
global, V5: 305
government, V5: 8, 305–306, 307,
　311–323, 361, 363
grading of, V5: 278–281
indenture, V5: 235
index funds, V5: 95
indexes of, V1: 478–479
inflation-indexed, V6: 239–240
insured, V5: 323, 338
interest rate risk, V5: 264–271
interest rate swaps, V6: 144n11
internal, V5: 304–305
internal rate of return and, V1:
　240, 257
introduction, V5: 233–235, 304
investment securities, V2: 365
as long-term liability, V3: 514–527
maturity, V5: 235–237
measurement scales for, V1: 271
moral obligation, V5: 322
mortgage, V5: 327
noncallable, V5: 246, 362
option-free, V5: 267, 524–528,
　529–532, 537, 548
options on, V6: 92
predicting ratings/yields, V3: 357
price behavior of, V5: 236, 264–269,
　520, 524–532 (*see also* duration,
　debt securities)
price calculation, V5: 404–415
price distribution of, V1: 421–422
price of, V3: 517
primary, V5: 330–331, 339–340
provisions for paying off, V5:
　243–248, 275–276
ratings/yields of, V1: 271n3
recovery rates on defaulted, V1:
　536–538
return sources in, V5: 448–449
returns on, V1: 272, 321, 384–390
revenue, V5: 322–323, 375–376
rights of bondholders (U.S.), V5:
　324–325
risk-free, V6: 22
risks of investing in bonds
　call risk, V5: 275–276
　corporate takeover/restructuring
　　risk, V5: 285
　credit risk, V5: 277–281
　currency risk, V5: 283

defined, V3: 182, 336
    interpreting, V3: 336–337
in income statements, V3: 141–142
margin ratios, V3: 385
gross sales: revenue recognition
    principles, V3: 152–154
gross-of-fees returns: GIPS
    requirements, V1: 147, 152, 154
Group of Five, V2: 503–504
Group of Seven, V2: 504
group research, standards for, V1: 81
Groupe Danone
    cash flow statements, V3: 281–283
    income statements, V3: 139–141
    operating profit, V3: 142
    reconciling GAAP, French/U.S., V3:
        167n31
grouping by function/nature in
    income statements, V3: 141
growth. *See also* expected growth rate
    accounting red flags and warning
        signs, V3: 578–579
    companies vs. stocks, V5: 176–177
    infinite period DDM and, V5:
        143–144
    investment strategies for, V6: 192
    price-earnings/growth rate (PEG)
        ratio, V5: 78
    rates of, V1: 209–211; V5: 132
    required rate of return estimation
        and, V5: 188
    sustainable rate of, V4: 57
    temporary supernormal growth, V5:
        144–146
growth investing, V5: 51, 178
growth investors, V3: 622
growth stocks vs. value stocks, V1:
    305–306, 500–501
Grupo Imsa: credit rating upgrade,
    V3: 9
GSCI. *See* Goldman Sachs Commodity
    Index (GSCI)
GSEs. *See* government-sponsored
    enterprises (GSEs)
GSMI. *See* Global Security Market
    Index (GSMI): Brinson Partners
GTC. *See* good-until-canceled (GTC)
    orders
guaranteed investment contracts,
    V6: 192
guarantees, performance, V6: 53

H
Hallett, Ross E., V1: 10
Hamermesh, Daniel, V2: 77
hand signals, traders', V6: 53n5, 63
harmonic mean, V1: 300
harmonic series, V1: 300n25

harmonized index of consumer prices
    (HICP), V2: 502
harvest fluctuations (example), V2:
    85–87
Harvey, Campbell, V4: 72
Hawawini, Gabriel, V5: 115
health insurance: as asset allocation,
    V4: 211
hedge funds
    advantages, V6: 230–232
    biases in, V6: 228–230
    classification system, V6: 221–224
    defined, V1: 271n4; V6: 219–221, 229
    fee structure, V6: 220–221, 229
    forms/uses of, V6: 18
    funds of funds (FOF), V6:
        224–225, 227
    indexes, V6: 227
    legal structure, V6: 219–220
    leverage in, V6: 225–226
    on nominal scale, V1: 271
    objective, V6: 219
    overview, V6: 218–219
    performance of, V1: 500n29; V6:
        230–232
    private equity investment by, V6: 213
    purpose, V6: 19
    selection bias, V1: 499–500
    unique risks, V6: 219, 226–230
hedged vs. unhedged returns, V5:
    157n11
hedges
    comprehensive income, impact on,
        V3: 184
    fair value hedge, V3: 527
hedonic price, estimating, V6: 203–205
held-for-trading securities: accounting
    for, V3: 651–652
held-for-use assets: impairment, V3:
    454–457
held-to-maturity securities, V3: 651–652
herd instincts, V2: 348
Herfindahl-Hirschman Index (HHI),
    V2: 114, 222, 235–236, 253
Hewitt Associates: balance sheets, V3:
    210–212
Hewlett-Packard (HP) Co. *See also* HP
    Compaq
    balance sheets, V3: 237–239
    cash flow comparisons, V3: 289–290
    computer components, V2: 219–220
    Dell vs., V2: 255–257
HICP. *See* harmonized index of
    consumer prices (HICP)
high quality bond grade, V5: 278
high yield fixed income composites,
    V1: 165
high-skilled labor, V2: 73

high-yield bond indexes, V5: 57, 58, 61
histograms, V1: 279–280
historical cost asset models for
    tangible assets, V3: 438–442
historical costs, V3: 111, 208
historical equity risk premium
    approach, V4: 53–55, 54n19
historical simulation, V1: 460
historical view
    derivatives, V6: 12–15
    futures contracts and markets, V6:
        50–51
    venture capital risk and return data,
        V6: 215
Hoffman-LaRoche: global forward
    markets, V6: 34–35
holding company, V5: 327
holding period return (HPR)
    bank discount yield and, V1: 254
    calculation of, V1: 245, 272
    currency exchange rate and, V1:
        272n5
    defined, V1: 245
    geometric mean return and, V1: 297
    holding period yield and, V1:
        254n13
    money-weighted rate of return and,
        V1: 247
    time-weighted rate of return and,
        V1: 247–252
    volatility and, V1: 452–454
holding period yield (HPY), V1:
    254–257; V5: 50
holdings list: fair dealing standard,
    V1: 57
HOLDRs (Holding Company
    Depository Receipts): exchange
    traded funds (ETFs), V6: 197
Holiday Inn, V2: 233
home bias, V5: 118
home insurance: as asset allocation,
    V4: 211
homeland security multiplier, V2: 448
homogenization of futures contracts,
    V6: 52
Hong Kong: budgetary surpluses in,
    V2: 433
Hong Kong Tracker Fund: exchange
    traded funds (ETFs), V6:
        193, 197
horizon return, V1: 254n13
horizontal common-size analysis
    balance sheet, V3: 232, 316
    defined, V3: 312n5
    income statement, V3: 179n38
hot issue securities, V1: 55
Hotelling, Harold, V2: 290
Hotelling Principle, V2: 290–292

level inventory, management of, V4: 121–123

level of significance, V1: 520–522

leverage. *See also* debt; financial leverage; interest; operating leverage
- beta estimation, V4: 59–61
- bond investments, V5: 250–251
- GIPS requirements, V1: 142, 147
- hedge funds, V6: 225–226
- margin transactions, V5: 26–29
- ratios of (*see* financial leverage ratios)
- real estate investments, V6: 201
- risk-return possibilities, V4: 272, 292
- suitability and, V1: 61

leveraged buyout investing, V6: 213

Levi, V2: 227

Levy, Efraim, V2: 151

liabilities. *See also* taxes
- accrued, V3: 216
- on balance sheet, V3: 38–39, 199, 207–212, 215–218, 224–225
- current/noncurrent, V3: 202–203, 215–218
- deferred tax liabilities, V3: 474–479
- defined, V3: 36, 37, 196, 199
- Federal Reserve, V2: 373
- financial liabilities, V3: 223
- financial reporting, V3: 36–37
- as financial statement element, V3: 36, 109
- IFRS *Framework*, V3: 649
- liquidity ratios, V3: 328
- measuring, V3: 207–212, 224–225
- nonfinancial, V3: 660
- nonpublic information release and, V1: 41
- tax base determination, V3: 481–484
- temporary (tax) differences, V3: 485–489
- working capital management and, V1: 238

LIBOR. *See* London Interbank Offered Rate (LIBOR)

licensing
- barriers to entry, V2: 191
- revenue recognition principles, V3: 147

lien, V5: 327

life cycle
- investment goals, V4: 213–214
- net worth, V4: 211–213

life insurance
- as part of investment plan, V4: 210–211
- as tax-deferred investment, V4: 226

lifestyles: effect on industries, V5: 172

LIFFE. *See* London International Financial Futures and Options Exchange (LIFFE)

LIFO. *See* last in, first out (LIFO) methods

likelihoods, V1: 394

LimeWire, V2: 93

limit buy orders, V5: 30. *See also* bids

limit moves, V6: 60

limit orders, V1: 370–371; V5: 25

limit pricing, V2: 254

limit sell orders, V5: 30

limit up/down, V6: 60

limited liability corporation (LLC), V2: 110; V6: 219–220

limited partnerships
- GIPS and, V1: 142
- hedge funds, V6: 202, 219–220
- real estate, V6: 212–213

limit-order books, V5: 30

limit-order processing: trading systems, V5: 31

line graphs for financial analysis, V3: 319

line item requirements in financial statements, V3: 114–115

linear interpolation, V1: 302

line-item veto, V2: 426

lines of credit, V4: 128–130

liquid asset ratio, V1: 577

liquid assets
- commercial banks, V2: 365, 367, 475
- defined, V4: 222–223
- requirements for, V3: 352
- savings and, V2: 363

liquidations
- corporate, V5: 325
- LIFO method, V3: 402–403, 579
- venture capital, V6: 216

liquidity
- balance sheet, V3: 203
- cash equivalents, V3: 38
- commercial banks, V2: 367
- defined, V2: 363; V3: 8; V4: 93, 222
- futures contracts, V6: 9n8, 51n4
- futures markets, V6: 9, 52
- importance of secondary markets for, V5: 12
- limited, V1: 61
- managing
  - defined, V4: 93–95
  - drags on liquidity, V4: 94–95
  - measuring liquidity, V4: 95–101
  - primary sources of liquidity, V4: 93–94
  - pulls on liquidity, V4: 94–95
  - secondary sources of liquidity, V4: 93, 94
  - working capital management, V4: 93–95

- as market characteristic, V5: 7
- market maker's role in, V5: 29
- measurement of, V5: 366n6
- REITs, V6: 202
- secondary bond market, V5: 341
- U.S. Treasury securities, V5: 362
- venture capital, V6: 215
- yield spreads and, V5: 374–375

liquidity preference theory, V5: 366–367

liquidity premiums, function of, V1: 183; V6: 189

liquidity ratios
- on balance sheets, V3: 239
- calculating, V3: 328–329
- defined, V3: 239, 320; V4: 96
- evaluating, V3: 330–331
- in financial analysis, V3: 328–331
- interpreting, V3: 329–331
- types of, V3: 329

liquidity risk
- about, V5: 281–282
- changes in, V5: 282–283
- in company analysis, V5: 190
- foreign security risk premium, V5: 157
- hedge funds, V6: 226
- marking to market and, V5: 282
- overview, V4: 109

liquidity-based presentations: balance sheet, V3: 203

living wage, V2: 51, 77

LLC. *See* limited liability corporation (LLC)

loads, V6: 190, 196

loanable funds, V2: 414, 441–443, 473–474, 478–479, 480–481

loans
- collateralized, V5: 250–251, 313, 318–320, 338, 364
- commercial banks, V2: 365
- conforming, V5: 318
- creating deposits by marking, V2: 374–377
- federal funds rate and, V2: 476
- mortgage, V5: 312, 313–316

local currency debt rating, V5: 306

local government bond issues. *See* municipal bond market

local laws and knowledge of the law, V1: 16

local market, V2: 116

locals (floor traders): futures contracts, V6: 62–63

location, measures of, V1: 283, 301–306

Lochhead, Scott, V4: 70

lockbox system, function of, V4: 117, 118

locked limits, V6: 60

skewness
of binomial distributions, V1: 428–429
CAPM, effect on, V4: 291–292
coefficients of, V1: 327n41
defined, V1: 268, 325
deviations and, V1: 287
formula, V1: 327–328
negative, V1: 323n38
of normal distributions, V1: 440, 440n17, 441
in return distributions, V1: 325–330
in t-test, V1: 527
SL. *See* straight-line (SL) depreciation methods
SL Industries (SLI): inventory accounting, V3: 625–627
SLF. *See* savings supply curve (*SLF*)
SLM. *See* Sharpe-Lintner-Mossin (SLM)
small cap growth composites, V1: 165
Small Order Execution System (SOES), V5: 31
small sample bias: mispricings, V5: 113
small stock investment strategy, V6: 192
small-cap growth index, V5: 51
Small-Cap Market (SCM), V5: 22
small-cap stocks. *See also* stocks
beta estimation considerations, V4: 58–59
performance vs. large-cap stocks, V5: 50
small-cap value index, V5: 51
small-firm effect
about, V5: 78–79
in beta estimation, V4: 290, 292
selection bias and, V5: 113
small-mid cap growth composites, V1: 166
smart card, V2: 360
smart money and technical analysis, V1: 579–581
Smetters, Kent, V2: 444, 445
Smith, Adam, V2: 46, 249, 347
SML. *See* security market line (SML)
smoothed pricing bias: hedge funds, V6: 228–229
smoothing techniques and cost of capital, V4: 58
social interest, V2: 38, 45, 220
Social Security
benefits for, V2: 444–445
CPI bias and, V2: 321
deficit in, V2: 443
federal budget and, V2: 428–432, 456–457
time bomb, V2: 444–445
Social Security tax
burden of, V2: 80, 84
federal budget and, V2: 428–429, 431

payment of, V2: 77–78
SS time bomb, V2: 444–445
tax wedge component, V2: 436
socially responsible investment (SRI) funds, V5: 51
SOES. *See* Small Order Execution System (SOES)
soft commissions, V1: 50
Soft Dollar Standards (CFA Centre for Financial Market Integrity), V1: 8
soft dollars, V1: 50
software development
costs, V3: 427–430
revenue recognition principles, V3: 146
solvency, V3: 8
solvency ratios
balance sheet, V3: 239
calculating, V3: 332–333
defined, V3: 239, 320, 331–332
evaluating, V3: 334–335
in financial analysis, V3: 331–335
interpreting, V3: 333–334
Sony Corporation
balance sheet, illustration, V3: 205–207
changes in shareholders' equity, V3: 228–230
SOPH. *See* Standards of Practice Handbook (SOPH)
sources
attributing, V1: 30, 31, 38
reliability of, V1: 37
South Africa: GIPS in, V1: 134, 135
South America: global derivatives exchanges, V6: 14
South Central Missouri Title Company: installment sales, V3: 151
South Korea: budgetary deficits in, V2: 433
sovereign bonds
about, V5: 305
credit risk, V5: 305–306
government security distribution, V5: 306–311
sovereign risk, V5: 285
sovereign yield spread, V4: 65–66
Spain
GIPS in, V1: 134
inflation targeting in, V2: 500
SPC. *See* Standards of Practice Council (SPC)
SPDRs. *See* S&P 500 Depositary Receipts (SPDRs)
Spearman rank correlation coefficients, V1: 549–552
Special Drawing Rights, V2: 373
special orders, V5: 26

special purpose entities (SPEs)
accounting red flags and warning signs, V3: 580
Enron accounting scandal, V3: 582–583
special purpose vehicle, types of, V5: 336–337
special redemption price, V5: 247
special situations investing, V6: 213
specialists. *See also* market makers
as exchange membership category, V5: 24
market role of, V5: 29–30
stock exchange, V5: 85–86
specific identification methods: inventory costs, V3: 158, 382–384, 393
speculation in derivative markets, V6: 19
speculative bond grade, V5: 278, 279, 329
speculative company, V5: 177
speculative stock, V5: 178
speculative value, options, V6: 99
spending phase: investor life cycle, V4: 212, 213
SPEs. *See* special purpose entities (SPEs)
spin-offs
illustration of, V3: 453
for long-lived asset disposal, V3: 452n12
spot price
commodity trading, V6: 266, 269
defined, V6: 6
futures trading, V6: 18
spot rate curve: yield spread measures relative to, V5: 471–479
spot rates
defined, V5: 368
non-treasury securities vs., V5: 422–423
short-term forward rates and, V5: 483–484
theoretical, V5: 466–479
valuation using, V5: 416–422
spread for life, V5: 462
spread products, V5: 368
spreads. *See also* yield spreads
bid-ask, V5: 8, 30, 115, 281–282
credit, V5: 277–278, 371–372, 422–423
for floaters, V5: 461–464
nominal, V5: 374, 472–476, 478, 479
option-adjusted, V5: 476–479
quality, V5: 371
swap, V5: 380–385
term structure, V5: 75
zero-volatility, V5: 472–476, 478, 479